D1243102

Library of Congress Catalog

Title: Establishment and Maintenance of Landscape Plants

Author: Whitcomb, Carl E.

Major Areas: 1. Transplanting
2. Plant establishment
3. Plant maintenance

Includes bibliographies and index

Library of Congress Catalog Card Number: 87-50632

ISBN: 0-9613109-4-4

Printed in the United States of America

Lacebark Inc.
P.O. Box 2383
Stillwater, Oklahoma 74076

This book is dedicated to the establishment and preservation of trees. Trees shade, protect, enhance, cool, beautify, screen, complement, soften, enframe, color, and provide a vast array of visual and physical benefits to man. Yet trees are poorly understoood by the general public as well as many professionals. If this book aids the establishment, health or preservation of a few trees, then it will have been worth the tremendous number of hours.

A special thanks to Cara Beer, Dr. Frank Carpenter, Susan Kenna, Ruth Ann Stuart, Andy Whitcomb, Benjamin Whitcomb, and LaJean Whitcomb for reviewing and editing the manuscript and offering suggestions. A good of this nature requires a great effort on the part of the author's family. Without their assistance it would have been far more difficult.

TABLE OF CONTENTS

ABOUT THESE BOOKS i

ABOUT THE AUTHOR iii

INTRODUCTION
Tree Physiology and the Urban Landscape . . iv

CHAPTER 1. Transplanting and Establishment
    A Summary of Procedures 2
    Pre-Installation 2
    Installation 3
    Literature Cited 6

CHAPTER 2. Methods of Plant Production
    Old Vs. New 9
    Bare Root 9
    Balled-in-Burlap 13
    Tree Spades 22
    Container Production 26
    The Unique Container 27
    Root Development/Root-bound . . . 28
    Root Development and Larger Plants . . 37
    The Future. RootMakers 41
          RootBuilders 44
          The Fabric Container 48
    Harvesting, Holding, and Planting . . 51
    Water Management of Newly Planted Trees . 53
    A "Can Opener" for Trees in Fabric Containers 58
    Container Size/Tree Size Relationships . . 60
    The Permanent Root System 62
    Literature Cited 66

CHAPTER 3. Holding Nursery Stock After Harvest
    Alternatives 69
    Overwintering Nursery Stock 71
    Methods of Protection 78
    Literature Cited 86

CHAPTER 4. Root Pruning: Pros and Cons
    A Practical Example 88
    Practices to Avoid 90

Practice With Care 94
Literature Cited 96

CHAPTER 5. The Planting Hole
Advantages of a Wide Planting Hole . . 99
Changing Soil Conditions 101
Establishment is a Two-part Process . . 101
Evaluating Drainage 102
Plant Tolerant Species 102
Plant Shallow or on Berms . . . 102
Provide Internal Drainage . . . 104
Fertilizing at Planting 109

CHAPTER 6. Soil Amendments
Dispelling Old Myths 112
Florida Sand and Soil Amendments . . 113
Amending Good Soils 117
Amendments, Clay Soils and . . . .
Supplemental Fertilizer . . 118
Why Soil Amendments Generally . . .
Are Not Helpful 121
Some Amendments Are Helpful . . . 125
A Lesson From Nature 125
Superabsorbents 127
Container Studies 128
Field Studies 130
Literature Cited 131

CHAPTER 7. Gypsum and Changes in Soil Structure
Gypsum and High Sodium 136
Gypsum and Low Sodium 137
Alternatives 138

CHAPTER 8. Establishment of Container-Grown Plants
Water Movement in Soils 141
Soil Amendments May Create Problems . . 146
Root Growth Out From Containers . . 147
Topdress for Better Establishment Success . 150
Disturb the Roots at Planting? . . . 152
Cuttings Vs. Seedlings 154
Disadvantages of Containers 155
Advantages of Containers 156
Literature Cited 159

CHAPTER 9. Spring Vs. Fall Planting
   Fall Planting for Container Stock . . . 161
   Research Findings I 161
   Research Findings II 166
   Literature Cited 170

CHAPTER 10. The Restricted Planting Hole
   Keys to Success 172

CHAPTER 11. Root Stimulators
   Supporting Research 183
   Literature Cited 188

CHAPTER 12. Top Pruning at Planting
   No Support for an Old Practice . . . 190
   Experiments and Answers 190
   Related Research 195
   Top-Root Relationships 195
   What Makes Roots Grow? 195
   Research Continued 196
   Summary 197
   Literature Cited 198

CHAPTER 13. Mulches
   Many Benefits from an Old Practice . . 201
   Traits of an Effective Mulch . . . 201
   Mulch Over Plastic 202
   Plant Response to Mulching 204
   Weed Barrier Fabrics 211
   Summary 214
   Literature Cited 216

CHAPTER 14. Establishing Azaleas and Other Sensitive Species
   Peat as a Soil Amendment 218
   Research to the Rescue 218
   Understanding the Effects of Peat . . 219
   Excessive Drainage 222
   Soil Tests 224
   Fertilizing Azaleas and Other . . .
         Salt-Sensitive Species . . 228
   Research Results 228
   Literature Cited 232

CHAPTER 15. Transplanting with Tree Spades
    Advantages and Disadvantages . . . 234
    Pulling Trees 235
    Comparing Transplanting Techniques . . 235
    Further Techniques Explored 240
    Literature Cited 249

CHAPTER 16. Transplanting Large Trees
    Clues from Smaller Trees 251
    Tree Size Vs. Stress 251
    A Transplant Study with Large Trees . . 258
    Moving Large Trees 262
    Literature Cited 270

CHAPTER 17. Staking Landscape Trees
    Stakes = Problems 272
    Literature Cited 283

CHAPTER 18. Competition Between Woody Plants and Grasses
    The Competitiveness of Grass . . . 285
    Trees Can Restrict Grass 288
    Grass-Shrub Competition 289
    Bermudagrass Competition 289
    Allelopathy or Chemical Growth Factors . 293
    Literature Cited 295

CHAPTER 19. Competition Between Woody Plants and Ground C
    A Study of Tolerance and Suppression . . 298
    Literature Cited 309

CHAPTER 20. Weed Control
    The Basics 311
    Pre-Emergent Herbicides 315
    Post-Emergent Herbicides 326
    Complications with Roundup . . . 331
    Root-absorbed Roundup 331
    Grass Specific Herbicides 334
    Chemicals to Avoid 334
    Soil Sterilization 334
    Charcoal and Herbicide Damage . . . 340
    Studying the Problem 340
    Incorporation of Charcoal Helps . . . 343
    Literature Cited 346

CHAPTER 21. Plants in Landscape Containers
    Containers Are Different 350
    Containers Without Bottoms . . . 351
    Containers With Bottoms 359
    Determining Drainable Pore Space . . 364
    Drains and Drainage 365
    Insulating the Root Zone 378
    Literature Cited 381

CHAPTER 22. Plant Nutrition, Soils and Fertilizers
    A General Summary of Fertilization
        Practices for Landscape Plants . . 384
        Soil Test 384
        Expressions of Soil Test Results . 388
        Build Reserves of Phosphorus . .
            and Potassium . . . 388
        Managing Nitrogen . . . 389
    Leaf Analysis 391
    Plant Nutrition and Fertilizers . . . 392
    Nutrient Absorption and Energy Distribution 395
    Sources of Nutrient Elements . . . 398
        Nitrogen 399
        Phosphorus 399
        Potassium 400
        Calcium 400
        Magnesium 401
        Sulfur 401
        The Micronutrients 402
    Why a Fertilizer Burns 402
    Nutrient Elements: Plant Response and Use 404
        Nitrogen 404
        Phosphorus 405
        Potassium 408
        Sulfur 408
        Calcium and Magnesium . . 409
        The Micronutrients . . . 411
    Relationship of Plant Nutrients . . . 416
    Fertilizer Salts and Salt Index . . . 419
    Literature Cited 423

CHAPTER 23. The Essential Nutrient Elements:
    The Macro Elements 426
        Nitrogen 426
        Phosphorus 428
        Potassium 430
        Magnesium 432
        Sulfur 438
        Calcium 439
    The Micro Elements 440
        Iron 440
        Manganese 442
        Copper 444
        Zinc 447
        Boron 447
        Molybdenum 448
    Literature Cited 450

CHAPTER 24. Fertilizing Landscape Trees
    Soil Test for Best Results 452
    When and Where to Fertilize . . . 453
    Where are the Roots? 457
    Summary 458
    Fertilizing Landscape Plants: Three Examples 461
    Literature Cited 463

CHAPTER 25. Plant Stress and Landscape Problems
    Trees and Stress 465
    Gradual Changes in Soil pH . . . 465
    Soil Compaction 467
    Improper Nutrition 468
    Water 470
    Literature Cited 473

CHAPTER 26. Solving the Iron Chlorosis Problem
    Calcium Sources 475
    Treating the Symptoms 475
    Treating the Cause 475
    Determining What Happened . . . 480
    A Landscape Example 483
    Water Changes Soil Chemistry . . . 484
    Summary 487
    A Technique for Solving Chlorosis Problems 488
    Literature Cited 493

CHAPTER 27. Protecting Existing Trees
    Protect It or Remove It 496
    The Adjustment Factor 497
    Misconceptions 498
    Helpful Practices 506
    Root Flairs Are Clues 510
    Manipulating Tree Roots 512
    Root Barriers 513
    Shifting Support Roots 515

CHAPTER 28. Cut, Fill and Other Grade Changes
    Cuts 518
    Fills 522
    Tree Wells 524
    Retaining Walls 529
    Shifting the Root System 533

CHAPTER 29. Light, Shade and Root Growth
    Light Duration 535
    Light Intensity 539
    Shade Effects Plant Growth . . . 540
    Literature Cited 550

CHAPTER 30. The Effects of Drought Stress
    Drought Is Not Always Bad . . . 553
    Watering During Drought 555
    Summary 557
    Literature Cited 558

CHAPTER 31. Pruning
    Tough Choices 560
    What to Do 565
    What Not to Do 570
    Wound Dressings 576
    Bracing and Cabling 578
    Literature Cited 584

CHAPTER 32. When Trees Compete with Turfgrass
    Tree Competition with Grass . . . 588
    Effects on Bluegrass Growth . . . 590
    Effects on Seed Germination . . . 598
    Literature Cited 601

APPENDIX
    Conversion Factors for the Nurseryman:
                    English and Metric .   602
    Calculating Solutions PPM   604
    Measures and Equivalents   605
    Approximate Toxicities of Various
        Chemicals Used in Nurseries .   .   607

GLOSSARY   609

INDEX   622

About These Books

College professors are generally held just below politicians at being able to "waltz around the question without ever giving an answer". While an undergraduate at Kansas State University, I came across a comedy record by 'Brother' Dave Gardner. At one point in a dialog with himself he made the statement, "Don't give me your doubts, I have enough doubts of my own. Tell me what you believe in!" Since I had encountered several professors, even at that early age, who would talk of various theories but would not tell what they believed, the statement stuck--permanently. In the ensuing years, it became more and more clear that when people ask a specific question they expect an answer that is reasonably specific, even from university professors.

These books are "What I believe in!" I have included some of the research, experiences or observations on which that belief is based.

No area remains unchanged over time. By the time this book is printed, some points may be subject to modification as horticulture is a rapidly changing field. You will also see articles and hear talks that suggest other views or ways of doing things. However, be cautious and make sure the new information is well founded and not a fluke or the result of poorly designed and conducted research or simply misinformation. The proverbial primrose path is wide and well traveled by people following misinformation. Everything included in this book has been tried and experienced by the author. This does not mean that it will work exactly the same way for you, but neither is it an untested theory.

In 1986 I first wrote *Landscape Plant Production, Establishment and Maintenance*. My view was to show the relationship between how a plant was produced, harvested, transplanted, established and grew. After one printing of the book and exposure to the nursery and landscape industries, it quickly became clear that there were two distinct interests: 1) production of landscape plants and 2) establishment and maintenance of landscape plants. As a result of those two distinct interest groups and the fact that there was additional material I wanted to add to the book anyway, two books now exist instead of one.

Production of Landscape Plants is an attempt to describe the various techniques used in the production process and offer suggestions for improvement. Clearly the better the root system,

i

the healthier the plants. Likewise, the healthier the plant, the fewer the problems in transplanting and establishment.

Establishment and Maintenance of Landscape Plants is an attempt to share many of the findings and feelings derived from a vast array of transplanting and maintenance studies done over a period of more than 30 years. Some of the current "horticultural" practices are wrong. In this book the correct way, as I currently know it to be, is presented along with the why! The more successful the performance of all landscapes, the greater the vitality of the nursery/landscape industry and the greater the beauty of our great country.

Carl E. Whitcomb
September, 1991

About the Author

Carl E. Whitcomb was a university professor 1967 to 1986. He has received patents on a solar-heated greenhouse, a micronutrient fertilizer (Micromax) and unique container designs for improving the root systems of container nursery stock, a capillary watering system, and other inventions. He has written over 400 technical and semi-technical publications on plant propagation from cuttings and seeds; plant nutrition and production, both in containers and field; and factors affecting the transplanting, establishment and performance of landscape plants. He is author of three other books, *Know It & Grow It II: A Guide to the Identification and Use of Landscape Plants, Plant Production in Containers*, and *Production of Landscape Plants*. He has traveled extensively throughout the U.S.A. where he is a frequent speaker at nursery meetings as well as Canada, Europe, Australia and New Zealand.

A native Kansan, he received a B.S. degree from Kansas State University and M.S. and Ph.D. degrees from Iowa State University. He taught and conducted research for five years at the University of Florida and 13 1/2 years at Oklahoma State University. He was the 1977 recipient of the Porter Henegar Award given annually by the Southern Nurserymen's Association for excellence in research; the 1983 recipient of the L.C. Chadwick Award, presented by the American Association of Nurserymen, "To an exceptional educator for superior teaching, guidance and motivation of students in the nursery and landscape arts and sciences"; in 1985 he was named Outstanding Oklahoma Nurseryman. In 1986 he was made Honorary Life Member of the Oklahoma Horticulture Society and received the Slater Wight Memorial Award for 1986 presented by the Southern Nurserymen's Association for "Outstanding contributions to the nursery industry." In 1987 he was named "Outstanding Industry Person" by the Florida Nurserymen and Growers' Association. In 1988 the original version of this book received the Award of Merit from the Garden Writers' Association of America. He was elected President of the International Plant Propagators' Society, Southern Region, 1988-89.

Currently, Dr. Whitcomb is a private research horticulturist/consultant/author/lecturer. He and his wife, LaJean, operate Lacebark Inc., Publications and Research, P.O. Box 2383, Stillwater, Oklahoma 74076.

Introduction

Tree Physiology and the Urban Landscape. *Mature trees are massive living organisms. Because they may become so large, yet are immobile, they are subject to an array of problems. Consider that most native trees begin life on a particular site because they are adapted to, and tolerant of, the conditions on that site. But as the tree grows older and larger, the conditions of the site change, usually under the influence of man. During the 20- to 100-year life of most trees, man's influence often plays a major role in the overall health of the tree. Areas that were once woods with an array of understory plants, natural vegetation, and litter on the soil surface become developments with modified drainage patterns, grass, irrigation systems and elevated temperatures (Figure A). Any native mammal would quickly leave a site with such an abrupt change, but trees cannot move, nor can they adjust their needs. Some trees tolerate urbanization fairly well. Live oaks, **Quercus virginiana**, and the many species of elms (**Ulmus spp.**) have a high level of tolerance. Black cherry, **Prunus serotina**, many pines, and some oak species quickly disappear from urban sites, from either direct or indirect problems.*

Another tree situation, sometimes equally devastating, is when the one- to five-year-old tree is introduced to the urban site. At this relative small size and early age the tree is more tolerant of changes in environmental conditions than ever again in its lifetime. How successful the tree will be often depends on the knowledge and understanding of the individual selecting the site for the tree. Unfortunately, many times the location is determined by the desire of the designer for a particular size, shape, color or texture of tree with little or no consideration for the requirements of the tree. Landscape architects and designers often try to dictate sites to trees, and often the trees respond by allowing them to make another choice as a replacement.

*How much more successful most man-made or modified landscapes would be if the requirements of the trees were given first priority instead of only passive consideration. How much more successful if the selection of trees for a site were based on the conditions for best growth of the trees instead of what they will **tolerate**. Many trees are placed in urban conditions that push the absolute limits of their tolerance. Such trees leave a favorable environment in the nursery and are plunged abruptly into an environment at the edge of their tolerance limits or beyond, and the result is poor performance and only marginally attractive*

iv

trees. Such trees are very susceptible to a host of secondary disease and insect problems that under reasonable growing conditions would be of only minor importance. These are the trees that require frequent sprayings for problems and promote the perception that trees require extensive maintenance. The right tree in the right place does **not** require extensive maintenance.

There is no question but that the healthier the plant, the fewer the problems. Plant health should be the all-important factor when selecting a plant for a specific site. If the plant is healthy on that site, it will be attractive and functional. But **the site must be modified to fit the plant, because the plant cannot adapt to fit the site.**

As we increase our understanding of how trees and other plants grow, we can increase, somewhat, their tolerance for certain environmental conditions, but these are minor changes relative to the overall requirements. For example, when turfgrass is present on the site where the tree is planted, the competitive-restrictive effect of the grass on the development of new roots by the tree is awesome. Kentucky bluegrass reduced the growth of maple roots by as much as 70% (5). Common bermudagrass reduced growth of Japanese black pine by as much as 60% (4). In neither case did any of the maples or pines die, but certainly they were under tremendous stress and subject to many other problems, compared to trees grown without the presence of the grass. By wisely using mulches and other techniques to keep grass competition away from newly planted trees, the stress level of the tree is reduced. The tree may still not grow and perform well on the site depending on the vast array of other conditions influencing plant health. But when one major stress factor is reduced, the chances are much better.

On any site there are many positive (beneficial) and negative (detrimental) factors influencing plant health. The plant response we see is the end result of the total factors. However, every negative factor that can be reduced or eliminated will mean a greater plant response to the positive factors. We tend to look at a tree or shrub, and because it is alive and green we assume it is healthy when, in fact, it may be just barely above the threshold point in the constant life and death struggle. If a technique existed whereby each plant could be evaluated for its stress level, we could be much more effective in managing plants in the landscape. Imagine a machine that gives a read-out that a certain tree is a plus 5, where 0 is the point of death and 10 is the absolute pinnacle of health and vigor for the species.

Perhaps plus 3 is the point where that species begins to have problems with secondary pests and diseases. If the specific plant were a plus 5, we would know that the plant is not in immediate danger, but wherever possible, steps should be taken to improve plant health. This might be additional or **less** fertilizer, especially less nitrogen, or adjustment in soil pH to increase the availability of micronutrients, or a replacement of the mulch on a species sensitive to high root zone temperature, and so on.

Unfortunately, at the present time, we do not know if a specific tree is a plus 2 or a plus 6. About all we can detect are the extremes. The pessimist says this is fiction and unrealistic. However, research conducted for many years with plant growth in containers where conditions can be manipulated has shown that plant health can be greatly improved, even though the plant was dark green and apparent-ly healthy to begin with. The opportunities are extensive.

For example, many years of trying to grow azaleas in the same soil mixture as was used for an array of other species always ended in frustration and poor quality (or dead) azaleas. Obviously the soil mix was over-watered or not sufficiently aerated or ------. Then one day while conducting an experiment on micronutrient nutrition, the azaleas were beautiful even though the soil mix was the same as before **if** the right combination of micronutrients was used (Figure B). All the frustrations regarding soil mixes of the past were gone. It had not been the soil mix, but rather a nutritional factor that restricted plant health. When the right nutritional combination was found, the supply of nutrients to the top of the plants in the proper proportion increased, which meant more energy was manufactured by the leaves. This, in turn, meant more energy to translocate to the root system which meant more root growth and absorption of nutrients and water to supply the top and so on (Figure C).

*Figure A. A native stand of post and blackjack oak (**Quercus stellata** and **Q. marilandica**) (above) and a similar site following development. The environment of both tops and roots of the trees has been radically altered.*

Figure B. Azaleas grown with different nutritional conditions but in the same soil mix. All plants were green and apparently healthy but there was a great difference in size (above). When the containers were removed, the size of the root system was even more striking than the size of the tops (below).

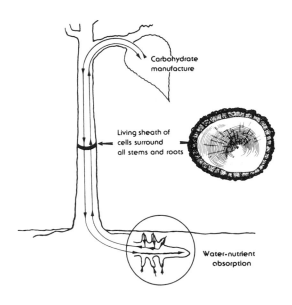

Figure C. *Water and nutrients are absorbed by the root tips and translocated upward through the most recent several years of internal growth rings (xylem) to the leaves. Energy from the sun captured by the leaves in the form of sugars is translocated downward through the phloem or outer sheath of tissues. The greater the supply of water and the entire complex of nutrients to the leaves, the more energy the leaves can manufacture so more energy can be returned to the roots for further growth.*

As years and experiments have advanced this point further, some fascinating aspects of plant growth have been uncovered. Just because a plant is dark green and growing does not mean it is at the plus 10 point on the scale of plant health. The most vigorous and healthy plant you know or can imagine may only be a 6 on this 1 to 10 scale. Another example to make the point: For many years growth rates of plants had been increasing as a result of many experiments and improvements of plant growing conditions. As a challenge, it was decided to try to grow a "slow-growing" oak tree six feet tall in a single growing season. All of the factors that could be controlled were controlled as accurately as possible. After three attempts, the goal was attained. The *shumard, bur and northern red oak seeds (**Q. shumardi, Q. macrocarpa** and **Q. rubra**, respectively) were planted in an unheated greenhouse in March and by the end of the growing season, late October in this location, the trees were truly six feet tall with good stem development and branching. To obtain this exceptional growth, an array of factors were synchronized as carefully as possible. Each factor contributed to the acceleration of plant growth. Likewise, if one factor was not synchronized with the others, the plants showed no "deficiency" symptoms. The leaves were just as green and of identical size, but the overall tree size was simply not as great. The point is that there are no visual indications when a factor or combination of factors is less than ideal. The plant simply does not grow as well. Were our six-feet tall oak trees the ultimate in plant growth, health and vigor? Absolutely not! In more recent years we have grown bur oak seedlings over seven feet tall in one growing season as we further improved or refined the vast complex of synchronized factors that affect plant growth, health and vigor. So what is the ultimate in plant growth? No one knows, but as we strive to improve growing conditions, the vast array of pest and disease problems become more and more obscure. Thus the conclusion that the healthier the plant, the fewer the problems.*

It seems appropriate at this early point to reaffirm that more does not necessarily mean better. Several examples quickly come to mind where we are in a sense killing our plants with kindness. Some examples:

*a) **Excess** nitrogen fertilizer, disproportionate to the levels of other nutrient elements and soil and environmental conditions, is more harmful than helpful. At the same time, a **deficiency** of nitrogen can be harmful to plant health.*

*b) "Additional phosphorus helps make a good root system" and "You can't get too much phosphorus" are quotes made by the misinformed. Excess phosphorus ties up micronutrients, especially iron and manganese and can **suppress** plant growth. Many older landscapes are literally low-grade phosphate mines, and unfortunately there is no practical way to remove excess phosphorus from a soil.*

*c) Each species **does not** have an "ideal" soil pH. Sample the soil where a species is truly native and have it analyzed. The results will surprise you. Over much of the USA east of the Mississippi River, the soils are very acid with pHs in the 4 to 5 range, and according to virtually all soils labs and extension service information, these soils should be heavily limed to raise* the pH to 6.5 to 7.0. **Not so.** Most trees will grow much better at the lower pH than at the higher pH. Just because corn, wheat and soybeans grow best at 6.5 to 7.0 pH does not mean that most trees, shrubs and other landscape plants have the same requirements. The list of factors that we impose on landscape plants in an attempt to aid their growth while in reality we are complicating their growth and health could go on and on. Each landscape site is unique. It must be considered as a unique situation relative to the existing conditions of climate, soils and water and what factors man is going to impose. Then and only then can the intelligent process of selecting plants that will grow and remain healthy in the combination of conditions that exist be made.

The assumption is often made that a tree is quite large and should be able to tolerate a great deal. **Not so**! As a tree (or other plant) grows larger and larger, the distance compounds must be transported from roots to leaves and return increases. In addition, the mass of living cells in the tree grows larger and larger and the balance between the capacity of the roots to absorb water and nutrients and the capacity of the leaves to capture the light in the various carbohydrates (energy) and provide for the respiration of all the living cells of the tree becomes a critical balance. The physiological processes important to growth and plant health include:

a) absorption of water and nutrients by the roots;

b) the capture of light energy in the process of photosynthesis in all green tissues;

c) hormone synthesis by roots, shoots, leaves, flowers and fruits;

d) respiration of all living cells;

e) nitrogen metabolism;

f) synthesis and activity of various enzymes;

g) the transport of various growth regulatory and energy compounds from the point of production to the point(s) of use; and

h) conversion of energy into new cells (2, 3,). This is an extremely complex system, dependent on an array of cultural and environmental factors over which man has an influence either positive or negative.

Trees store large quantities of energy. Over 75% of the dry weight of a tree consists of various transformed sugars (energy). Trees use both currently produced energy as well as stored reserves of starch during various times of the year. Energy levels in trees drop rapidly with the beginning of a flush of growth then slowly recover as the new tissues mature and begin to manufacture more energy than they use. Attempting to transplant trees after they have begun a flush of growth and energy levels are naturally reduced is asking for trouble and stress levels that **invite** secondary problems.

When buds begin to swell in the spring, a strong chemical signal can be followed down the stem to the roots. If part of the top of the tree is removed by pruning, the strength of the chemical signal is decreased. If the bark is cut or injured, cambial growth below the blockage stops abruptly, largely as a result of reduced levels of growth regulators (1, 2).

Water is a key factor in tree health. It serves as a solvent for the transport of energy and growth regulatory compounds, as the major constituent of protoplasm in the cells, and as the coolant for the leaves and other plant parts to prevent overheating. Plants sweat and are cooled by sweat, although it is generally referred to as transpiration. When man can no longer sweat, his temperature quickly goes up and may reach the lethal point. A similar situation occurs in plants. On the other hand, excess water can be as harmful as the proper amount is helpful. Roots can be suffocated by excess water or by soils so compacted that insufficient gaseous exchange between soil and air can occur. The functions of roots in soils, because they cannot be seen, generally go unnoticed and receive little care or consideration (Figure D). This is unfortunate because, as the root system goes, so goes the plant! (Figure E.)

Figure D. The large tree (above) was on the site before construction began. The tree was "saved" by allowing some "extra" space in the parking lot (below). The trees died, but trees can sometimes get revenge (see Figure E on the next page).

Figure E. The roots of this tree were suffocated by the parking lot created beneath it and at a point could no longer support the top. Appropriately, the truck belonged to the owner of the site that had destroyed the trees roots. In this case, no one was injured, but sometimes this is not the case.

In summary, "accentuate the positive" should be the watch phrase. Do everything, which may mean doing nothing, to accent tree health. Time and effort spent to prevent problems is much more effective and efficient than time and effort to correct problems. By concentrating on improving and maintaining factors that aid tree health, other problems are minimized. There is much to be gained in the positive approach to tree health. Remember that the only 100% effective insecticide or fungicide is the one that is still on the suppliers shelf! The natural defenses of plants will do a tremendous job if we work with them instead of against them. And remember, as the root system goes, so goes the plant.

People of all ages are keenly interested in, and enjoy, plants (Figure F). If grown, transplanted and cared for properly, plants can grow for many years and provide a host of rewards. As the poem goes, "Only God can make a tree", thus the emphasis on preserving and caring for trees should be considered appropriately (Figure F).

Figure F. Youth, both in plants and people (above). Maturity can also be graceful, useful and functional in both people and trees (below).

Literature Cited

1. Evert, R.F. and T.T. Kozlowski. 1967. Effects of isolation of bark on cambial activity and development of xylem and phloem in trembling aspen. Amer. Jour. Bot. 54:1045-1055.

2. Kozlowski, T.T. 1985. Tree growth in response to environmental stress. Jour. of Arboriculture 11:97-111.

3. Kramer, Paul J. and T.T. Kozlowski. 1979. Physiology of woody plants. Academic Press, New York.

4. Whitcomb, Carl E. 1981. Response of woody landscape plants to bermudagrass competition and fertility. Jour. of Arboriculture 7:191-194.

5. Whitcomb, Carl E., Eliot C. Roberts and R.Q. Landers. 1969. A connecting pot technique for root competition investigations. Ecology 50:326-329.

CHAPTER 1

TRANSPLANTING AND ESTABLISHMENT

A Summary of Procedures - - - - - - - - 2

Pre-Installation - - - - - - - - - - - - 2

Installation - - - - - - - - - - - - 3

Literature Cited - - - - - - - - - - - - 6

Transplanting and Establishment

A Summary of Procedures. Research findings and new technology are slow to be incorporated into nursery and landscape practices. Tradition is important and has a distinct place in our society, however, blind allegiance to tradition stymies progress. In 1968, a study was begun to determine the "optimum" amount of soil amendments to use in the planting hole since recommendations varied from 5% to 50% by volume. The optimum amount turned out to be none. The findings were such a contrast to tradition, the question arose, "If tradition was in error regarding soil amendments, what about other practices?" This has led to numerous studies relative to reducing stress and accelerating growth of landscape plants. The following is a brief summary of the new technology in landscape plant establishment and care including one or more supporting references. If you simply want to know **what** to do, follow this outline. The **whys** are in the following chapters.

Pre-Installation.

A. Match the requirements of the plant with the conditions on the site carefully; consider the size and shape of a tree, color of bloom, and growth requirements. For example, wet or dry site, exposed or somewhat shaded by buildings or other trees. Matching the conditions on a planting site with a plant that will tolerate those conditions is the single most important factor influencing plant success (13).

B. The condition of the plant at time of digging and planting plays a key roll in transplant success. New root growth is dependent on stored energy reserves and conditions **inside** the plant; without sufficient energy, all of the subsequent steps will be of little benefit (12).

C. Evaluate soil internal drainage with a percolation or drainage test. Dig a hole 10 to 12 inches deep. Fill with water, twice the same day---wait 24 hours from last filling and note water level. If water is still present, **drainage must be provided**.

D. Conduct soil tests for chemical analysis of fertilizer needs. Simply spreading fertilizer can be as hurtful as helpful.

E. Have water quality (chemical analysis) determined. All dissolved minerals in the water can influence plant growth and should be considered in the overall management of the landscape.

Installation.

F. Install drainage if needed as determined by percolation test.

G. Incorporate any fertilizer necessary as shown by soil test--especially calcium, phosphorus, magnesium, or sulfur, or as needed to compensate for the irrigation water quality.

H. All planting holes must be dug at least three times as wide as the root ball or wider but no deeper than the root ball to avoid settling. Where drainage is marginal, all plants should be planted shallow or in mounds or berms. Replace existing soil around all plants to a firm, but not compacted, condition. Aeration of the soil is very important, yet large air spaces are to be avoided.

I. Use no soil amendments except in very specific condi-tions of raised or amended beds for plants with very limited root systems. If the existing soil is very poor, remove and replace with good field soil or place at least six inches of good field soil on the surface. However, you should match soil types as backfilling with a good sandy loam in a heavy clay will serve as a collection point for water and the roots will suffocate. Soil amendments in a small planting hole **do not** assist plant establishment and growth (5, 9, 14). It is better to use the amendments as a mulch. The only exception is where the entire plant root zone for many years can be amended. Water thoroughly while backfilling to avoid leaving air pockets. Do not pack soil excessively yet firm the soil so the plant is adequately supported. Make certain that any burlap, or if container-grown, the top of the root ball, is covered by approximately one inch of topsoil, but do not "bury" the plant as aeration is a key ingredient in active root growth.

J. If the plant has been dug balled-in-burlap, remove plastic cover, if any, and the burlap from the sides of the ball after placement in the planting hole. If container-grown, remove the container exposing the root ball as little as possible to air. The white growing root tips are the key to rapid establishment in the landscape, but are killed or injured by even brief exposure to air.

K. Trees dug with a tree spade **should not** be planted into a tree spade-dug hole. The development of new roots at the face of the root ball and into the surrounding soil require considerable aeration, thus the need for a larger planting hole with a well-aerated soil (1, 4).

L. Mound the remaining soil into a dike or berm to hold water around the tree where rainfall can be limiting and soils are fair to good. With heavy soils it is advisable to break the dike to avoid excess water and suffocation of roots during wet weather, yet the dikes can readily be repaired to facilitate watering during dry weather. In areas of frequent rainfall and heavy soils, it is better to plant shallow or create berms to drain excess water away and avoid root suffocation (9, 14).

M. Plants container-grown with good nutrition and planted in the fall while the soil is warm, establish roots very rapidly. The following summer the plants have many more roots to support the plant and reduce moisture stress. This technique has worked extremely well, however, how far north fall planting can be done remains to be determined (2, 9). "Fall" may be late August in Minnesota and November along the Gulf Coast.

N. Stake only when necessary. On certain soils, on windy sites, or when trees or shrubs are quite large, staking may be required to hold the young plant upright until it becomes established. Two stakes should be placed on either side of the plant and as low as possible (generally 12 to 18 inches above the soil). Attach stake to stem using wire or cord and an effective cushion/insulator or an eye screw or eyebolt of a size proportionate to the plant (this does little harm to the tree). Do not wrap wire or rope snugly around the stem as it frequently causes damage to the stem. Remove stakes after one growing season in most cases. If eye screws cannot be readily removed, leave them in place (3, 9).

O. Install expandable stem protectors on all trees and any shrubs with exposed stems that may be damaged by string trimmers (weed eaters).

P. Following planting of bare root, balled-in-burlap or container-grown trees, remove only damaged branches or to aid branch spacing and development and appearance. Do not shear or prune branches indiscriminately. Evaluate branching carefully, consider spacing around the stem as well as vertical spacing and appearance. Remove branches that have very narrow forks as these will become particularly subject to wind or ice damage as they grow larger. These suggestions also apply to shrubs. There is no advantage to indiscriminately pruning one-third of the top of the plant as has long been recommended (15).

Q. There is no benefit to the tree from painting pruning wounds. The tree will wall-off or compartmentalize decay if the tree is healthy (6). If pruning **is** done, do not cut too close to the main stem to avoid disturbing the branch collar (7).

R. No root-bound container-grown plants should be accepted.

S. If trees and shrubs must be transplanted during the growing season, plants grown or established in containers or in fabric containers should be used. Or if transplanted B&B in full leaf, strip off all leaves if necessary (except conifers and broadleaf evergreens that hold leaves for more than one growing season). Leaf removal is recommended only when the stem tissue is physiologically mature.

T. Several hours after planting, re-water thoroughly to assist soil in settling around the root ball and to eliminate air pockets.

U. Water thoroughly once each five to seven days during the first growing season when there is insufficient rainfall. However, **do not drown the roots!**

V. Proper watering is critical to the establishment of plants in the landscape. Excess water, especially where drainage is marginal or poor, can be as undesirable as insufficient water. Container-grown plants must be watered at a moderate rate **frequently** to aid rapid establishment.

W. Fertilize all landscape plants as soon as installa-tion and one thorough watering are complete. If soil tests have been conducted and phosphorus and other non-leaching fertilizers have been incorporated, only nitrogen should be applied. Fertilize the plant on the soil surface immediately after planting (spring or fall) or use slow-release fertilizer in the planting hole. Fertilize at the rate of about one pound of nitrogen per 1000 square feet of soil surface area. Spread the fertilizer over the area which has been kept clean of weeds and grass and has been mulched. Repeat fertilization procedure two to three times during the growing season but especially in the fall when soils are warm and roots are especially active (8, 9).

X. Mulch all exposed soil surfaces no less than two inches and not more than four inches deep with a coarse, well aerated mulch. Porous weed barrier fabric may be placed under mulches and provides some benefits. Do not allow the placement of plastic sheeting beneath any mulch.

Y. Keep grass and weeds away from young trees (11). It is best to clear a five- to seven-foot diameter circle around the tree and mulch heavily (three to four inches) but do not bury the base of the trunk so that bark suffocation occurs. This will aid in keeping out grass and weeds, will conserve soil moisture and protect the root ball from drying out, and keep the soil cooler in summer and warmer in winter. Remember, too much of a good thing is generally undesirable; three to four inches of mulch is about right. River gravel, pine bark, leaves, redwood nuggets, etc., may be used as a mulch, but do not bury the above-ground stem with mulch. Leave a depression in the mulch around the stem. **Do not** place black plastic below the mulch as it restricts oxygen reaching the roots; porous weed barrier fabrics are far superior. Do not use limestone rock as a mulch due to the pH factor (10).

This summary is intended to be a quick "what to do" guide only. The details and support for these recommendations are in the various chapters. As you read the rest of the story, the basis for the recommendation will become clear.

Literature Cited

1. Bridel, Robert, Carl E. Whitcomb, and B.L. Appleton. 1983. Improving performance of tree spade-dug trees. Jour. of Arboriculture 9:282-284.

2. Dickinson, Sancho M. and Carl E. Whitcomb. 1977. The effects of spring vs fall planting on establishment of landscape plants. Nursery Res. Jour. 4(1):9-19.

3. Neil, P.L. 1969. Growth factors in trunk development of young trees. Proc. Int. Shade Tree Conf. 45:46-59.

4. Preaus, Kenneth and Carl E. Whitcomb. 1980. Transplanting landscape trees. Jour. of Arboriculture 6(8):221-223.

5. Schulte, Joseph and Carl E. Whitcomb. 1975. Effects of soil amendments and fertilizer levels on the establishment of silver maple. Jour. of Arboriculture 1:192-195.

6. Shigo, Alex. L. 1977. Compartmentalization of decay in Trees. USDA Bulletin #405. 73 pages.

7. Shigo, Alex L. 1980. Branches. Jour. of Arboriculture 6:300-304.

8. Whitcomb, Carl E 1978. Effects of spring vs. fall fertilization on the growth and cold tolerance of woody plants in the landscape. Okla. Agri. Exp. Sta. Nursery Res. Rept. P-777 pp. 11-12.

9. Whitcomb, Carl E. 1979. Factors affecting the establish-ment of urban trees. Jour. of Arboriculture 5(10):217-220.

10. Whitcomb, Carl E. 1980. Effects of black plastic and mulches on growth and survival of landscape plants. Jour. of Arboriculture 6:10-12.

11. Whitcomb, Carl E. 1981. Response of woody landscape plants to bermudagrass competition and fertility. Jour. of Arboriculture 7:191-194.

12. Whitcomb, Carl E. 1982. Why large trees are difficult to transplant. Jour. of Arboriculture 9:57-59.

13. Whitcomb, Carl E. 1985. *Know it & Grow It II: A Guide to the Identification and Use of Landscape Plants.* Lacebark Publications, Stillwater, Ok. 740 pages.

14. Whitcomb, Carl E., Robert L. Byrnes, Joseph R. Schulte and James D. Ward. 1976. What is a $5 planting hole? Amer. Nurseryman 144(5):16, 111, 112, 114, 115.

15. Whitcomb, Carl E., Steve Shoup and Rick Reavis. 1981. Effects of pruning and fertilizer on the establishment of bare root deciduous trees. Jour. of Arboriculture 7:155-157.

CHAPTER 2

METHODS OF PLANT PRODUCTION

Old Vs. New - - - - - - - - - - - - - - - - 9

Bare Root - - - - - - - - - - - - - - - - 9

Balled-in-Burlap - - - - - - - - - - - - - 13

Tree Spades - - - - - - - - - - - - - - - 22

Container Production - - - - - - - - - - 26

The Unique Container - - - - - - - - - - 27

Root Development/Root-bound - - - - - - 28

Root Development and Larger Plants - - - 37

The Future. RootMakers - - - - - - - - - 41
       RootBuilders - - - - - - - - - - 44
       The Fabric Container - - - - - - - 48

Harvesting, Holding and Planting - - - - 51

Water Management of Newly Planted Trees - 53

A Can opener for Trees
       in Fabric Containers - - - - - 58

Container Size/Tree Size Relationships - 60

The Permanent Root System - - - - - - - 62

Literature Cited - - - - - - - - - - - 66

Methods of Plant Production

In order to make sound decisions regarding transplanting and establishing landscape plants, some knowledge of how they are produced is required. This chapter on methods of plant production is included to support that knowledge. For example, to order and obtain bare root nursery stock in the fall would, in nearly every situation, be disastrous. Likewise, to miss planting container nursery stock in the fall, if the project is ready, would be unfortunate.

Old Vs. New. Landscape plants have been grown in field soils then dug and wrapped or tied in some way since man began caring about his immediate surroundings. The classical bare root or balled-in-burlap (B & B) technique for transplanting plants grown in the field has remained unchanged for many years. As labor costs increase and the size and quality of nursery stock grown in containers improve, the demand for bare root and balled-in-burlap plants has decreased. In addition, the general performance of bare root or balled-in-burlap trees following transplanting is only fair on marginally suitable landscape planting sites or where planting cannot be done at the time of year most favorable for plant establishment.

As the nursery and landscape industries have grown in size and sophistication, so have the general expectations of consumers. Plants that require a growing season or more to establish and lend the full desired effect to the landscape are no longer acceptable.

Recent work showed that up to 98% of the roots of field-grown trees are lost when dug conventionally (balled-in-burlap or with a tree spade). This is probably the single most important factor in understanding the marginal performance of plants grown conventionally in the field and dug and transplanted bare root or balled-in-burlap.

Bare Root.
The advantages of handling trees and shrubs bare root are:
a) The investment per plant is low.
b) Cost of plants to the consumer is low.
c) Plants are lightweight without soil, making shipping economical.
On the other hand, the disadvantages are:
a) The time appropriate for digging and transplanting is short.

b) Only those deciduous species easy to transplant are tolerant of the technique.
c) Since all fine roots are killed during digging, handling and storage, no root activity occurs until bud swell in the spring. Consequently, planting in fall or winter is generally not suitable due to bud and twig dehydration. In many geographic areas, the lowest humidity of the year occurs during the winter.
d) Small plants can be handled bare root with acceptable survival rates, whereas larger plants generally have more problems.
e) Only those plants very stress-tolerant and capable of rapid recovery following transplanting can be handled successfully.

Most plants dug bare root are grown in sandy loam field soils so that the soil can be easily removed from the roots. This is normally done by mechanical diggers using a U-shaped blade with a lifting unit or fingers that lift and agitate the soil (Figure 2.1). In some cases a modified potato harvester is drawn behind the U-shaped blade to further lift and shake the plants and soil to hasten separation (Figure 2.2). The plants are either loaded onto trailers and taken to a storage area where they are later graded and sorted as to size and quality or in some cases, they are rough sorted and tied into bundles in the field (Figure 2.2). With either procedure, sufficient dehydration occurs to kill all fine roots leaving the larger roots roughly 1/8-inch or larger to re-establish the plant on the new site. Fortunately, the energy level inside the plant is generally good, which further aids re-establishment on the new site. Handling plants bare root can work well if the storage time is brief or non-existent. **The greatest problem with bare root nursery stock is the storage rather than the digging process.**

Figure 2.1. A U-shaped blade is used to cut the roots on three sides of the plant (above). Most units have some type of lift or finger apparatus attached to the back of the U-blade to further shake or move the soil to aid separation. A crawler tractor was modified to give more belly clearance for stradling the rows while digging with a U-blade (below).

11

Figure 2.2. A modified potato harvester is drawn behind the U-blade to further aid in soil separation (above). The potato harvester shakes the plants and soil vigorously and in many soil/soil moisture situations, leaves the roots relatively clean. The plants may be taken directly to a storage area or rough-graded and tied in the field (below).

12

Balled-in-Burlap. Balled-in-burlap (B & B) is the time-honored method of transplanting most field-grown nursery stock, primarily during the dormant period. The plant is carefully dug with a block of soil surrounding the base of the plant. The soil is generally wrapped in burlap, secured with pinning nails and/or wrapped with twine (Figure 2.3). If the process is completed correctly, the soil ball is held securely and is not broken or allowed to shift during shipping, handling and planting into the landscape. Because only a very few active root tips are present in the soil ball they must sustain the plant until it is planted into the landscape and new roots develop from the cut ends of the larger roots (Figure 2.4). Breakage or disruption of these few small roots may mean the plant dies.

Advantages of the B & B method are:
  a) Digging and transplanting season is extended compared to bare root.
  b) Plants with poor survival when handled bare root can be transplanted with moderate satisfaction. In particular are the broadleaf evergreens and conifers: pines, spruce, fir, hollies, etc.
  c) A soil ball placed in the landscape creates minimal textural and water movement differences compared to container-grown plants in soilless mixes where the texture of the mix and the soil at the planting site are vastly different and create greater water stress problems.
  d) Plants may be dug ahead of time and held for moderate periods of time above ground if handled properly, thus extending the transplanting time.

Note: Transplanting with tree spades and other mechanical digging devices would have the same advantages and disadvantages as the B & B method.

13

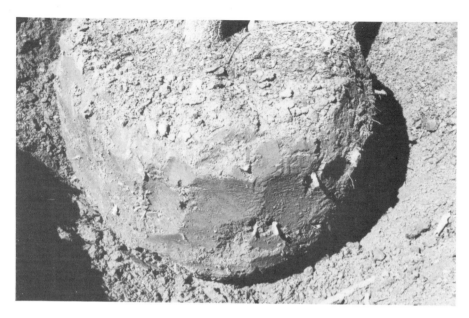

Figure 2.3. Once the ball of soil is shaped (above), burlap is used to hold the soil ball in place around the roots during digging, handling and planting (below). Pinning nails are used to secure the ends of the burlap. Twine may or may not be needed to further secure the burlap and soil mass depending on the specific soil.

Figure 2.4. Plants dug bare root, B & B, or with tree spades must be sustained by the very limited absorption of water by the sections of large roots and the few fine roots. New roots develop just behind the cut surface of the root end in most cases. These roots are slow to develop following planting, thus considerable care and maintenance is required. The plant on the left was grown in a fabric container that stimulates root branching. The plant on the right has an excellent root system for a plant dug B & B.

Disadvantages are:
a) 98% or more of the roots of the plant are lost at digging (11).
b) Digging is limited to the dormant season for all but a few of the very tolerant species.
c) Some species still cannot be transplanted with satisfactory survival percentages using this technique. Examples: Kentucky coffee tree (*Gymnocladus dioica*), blackgum (*Nyssa sylvatica*), sassafras (*Sassafras albidum*), and gums or eucalyptus (*Eucalyptus* spp.).
d) considerable labor is required, and the labor must be skilled at this technique (it is not as easy as it looks or sounds and balls are different sizes (Figure 2.5).

15

e) Soil moisture conditions can limit digging. Very dry or very wet soils are unsatisfactory.

f) The root balls are heavy and awkward to transport, yet if broken or allowed to shift, chances of plant survival decrease.

g) Root balls must be kept moist but not overly wet during handling and shipping (Figure 2.5) Soil balls with excess water may end up shaped like pancakes after being hauled considerable distance.

h) Heavier soils work best since the soil ball is less likely to break and damage the few small roots that must sustain the plants until replanting. Some species, such as redbuds, dogwoods, pines, and other conifers in particular, grow best on well-drained, sandy loam soils. However, since they are are often dug B & B, they must be grown on soils sufficiently heavy for satisfactory digging.

i) Planting should be completed in the spring before natural bud break for the species (elongation of the buds at the ends of the many twigs and branches). The growth regulating chemicals sent downward by the expanding buds are responsible for the development of new roots from the cut ends of the larger roots. This early root development plays a major role in reducing the stress experienced by the plant during the critical first growing season.

Many plants are dug B & B and "heeled-in" (placed above-ground and surrounded with mulch such as sawdust, bark or straw) to protect the roots in the ball of soil (Figure 2.6). These plants are often held for planting after the normal spring flush of new growth for the species. Under these conditions, the major development of new roots occurs into the mulch material. When plants are removed from these conditions, many of the new roots outside the original soil ball are damaged or killed, either by exposure to air or physical breakage. When the initial spring bud break is past, there is less chemical signal to stimulate a new burst of roots to rapidly establish the plant in the new site. Consequently, the plant has new foliage, with a high rate of water loss, with an extremely limited root system and no major chemical signal to develop new roots until the following spring. Conditions are further complicated by the fact that the energy level in the plant drops substantially with the extension of the new top growth. Also, because of the very limited root system,

16

the supply of water and nutrients to the leaves will be minimal throughout the growing season which prevents the normal replenishing of energy in the plant following the initial spring flush. Energy levels in the plant decrease sharply during spring growth then slowly build to a peak in fall just before leaf drop, with only a slight decline during winter until the spring flush again (6, 9, 11).

Energy (carbohydrate) and growth regulator levels of root tissue are probably the limiting factors in new root growth when trees are transplanted during the spring shoot growth period (8, 13).

All these factors strongly emphasize the importance of: a) planting B & B plants **before** the spring flush of growth, or b) holding these plants in some type of container to minimize the disruption of the new roots produced prior to time of planting in the landscape.

To say that balled-in-burlap does not work would be in error because it can work if done properly and timely. However, the vast loss of roots means the plant will be under severe stress for some time and thus requires considerable attention and maintenance. At this point we have techniques for growing plants with superior root systems that reduce or eliminate most of the stress associated with transplanting.

Figure 2.5. Trees dug balled-in-burlap ready for sale or shipping. Frequently the root balls are of different size, shape, and weight, making handling and shipping awkward (above). Watering must be done carefully. Because the root ball is small in comparison to the top and the burlap further promotes evaporation, the root balls can dry out very quickly (below).

18

Figure 2.6. Trees heavily mulched to protect the roots from heat and cold and to help stabilize soil moisture. Unfortunately, if the trees remain in this position very long, the burlap deteriorates and roots grow into the mulch or into the soil below, making further movement of the ball difficult and increasing plant stress.

When first considered, placing plants dug B & B into containers for holding seems like a very desirable alternative (Figure 2.7). However, several factors must be considered to avoid complications. Every container has a perched water table caused by the bottom restricting the normal downward movement of water. This is why very porous soilless mixes are used almost exclusively for producing plants in containers. When the ball of field soil is placed in the container, the potential for a very high perched water table and rapid suffocation of roots exists (Figure 2.8). If the ball of field soil is surrounded by a suitable soilless growth medium such as would be used if the plant had been grown in the container, drainage of excess water proceeds normally and the plants can be held for considerable time under these conditions. On the other hand, if the soil ball is placed

19

in a container and surrounded by additional field soil, water management must be precise. In most cases, plant losses, particularly of sensitive species, are great. Given two trees dug B & B and placed in containers the same diameter and depth, one surrounded by soil while the other is surrounded by a suitable mix for the depth of the container, the one with the soil may lose part or all of its root system to suffocation. Taxus, pines, and other conifers, as well as dogwoods, redbuds and certain other hardwood species are especially sensitive (15). The soilless mix used around the B & B soil ball should contain reasonable levels of all nutrients required for plant growth. For a discussion of soilless mixes and nutrition of these soil substitutes, see *Plant Production in Containers* by Carl Whitcomb (14). Proper nutrition of B & B trees held in containers greatly reduces the stress experienced by the plants before, during and after transplanting.

Figure 2.7. These upright junipers were dug in the field and placed into paper mache pots for holding or shipping. This can be an acceptable practice if water is managed carefully but often it ends in plant death due to root suffocation.

20

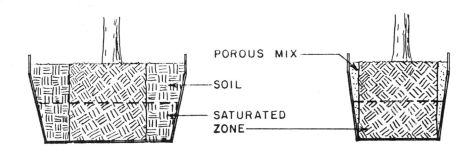

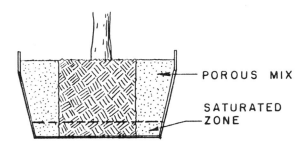

Figure 2.8.   If the root ball is surrounded by soil, the saturated zone in the container will be deep (above, left).   Likewise, if the sides of the root ball are large enough to touch the sides of the container, the saturated zone will be deep and many roots are likely to suffocate (above, right).   However, if the root ball is surrounded by a porous mix, the saturated zone will be shallow and plant performance will be good (below).

Both bare root and balled-in-burlap plants are most effectively dug and planted in early spring before growth begins. This greatly limits the length of time nursery plants can be offered for sale.   Therefore, various techniques such as cold storage, shade and heeling-in with sawdust, bark, straw or similar materials are used to extend the digging and selling season. These techniques are successful to varying degrees.   However, the consuming public does not understand the limitations of these techniques and sufficient plant losses occur to discourage many gardeners.

Tree Spades. Many trees are dug with a mechanical tree spade, then placed in wire baskets lined with burlap to better secure the root ball for shipping and handling (Figure 2.9). This technique adds considerable harvest expense, but does help in keeping the soil around the roots from shifting.

The effect of the wire basket on future root growth and plant health has been questioned. In order to observe this closely, several trees were dug that had been placed in wire baskets for transplanting six years earlier. The wire baskets were in very good condition even though they had been in the soil for six years and were made of painted, not galvanized, wire. Root restrictions and injury as a result of the wire could be observed at several locations (Figure 2.10).

Lumis and Stroger (7) report that the regrowth of tissue has the capacity of enclose sections of wire baskets completely. They note, "If vascular and cambial function is partially or fully restored, the concern about the detrimental effects of wire baskets may be over-stated."

The effect of the wire on the future health of the trees remains to be seen. However, the many roots partially restricted, and the limited deterioration of the wire, suggest that the wire baskets do somewhat jeopardize plant health. Whether the benefits of the wire baskets in moving larger plants and keeping the soil ball from breaking or shifting, justifies the restriction of a portion of the lateral root growth even if for a limited time remains to be determined. Many nurserymen and landscape contractors are either for or against wire baskets based on their own feelings and observations. Until a good study is made of the long-term effects of wire baskets on tree growth and health, the jury is still out.

One of the most costly practices for both B & B and tree spade harvest field nurseries is the hunt-and-harvest practice. If all of the trees are of a consistent size and quality so that they can all be harvested at one time, mechanical digging with tree spades works fairly well. However, if only an occassional tree is salable, so that either the machine operator or B & B digging crew must hunt for an acceptable tree, the cost of harvest goes up dramatically (Figure 2.11).

Figure 2.9. A field-grown tree is dug with a tree spade (above). The root ball is placed in a wire basket lined with burlap and tied securely. By making crimps or twists in the wire the burlap can be drawn securely around the root ball to reduce the likelihood of shifting or breaking during shipping and handling (below).

Figure 2.10. Root growth of a sycamore tree in relation to a wire basket. Several roots have been partially restricted by the wire (above). Looking at the overall root system (see arrows, below) several roots have been partially restricted but they represent only a small portion of the supporting root system on this six-inch caliper tree. The painted wire basket had been in the ground six years, yet little deterioration had occurred except near the soil surface.

Figure 2.11. If all of the trees are of marketable size and quality such that all can be dug at one time, labor/ machinery efficiency is good (above). However, if only an occasional tree is of marketable quality, the cost per unit to harvest is much greater and space use efficiency in the field is decreased (below).

25

Container Production. After World War II a new nursery industry began developing in southern California where techniques common to greenhouse production of pot plants were used. Because temperatures were mild and moisture fell only when the irrigation system was on, container production procedures which worked in the southern California sun lead to disaster when employed elsewhere. Southern California is unique in that it provides an outdoor environment similar to the climate in greenhouses in other parts of the world, but **little** rain.

Despite numerous setbacks and frustration for growers outside southern California, the production of a wide assortment of plants in containers continued to increase. The consuming public eagerly purchased them for several reasons:

   a) Plants were in full leaf and sometimes flowering when offered for sale, thus the stigma of buying a "dead" (dormant) plant was removed.
   b) The container provided a neat package, easily displayed, handled, and transported in the trunk or back seat of an automobile.
   c) In general, container-grown plants could be planted anytime during the growing season, instead of just during a limited period in the spring.
   d) For the less informed public, the container-grown plant provided a greater chance of success.

By the early '60s, container production of nursery stock had spread throughout the southern United States and in other parts of the world. However, many problems existed because the unique environment of the container was not understood. Productive field soils failed to support good plant growth in containers. Peat and sand were frequently added to field soils to try to improve drainage but with little benefit. During this period, growth of plants in containers was slow because of poor nutrition and losses were high due to root rot organisms such as *Phytophthora* and *Pythium* which flourished in these overly wet and poorly aerated conditions. With each improvement in container plant production techniques, the weeds grew better than the crop plant, and because the roots of the crop plant were confined to a limited volume, the growth restrictions due to weeds were tremendous. (For detailed information regarding containers, see *Plant Production in Containers*, 1989)

The Unique Container. Growing plants in containers does not alter the basic physiological principles involved in the production of any crop. Neither are the genetics of the plant altered (Figure 2.12). On the other hand, the conditions in the container are unique compared to any other plant production system. Consider that no plants have evolved in containers as compared to the immense diversity of climatic conditions and soils that exist in nature. Plants are grown in containers for the convenience of man, **and** only when conditions in the container have been highly refined and carefully maintained, do the plants grow well.

The length of time a plant can be grown or held in a container without repotting, is limited. The air spaces in the container growth media (soil mix), so essential to active root growth, are rapidly filled by roots as the plant grows. In a sense, the plant restricts itself as the demand for aeration due to growth of the root system increases and the availability of air decreases due to filling of the air spaces with roots and settling and decomposition of the media. When the aeration level in the mix declines beyond a certain point, root activity declines, and, unless shifted to a larger container with new mix, the plant will stop growing, regardless of additional fertilizer or water. This is especially true for woody plants. A further complication is the fact that with conventional containers, 90% or more of the roots of most plants are in the outer sheath of growth medium next to the inner container wall. The vast proportion of the medium provides little towards plant health and vigor other than serving as a water reservoir and ballast to hold the plant upright. Because of this container/root/ media/aeration relationship, the time a plant can remain in a specific container is limited. Thus the point is reached where container-grown nursery stock must be sold, shifted into a larger container, or thrown away.

Figure 2.12. These small trees were field-grown then dug when dormant in the fall and placed in storage. Before spring growth began, they were placed in containers with a good growth medium. These field-grown plants are now "container-grown" (once a good root system has developed). The growth characteristics of the plant are not altered, but the environment of the root system has been radically changed. If the container growth medium is correct, plant top and root growth will be excellent. However, unless the container conditions are understood and managed correctly, disaster can occur.

Root Development/Root-bound. The question frequently arises, "When does root development in a container reach the point of being 'root-bound'?" The answer is not simple. Root-bound begins at that point where the growth rate of the plant begins to decline due to a decrease in available space in the container for further root development. It continues to the point where plant growth

28

cannot be stimulated to proceed at even modest rates, regardless of fertilizer, water, light, or temperature conditions. The greater the decline in plant growth and vigor, due to decreased root activity, the more difficult establishment of the plant will be in a larger container and especially in the landscape. At some point, the plant becomes so stunted that the only value remaining is as organic matter in a compost heap. **Being root-bound is, therefore, not a specific point or condition but rather a progressively undesirable condition from the ideal state of root development to the very undesirable point where the plant should be thrown away.** The point where the plant should be discarded varies with species and, to some degree, how the plant was propagated, but in general, if no white root tips are visible on the surface of the root ball when the container is removed, establishment and subsequent growth in the field or landscape will be poor at best and losses are likely to be substantial.

Plants that are propagated from cuttings develop secondary roots more readily than those grown from seed. The roots that form on the base of a cutting are secondary or adventitious roots. The fact that these form rather easily and quickly also means that as roots restrict roots, secondary roots are formed, thus slowing somewhat the rate at which a plant reaches the severe root-bound condition, where no white root tips are visible when the container is removed. Plants grown from seed generally do not develop secondary roots readily, therefore, as the initial root growth progresses to the point where space becomes limiting to plant root growth, the decline in numbers of white root tips is rapid. A tree grown from seed in a container with no white root tips is unlikely to grow following transplanting into the field or landscape. A higher percent of these undesirable trees will survive if shifted into a larger container if they are managed very carefully, essentially as a large cutting. However, their growth will be slow, problems many, and their value will be minimal.

A key point to remember is that once normal growth is restricted, for any reason, the plant will never catch up with plants that have not been restricted--assuming all other factors are equal. This can be readily observed in the photos in this chapter dealing with the time of transplant of tree seedlings. The ideal point of transplant to avoid any root-bound stress is as soon as the root development has progressed so that it will hold the soil mix together, no more. This is **much** sooner than would normally be anticipated from observing the root system.

29

The emphasis on white root tips, visible when the container is removed, cannot be over-emphasized. The white root tips play a key role in establishing the plant in the field or landscape. Unfortunately, not all of the white root tips visible when the container is removed grow out into the surrounding soil. In studies with several species only 38% to 61% of the white root tips continued to grow following transplanting. In these studies care was taken to assure that the root tips did not dry out while the counts were being made or during the transplanting process. The reason for an apparently active and white root tip to cease to extend following transplanting is not understood. See the chapter on spring vs. fall transplanting and the book, *Production of Landscape Plants* for further information on this topic.

Figures 2.13, 2.14, 2.15, 2.16, 2.17, 2.18, 2.19 show plants with root development from near ideal to severely root-bound. Perhaps the best advice is simply, "If in doubt, throw it out". To put it another way, it is far better and more economical to throw it out than to go to the expense of planting only to have it die and have to be replaced. Plants that perform poorly or die after installation in the landscape are "black eyes" to the nursery and landscape industry and related businesses. The "man on the street" generally attributes a dead or dying plant to something, the lack of rain, too much rain or irrigation, "that particular species won't grow here", poor planting procedures by the contractor or nursery, and on and on. On the other hand, plants are supposed to be green and healthy so little notice is given to good plant performance. One dead or dying plant in a landscape probably does more harm to the image of the industry than the favorable appearance of several hundred healthy ones. Once container-grown nursery stock gets root-bound beyond a certain difficult-to-define point, it becomes a liability, not an asset. **When a plant reaches the point of optimum root growth it** should be sold or shifted into a larger container. If not, at some point shortly thereafter a point is reached where its value and performance decreases very rapidly. That is the price for the convenience of plant production in containers.

Figure 2.13 Nearly ideal root development in a conventional container prior to transplanting. Note the white root tips on the sides and bottom of the root ball which will extend and support the plant physically as well as with water and nutrients.

Figure 2.14. The pyracantha (above) has visible white root tips, but they are mostly at the base of the root ball and the root mass around the sides is very tangled. This plant will likely survive in the landscape and because it is from a species that develops secondary roots with relative ease, will probably function for a reasonable time, although its life will be shortened by the root-bound condition. The roots of the juniper (below) will mean poor establishment and landscape performance if it survives at all.

32

Figure 2.15. This ligustrum is very root-bound and will be slow to establish in the landscape. Like the pyracantha in the previous figure, if it survives the transplant stress and does eventually get a few roots out into the surrounding soil, it will probably function for a moderate period of time. Keep in mind that a ligustrum or pyracantha are much more tolerant to the undesirable root-bound condition than many other species.

Figure 2.16. The oak tree (above) is severely root-bound and will never make a good tree with adequate anchorage even if it does survive transplanting. Throw it away, is good advice. The roots of this elm tree (below) are so intermingled that it would be permanently stunted to some degree even if it survived transplanting. There were no white root tips visible on the outer surface of the root ball, thus intensive, extended care would be required in order to get this tree to survive in the landscape. If it survived, it would be poorly anchored and stunted, thus subject to disease and insect problems and blow-over.

Figure 2.17. With the spring flush of growth, many root-bound plants will develop some new actively growing root tips. On the outer surface of the root ball, only a few white root tips can be observed (above). These are the key to survival of the plant. Unfortunately, for every active white root tip, there are masses of roots showing no activity (below). The bottom photo is a close-up of the center of the bottom of the above plant.

Figure 2.18.   In many cases, if a root-bound container-grown plant is planted either in a field nursery to grow on or a landscape, its performance is poor and its life is short.   The oak (above) was grown in a three-gallon container for one year, then planted in the field.   When it was dug two years later, the only roots that grew out from the container root mass were from the bottom and on one side (with one exception, see left, center).   Once the tree reaches any appreciable height and a strong wind blows from left to right...., as there were no roots growing downward either. This has nothing to do with a tap root, but rather with container design.

Figure 2.19. These two trees are the same age and the difference in container volume is only about 20% (5-gallon poly bag, left, and 4-gallon rigid plastic container, right), however, note the many white root tips on the tree grown with the poly bag which stops root circling and stimulates root branching as opposed to the poor root system with most roots at the very bottom of the container. Container design can have a great influence on root development and plants becoming root-bound.

Root Development and Larger Plants. Many containers and other root modification techniques have been tested and reported. However, a major clue as to the importance of the number of roots at the root/stem interface resulted from an unplanned experiment. A study had been planned with considerable care since differences in plant response to treatments was expected to be relatively small. Four species were selected and 180 trees of each species were planted in the field. In order to have very uniform plants in the beginning, about 300 trees of each species had been grown in two-gallon polyethylene bag containers. The 180 most uniform trees were selected for the study. Two years later and three unsuccessful attempts to establish various treatments among the trees ended in a great deal of difference in tree size and quality but without any treatments. Since the trees were very

37

uniform when planted, the vast difference in tree growth was a surprise and mystery.

At the end of the second growing season, all of the trees were dug using a 24-inch backhoe, and the soil removed in order to see if a relationship existed between root development following planting and top growth. All large trees had many small to medium-sized roots, whereas, some small or medium-sized trees had a few large roots. Counts of large roots (over 3/4-inch or more in diameter at the root/crown interface) were not correlated with stem diameters of tree height. Likewise, counts of various sizes of roots alone or in combination at a point approximately 18 inches out from the stem revealed only poor correlations with stem diameters and tree height. However, when counts of roots, approximately 3/16 inches (5 cm.) or larger arising from the root/stem interface were taken, a striking correlation resulted (Figures 2.20 and 2.21)

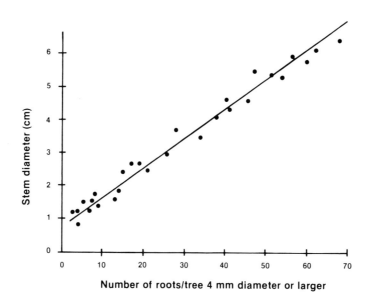

*Figure 2.20. Relationship of number of roots arising from the root/stem interface and stem diameter of lacebark elm (**Ulmus parvifolia**) trees. It is striking how the relation-ship between number of roots and stem diameter of the trees exists since all values are very close to the line.*

Figure 2.21.   Uniform trees of lacebark elm (**Ulmus parvifolia**) *were planted in the field from two-gallon containers then dug two years later.   The vast difference in tree size as affected by the number of roots arising from the root/stem interface shows the importance of proper root development on plant growth in the landscape.*

This suggests that the number of roots arising from the root/stem interface is more important to tree growth than the number of roots developed on the ends of a few larger roots as a result of root pruning or other techniques.   Looking back, this was somewhat suggested by earlier studies, but the relationship was missed in evaluating the results of those studies (1, 2, 3, 4, 5, 10).

The fact that the trees were uniform in age and size when the study began points up a pronounced weakness in evaluating container-grown plants using only the visual quality of the top. With the luxury of water, root zone aeration and nutrition in a well managed container production system, a plant of good size and visual quality can be produced with a poorly formed root system (Figure 2.22). Following transplanting into a less favorable environment, the quality of the root system greatly influences root proliferation and soil contact on the new site and gradually plants with superior root systems grow faster because of the additional water and nutrient absorption.

The striking relationship between the number of relatively small roots arising from the root/stem junction and plant growth in the landscape suggests several management practices:

a) Root pruning of bed-grown seedlings should be done earlier and shallower than is currently practiced.

b) Tree seedling containers should be relatively shallow in order to stimulate root branching at or near the root/stem junction (as opposed to the deep containers sometimes used). Transplanting should be prompt and much earlier than is normally practiced.

c) Trees that can be propagated from cuttings with a substantial numbers of roots stimulated on the base of the cutting should have superior growth compared to the same species grown from seed. Hickman and Whitcomb (5) observed far better growth with several cultivars of lacebark elm propagated from cuttings compared to the best seedlings. They concluded that the difference was due to the genetic superiority of the cultivar propagated from cuttings as opposed to the seedlings. In retrospect, the difference may have been equally or more related to the number of roots developed at the root/stem interface. Similar growth differences have been obtained using red maple (*Acer rubrum*), osage orange (*Maclura pomifera*), and London planetree (*Platanus acerifolia*) (unpublished data).

Figure 2.22. Root development of two English oaks as a result of root-modifying seedling containers. However, due to the abundance of nutrients, water and aeration in the larger containers, the tops of the two trees grew similarly while having vastly different root systems. If these trees were planted into the landscape, their performance would be very different.

The Future. RootMakers. New container designs force the root system on a seedling to branch at the desired root/stem juncture. They stop root circling or wrapping and stimulate root branching. This container is 2.6 inches square and 4 inches deep (Figure 2.23). The bottom is designed to air-root-prune the taproot of seedlings and stimulate secondary root branching. It works like a bottomless container only has a bottom for ease of filling and handling. In addition, the offset edges or shoulders are tapered to direct secondary roots into openings in the sidewall for further air-root-pruning. The container is called the RootMaker and is patented. A One-gallon size is available to continue the process. For more information, contact Lacebark Inc. P.O. Box 2383, Stillwater, Oklahoma 74076.

41

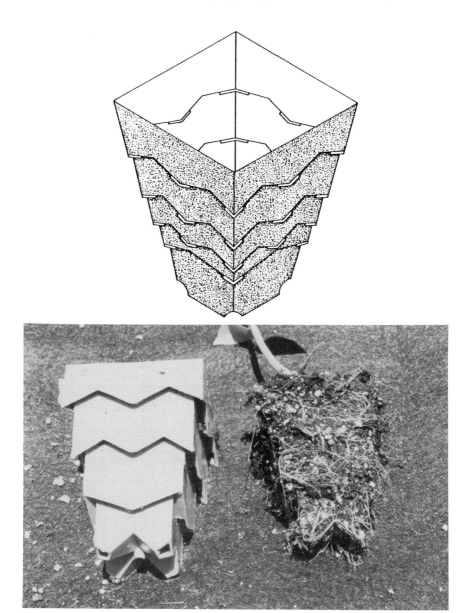

Figure 2.23. The RootMaker container as originally conceived (above) and as is currently manufactured (below). As roots develop on a seedling or cutting and reach the bottom of the container, they are air-root-pruned. By limiting the depth of the container, secondary root branching occurs back to the base of the stem. As secondary roots reach the sides, they, too, are air-root-pruned. Root system quality transplantability and stress tolerance are all improved by this unique container.

Containers with taper are very subject to being blown over, especially when trees are grown (Figure 2.24). Taper in round conventional containers is to allow stacking or nesting for shipping. Taper in wooden boxed trees is to prevent the root ball from falling out when the tree is lifted and the bottom has rotted. In addition, the spaces between the tapered containers allows cold air readily to dissipate heat and damage roots if the temperature is sufficiently low. A square container with no taper would need to have either a non-deteriorating bottom or some mechanism to hold the root ball in place if a wooden bottom that might decay was used. In addition, trees that are grown in, or placed in conventional containers with smooth inner walls have wrapped, twisted and entangled roots.

Figure 2.24. These trees in boxes have been placed on individual concrete pads so they may be tied down to prevent blow-over. It also serves to prevent roots from growing into the soil below.

43

RootBuilder. First came the concept of a box with no taper and a locking apparatus at the corner (Figure 2.25). Next came the idea of a root-trapping design built into the sidewalls to prevent root wrapping and to further stimulate root-branching (Figure 2.25). The sidewalls consist of injection-molded panels with diamond shapes and a sloping section from top to bottom that creates a triangular root-trapping point (Figure 2.26). This provides physical strength for the sidewall while using a minimum of plastic. Superior root systems are created by these container designs. Plants grown with these techniques will establish faster and have fewer losses/problems in the landscape.

After an assortment of attempts to make a less expensive version of the root-pruning box, a workable modification resulted. The RootBuilder expandable or modular container (U.S. patent #4716680) consists of individual modules or panels, each 19 inches long and 14 inches tall with a self-contained lock to form a container. The length of the panel is simply six inches by 3.1416 (pi) so that the container increases six inches in diameter with each unit added. Thus two panels make a 12-inch diameter container, three equals 18 inches, four equals 24 inches, and so on (Figure 2.27). Each panel consists of 200 hexagonal funnels in the side wall, open at the tip. These funnels direct roots to the open tip where they are air-pruned. The funnel design prevents root circling and the air-pruning stimulates root branching. The 200 openings in the funnels on a panel amount to only three percent of the side wall surface area, thus watering is virtually the same as with a conventional container of comparable size.

The bottom of the RootBuilder can be any material impervious to roots. Plastic or roofing paper works well. If the trees are to be shipped some distance, place weed barrier fabric over the plastic or roofing paper before placing the RootBuilder and filling with a good container mix. The roots will grow into the weed barrier fabric and knit the unit together. When trees are established in these containers, the weed barrier fabric and the panels can be moved as a unit. At planting, remove the fabric from the bottom, unlock the panels for re-use and plant the plant. Because the root ball is wider than normal and has a flat bottom, only very tall trees need staking.

The size of the container can be adjusted to fit any size tree. Two panels equals 12-inch diameter, 7-gallon container; three equals 18-inch, 15-gallon; four equals 24-inch, 25-gallon; five equals 30-inch, 40-gallon; six equals 36-inch, 60-gallon; seven equals 42-inch, 84-gallon; eight equals 48-inch, 110 gallon.

44

Since all panels are the same size, they can all be in use whether the need is for 15-gallon or 85-gallon container. They are shipped flat, 100 per carton, and require a minimum of storage space. Since there is no taper to the side wall, they are much less subject to blow-over than conventional containers and have more earth contact to provide a temperature buffer during the winter.

It should be noted that when six or more units are locked together, the top and bottom of each unit should be secured by a strip-lock tie such as is used to secure a bundle of wires. The self-contained lock works well on level surfaces but on uneven surfaces and with six or more units, extra pressure on a connection can allow the RootBuilder to release.

When the first experimental RootBuilder containers were opened to inspect the roots, it was surprising. Containers with metal liners inside to create a smooth interior side wall (for comparison) were opened first. As expected, many roots were visible at the outer surface of the mix and some were pencil size or larger. When the RootBuilder was opened, only upon close inspection were a few white root tips visible, nothing more. However, when approximately one-half inch of mix was brushed away, masses of fine roots were visible. Even more striking was the fact that healthy roots were present on the southwest side of containers exposed to full sun. Apparently the design of the side wall with the network of hexagonal funnels reflects and shades enough of the side wall surface to limit heat stress.

When RootBuilder containers were filled with field soil and watered, the drainage was poor and the weight was excessive. However, when a good container soil mix was used around the root ball of a tree dug in a fabric container (then fabric removed) or B & B, drainage was good, water management was simplified, and the weight of the overall root ball was reduced.

The RootBuilder container builds a root system superior to any conventional container. Since the root branching occurs back in the mix, roots are less subject to stress of heat and cold. Likewise, when a tree is planted, the roots are poised to grow horizontally and anchor and establish the tree quickly. This is a new product, but results suggest it solves a number of problems.

Figure 2.25.   First came a box with no taper and easy-locking corners (above).   This would allow the box to be removed by pulling opposite pins.   This removal procedure thus allowed for a container sidewall that otherwise would not work.   The diamond shapes have a sloping section from top to bottom that creates a triangular root-trapping point.

As of this writing, no one has had any experience with shipping trees grown in this unique container. Can they be placed horizontally? Must they remain upright? Overwintering techniques also remain to be determined. Wrapping an insulating material such as heavy microfoam around the outside of the RootBuilder will help a great deal. How thick does the insulation need to be for a given geographic area? As answers to these and other questions are worked out they will be made available.

Figure 2.26. The RootBuilder panels locked together to form an 18-inch, 15-gallon container. In this case they are setting on roofing paper and are watered by "spray stakes" from a central line. This container design forms a very fibrous root system that allows plants to establish quickly in the landscape.

The Fabric Container. In 1982, a new system became available for producing trees and shrubs. It essentially combined the advantages of growing a plant in a container with the buffer, safety and simplicity of producing plants in the field. The system consisted of a porous fabric container that allows plant roots to penetrate the fabric as they extend outward. However, as the roots grew in diameter, they were restricted by the physical strength and resistance to expansion of the unique fabric. Because absorption of water and nutrients is almost exclusively at the root tips, the more fibrous the root system, the more plant growth and health is enhanced. Likewise, since the translocation of water and nutrients from the root tips to the leaves is through the xylem (the central core of the root and stem) the fabric provides little restriction. However, the physical restriction of the fabric causes the root system to branch inside the fabric container and restricts the downward flow of energy (carbohydrates or soluble sugars) from the leaves at the inner surface of the fabric container, since the downward flow of energy is in the phloem (the outer sheath of the root and stem) (Figure 2.27).

Figure 2.27. Root development inside a fabric container. In this case the tree was dug, the bottom removed, and the soil washed away while leaving the fabric/root complex undisturbed. Trees grown conventionally and dug balled-in-burlap have a more inferior root system.

With this unique system, plants can be dug and transplanted over a much longer time during the year than bare root plants or those dug balled-in-burlap. The root ball is generally smaller than B & B, making handling and shipping easier. Some roots are lost at time of harvest, but these nurse roots have been mostly deprived of energy from the leaves since they are outside the fabric wall and are of minor consequence (Figure 2.28). The plants re-establish very quickly because of the tremendous root systems and energy storage within the roots. These "containers" cannot blow over like conventional above-ground containers, and because of the tremendous insulating effect of the soil, the plants' roots are in their natural environment, protected from the extremes of heat and cold that are so devastating to plants in conventional above-ground containers.

Figure 2.28. Root development of a white ash tree grown conventionally and dug with a 30-inch tree spade (left). The root ball weighed about 350 pounds. The root system of the same age and species of tree grown in an 18-inch fabric container (right). The root ball weighed about 150 pounds.

49

On the inside of the fabric, nodules form (Figure 2.29). These nodules are quite firm as a result of many small cells with very thick walls. Consequently, they are not easily damaged in handling and are probably more resistant to dehydration than other root tissues. Microscopic examination of these nodules and root tissue just behind the nodule shows vast quantities of starch. This is the stored energy source that supports the tremendous burst of new root growth following transplanting. It is uncertain whether or not root primordia (dormant root buds) are present in the nodules and adjacent root tissue. However, the extremely rapid production of new roots following transplanting suggests this. New root production from the end of a cut root on a plant grown conventionally takes several weeks. The much more rapid root development with this technique shows that a very different and more responsive root production system has been created.

Figure 2.29. The pine root (above) shows the nodule caused by the physical restriction of the fabric which causes an accumulation of energy in the root at that point. Following transplanting, a tremendous number of roots develop very quickly from these nodules.

At some point in time, growth of a tree or shrub in a given size of fabric container will be restricted. However, the restriction is quite different from a "root-bound" plant in a conventional above-ground container. In a conventional container the plant becomes stunted and internally starved. On the other hand, in the fabric container the plant eventually becomes dwarfed, but internally it is gorged with energy. This is reflected in fullness and overall thrifty appearance of the top and the continued increase in stem diameter long after further height growth has slowed to a fraction of its earlier rate. It is not surprising then, that trees that have been dwarfed by considerable periods in fabric containers resume normal growth quickly following digging, removal of the fabric, and transplanting. The extensive root system with the capacity to establish quickly in a limited volume of soil, allows a much larger tree to be harvested and transplanted successfully with a smaller and lighter ball than is required using conventional techniques. It is not the size of the root ball, but rather what is in the root ball that counts. The combination of more roots and more energy to produce new roots sets the container system apart from all others.

Harvesting, Holding and Planting. From the various studies conducted and the thousands of trees harvested, held, and established with the fabric container system, several points are clear:

    a) Trees may be harvested and transplanted **as soon as growth hardens.** River birch and pine, which have reputations for being difficult to transplant, perform well when fall-dug and transplanted using this method.

    b) Trees may be harvested and transplanted any time during the dormant period.

    c) Some species of trees may be harvested and transplanted after bud break in the spring with excellent root development following, either in large containers or the landscape.

However, how late and how long new growth can proceed in the spring and still have successful harvest and transplant, depends on the species involved, the geographic location and associated weather factors. Care the tree receives before, during and after transplanting also plays key roles. It may also be that what was successful one year may not be successful another year because of subtle differences in plant response to the season.

There is a definite time when trees grown in the fabric container should **NOT** be dug. When active new growth is present and spring temperatures increase and in some areas become sufficiently high so as to suppress relative humidity, digging should not be attempted. If moisture stress on the new shoots and leaves is sufficient to stop all extension and leaf activity, the continuing chemical signal from the new growth will be partially or completely eliminated and rapid root growth following transplanting will probably not occur (Figure 2.30). This **unfavorable** condition for digging **extends until** all new growth has ceased. This may be in late summer when all leaves are fully expanded and buds on the current flush are mature. However, with flush-type growers, after one flush of growth has matured and before another flush of growth begins, generally the trees may be successfully harvested and transplanted as long as watering is done carefully and timely (Figure 2.31).

Figure 2.30. The dieback in the top of this Chinese pistache is due to leaf and branch desiccation following a harvest date of August 8. Leaves near the tip were only partially expanded; the leaves at the base were fully matured. Note the dieback stopped at the point where mature leaves and buds were present.

Figure 2.31. The current flush of growth of this oak has hardened; that is, all leaves are full size and axillary and terminal buds are mature or nearly mature. This tree can be harvested in the fabric containers with good success even though it may be early or mid summer as long as water is carefully managed. On the other hand, when leaves are present that are not fully expanded, harvesting is not encouraged.

Water Management of Newly Planted Trees. The following resulted from a visit with a young landscape contractor. The problem was the loss of 18 trees on a landscape job. The trees had been grown in fabric containers ("gro-bags"). They had been held above ground for six weeks prior to planting and, "They all looked good at time of planting". He said his employees watered the trees daily which were were about three-inch caliper live oaks from 18-inch containers. All fabric had been removed and the root balls "looked OK" at planting. "The trees were dead in about four days" was the complaint.

Advice was sought as to what happened and why. I first asked about other plants on the site, suspecting something directly toxic. "All the shrubs and flowers around the trees look fine", I was assured. That leaves improper watering as the suspect. "They were watered every day and the shrubs were doing OK under the same watering scheme," was the reply.

My opinions as to what happened and why are as follows:

1) If the trees survived for six weeks above-ground after harvest, the cause of death was lack of water.

2) The quantity of water lost during a 24-hour period by a three-inch caliper tree in full leaf probably 12 feet or more in height, is vast.

3) Trees sweat just like people do; the technical term is called transpiration but the end result by either name is evaporative cooling. If you are working and sweating on a hot day, the natural evaporative cooling process prevents overheating. But, if you stop sweating, it is time to find a shady spot and a cold drink or your temperature will exceed the normal limit and heat sickness will result.

Plants can suffer similar repercussions, but being immobile can take no action. When available moisture in the root zone (or root ball) is gone and the leaves can no longer "sweat", the evaporative cooling process stops as the stomates close and very quickly the temperature of the leaves can rise above the lethal point. Once this occurs, there is no recovery for those leaves. Some species such as river birch and sycamore will drop some or all of the leaves very quickly as a water-conserving measure. When water is again available, buds expand and new leaves appear. However, in the example of live oaks, the "evergreen" leaves do not drop so continue to lose water until all buds and twigs are dehydrated to the point of no recovery.

4) Why were the trees killed and not the shrubs, must also be addressed. The amount of leaf surface area on the shrubs proportionate to the roots and root/soil container volume is much less than with the trees. Trees lose water mostly from the leaves, but some is lost from buds, twigs, and the main trunk. Nick the trunk of a tree with a knife or a branch with you finger nail and green tissue containing much water can be observed.

5) The higher in the air, the greater the wind and the greater the water loss by leaves. This is true even in Florida where the humidity may be 90%. A breeze cools you by speeding evaporation of moisture from the skin, the same occurs with a tree. A shrub, being closer to the soil surface would lose less

54

moisture per leaf than a tree would during the same 24 hour period in most cases.

6) When the surrounding soil is dry, water is rapidly drawn away from the moist root ball in all directions by capillarity, "the ink blotter effect". It had been extremely dry in central Florida with near record high temperatures which further depressed the humidity and accelerated water loss from the leaves.

Combine the water loss from the leaves of the trees and the dry surrounding soil wicking water away and it is extremely easy to underestimate the quantity of water needed per tree and the frequency of re-application needed.

The same complications can and do occur with container-grown and B & B or tree spade-dug trees. With trees grown in containers, they generally have considerably less foliage than a field-grown tree. B & B and tree spade-dug trees are either not moved during August or September, or are moved with huge soil balls proportionate to the size of the top.

Growing and transplanting trees from fabric containers is a double-edged sword. On the one hand, the root ball is much lighter (in this case about 200 pounds per tree) than a B & B tree of comparable stem diameter and height with a root ball that weights 500 pounds or more. Trees in fabric containers are much easier to harvest, the harvest season is much more flexible, and the recovery of the tree following transplanting is faster **IF**, the root ball is kept moist during harvest, handling, shipping, and **after planting** for several weeks.

The lighter root ball and extended and easier harvesting comes with a price and that price is attentive watering, and careful water monitoring following transplanting.

In my opinion, the contractor referred to previously, erred by not watering properly. With sizable trees, in full leaf, during a hot dry summer, when Mother Nature is providing no assisting rainfall or higher humidity, watering several times a day may be required to meet the moisture requirement of the tree. The good news is that if proper watering is done, the tree will produce an abundance of new roots in a few weeks and the watering frequency can be reduced.

Perhaps the best summary is the age-old phrase, "There is no free lunch". Someone must pay to provide the care necessary for the tree to survive **if** trees are to be dug and transplanted during the hostile conditions of summer. A tree uses thousands of times more water to survive, than any other item. Certainly water is most often the limiting factor affecting plant growth and health!

The fabric container allows rapid growth of new roots following transplanting later in the spring and earlier in fall (or under some conditions, late summer). As more experience using this technique for growing and transplanting trees is gained, the length of the unfavorable "window" when transplanting should **not** occur, can be better defined for various species and environmental conditions.

Unlike trees grown conventionally and dug B & B or with tree spades, trees grown in the fabric containers retain their quality above ground. Conventional techniques of mulching harvested trees with sawdust, bark, straw or similar materials work well. Since the fabric does not decompose, there is never the need to reburlap as is so often required with trees dug B & B and held for more than a few weeks.

Trees harvested in fabric containers may be tied with twine or other cord to secure the top of the fabric over the exposed soil at the surface where the soils are sandy. Such tying should **never** include the stem of the tree where girdling could occur if the cord is not removed at planting.

Trees may be harvested during the favorable periods, fabric removed and placed in various types of above-ground containers for sale at times when they should not be dug (Figure 2.32). A key factor to remember here is the size of the root ball relative to the size of the container. If the root ball contacts the interior sides of the container at or above the drain holes, 50% or more of the soil will remain saturated following watering and a major portion of the root system may be lost due to suffocation. The same thing may occur if the container is large enough but field soil is used to fill in the space around the root ball. On the other hand, if space exists between the root ball and container and a porous mix suitable for plant growth in the particular depth of container is placed around the root ball, the plant will remain healthy (Figure 2.33).

Figure 2.32. This loblolly pine was dug before spring bud break and placed in a large container. However, if the tree remains in the container too long, the roots will begin to circle in round containers and may quickly become "root bound".

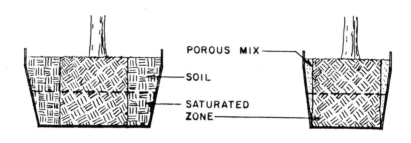

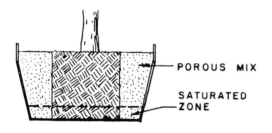

Figure 2.33. When placing a root ball of soil in a container, be sure there is at least one inch of space between the side of the soil ball and the side of the container. If space is present and if a porous mix is used to fill in the space, the plant will remain healthy. however, if the space is filled with soil or the soil ball contacts the sides of the container (above), the saturated zone will be much deeper and many roots will likely be suffocated.

A "Can Opener" for Trees in Fabric Containers. One of the problems with the fabric containers has been getting the fabric off when planting in the landscape. Because of the difficulty in removing the original black fabric, some have opted to simply cut or slit the fabric several times during the planting process and leave it in place. In my opinion this is an error.

In order to get the full benefit from the system the fabric must be removed in order to get the maximum root growth into the surrounding soil in the shortest time. This root growth is what gets the plant through the transplanting transition and on its way to becoming established. Leaving ANY fabric on the sidewall slows total root growth and increases complications.

The "can opener" for fabric containers consists of a T handle and two sharpened pieces of flat or round steel that form a yoke like on the front of a bicycle or two tines of a fork. The opening of the yoke should be about 1/4 inch and the length should be about 14 inches.

With a tree in a fabric container standing upright, one tine of the yoke is stabbed down inside the fabric wall. The other tine remains on the outside. About two inches back from this point, cut the fabric vertically and begin to twist the handle. As the fabric is collected on the two tines, the fabric is pressed against the ball and the fabric not yet removed on the one side. At the same time, the fabric is pulled away from the soil and roots on the other. Only a smooth twisting action is required and the fabric is quickly and easily removed with NO jerking, pulling, or disturbance of the root ball.

With the old black fabric containers the poly bottom tears away as the fabric is removed, thus in most cases, only one vertical cut in the fabric is required. With the gray or knit fabric containers an "X" cut across the bottom of the ball is needed in addition to the vertical cut.

As the old saying goes, "Try it you'll like it". This is a simple and inexpensive tool that can eliminate frustrations in getting the fabric off at planting time. In so doing, the roots are not disturbed and the fabric is fully removed, thus improving landscape performance.

Backfill with the existing soil unless a large area can be changed to a better soil. Soil amendments are of no benefit except under very unique conditions. Staking is required as with most trees transplanted on most sites. However, because of the rapid root growth into the surrounding soil, the stakes may be removed after a few months.

Container Size/Tree Size Relationships. Success in transplanting relatively large trees with small root balls raises the question of container size vs. tree size and grades and standards. Clearly, this technique is very different from B & B and tree spades. The root system is not only more fibrous but also is primed with energy for rapid growth of new roots following transplanting. But how small can the root ball be for a given size of tree? The answer lies in the conditions and care when the tree is grown and harvested, time of year, care after planting, tolerance of the species and other factors (Figure 2.34). What will work successfully in Pennsylvania or Oklahoma may not work in Florida.

Interestingly, there is no difference in actual soil/ root volume between an 18-inch fabric container and a 24-inch Vermeer tree spade which meets American Association of Nurserymen Grades and Standards for a two-inch caliper tree. The cone shape of the soil ball with the tree spade contains about two cubic feet of soil while the 18-inch fabric container 14 inches deep contains the same volume (Figure 2.34).

In the case of a three-inch caliper tree, the grades and standards call for a 30-inch soil ball. At first, a three-inch tree in a 22-inch fabric container looks out of proportion. However, when the soil depth in the 22-inch fabric container is 15 inches deep, it contains 3.3 cubic feet. A 30-inch Vermeer tree spade contains 4.0 cubic feet but 0.5 cubic foot is below the 15-inch soil depth and contains few, if any, functional roots. In comparing the functional root zone, the soil volumes are about the same.

When these comparisons are related to the improved root branching and capacity to produce new roots following transplanting, the "small" fabric containers are reasonable. A key factor to remember is that it is not the quantity of soil moved but what is in the soil that is important.

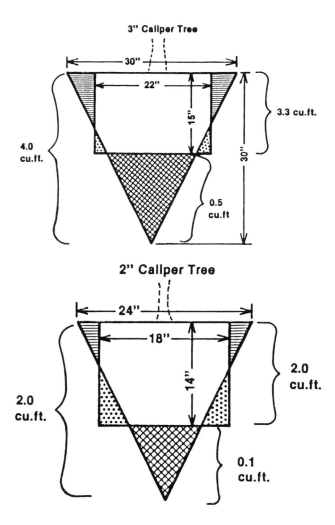

*Figure 2.34. The actual volume of an 18-inch fabric container, 14 inches deep, is the same as a 24-inch Vermeer tree spade which meets American Association of Nurserymen grades and standards for a two-inch caliper tree. The actual volume of a 22-inch fabric container 15 inches deep does contain 0.7 cubic foot of soil less than a 30-inch Vermeer tree spade (below). However, 0.5 cubic foot of soil dug by the tree spade is below the active root zone of the tree and contributes nothing to transplant success. Therefore, with a three-inch caliper tree, the **effective** root ball is about the same volume for both techniques.*

61

The Permanent Root System. Trees and shrubs grown in fabric containers develop tremendous root systems compared to conventional field-grown nursery stock. Because of the fibrous root system and energy reserves present at time of harvest, new root growth into the surrounding soil is very rapid. Vast quantities of new roots are produced (Figure 2.35). But how will these roots function after a few years and what about the long-term health of the plant?

In August 1982, river birch, loblolly pine and green ash trees (all having calipers of about two and one-half inches) were dug. The river birch and green ash had been grown in 20-inch, and the loblolly pine in 16-inch, fabric containers. The fabric containers were removed when the trees were planted the following day.

After two full years had gone by, the river birch and loblolly pine had grown well. (The green ash had been dug in an earlier study). By excavating these trees, the question regarding the permanent root system of trees grown in fabric containers following transplanting into the landscape could be answered. The pine and a river birch were dug using an 80-inch tree spade. The soil was removed by shaking and washing. Both had trunks in excess of five-inch stem caliper by this time. For comparison, river birch and loblolly pine of similar size and age but grown without the container were also dug for root evaluation.

Figure 2.35. A sycamore tree with 2.5-inch diameter stem, dug in the spring and transplanted with the fabric removed. One month after planting, the tree was dug and the soil washed away. Some of the new roots were over 10 inches long and every white root visible in the photo is less that 30 days old.

Following digging, soil was easily removed from the roots of the trees grown conventionally. Extensive efforts of shaking and washing were required to expose the root systems of trees grown in the fabric containers. Comparisons of the root systems provide a striking contrast (Figure 2.36).

Since water and nutrient absorption occurs almost exclusively at the root tips, a larger number of root tips will increase the growth and overall health of the top. Anchorage by many small roots is equal to or greater than that of a few large roots.

Figure 2.36. Roots of five-year-old loblolly pines (above) and a river birch (below) grown with (left) or without (right) benefit of the fabric container. Both trees began as seedlings in small bottomless containers for the first three months, then were transplanted into two-gallon containers for the remainder of the first growing season. The pine and birch on the left were grown in the fabric containers in the field for two years then dug, fabric removed, planted, and allowed to grow for two more years. The control trees on the right were planted directly from one-year-old two-gallon containers into the field and allowed to grow four years before being dug.

The fibrous root system created by the fabric container may provide long-term benefits to tree health in addition to the obvious advantages of ease of transplanting and rapid establishment. Evidence continues to mount as to the detrimental effect of twisted and distorted root systems on long-term tree health. In this case, with species grown in the fabric containers, the likelihood of root girdling or strangulation is remote, since water and nutrient absorption is accomplished by a mass of small roots as opposed to a few major roots. In addition, no roots from trees grown in the fabric containers will ever get as large as when the same species are grown conventionally, reducing the likelihood of damage to sidewalks, driveways or foundations. The fibrous and compact root systems of the trees from the fabric containers also lend themselves readily to planting pits and other landscape situations where horizontal root development is restricted. Anchorage of the trees from the fabric containers should be equal to or better than conventional trees since the many small roots act much like the many fine strands of steel in a cable vs. a solid steel rod of the same diameter.

Trees grown in the fabric containers then transplanted and grown to a larger size would be better candidates for large trees to be moved either conventionally or with large tree spades. The root systems in Figure 2 and the effort required to dislodge the soil from both root systems emphasize their greater tolerance for moving than that of trees grown conventionally.

Evidence such as this suggests that trees grown in the fabric container system will not only transplant easier and with less effort than conventionally grown trees, but will have a superior root system for life. Such compact, fibrous root systems are more compatible with today's urban landscape, restricted spaces and limited soil volumes for root growth. Only the future and further study and observation will provide certain answers regarding the performance of trees grown with this system. However, keep in mind that watering is a key factor in the success of this technique when transplanting. Because of the large top and somewhat smaller root/soil ball, it will dry out faster than plants dug B & B. **Proper watering has always been, and always will be, the number one item in transplanting success.**

Literature Cited

1. Appleton, Bonnie L. and Carl E. Whitcomb. 1983. Effects of container size and transplanting date on the growth of tree seedlings. Jour. Environmental Hort. 1:89-93.

2. Davis, Randy E. and Carl E. Whitcomb. 1975. Effects of propagation container size on development of high quality seedlings. Proc. Int. Plant Prop. Soc. 25:448-453.

3. Gibson, John D. and Carl E. Whitcomb. 1980. Producing tree seedlings in square bottomless containers. Ornamentals South 5:11-15.

4. Hathaway, Robert D. and Carl E. Whitcomb. 1984. Nutrition and performance of container-grown Japanese black pine seedlings. Jour. Environmental Hort. 2:9-12.

5. Hickman, Gary, Bonnie Appleton and Carl E. Whitcomb. 1982. Vegetative propagation and evaluation of five *Ulmus parvifolia* selections. Okla. Agri. Exp. Sta. Res. Rept. P-829:16-18.

6. Kramer, P.J. and T.T. Kozlowski. 1960. Physiology of Trees. McGraw-Hill Book Co., New York.

7. Lumis, G.P. and S.A. Struger. 1988. Root Tissue development around wire basket transplant container. HortSci. 23:401-402.

8. Reich, P.B., R.O. Jeskey, P.S. Johnson and T.M. Hinckley. 1980. Periodic root and shoot growth in oak. Forest Sci. 26:590-598.

9. Siminovitch, D., C.M. Wilson and D.R. Briggs. 1953. Studies of the living bark of the black locust in relation to its frost hardiness. IV Seasonal transformations and variations in the carbohydrate: starch-sucrose interconversions. Plant Physiology 28:383-400.

10. Stoner, David and Carl E. Whitcomb. 1969. Root development of *Parkinsonia* seedlings. Nursery Field Day memo. Univ. of Florida. 22 pages.

11.   Wargo, Philip M. 1979.   Starch storage and radial growth in woody roots of sugar maple. Can. Jour. Forest Res. 9:49-56.

12.   Watson, Gary W. and E.B. Himelick.   1982.   Root distribution of nursery trees and its relationship to transplanting success. Jour. of Arboriculture 8:225-229.

13.   Watson, Gary W. and E.B. Himelick. 1982.   Seasonal variation in root regeneration of transplanted trees. Jour. of Arboriculture 8:305-310.

14. Whitcomb, Carl E. 1988.   *Plant Production in Containers.* Lacebark Publications, Stillwater, Ok.

15.   Whitcomb, Carl E. 1985.   *Know It & Grow It: A Guide to the Identification and Use of Landscape Plants.*   Lacebark Publications, Stillwater, Ok.

CHAPTER 3

HOLDING NURSERY STOCK AFTER HARVEST

Alternatives - - - - - - - - - - - - - - - 69

Overwintering Nursery Stock - - - - - - 71

Methods of Protection - - - - - - - - - 78

Literature Cited - - - - - - - - - - - - 86

Holding Nursery Stock After Harvest

Alternatives. An additional technique that deserves more attention is the placing of B & B, bareroot, or fabric container-grown trees and shrubs in large containers following harvest. The initial reaction is generally one of, "Additional expense that can't be justified". However, consider the following "normal" sequence of events:

1) Trees or shrubs are dug in the field and at this point the plants are at their prime relative to transplant success.
2) The plants are held at the field production site for several days or weeks, and the drying out and quality deterioriation begins.
3) During shipping and handling, further drying and deterioration continues.
4) The plants are often placed in a holding area either by the wholesale or retail nurseryman, garden center or landscape contractor. The plants may remain here from a few days to several months before being installed in the landscape.

From the time the plants are harvested in the field, there is no opportunity for recovery to begin until planting. If the root ball dries out at any point during this process, roots are damaged thus further delaying root development. If the root ball is maintained overly wet, root suffocation may occur or the soil may slump during shipping, breaking some of the fine roots in the ball. If roots grow out into the mulch material while in a holding area, when the plants are finally moved, many of these new roots are lost or damaged. **The plant spent precious energy to grow those roots yet in a matter of minutes they are often lost. Unfortunately, many of the roots that develop in a loose mulch are very course, poorly branched and easily broken. These large coarse roots are the result of excessive aeration, are brittle and watery and as a result, dehydrate quickly or if broken, are easy entrances for disease organisms.**

The end result is a plant that was of excellent quality when dug in the field but may be stressed and of mediocre quality at best when it goes into the landscape. If the plant is to survive, it must produce additional roots in the landscape site. Because the energy level in the plant is lower and the most active root buds are already spent, establishment is often slow which predisposes the plant to a host of other disease, insect, and stress problems.

On the other hand, consider the events if the plants are placed in containers, especially one with a root-trapping configuration such that root branching is stimulated and as a result of nutrients added, proper aeration, and watering, recovery can begin:

1) Trees and shrubs are dug in the field either bareroot, balled in burlap, or in fabric containers.

2) They are placed in containers. Any twine around the stem (Figure 3.1) removed and in the case of the fabric container, the fabric is removed.

3) The space around the soil ball is filled with a soilless container mix suitable for the depth of the container. Remember that drainage from a container (and aeration) is controlled by the depth of the container and the porosity of the mix not the drain holes. If the mix is correct, water will drain around the root ball of soil such that existing roots in the soil and new roots produced can function well.

4) By either incorporating nutrients into the mix or top-dressing immediately after arrival at the holding site, the few roots in the soil ball and any new roots produced, can begin absorbing nutrients and supporting the top, even if the top is dormant (except for bare root).

5) As new roots grow out into the mix considerable nutrients are absorbed. If a root-pruning container is used, when roots contact the sides of the container they are pruned. When root pruning occurs apical dominance is removed and root branching occurs, which in turn, improves nutrient absorption.

6) Since these root-pruning containers have vertical sides, the plants are less subject to blowing over than if they were in either tapered round containers or mulched-in in the classical fashion used on B & B nursery stock. In addition, since containers have greater contact with the earth the adverse effect of severe temperatures is reduced. Contrast this arrangement with either round tapered containers or square, tapered containers where air can move readily among the containers unless further mulching is done.

7) When the container is removed at planting time, the plant has recovered substantially from the harvest shock, has produced new roots which are supporting the top. With the root-pruning RootBuilder container, the roots are positioned to grow laterally in all directions with no wrapping or spiralling.

Trees and shrubs handled in this way will establish quickly in the landscape and shrinkage (losses) in the holding area will be vastly reduced. In addition, the plants have increased in value and health during the holding procedure instead of decreased. This procedure does require capital ($) but in the long run will pay substantial dividends. See Figures 2.24, 2.25, and 2.26 in Chapter 2 for further details.

Figure 3.1. Plastic twine or string that is not removed during the planting process will restrict plant growth. In most cases, the stem grows above the twine, further obscuring it from view. The restriction seen here is from one growing season.

Overwintering Nursery Stock. Roots of plants growing in field nurseries or in the landscape are insulated by the soil mass and to some extent, heated by warmer temperatures deeper in the earth. Even when the soil freezes, the actual temperature of the soil rarely drops more than a few degrees below the freezing point except very near the surface. If the soil is insulated by vegetation, leaves, or snow cover, the soil may not freeze at all even when air temperatures are far below freezing.

For the temperate and sub-temperate zone species, it is not the freezing process that injures roots in containers, or balled-in-burlap (B & B) plants above ground, but rather the specific temperature. The tops of most temperate zone species have the capacity to harden (increase cold tolerance) with the decreasing day length and cooler temperatures in the fall. By contrast, roots have little, if any, capacity to increase their tolerance to cold. For example, the top of a Chinese holly (*Ilex cornuta*) can survive air temperatures of -10 degrees F (-26 C), whereas the roots of the same plant in a container will be killed when temperatures drop to 15 degrees F (-8 C). The small roots are more vulnerable to injury than larger roots and the injury may go unnoticed if the plant survives. This is often observed in the spring in the form of stunting or very slow growth as new small roots must be produced in order for the plant to resume normal growth. If enough of the small roots are killed, the plant is essentially bare-rooted if it is sold and planted into the landscape before some root recovery occurs. **Any plant held above ground with the roots exposed to unnatural low temperatures is subject to root injury or death. Plants balled-in-burlap have somewhat more buffer than do plants in containers because of the soil density and water in the soil, but the same type of cold injury or death can occur.** B & B trees are vulnerable to cold injury of roots as well.

Plants grown in containers are especially vulnerable to cold injury because with conventional round containers, the bulk of the roots are in the outer sheath of growth medium against the inner wall of the container (Figure 3.2). Therefore, the only insulation is the thickness of the sidewall of the container. When temperatures drop below the lethal point for a few hours, the roots contacting the inner surface of the container may be killed. In such cases, the roots may re-grow from the surviving roots in the center of the growth medium and at the base of the plant. However, if the temperature stays at or below the lethal point long enough, the temperature of the entire mass of growth medium will eventually reach the lethal temperature, killing the entire root system. Unfortunately, there is no easy way to determine the extent of the root injury until the following spring. This is because the top of the plant is alive and only when desiccation occurs is the complete effect of the root injury realized. One technique that does work is to place plants suspected of suffering moderate to severe root injury in a heated greenhouse well in advance of spring planting. If the tops of the plants quickly die, little doubt remains. However, if the top survives and begins slow to moderate growth, the survival and performance of the plant in the landscape is still somewhat in question. This is because the stress level in the field or landscape is generally greater than that experienced in the greenhouse.

72

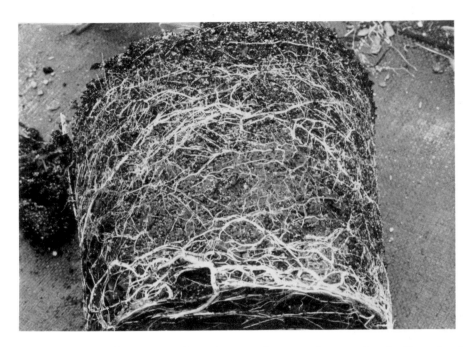

Figure 3.2. With conventional round container, the bulk of the roots are in the outer sheath of growth medium against the inner wall of the container making them extremely vulnerable to both low and high temperatures.

One of the major factors limiting the use of containers by the nursery industry in the northern states is root damage when ornamentals are held above ground in containers (2). Until recently, most winter injury has been attributed to desiccation of the top when the root mass is frozen. To prevent desiccation, relatively inexpensive, unheated, plastic-covered greenhouses are often constructed to protect the plants from drying winds, scorching sun, and rapidly fluctuating temperatures (Figure 3.3). To reduce heat buildup during warm winter days and in the early spring, the greenhouses are either covered with opaque white plastic or sprayed with white latex paint. However, even in the protection of these greenhouses, roots of many species of ornamentals may be damaged during severe winters and the injury may go unnoticed until late spring or early summer.

The difference in winter hardiness of plants growing in soil and of the same species growing in containers or planters has been a difficult-to-resolve problem. Winter injury is seldom a problem in these species when the plants are grown in the nursery field or landscape. Several studies have demonstrated that winter injury of many species of plants growing in containers can be attributed to lack of root hardiness.

The age and maturity of roots influence their cold hardiness. Mityga and Lanphear (7) found that young white roots of *Taxus* X *media* 'Hatfieldi' were killed at 27 degrees F (-3 C), secondary roots, red to brown in color were killed at 20 degrees F (-7 C) and the mature roots near the base of the stem were not killed until 12 degrees F (-11 C).

Studer et al. (8) published lists of several species and the killing temperature of immature roots (Table 3.1). Havis (6) and Studer et al. (8) have also listed the killing temperatures of mature roots of several species. Their findings have been combined in Table 3.2.

These values can be useful in determining the sensitivity of a species, its vulnerability to brief periods of cold and the tolerance when used in landscape containers and root top gardens.

The average air temperature in an overwintering structure or holding facility for container-grown or B & B plants is generally less critical than the extreme temperature experienced by the root. Plants along the outer edge of a block of plants are more likely to be injured than those in the center (Figure 3.4). It may be practical, in some cases, to place plants with more cold-tolerant roots around those with less cold-tolerant roots for insulation.

Figure 3.3. Above, quonset polyethylene-covered structures provide good overwintering protection. If additional protection is needed, a layer of polyethylene or microfoam laid over the tops of the plants inside the houses will greatly increase protection against cold. Below, plants closely spaced in a polyethylene-covered quonset-style structure. The center support posts provide greater snow loads with wider houses. It is much easier to use center supports and sleep well than to leave them out and wonder.

75

Table 3.1. Root killing temperatures of immature roots.

Species	Killing temperature	
	degrees F	degrees C
Buxus sempervirens	26.6	- 3
Cotoneaster microphylla	24.8	- 4
Cotoneaster dammeri	23	- 5
Cornus florida	21.2	- 6
Euonymus alatus 'Compacta'	19.4	- 7
Euonymus kiautschovica	21.1	- 6
Ilex cornuta 'Dazzler'	24.8	- 4
Ilex crenata 'Helleri'	23	- 5
Ilex 'Nellie Stevens'	23	- 5
Ilex opaca	23	- 5
Juniperus conferta	12.2	-11
Juniperus horizontalis 'Plumosa'	12.2	-11
Juniperus squamata 'Meyeri'	12.2	-11
Kalmia latifolia	15.8	- 9
Koelreuteria paniculata	15.8	- 9
Leucothoe fontanesiana	19.4	- 7
Mahonia bealei	24.8	- 4
Magnolia stellata	21.2	- 6
Pieris japonica	15.8	- 6
Pyracantha coccinea 'Lalandi'	24.8	- 4
Rhododendron 'Purple Gem'	15.8	- 9
Rhododendron schlippenbachii	15.8	- 9
Taxus X media 'Hicksii'	17.6	- 8
Viburnum plicatum tomentosum	19.4	- 7

Table 3.2. Root killing temperatures of mature roots.

Species	Killing temperature	
	degrees F	degrees C
Acer palmatum 'Atropurpureum'	14	-10
Cornus florida	19.9	- 7
Cornus florida	10.4	-12
Cotoneaster horizontalis	15	- 9
Cotoneaster microphylla	8.6	-13
Cryptomeria japonica	16	- 9
Euonymus alatus 'Compacta'	6.8	-14
Ilex cornuta 'Dazzler'	17.6	- 8
Ilex crenata 'Convexa'	19.9	- 7
Ilex crenata 'Hetzi'	19.9	- 7
Ilex 'Nellie Stevens'	14	-10
Ilex opaca	19.9	- 7
Ilex opaca	8.6	-13
Juniperus conferta	- 9.4	-23
Juniperus horizontalis 'Plumosa'	- 4	-20
Juniperus horizontalis 'Plumosa'	0	-18
Juniperus squamata 'Meyeri'	- 0.4	-18
Koelreuteria paniculata	- 4	-20
Leucothoe fontanesiana	5	-15
Magnolia X soulangeana	23	- 5
Magnolia stellata	23	- 5
Magnolia stellata	8.6	-13
Mahonia bealei	10	-12
Pieris japonica 'Compacta'	15	- 9
Pyracantha coccinea	17.9	- 8
Pyracantha coccinea	17.6	- 8
Rhododendron carolinianum	0	-18
Rhododendron catawbiense	0	-18
Rhododendron 'Hinodegiri'	10	-12
Rhododendron 'P.J.M. Hybrids'	-10	-23
Taxus X media 'Hicksii'	- 4	-20
Viburnum carlesii	15	- 9

*Figure 3.4. Aluminum plants (**Pilea** spp.) are killed at temperatures about 32 degrees F (0 C). In this case, the heater in the greenhouse went out and the plants around the edge were killed or severely injured, whereas, the plants in the center were not injured. This emphasizes the cooling effect of the edge. Also note that more plants on the left hand side of the photo (north) were damaged than on the right hand side (south). This was probably due to a very small difference in temperature in the container and surrounding surfaces on the side exposed to the low angle of winter sun.*

Methods of Protection. **These methods are included to show techniques that work in protecting the root system. The application when dealing with plants for a landscape job may be smaller, but the practical techniques the same.** Gouin (4) worked extensively with microfoam insulating blankets over container nursery stock as a means of insulating roots from lethal temperatures. This technique can also be used with plants dug B & B or in fabric containers. In one study, plants were over-wintered in polyethylene-covered structures as compared to covering with microfoam. Both groups of plants showed no visible injury to the tops, but the roots of the plants from the polyethylene-covered structure were damaged. By early summer the plants could be easily distinguished by the size of the current season's growth, which was nearly double with the microfoam insulation as compared to the polyethylene-covered structure.

Microfoam is a white, pliable, styrofoam-like packaging material available in rolls of various thicknesses and widths. It is light in weight, has considerable insulating value, and reduces light intensity by about 50%. Gouin (3) suggests the following steps when using microfoam for protecting nursery stock. First water the plants thoroughly. Then in a well-drained area, lay upright plants on their sides and leave spreading plants standing. Pack the plants tightly together, but expose as much of the foliage to light as possible. Cover the plants with a layer of microfoam so the edges touch the ground. Several sheets may be taped together to form a wide blanket. Cover the microfoam with white polyethylene plastic and seal its edges to the ground. In late winter or early spring, uncover the plants and stand upright any that were laid on their sides. **Do not wait too long to uncover** in late winter or early spring. If the buds break (begin growth) beneath the microfoam, the tissues will be weak and quickly damaged when uncovering occurs. This technique can be used for a few days or a month or more as long as the weather is cold. The key factor to remember is **it only takes one cold period below the lethal point to cause death of the roots of the species** (Figure 3.5). It is equally important to remember that with a few sunny days the temperature beneath the microfoam can reach 90 degrees F or more and plant growth begins. The microfoam technique probably has much more application in areas with severe winters than in the South where sunny skys and 70 degrees F can occur during any month. Replacing containers or B & B nursery stock that have roots killed by cold is embarassing as well as expensive.

In some areas, and especially with trees and large plants that have more cold-tolerant roots, simply spacing the containers or root balls very close together and surrounding with straw or similar materials will provide sufficient protection for the winter or for brief cold periods until the material can be planted (Figure 3.6). If straw is to be used, remember:

a) rodents love it,

b) there will always be some grain that will pose a weed problem if herbicide protection is not provided and the plants have not been planted when spring arrives. Treflan (trifluralin) works very well if applied to the surface of the containers or soil root balls before the straw,

Figure 3.5. In this case, orders of container nursery stock were taken from their protected environments and assembled ready for shipping. It only takes one night with sufficiently low temperatures to kill part, or all, of the roots of plants above ground. It sometimes occurs in a holding/staging area such as this or at the unloading point before protection is provided. The key point to remember is that the roots of container-grown and B & B plants must be protected from cold below the lethal point at all times.

     c) a layer of straw that looks like more than adequate will settle and provide little protection after a rain or heavy snow (Figure 3.6). Straw must be four to six inches thick to provide appreciable protection (Figure 3.7).

Figure 3.6. Above, barberry plants closely spaced and surrounded by a heavy layer of straw. In Oklahoma, this will provide adequate protection for the roots of this species. In this case, the straw compacted after a heavy snow leaving some containers with little or no protection. Below, using Treflan or a similar herbicide before spreading straw, controls weeds.

Figure 3.7. Roots of two plants of the same species in the spring. Roots of the plant on the left (P) were protected by styrofoam insulation, whereas, the plant on the right (M) was mulched with an insufficient amount of straw. Both plants lived, however, the extent of the early flush of growth was about four times greater where the roots were not injured by the cold.

In summary, several factors are especially important in protecting the roots of nursery stock:

a) Allow plants to harden normally in the fall. Do not apply excessive fertilizer in the fall and extend the plant growth too late into the season. At the same time, plants under nutrient stress are more likely to suffer injury. Moderation is the best advice.

b) Water plants thoroughly before any prolonged freezing weather. The specific heat of water is quite high; therefore, the more water in the container or root ball, the longer the cold period must be before freezing occurs.

c) Don't place plants in polyethylene-covered structures or under microfoam too early as this may encourage growth due to increased air temperatures. Likewise, don't wait too long as **it only takes one cold night**.

d) A double layer of polyethylene over a structure with air inflation provides greater insulation than a single layer and will tolerate more wind stress.

e) Ventilate polyethylene-covered structures on sunny days to prevent excessive heat buildup. This is more critical in areas with considerable winter sunshine. Remember to water from time to time when the containers are not frozen, to replace water lost during the ventilation process.

f) In more severe climates, cover plants inside polyethylene-covered structures with a second layer of poly or microfoam over the tops of the plants to provide additional protection.

g) In more northern areas, milky polyethylene is generally recommended, whereas, in milder climates, milky or clear poly has been used satisfactorily.

h) With the first break in the consistent cold, emphasis must be placed on ventilation of polyethylene structures to prevent heat buildup. Once the buds of most plants have received sufficient chilling, growth will begin abnormally early if the polyethylene-covered structure is not kept cool. This is one of the major drawbacks to overwintering in polyethylene-covered structures or under microfoam (Figure 3.8).

i) Exposure to wind will increase both the desiccation of the tops plus cause the container or root ball to cool down more quickly to the lethal point. Wind protection of containers can sometimes mean life or death to the plant (Figure 3.9).

j) Plants of the same species and cultivar grown in containers will be more subject to cold injury than plants in fabric containers or B & B above ground. This is because most of the roots of container-grown plants are against the inner wall of the container (Figure 3.2). However, if the temperature drops to the lethal point for the species and stays there long enough for the entire root mass of both the container and B & B root ball to reach the lethal point, both plants will be killed.

Figure 3.8. A dormant bud of photinia (above) will tolerate temperatures below 0 degrees F (-18 C). However, once bud break occurs (below), the new growth will be killed or damaged at temperatures at or just below freezing. The very early bud break in polyethylene-covered structures generally means that the plants cannot be planted out-of-doors until the frost-free date is reached.

Figure 3.9. Above, container-grown plants left unprotected. All plants on the northern edge were killed while many plants which enjoyed the protection of the other containers survived. Below, in some cases a layer of heavy paper to prevent wind movement among the container can reduce or root injury. However, this does not work when temperatures are severe.

Literature Cited

1. Foster, Stanley. 1977. Winter plant protection at Greenleaf Nursery Co. Oklahoma Division. Proc. Int. Plant Prop. Soc. 27:298-299.

2. Gouin, Francis R. 1973. Winter protection of container plants. Proc. Int. Plant Prop. Soc. 23:255-258.

3. Gouin, Francis R. 1974. A new concept in over-wintering container-grown ornamentals. The Amer. Nurseryman 140(11):7, 8, 45, 48.

4. Gouin, Francis R. 1976. Soil temperatures of container plants overwintered under microfoam. The Amer. Nurseryman 44(8):9, 82.

5. Havis, J.R. 1972. Winter injury. In Nursery Container Production. U. of Mass. Coop. Ext. Serv. Pub. 73:35-37.

6. Havis, J.R. 1976. Root hardiness of woody ornamentals. HortSci. 11:385-386.

7. Mityga, H.G. and F.O. Lanphear. 1971. Factors affecting the cold hardiness of *Taxus cuspidata* roots. Jour. Amer. Soc. Hort. Sci. 96:83-87.

8. Studer, E.J., P.L. Steponkus, G.L. Good and S.C. Wiest. 1978. Root hardiness of container-grown ornamentals. HortSci. 13:172-174.

9. Tinga, J.H. 1977. Factors affecting physiology of roots in winter. Proc. Int. Plant Prop. Soc. 27:291-293.

CHAPTER 4

ROOT PRUNING: PROS AND CONS

A Practical Example - - - - - - - - - 88

Practices to Avoid - - - - - - - - - - 90

Practice With Care - - - - - - - - - - 94

Literature Cited - - - - - - - - - - - 96

Root Pruning: Pros and Cons

Root pruning has been promoted and used either actively (doing it) or passively (talking about doing it) by most of the nursery industry growing woody plants in the field for many years. The point is often put forth that "these trees have been root-pruned" with the implication that they will transplant and grow "better" on the new landscape site. But will they? As with many things, it depends! The following discussion is an attempt to clarify when root pruning is beneficial and when it is harmful.

A Practical Example. Consider trees in a field, growing reasonably well, with good internal energy (carbohydrate) levels and no particular complications with diseases, insects or severe competition from weeds. The decision is made to root-prune for three reasons: 1) improving the root system, 2) making the trees easier to dig and transplant and 3) improving performance (growth and visual appearance) after transplanting. This sequence of events probably occurs:

a) Healthy plants are grown with good energy levels.

b) Those plants are root-pruned.

c) Abruptly the top of the plant is subjected to stress. First there is moisture stress due to loss of a major portion of the fine roots, then within a few hours or days the top of the plant also suffers stress from the greatly reduced nutrient absorption capacity since nearly all nutrient absorption occurs at the root tips. However, with the closing of the stomates due to moisture stress and blocking of the entrance of carbon dioxide, the leaves can utilize very few nutrients until the moisture stress subsides.

d) Since respiration (the use of energy by all living cells) continues, while manufacture of energy by the leaves has been greatly reduced, the plant soon suffers an internal deficiency of readily available energy. There are no doubt substantial quantities of energy in the forms of starches, proteins and other storage forms. However, these cannot be mobilized quickly enough to prevent at least short-term energy stress.

e) The cut ends of roots probably undergo a wounding reaction, followed by callus formation at the severed root end and eventually (the length of time depends a great deal on the nature of the species, soil conditions and time of year) new roots form.

f) New roots develop at the ends of severed roots only (Figure 4.1). Only a few species such as *Salix* or *Populus* form secondary roots other than at the very tip of the cut root.

g) Slowly, as the new roots extend out into the surrounding soil, the moisture stress of the top subsides. Nutrient absorption resumes with the extension of new root tips.

h) If the leaves were not lost as a result of the initial moisture stress following root-pruning, they gradually accelerate in the manufacture of energy as water and nutrient supplies increase.

i) Levels of soluble energy within the entire plant begin to build towards previous levels. However, since the transfer of energy from the leaves back to the roots is through living cells, energy levels in the roots are the last to be replenished.

j) At some point and subject to influences by an array of soil temperature and other environmental conditions, the plant may reach the total level of soluble energy as before root pruning (2, 3). Determining the point the energy level will reach the point prior to root pruning is difficult. But this may or may not be a major complication (4).

Figure 4.1. Root growth from a cut-root end. New root production occurs only at the cut end. In addition, considerable time is required from the time the cut occurs until new roots emerge.

Practices to Avoid. Now consider the internal condition of the plant in the following four examples:
   1) dug before maximum recovery is reached,
   2) dug with a root ball the same dimension (depth and width) as the apparatus used to root-prune,
   3) root-pruned too late in the season for maximum recovery of energy before leaf drop or cold weather in the case of evergreens or
   4) when the soil remains dry following root pruning.
   Example 1. If the tree is dug before maximum recovery of soluble energy, the transplant stress may be much greater than if no root pruning had occurred. **New roots cannot be produced without energy** and if the plant just spent a substantial portion of its supply of readily available energy for new roots as a result of root pruning, and the top has not recovered in its capacity to manufacture energy, the plant will be forced to initiate new roots again following transplanting (with minimal reserves). If the level of soluble energy in the plant and particularly in the roots has not recovered, development of more new roots into the surrounding soil following transplanting may be

very slow, and as a result the plant may experience stress to the point of death.

Example 2. If the tree is dug with a root ball about the same size as the instrument used for root pruning, all of the new roots may be lost. Look at the point of new root development as shown in Figure 4.1 again. Note that all new roots develop **at** the cut ends, not behind the cut ends. Therefore, unless the root ball at transplanting is substantially larger than the root pruning dimensions, the roots produced as a result of the pruning process will be lost (Figure 4.2). This is a common error.

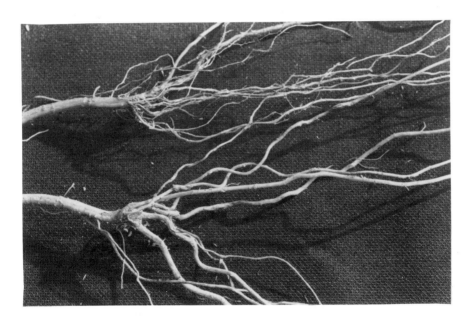

Figure 4.2. New roots grew from the ends of pruned sycamore roots. If the soil ball is dug at the same point as the root-pruning, no benefit will be derived. However, if the soil ball is dug considerably larger than the point of root pruning, many of the new roots will be retained.

If the root ball at transplanting is not large enough to contain most of the roots produced in response to pruning, **and** the tree is dug before the recovery of internal energy levels near to that before root pruning, the plant will suffer more stress more rapidly than had it never been root-pruned (Figure 4.3).

Figure 4.3. This tree was root-pruned on all four sides using a trenching machine (note the straight digging line to the outside of the ball). The tree was watered and maintained for about two months before digging. Because the final root ball was substantially smaller than that cut by the trencher, no benefit was gained from the root-pruning. Probably the tree would have been better off to have been moved when the original trenching was done.

Example 3. If the tree is root-pruned late in the season and as a result of time of year, drought, or some other complicating factor, the internal energy level never recovers. The plant may suffer more winter injury than if it had not been root-pruned. If these conditions occur and the tree has also been dug and/or transplanted, the stress level and likelihood of winter injury are further increased.

Example 4. If the soil remains dry following root pruning, even though new roots develop, their capacity to extend into the surrounding soil and absorb water and nutrients is limited, causing a great deal of stress to the plant. Since the weather is often very unpredictable, and short-term droughts may occur almost anywhere, a drought of only a few weeks may delay recovery and increase the likelihood of injury from cold weather.

On the other hand, **if root pruning is practiced at a point well inside the dimension of the final root ball at time of digging, and the energy level inside the plant has recovered to near the level prior to root pruning as a result of favorable moisture, temperature and other conditions, then root pruning may be beneficial** (Figure 6.2).   If root pruning is to be practiced, it should be done frequently when the plants are young (perhaps as often as every six to eight weeks) in order to stimulate root branching near the stem.   Each successive root-pruning should be at least four to six inches beyond the last.   Any more than three root-prunings is probably counter-productive, even if all the previous mentioned factors are met (Figure 4.4).

Figure 4.4. Palms are monocots or enormous "grass" plants. Their root system is very different from dicots or woody hardwood and softwood trees.   There is probably no advantage to root-pruning a palm.   In this case, a large Canary Island date palm (Phoenix canariensis) is being planted at Busch Gardens in Tampa, Florida. Note that lifting is by the root ball as well as the stem.   Since there is no cambium just under the bark, the likelihood of stem damage to a palm is less likely, although it can occur.

Practice With Care. Unfortunately, root pruning can sometimes be more detrimental than beneficial. Like many other time-honored horticultural practices, root-pruning sounds very desirable in print or without a thorough evaluation. It is virtually impossible, at the present time, to evaluate the degree of recovery of energy levels in the plant following root pruning. One can only make an "educated" guess as to the extent of recovery, and educated guesses are just that--guesses. Until a plant makes a flush of growth, internal energy levels cannot be measured. For example, Whitcomb and Appleton (16) treated two species of container-grown nursery stock that had been fertilized using only liquid nitrogen (N), phosphorus (P) and potassium (K) sources, with either none or three levels of slow-release N, P, K fertilizer in late spring, after the first flush. After six weeks, the plants were transplanted and root growth determined three weeks later. The two species had 18% and 25% more root growth as a result of the added slow-release fertilizer. However, since the first flush of growth in the spring was over at the time the slow-release fertilizer was applied, and no new growth had begun, no visual differences could be detected between the plants that received no slow-release fertilizer and the plants which received the moderate level of slow-release fertilizer. The difference in root growth was a result of internal energy that could not be visually detected, yet the root growth response was quite different.

Kramer and Kozlowski (8) contend that each species has a characteristic root:shoot ratio which remains relatively constant but gradually shifts with plant age and size. Root-pruning reduces this ratio or proportion of root vs top growth by additional root growth at the expense of shoot growth. The length of time for the root:shoot balance to be restored depends on the species involved, time of year and a host of moisture, temperature and other environmental and cultural conditions. Rook (13) noted that 80 days were required for Monterey pine seedlings to resume normal root growth while several months were required for white pine (14). Rohrig (12) found that in oak seedlings, growth rates of shoots and roots recovered to be about the same several weeks after root-pruning. However, root-pruned plants were 20% to 30% smaller when the study was concluded indicating stress caused by the root pruning process. Kramer and Kozlowski (8) felt the reduction in plant size was due to water stress. Shoot growth may be inhibited by water stress induced through root pruning (3, 8, 9). Perhaps in conjunction with the water stress, nutrient absorption is also restricted due to root pruning (7, 13). Geisler and Farree (4) observed that shoot growth of young apple trees was reduced as the result of root pruning. This has been reported for other species as well (1, 2, 3, 7, 9, 11). Recent research by Gillman and Yeager (5) notes that "for each species, root pruning stimulated root regeneration compared to the unpruned controls, but the number varied significantly among species. *Platanus* had an average of 32 new roots on each pruned root, but *Quercus* and *Ulmus* had fewer than 10". They also observed that root pruning stimulated growth of **existing** lateral roots that are behind the severed roots. Watson and Sydnor (15) reported that root pruning landscape-size Colorado blue spruce five years before transplanting increased the number of roots and the root surface area in the root ball. Root-pruned trees had 11.8% of the whole root system in the root ball compared to 5.8% for the non root-pruned trees. They concluded that the additional roots **should** increase survival and reduce transplant shock.

Gillman and Kane (6) studied root pruning in depth as it affects southern magnolia. They root-pruned during dormancy, during the first shoot flush, after the second flush or twice during those times. By the end of the growing season, root-pruning at all stages of growth **reduced** leaf number, tree height, trunk caliper, and total tree leaf area and weight compared with the unpruned trees. Root pruning **did** increase the proportion of fine roots to coarse roots. It is interesting to note that "root-pruned trees grew at a faster rate following transplanting than unpruned trees. Despite these initial differences, trees in all treatments were the same size one year after transplanting." The growth restrictions may generally be explained by a combination of:

  a) limited water absorption,
  b) reduced nutrient uptake,
  c) reduced hormone synthesis,
  d) an increased proportion of energy translocated to the roots (3) and
  e) insufficient recovery time from the point of root-pruning until transplanting.

All this confirms that **if** root pruning is practiced, and **if** the proper time is allowed between root pruning and digging, some benefits may occur. However, with the multitude of factors involved, both internally in the plant and environmentally, the likelihood of striking the right combination is challenging. At this point root pruning may be one of those techniques that is best to talk about rather than practice.

Literature Cited

1. Alexander, D.M. and D.H. Maggs. 1971. Growth responses of sweet orange seedlings to shoot and root pruning. Ann. Bot. 35:109-115.

2. Fuchigami, L.H. and F.W. Moelle. 1978. Root regeneration in evergreen plants. Proc. Int. Plant Prop. Soc. 28:39-49.

3. Geisler, D. and D.C. Ferree. 1984. Response of plants to root pruning. In Hort. Reviews 6:156-188.

4. Geisler, D. and D.C. Ferree. 1984. The influence of root pruning on water relations, net photosynthesis and growth of young 'Golden Delicious' apple trees. Jour. Amer. Soc. Hort. Sci. 109:827-831.

5. Gillman, E.F. and T.H. Yeager. 1988. Root initiation in root-pruned hardwoods. HortSci. 23:775.

6. Gillman, E.F. and M.E. Kane. 1990. Growth and transplantability of *Magnolia grandiflora* following root-pruning at several growth stages. HortSci. 25:74-77.

7. Humphries, E.C. 1958. Effect of removal of part of the root system on the subsequent growth of the root and shoot. Ann. Bot. 22:251-257.

8. Kramer, Paul J. and T.T. Kozlowski. 1979. Physiology of woody plants. Academic Press. New York.

9. Maggs, D.H. 1965. Growth rates in relation to assimilate supply and demand. I. Leaves and roots as limiting regions. Jour. Exp. Bot. 15:574-583. II. The effect of particular leaves and growing regions in determining dry matter distribution in young apple trees. Jour. Exp. Bot. 16:387-404.

10.   Randolph, W.S. and C. Wiest. 1981. Relative importance of tractable factors affecting the establishment of transplanted holly. Jour. Amer. Soc. Hort. Sci. 106:207-210.

11.   Richards, D. and R.N. Rowe. 1977. Effects of root restriction root pruning and 6-benzylaminopurine on the growth of peach seedlings. Ann. Bot. 41:729-740.

12. Rohrig, E. 1977. Wurzelschmitt an eichensamlingen. Forest Archives 48:24-28.

13. Rook, D.A. 1971. Effect of undercutting and wrenching on growth of *Pinus radiata* seedlings. Jour. Applied Ecology   :477-490.

14. Stephens, G.F. 1964. Stimulation of flowering in eastern white pine. Forest Sci. 10:28-34.

15.   Watson, Gary W. and T.D. Sydnor. 1987.   The effect of root pruning on the root system of nursery trees.   J. of Arbor. 13:126-130.

16. Whitcomb, Carl E. and Bonnie Appleton. 1984. Establishment of container grown ornamentals. SNA Nursery Res. Conf. Proc. 29:106-108.

CHAPTER 5

THE PLANTING HOLE

Advantages of a Wide Planting Hole - - - 99

Changing Soil Conditions - - - - - - - 101

Establishment is a Two-part Process - - 101

Evaluating Drainage - - - - - - - - - 102

Plant Tolerant Species - - - - - - - - 102

Plant Shallow or on Berms - - - - - - 102

Provide Internal Drainage - - - - - - 104

Fertilizing at Planting - - - - - - - - 109

The Planting Hole

Advantages of a Wide Planting Hole. Throughout many experiments over the past 20 years, the factor always associated with good transplant success and plant growth is soil aeration. In poor heavy clays the benefit of loosening the soil surrounding a new tree or shrub is tremendous but the benefit does not stop there. Any tree or shrub will benefit from loosening and aerating the surrounding soil in every landscape situation. It seems ironic that in this age of science and technology that one of the most beneficial things to be done when planting is simply to dig a wider hole. The key word is **wider, not deeper.** The active and supportive root system of most plants is in the upper 10 to 12 inches of soil. There is little, if any, benefit from digging the hole deeper and there is a good likelihood of increasing plant stress. No two soils are exactly alike, thus it is very difficult to determine how much a soil removed from a planting hole will settle when placed back into the hole during the planting process. Frequently the soil settles more than anticipated, and the plant ends up in a depression. Under arid conditions this may be desired, but in regions of moderate to high rainfall during periods of normal planting, this may mean root suffocation, plant stress and a high likelihood of secondary disease problems. Many publications suggest digging a deep planting hole, then packing the soil in the bottom to avoid settling. Since aeration is a key factor affecting root function, it makes no sense to dig the soil out, then pack it back.

On the other hand, if efforts in digging the planting hole are spent on making the hole wider but not deeper, the potential problem of settling and root suffocation can be avoided and a more favorable environment for rapid development of horizontal roots is created (Figure 5.1). In addition, it is much easier to dig in the top 8 to 12 inches of soil vs. at greater depths. Soil amendments added to the backfill are generally either of no benefit or are harmful.

Right

Wrong

(Result)

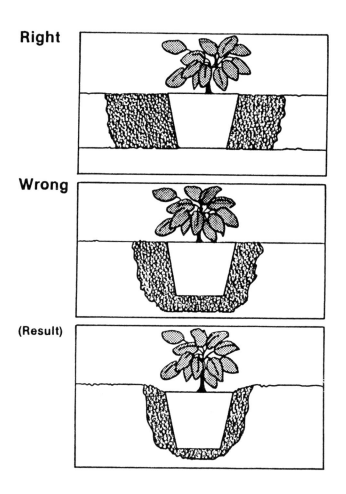

Figure 5.1.   If the planting hole is the same depth as the root ball, no settling occurs (above).   This does not restrict plant establishment and growth since the active root system is in the upper 10 to 12 inches of soil.   However, if the planting hole is dug deeper than the root ball (center) settling generally occurs, thus leaving the plant in a pit and subject to root suffocation during wet periods.   Stem damage can also occur if soil or silt fills in around the stem and suffocates those tissues.

Changing Soil Conditions. The question sometimes is asked, "Why is loosening the soil so important because after a few months the soil seems as hard as before planting?" It is true that soil settles at or near its original consistency after a growing season or so, but several factors are modified: a) if the soil was compacted from equipment during construction, even though that may have been years ago, the soil will settle to the point of its original texture, density, and consistency, not the compacted density. b) If the compaction was the result of foot traffic, the new planting may prevent foot traffic in the area, and c) the needs of plants are different during the first few weeks or months following transplanting as opposed to later when they are established.

Establishment is a Two-part Process. Over the years, it has become clear that the establishment of a plant on a new site is a two-part process. **First** there is the initiation of new roots from the cut or damaged old roots on the plant. **Second** is the extension of those roots through the surrounding soil.

It was from the transplanting studies with tree spades (see Chapter 15) that this factor first became evident to me. Simply digging a bigger hole, even in terrible subsoil clay, made a remarkable difference in the subsequent growth of the trees. Yet at the end of the first growing season, the soil density was virtually the same in and around the trees vs. the surrounding soil that had not been disturbed.

The initiation of new roots is much like the process of rooting a cutting. In the process of rooting cuttings, a very porous mix is used. The mix is much more porous than is practical to use to grow the plant once the cutting has rooted. The reason for the very porous mix is to provide an abundance of oxygen to the areas where new roots will form. The respiration of the plant tissues at the base of the cutting is high as is the requirement for oxygen. However, once the new roots have formed and begin extending into the soil, the requirements of the roots for oxygen is no higher than is typical for the species. Some plants do require greater oxygen in the soil than others. Flowering dogwoods and redbuds are classic examples of plants that must have good soil aeration or they die. But even with these species, the oxygen requirement following transplanting for the initiation of new roots is higher than for subsequent root growth into the surrounding soil.

The practical benefit of loosening the soil in a sizable area around a newly planted tree or shrub is to provide much improved aeration for the initiation of new roots which occurs during a period roughly from one to three months following planting. In the process of watering, rains and settling of the soil, the soil conditions gradually return to "normal" but by the time "normal" condi-tions for a particular soil are reached, the root initiation process is over and root extension proceeds at a pace typical for the plant species involved and establishment is well underway.

Evaluating Drainage. Where soils are heavy or compacted and water percolation is very slow, additional drainage may be required. A percolation or drainage test is the only way to know for sure. Simply dig a hole 10 to 12 inches deep, fill it with water several times during the day to wet the soil then fill again in the evening. If water is still in the hole after 24 hours, one of the three following precautions should be taken:

a. **Plant tolerant species.** Plant only those species that are tolerant to poor drainage. Even here be cautious as some species that will tolerate poor drainage once established, are not tolerant of poor drainage at the time of transplanting.

b. **Plant shallow or on berms or mounds.** Placing a poorly drained soil above the existing grade will greatly increase the rate of water movement through the added soil. In some cases, planting only three to four inches deep and mounding soil up around the root ball will greatly increase the chances of survival and rate of establishment. Berms or mounds may be the only practical way to grow some species on sites where drainage is poor and/or the water table is high during parts of the year. However, it is a mistake to place a sandy well-drained soil in a berm or mound if droughts occur at any time during the year. A coarse-textured sandy soil above a fine-textured clay soil will be very subject to drought due to the greater capillary attraction of water by the finer clay-textured soil below. In such a situation, it would be better to use a moderately heavy soil to create the berm.

When soils are heavy or compacted, the percolation of water into the soil is modified as a result of the planting process. The soil that was loosened during planting allows water to enter more readily than the surrounding soil. In many landscape situations, the rough grading is done then "top soil" is placed over the site. The top soil is relatively porous compared to the subgrade. During rain or heavy irrigation the water moves into the top soil readily but into the subgrade more slowly (Figure 5.2). Because the planting holes are often deeper than the top soil, some of the water in the surrounding soil will move laterally at the surface of the subgrade and enter the planting hole. **This always occurs to some degree.** It becomes a problem only when the planting hole retains this "extra" water for prolonged periods because there is no exit and restrictions to root functions occur.

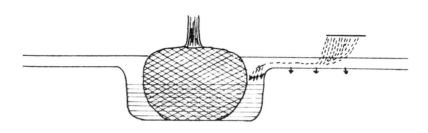

Figure 5.2. In the planting process, soil is often disturbed below the more porous layer of top soil. During periods of heavy rain or excessive irrigation, water may penetrate the top soil readily. Because the water enters the subgrade slowly, the "extra" water may move horizontally and begin to fill the planting hole creating the "bathtub" effect. Where this creates a problem, drainage must be provided as noted in Figure 5.4.

The assumption is often made that because the surface on the site slopes, drainage will not be a problem. If internal drainage through both the top soil and the subgrade is good, this is correct. However, if the subgrade drains poorly, the conditions on a slope may actually be **worse** than on a relatively level surface. Where the surface slopes, water may percolate through the top soil down the slope and into the planting hole (Figure 5.3). Where percolation of water through the subgrade is slow, the planting hole can fill with water and suffocate roots very quickly.

One practical solution to this problem is to remove the triangular area of soil just below the planting hole (Figure 5.3). If the soil is removed and loosened to the depth of the planting hole, water will continue to percolate down the slope without creating the "bathtub" effect.   By the time the soil settles to its natural density, the plants are established and the likelihood of future problems are few.

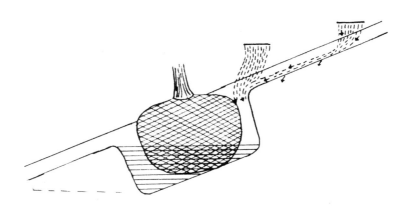

Figure 5.3. On slopes, water may enter the topsoil above the planting hole, move horizontally and accumulate around the root ball restricting or killing roots.   In some cases, the problem is more severe on a slope because water may move many feet down the slope and accumulate in the planting hole.   One practical solution is to remove and loosen the triangular area of soil below the root ball.   If this is done to the depth of the planting hole, water will percolate further down the slope and will not cause problems.

c. **Provide internal drainage systems** to carry away excess water. Whenever possible, drainage systems to a lower area are the most permanent and practical way to provide for plant growth on poorly drained sites (Figure 5.4). Since most of the roots of trees are in the upper foot of soil, the drainage system does not have to be deep to be effective and it can be the reverse. If a drain tile is placed three feet deep, water must percolate through the column of soil before entering. On the other hand, if the drain tile is placed only two feet deep, water has less soil to move through before entering the drain and more rapid drainage will occur. The shallower tile works well where soils are poorly drained only during the rainy season. In every case, the drain must be placed so the root zone of the plant is **above** the saturated zone as noted in Figure 5.4. An exception would be when the water table is high at all times. Under these conditions, it may be better to place the drain deeper. It is better to trench a considerable distance and insure good plant performance than to save a few dollars and have plant losses (Figure 5.5).

Where there is no lower area to allow for gravity drainage, a sump or pit equipped with a sump pump may be the only answer. In this case, a large hole or sump should be dug and filled with gravel except for a vertical opening large enough for a porous casing (pipe) to contain the sump pump. This sump should be located in low area to accommodate drain lines from surrounding plantings. A sump pump with a float switch will turn on automatically whenever the water reaches a set depth. Water may be pumped to any lower area, storm drain, or other suitable area.

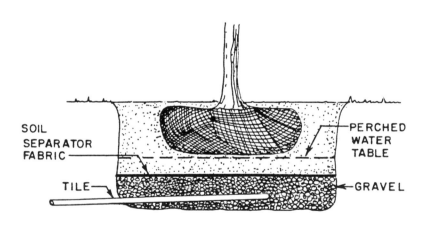

Figure 5.4. A drainage system for a planting hole in heavy clay soils. The root ball should be entirely above the upper limit of the perched water table caused by the gravel. The gravel layer should be no more than four to six inches deep. More gravel is not better and simply raises the upper limit of the perched water table. Water will enter the tile drain only when the soil is very wet, however, this technique will generally eliminate root suffocation.

105

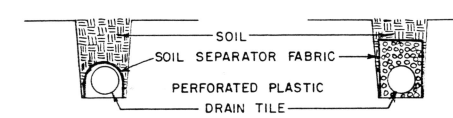

SOIL

SOIL SEPARATOR FABRIC

PERFORATED PLASTIC

DRAIN TILE

Figure 5.5. Examples of drainage systems. Left, drain tile with only soil separator fabric over the drain tile. With a gravel bed, right, the gravel simply increases the cross-sectional area of the drain (makes it bigger). Only free water will enter the gravel or the drain tile and this does not occur until the surrounding soil is saturated.

French or gravel drains work well where drainage conditions are not severe and a good soil separator fabric is used to prevent silt from filling in the spaces among the gravel. One technique that works well is to line the trench with soil separator fabric before adding the gravel and allow for a double layer of fabric near the surface where the two sides overlap. This gives maximum protection against silt entrance with ease of installation. Gravel drains are best constructed of quartz or other insoluble material to minimize the soil alkalinity problem that would occur if limestone were used (Figure 5.6 and 5.7).

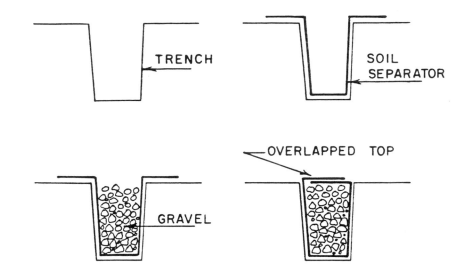

Figure 5.6.   An example of a simple surface drain.   Since the gravel is open to the surface, water will readily enter the drain without entering the surrounding soil.   This technique works well for removing surface water from some low areas.   It is especially effective since water does not have to enter the soil to enter the drain.

Figure 5.7. This site has good surface drainage but is very heavy clay. Several trees died until drains were incorporated into the planting holes. The drain only needs to be long enough so that the outlet end is slightly lower than the bottom of the planting hole. In this case, the drain lines were short but very effective.

A procedure often recommended is to auger or dig a sump in the bottom of the planting hole several feet deep. This is filled with gravel and covered with weed barrier/soil separator fabric before planting. This practice is not recommended unless a sump pump is also installed. The problem with this procedure is that it provides only a limited reservoir for excess water. Once the reservoir is filled with excess water, as happens quickly during rainy periods, the plant roots suffocate. This is analogous to having $500 in insurance when $50,000 is needed. Insurance was provided, but not enough to be of any real benefit.

The ideal planting hole is wide, well-drained and contains moderate fertility to support rapid root and top growth to establish the plant. Even in very poor soils, attention to these three factors can greatly improve plant performance and likelihood of success.

Fertilizing at Planting. Much has been said and written about the detrimental effect of adding fertilizers in the planting hole. This statement is probably based on experiments in the 1920s and '30s when the principal form of nitrogen fertilizer available was sodium nitrate. Sodium nitrate has one of the highest salt indexes of any fertilizer material. The salt index of a fertilizer is a relative measure of the water absorptive capacity of a salt and all fertilizers are salts. When a fertilizer with a high salt index is placed into the planting hole and moisture becomes limiting, a struggle develops between the plant and the salt for the available water and the salt always wins. Thus the term, "fertilizer burn" which is really the result of a drought or water stress condition created by the salt.

However, sodium nitrate is almost never used today. It is important to look at the specific needs of a soil based on a soil test and the salt index of the fertilizer considered. For example, if the soil on a particular site is very low in phosphorus, it would be very beneficial to incorporate a phosphate fertilizer into the planting hole, but which one? A quick look at the salt index table shows that the salt index of triple superphosphate 0-46-0 is only 10. On the other hand, the salt index of diammonium phosphate, 18-46-0 is 34. Neither of these fertilizers approach the salt index of sodium nitrate which has a value of 100 or potassium chloride with a salt index of 116. It is even more important to look at the salt index per unit of nitrogen. The salt index per unit of nitrogen for sodium nitrate is 6.4, however, the salt index per unit of nitrogen for urea (46-0-0) is 1.6. Therefore, if one pound of nitrogen is applied per 1000 square feet of soil, the sodium nitrate will supply four times as much salt as the urea. It is unfortunate that the recommendation of no fertilizer at planting has been perpetuated when the conditions and/or fertilizers have changed. The development of slow-release or controlled-release fertilizers such as Osmocote, sulfur-coated ureas, ureaformaldehyde and IBDU have further reduced the likelihood of creating a salt problem in the planting hole while supplying moderate levels of nitrogen for plant growth. However, do not think that these materials can be used indiscriminately since at excessive rates, they too can cause salt problems.

Another factor that must be considered when determining whether or not to add fertilizer to the planting hole is the time of year and soil temperature. Urea, 46-0-0 can be safely added to the planting hole when the soil is cool with little likelihood of plant injury. However, when the soil is warm, caution is advised since the urea breaks down much quicker and thus the salt concentration may be high for a short period. This still may not be a problem if the area is irrigated and moisture stress is unlikely to occur.

A rule of thumb is the higher the salt index of the fertilizer, the less favorable it is for incorporating into the soil near salt-sensitive plants and the greater the need for supplemental water when the soil begins to dry.

Only a soil test will tell what needs to be added to the soil for best support of plant growth. In some cases, phosphorus and nitrogen may be very beneficial, whereas, in other cases they may be harmful. Guessing invariably leads to problems. **Applying soluble fertilizers to the soil surface after planting is a good practice as long as the rate is not outrageous. The key is to not deprive the plant of nitrogen or other nutrients following planting without creating a complication with excess salts.** As soon as any root function begins on the new site, nutrient absorption can occur if the nutrients are present. The better the supply of nutrients to the top, the greater the energy level in the plant and the greater the energy level, the more rapid the roots grow and overcome the trauma of transplanting. Slow-release fertilizers are extremely safe for application immediately following planting.

CHAPTER 6

SOIL AMENDMENTS

Dispelling Old Myths - - - - - - - - - - 112

Florida Sand and Soil Amendments - - - 113

Amending Good Soils - - - - - - - - - 117

Amendments, Clay Soils and
           Supplemental Fertilizer - - 118

Why Soil Amendments Generally
           Are Not Helpful - - - - - 121

Some Amendments Are Helpful - - - - 125

A Lesson From Nature - - - - - - - - - 125

Superabsorbents - - - - - - - - - - - 127

Container Studies - - - - - - - - - - 128

Field Studies - - - - - - - - - - - - 130

Literature Cited - - - - - - - - - - - 131

Soil Amendments

Dispelling Old Myths. One of the most widely held practices in all of horticulture is the incorporation of organic matter during the planting process. In 1938 Jacobs (24) wrote that the uncertain qualities of topsoil may be improved by the addition of peat moss. Thompson (32) noted that "experienced plantsmen" are emphatic about the necessity for adequate humus content of the soil to be used as backfill. The practice extends back infinitely into the past as it seems very logical and practical.

As an undergraduate student at Kansas State University, my interest in planting procedures began to develop, especially soil amendments. The Kansas Highway Commission required 25% organic matter in all planting holes at that time. Later, work with the Iowa Highway Department revealed a requirement of 15% organic material for all planting. Still later, work with the Florida Department of Transportation revealed a 50% organic material requirement for all planting.

The story of the 50-cent plant in the five-dollar planting hole being superior to the five-dollar plant in the 50-cent hole is as old as horticulture. For many years, however, scientific evidence of what makes a five-dollar planting hole was limited.

In developing a landscape, establishment of woody ornamentals is a major concern. Most recommendations include the use of some form of soil amendment (2, 5, 6, 28, 32). Others go so far as to recommend digging the planting hole a year in advance and filling it with leaves and organic matter to form a composted planting media (4). However, recommendations are seldom referenced by research findings.

The same is true for the addition of fertilizers. Some authors maintain fertilizer should not be applied to newly planted landscape material the first year. They state that it takes a year for new feeder roots to develop (5, 6, 13, 14). Obviously they have never dug up trees or shrubs a few weeks after planting! Others advocate the use of diluted solutions of soluble fertilizers but fail to mention rate and frequency of application (12, 15, 32).

Using sawdust for soil improvements caused harmful effects on crop yields when sawdust was applied alone (1). It depleted nitrogen in the form of ammonia and nitrates. Work with several species of plant material and various mixes of hardwood bark, soil, and perlite caused a severe nitrogen deficiency that was not corrected by normal fertilization practices (16, 17). It was

112

demonstrated that a slow-release fertilizer incorporated in bark-amended mixes prevented nitrogen deficiencies (17).

Moisture characteristics and crop yields from sandy loam soils amended with farmyard manure and peat showed yield differences between the peat and control plots were small and inconsistent (29). The moisture absorbing and retaining capacities of peat:soil mixtures alone should not be the basis for incorporating peat with soil (14). Peat was not recommended as a soil amendment.

The addition of peat, vermiculite or sawdust to the soils of central Minnesota resulted in no better growth of landscape plants than unamended soil (27). A 50% sandy loam soil and 50% peat mixture was tested as a soil amendment on the growth and productivity of highbush blueberries. The unamended control plot yielded larger plants and better fruit over a five-year period than the peat-amended soils (34).

Florida Sand and Soil Amendments. In 1970, a study was begun to try to determine the optimum amount of organic matter to add to the planting hole to aid establishment of woody plants (7, 35). The study was conducted on the sand soils of North Florida using Canadian peat, vermiculite, pine bark, and colloidal phosphate (a clay-like material that holds considerable water), each at rates of 0%, 10%, 20%, 30%, 40%, and 50% by volume of the planting hole. The study was conducted both with supplemental overhead irrigation and with only normal rainfall. The test plants were uniform pittosporum (*Pittosporum tobira*) or mockorange grown in one-gallon containers. The planting holes were 18 inches in diameter and 12 inches deep. To insure thorough mixing, the soil and soil amendment for each treatment were mixed in a small cement mixer. The study continued for nine months, then the plants were measured, dug, and roots and tops evaluated and weighed.

There was no benefit from any soil amendment at any rate either in the irrigated or non-irrigated area (Table 6.1). Pine bark and to some degree, peat, restricted plant growth. Vermiculite had neither a beneficial nor detrimental effect. Colloidal phosphate was somewhat beneficial but inconsistent. All plants with all treatments in the irrigated plots were larger than those in the non-irrigated plots. However, the plant response to the treatments were about the same.

Table 6.1. Response of pittosporum shrubs to peat-amended soils. Values are expressed as percent of control, where the untreated control is considered 100% and other treatments are calculated as a proportion of that value.

| | % of peat in the backfill | | | | | |
	0	10	20	30	40	50
Growth index	100	100	84	81	74	76
Fresh top weight	100	98	89	85	80	81
Fresh root weight	100	88	85	88	64	70

The first plants terminated were dug by hand. A profile of roots confined to the soil-amended area could be easily seen (Figure 6.1). The need for a mechanical digger soon became clear since there were over 500 plants in the study. Digging plants with a backhoe revealed the root restriction to the planting hole even more dramatically (Figure 6.2). The plant roots were white and healthy in appearance in both the unamended and soils amended with the various materials and rates. The difference in plant response was one of plant size and extent of root growth. Soil tests of the various amended soils provided little help in explaining the plant response.

The first paper given at a technical meeting on these findings revealed the depth of the belief in soil amendments. The research findings were presented and questions answered. The moderator of the meeting returned to the microphone, hesitated and said, "I'm sure not going to ask what he thinks about apple pie or motherhood!" Other comments suggested that the response was true only in the extremely sandy soils of Florida and would not apply in other geographic areas or soils. Correspondence reported, "It doesn't work that way in the landscape." Reporting the results of the research was the easy part. Determining "why" proved to be much more difficult. One of the whys could be noted when the plants dug in the soil around the amended zone contained more moisture than in the zone. It had been three days since the last rain. Instead of the peat-amended soil holding more water, it contained less. More on this phenomenon later.

Figure 6.1   When the study was terminated, a profile was dug to determine the extent of root development.   With nearly all of the soil amendments, a mass of roots could be observed in the amended backfill with few roots extending into the surrounding soil.   The shrubs had grown from about 10 inches in height and spread when the study began, to over 20 inches tall with 30-inch spread in the nine months.   Plants with no soil amendments had roots extending three or four feet from the original root ball, whereas, those with soil amendments were mostly confined to the planting hole. This influence of soil amendments was the same whether the plants were irrigated regularly using overhead sprinklers or after the initial establishment period received only natural rainfall. Irrigation greatly increased top growth, but did not influence lateral root distributions.

Figure 6.2.   Above, the original planting hole was 18 inches in diameter and 12 inches deep.   Below, the planting hole in reverse showing the root distribution of **Pittosporum tobira** *in soil with 40% peat added.   The plant had previously been growing in a one-gallon container.   Notice that the roots did not extend beyond the amended soil. Roots developed well in the   amended soil, but not* **beyond** *the amended soil.*

116

Amending Good Soils. During 1973-1976, studies were conducted in Oklahoma on clay loam soils and subsoil clays. The subsoil clay site was a new housing development where all of the top soil had been removed to fill a wash and level the site. Soil fertility was very low and water percolation through the red clay was very slow. Schulte and Whitcomb (30) used silver maple (*Acer saccharinum*) and Chinese pistache (*Pistacia chinensis*) in one study with peat, pine bark, vermiculite and sand added to a clay loam soil and a clay subsoil at proportions of 0%, 20% and 40% by volume in a planting hole 18 inches in diameter and 12 inches deep. Mid-way through the second growing season the experiment was terminated and plants were evaluated for both top and root growth. **Plants with no soil amendments were consistently larger than those with soil amendments.** Pine bark at either 20% or 40% was most detrimental (Figure 6.3) followed by peat, sand and vermiculite. In all cases, vermiculite was neither helpful nor detrimental to plant growth. These findings were true on the clay loam soil as well as the subsoil clay.

It is important to note that during these studies there were few, if any, visual signs of stress, deficiencies, or other problems. The plants with amended soils were simply smaller. This is probably why the practice persisted for so long unchallenged or unquestioned. If all the plants on a site received peat in the planting hole and there is no comparison without peat, all appear to be fine. It is also important to note that few plants died from the soil amendment treatments in any of the studies, thus success or failure is not at question, simply degree of success (and, of course, money spent). It is also of interest that there was no "magical" treatment to make a poor subsoil clay into a productive soil.

117

Figure 6.3. Growth of silver maple trees with 20% ground pine bark incorporated into the soil at planting (left) and with no soil amendments (right). It is important to note that leaf size and color was the same on both trees, only the height, stem caliper and root system were greatly affected. The background is two sheets of 4' X 8' paneling..

Amendments, Clay Soils and Supplemental Fertilizer. Further studies concentrated on adding supplementary nutrients to the planting hole to replace those lost when a proportion of the soil was removed and replaced with organic matter which contains few nutrients. One hundred eight trees were planted in a good clay loam soil with a pH of 5.8 and 108 trees, in a nutrient-deficient clay subsoil with a pH of 7.1. None of the supplementary fertilizer treatments improved plant growth in the amended soils to the level of trees in unamended soils. Adding supplementary nitrogen to soils amended with pine bark did improve the growth somewhat suggesting that the nitrogen tie-up of the decomposing pine bark does influence plant growth (Figure 6.4). However, there was no evidence to suggest pine bark was toxic to the trees.

Trees in the unamended clay loam soil grew well, and the roots had a well balanced distribution with roots extending well beyond the limits of the planting hole. Trees planted in soils amended with peat moss had very fibrous roots but very few developed beyond the amended planting hole regardless of supplemental fertilizer.

Poorest roots were observed on trees grown in soils amended with pine bark. A few roots extended out of the pine bark-amended soil, but few secondary and fibrous roots were observed. With the 40% bark treatment, the majority of trees were dead by mid winter following the first growing season, when the trees were dug and evaluated. This was the only treatment where some of the trees died.

Growing conditions in the clay subsoil were very poor. Growth differences were small for the varying fertilizer rates or amendment level treatments. Plants grew equally well in the unamended, as in the amended clay subsoil.

Since that time, further studies have been conducted by several researchers. Corley in Georgia planted azaleas and flowering dogwood in an old roadway with and without soil amendments and found no benefit from amending the soil on either species (8, 9, 10). Later studies on several sites with an assortment of soil amendments and mulching treatments led him to conclude, "No consistent, positive responses were derived from traditional backfill amendments" (11, 12). Recently our early work in Florida was repeated and it was concluded, "Amendment of backfill soil at planting with peat moss, fired montmorrilonite clay or a superabsorbent gel had no significant positive influence on growth and establishment of container-grown sweet gum trees placed in well-drained arredondo fine sand soil" (19). In other words, it did not work!

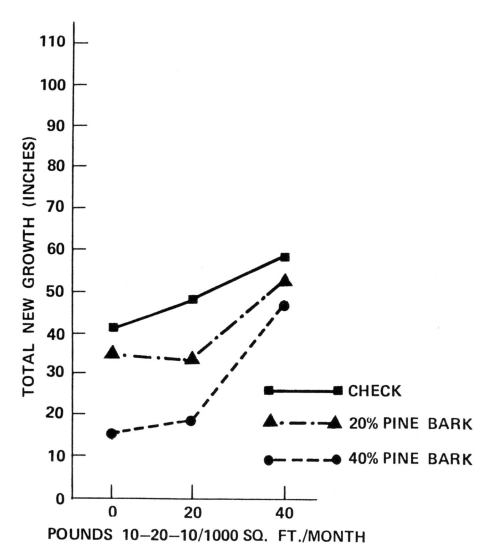

Figure 6.4.   Growth of silver maple with 0%, 20% or 40% of pine bark added to the soil at planting and three levels of fertilizer. Additional fertilizer reduced the detrimental effect of the pine bark, but growth was still less than the control with no soil amendment.

Why Soil Amendments Generally Are Not Helpful. The reason for the poor performance of plants in small areas of soils amended with organic matter is primarily one of water relations. Peat does hold substantial quantities of water. However, when mixed with soil, it increases the porosity of any soil. Through the process of capillarity (the ink blotter effect), water readily moves from a coarse material to a fine material unless the system becomes saturated. Therefore, the soil amended with organic matter **does** absorb water readily following irrigation or rainfall but quickly loses most of the water since the surrounding soil has a finer texture and a greater capillary attraction (Figure 6.5). This movement of water out of the soil made more coarse-textured by the amendment and into the surrounding finer soil occurs very rapidly when the surrounding finer soil is relatively dry as frequently occurs during the summer and fall. During this time of relatively high temperatures and low humidity, the water loss from the top of the plant is very rapid and the limited volume of water held by the amended soil is quickly lost. The amended soil may be sufficiently dry to cause plant stress while the surrounding unamended soil is still quite moist, but because of the textural differences, the moisture will not move back into the amended soil and since few, if any, roots have extended out into the unamended soil, the plant suffers from drought.

If the plant survives the drought conditions accentuated by the soil amendments, the roots will eventually grow beyond the amended soils and little further effect of the soil amendments occurs. However, with species slow to develop horizontal roots such as azaleas, the additional moisture stress caused by the soil amendments may continue for several years.

When planting without the use of soil amendments, the roots grow into loosened and aerated soil of the same texture as the surrounding soil, and a textural difference and dry zone does not occur. Even though the soil is loosened in the planting process, the texture of the soil is not changed.

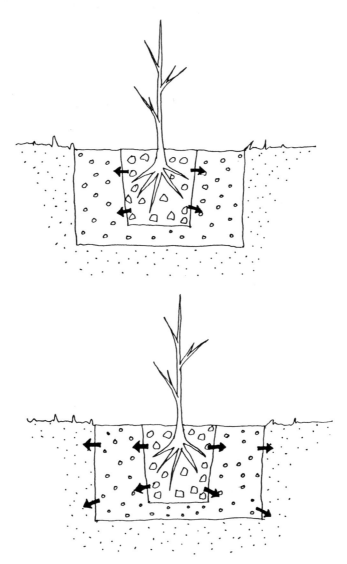

Figure 6.5.   When the backfill around the plant is soil, water is drawn out of the container mix and into the loose soil (above). However, as roots grow out into the surrounding, loosened soil, moisture is generally available.   On the other hand, if the soils around a container-grown plant are amended, water is drawn out of the container mix by the amended soil (since it is finer in texture), and in turn, water is drawn out of the amended soil by the unamended soil (below).   This leaves the plant "high and dry" because moisture will not move from the moist unamended soil back into the amended soil.

Another problem with soil amendments and plant growth may occur when soils that drain poorly are amended (Figure 6.6). Water percolates into the more coarse-textured amended soil more rapidly than the surrounding soil, thus a "bathtub" effect occurs and the roots may be suffocated directly or killed by the indirect effect of disease organisms that are favored by the poor drainage. Under such conditions, not adding soil amendments also increases the rate of infiltration into the loosened soil. However, the problem is generally much less severe. The most practical solution to this problem is to plant partially or entirely above the existing soil level, depending on the severity of the problem. Placing poorly drained soil above the existing grade of an otherwise poorly drained soil will greatly increase the drainage and aeration of that soil mass because of the increased depth of the soil column through which the moisture moves. Consequently, mounds or berms are excellent sites for plant growth in poorly drained soils.

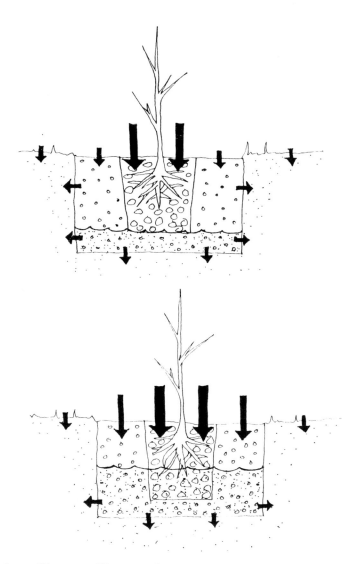

Figure 6.6.   Water will percolate into a coarse-textured material (soil) more quickly than a fine-textured material (soil).   When a container-grown plant is placed in a heavy soil, water will percolate into the planting hole through the container mix faster than the loosened, heavy soil (above).   However, if soil amendments are added to the heavy soil, water percolates faster into the planting hole from the more coarse-textured soil (below). This may cause a sufficient "bath tub" effect to suffocate plant roots.

Some Amendments Are Helpful. Soil amendments are **not always** undesirable. When the plant's entire potential root zone can be amended with organic matter or other materials, the results may be beneficial, **IF** water is carefully monitored and proper nutrition is provided, since most soil amendments hold fewer nutrients per unit volume than a good soil. Examples would be any size container where a perched water table is created by the bottom, thus a more coarse growth medium must be devised to provide adequate drainage and aeration. In some cases, raised beds for azaleas and rhododendrons, without bottoms, also benefit from soil amendments, especially peat and leaf litter or compost. However, the benefit is due more to the acidification of the soil and release of micronutrients than from the change in soil texture. For confirmation one need only travel through the Deep South and observe azaleas growing well on moderate to heavy soils with good surface drainage only, but a low soil pH which provides for good availability of the micronutrients. (See also the chapter on establishment of azaleas)

Soils in field nurseries are routinely amended with organic matter by green manure crops such as hybrid sudan, sudex, hay grazer, soybeans or other rapid-growing crops. In this case, however, like the raised beds, the entire root zone of the plant is amended, thus no barrier to water movement exists except at the very edge of the field. The incorporated organic matter amounts to only a small percent in the top six to eight inches of soil, whereas, in landscape situations soil amendments often amount to 20% to 40% or more.

A Lesson From Nature. In understanding why soil amendments are generally not beneficial to plant establishment and growth, a good lesson can be observed in nature. The litter on the forest floor is composed of leaves, twigs, fruits, bark and other organic debris (Figure 6.7). In temperate climates there are generally identifiable remains of plant parts from the last three years. Between this debris and the surface of the soil are further layers of organic matter in progressive stages of decomposition. Earthworms, some insects and other organisms incorporate a small portion of this organic into the surface of the soil. However, most remains **on** the soil surface, not **in** the soil.

*Figure 6.7. The natural litter on the forest floor provides a very beneficial mulch of organic matter **on** the soil surface, not **in** the soil.*

This organic mulch plays a key role in maintaining the natural nutrient cycle in an undisturbed forest, woodland or prairie. In addition, organic matter on the soil surface a) insulates the soil and the plant roots from becoming too warm in summer and cold in winter, and b) serves as a highly absorptive mat or blotter which captures most rainfall and allows more to percolate into the soil while slowing any run-off and reducing erosion. Rainfall on exposed soil has a tremendous compacting effect and generally breaks up the aggregate soil particles, thereby altering the porosity of the soil and ultimately restricting the normal exchange of carbon dioxide out of and oxygen into the soil.

The loose and porous natural organic mat on the soil surface provides a favorable environment for a tremendous range of microorganisms. In well-aerated conditions, the vast predominant microorganisms assist plant growth. However, as the organic layer on the soil surface is lost or removed and the soils become more compacted, there is an increase in the population of microorganisms unfavorable to plant health. It is impractical and nearly impossible to maintain sterile conditions, (what better place to contract a disease than in a hospital?) Therefore, it is of the utmost importance to maintain all factors favorable to the beneficial microorganisms. In so doing, potentially detrimental microorganisms are suppressed and plant health is increased. Shifts in microorganism populations are generally slow and very subtle, therefore it is important to develop an awareness of even slight changes in conditions that can influence plant growth at all times.

Remember that with the exception of 40% pine bark backfill, no plants were lost from any of the soil amendment treatments on an array of sites and growing conditions of these experiments. Adding soil amendments did not mean success or failure in the survival of the plants but it did affect the degree of success. Nature places the organic matter only on the soil surface where it serves very effectively as a mulch. We should all take more lessons from the natural plant communities.

Superabsorbents. In recent years, several superabsorbent compounds with horticultural applications, generally referred to as hydrogels, have become available commercially. These hydrophilic (water-loving) starch derivatives are identified chemically as "hydrolyzed starch-polyacrylonitrile graft copolymers." Initially research was conducted by the U.S. Department of Agriculture, but several private companies now have products available. Some of the more publicized trade names are Super Slurper, Viterra Planta-Gel and Terra-Sorb.

Superabsorbents absorb 200 to 5,300 times their weight in water under laboratory conditions. One common product (Terra-Sorb 200) reportedly absorbs 50 times more water per unit volume than peat moss. This water-holding ability is said to last six months or longer, depending upon the frequency of watering and the decomposition of the starch by microorganisms. Most products expand 20 to 30 times their original size upon wetting, thus may have the potential to increase aeration when incorporated into a plant growth medium or soil.

Among the proposed horticultural uses for superabsorbents are: seed coating, transplant dips for roots, pre-treatment of soil for sodding, incorporation into container media, hydraulic mulching and as landscape soil amendments.

Container Studies. Several products were obtained for use in an experiment to determine potential phytotoxicity to two greenhouse crops, and to evaluate their ability to reduce water stress and wilting (3). Because manufacturers' recommendations varied considerably, all products were tested at two common rates.

Nine superabsorbents were incorporated dry, into a peat-perlite medium (1-1 by volume) at rates of one and two pounds per cubic yard. A control treatment contained no super absorbent. All treatments received seven pounds per cubic yard of 19-6-12 Osmocote, four pounds cubic yard of 18-6-12 Osmocote, and one pound cubic yard of Micromax. Superabsorbents used were:

1) Stasorb, A.E. Staley Manufacturing Co.
2) Aqua-Terre, Stout Products
3) Aquastor, Absorbent Industries
4) Permasorb, National Starch and Chemical Corp.
5) Super Slurper, Super Absorbent Co.
6) Viterra 2, Nepera Chemical Co.
7) SGP 104, Henkel Corp.
8 & 9) Terra-Sorb 200 and 150, Industrial Services Int'l.

Rooted cuttings of poinsettia 'V-14' were planted in six-inch containers on October 8 and seedlings of geranium 'Sprinter Scarlet' on October 22. Containers were placed on the floor of a hot water floor-heated greenhouse. All plants were watered the same on a regular basis with no attempt made to initially test the water-holding and releasing ability of the super absorbents during the production phase of the study. On December 28, the poinsettias were watered for the final time, then the number of days to "plant wilt" determined. The geraniums were watered for the duration of the experiment.

In the geraniums, some interveinal chlorosis developed predominately on younger leaves, but a visual rating of chlorosis on December 21 showed no consistent difference between treatments and/or rates. The chlorosis was no longer visible when the study was terminated. The control plants never showed any chlorosis.

On January 27, approximately three months from planting, the number of flower heads per plant and fresh top weight were determined for the geraniums. There was no difference between treatments and/or rates of the superabsorbents and the control for fresh top weight of the plants or number of flower heads per plant, or overall visual quality.

The poinsettias grew very well in all treatments and were all of salable quality. Following the last watering, they took from 20 to 39 days to wilt. For this experiment, wilt was visually determined to be the point when flower bracts and a minimum of the two uppermost leaves were no longer turgid (became limp). Despite the warm floor temperature and unseasonably warm air temperatures, and the fact that poinsettias are fairly sensitive to moisture, there was no difference among the 18 superabsorbent/rate combinations and the no-absorbent control in time required to wilt.

Geraniums and poinsettias were selected as test plants due to their sensitivity to moisture extremes. No rotting of roots attributable to excess moisture for any specific product/rate combination could be detected, nor any more wilting in the no-absorbent control.

No medium volume changes were noted in the absorbent treatments, and no phytotoxicity was evident except for the erratic chlorosis when the geraniums were young. The products should not have decomposed in the three months of the experiment. Had decomposition started, a treatment effect might have developed because the products varied considerably in their particle size so decomposition would be expected at different rates. With the test plants used, and under these experimental conditions, no benefit was seen from the use of these relatively expensive products.

Tomlinson and Bilderback (33) compared the growth of 'Nellie Stevens' holly and leyland cypress in soil mixes with varying amounts of Terra-Sorb 200 at two pounds per cubic yard and Viterra Planta-Gel at 3.5 pounds per cubic yard to a pine bark and sand control. They found no growth response or benefit from the superabsorbents when plants were watered once daily, every three days, or every four days. They offered no explanation for the lack of benefit from the superabsorbents when watering frequency was decreased. If water was held by the superabsorbents and was available for plant use, then some response should have occurred.

Ingram and Yeager (23) used a water-absorbing polymer, Moisturite, in a bark, peat, sand container mix at different rates. They found no increased water retention or benefit in terms of growth of *Ligustrum japonicum.* They concluded that scheduling of watering was a key factor in growing and maintaining plants in containers.

Taylor and Halfacre (31) observed a similar response and noted that the gel was less effective as the fertilizer rate increased. Paul, et. al. (26) reported that an increase in moisture content as a result of the gel occurred only in the **absence** of fertilizer salts. In another report the authors noted, "None of the hydrogels functioned as advertised" (37).

Field Studies. Hummel and Johnson compared the effect of soils amended with peat, a fired clay, or a superabsorbent at manufacturer's recommended rate, on the growth of sweet gum trees. The sandy soils of North Florida which were used have very low water holding capacity and should have been a good test site. The researchers observed no benefit in growth or survival of the trees from the addition of peat moss, fired clay or superabsorbent to the planting hole (19). Hensley and Fackler found no benefit from root dips of superabsorbents when transplanting tree seedlings (18). They concluded that little benefit is likely where rainfall is adequate or where supplementary irrigation is available.

On the other hand, Ingram and Burbage (20) reported a slight benefit to plant growth from Terra-Sorb added to the planting hole. They worked with four-inch caliper live oaks transplanted in August in the deep sands of central Florida. However, tree survival was 55% when watered weekly, 65% when watered daily but only 54% when Terra-Sorb was used.

The general use of superabsorbents in the landscape is questionable. Greenhouse and indoor landscape use may have some merit, but not without further studies or improvement in the products. The theory seems very sound and the water absorbing effect of the superabsorbents in a glass of water is real. However, their performance in soils and soil mixes are apparently quite different. Where soils are sandy to pure sand, superabsorbents can provide benefits if the proper rate is used in proportion to the particle size/aeration characteristics of the soil and their functions are not affected by fertilizers. In many cases with sandy soils, the limited benefit from superabsorbents was probably due to too little or too much being added. Excess water holding capacity can suppress plant growth, just as surely as insufficient water. On the other hand, it is doubtful that these products will be of assistance on heavier mineral soils with moderate to good water-holding capacity.

Literature Cited

1. Aldrich-Blake, R.N. 1929. Recent research on the root system of trees. Forestry 3:66-70.

2. Anonymous. 1961. Getting a head start on tree planting. Organic Gardening and Farming, 8:48-49.

3. Appleton, Bonnie L. and Carl E. Whitcomb. 1982. Using superabsorbents to reduce wilting and water requirements of container-grown plants. Okla. Agric. Exp. Sta. Rept. P-824:63-64.

4. Barrows, D. 1967. It pays to give a tree a proper start. Home Garden, 54:40.

5. Baumgardt, John P. 1974. How to care for shade and ornamental trees. Kansas City, Missouri: Intertec Publishing Corp.

6. Bush-Brown, James and Louise. 1958. America's Garden Book. New York: Charles Scribner & Sons.

7. Byrnes, Robert L. 1976. Effects of soil amendments in variable ratios and irrigation levels on soil conditions and the establishment and growth of *Pittosporum tobira*, M.S. Thesis, Univ. of Florida, Gainesville, Fl.

8. Corley, W.L. 1978. Backfill tests in the Georgia Piedmont. SNA Nursery Res. Conf. Proc. 23:60-63.

9. Corley, W.L. 1979. Backfill tests in the Georgia Piedmont II. SNA Nursery Res. Conf. Proc. 24:79-80.

10. Corley, W.L. 1980. Backfill tests in the Georgia Piedmont III. SNA Nursery Res. Conf. Proc. 25:79-81.

11. Corley, W.L. 1980. Rhododendron backfill tests in the Georgia Piedmont. SNA Nursery Res. Conf. Proc. 25:82-83.

12. Corley, W.L. 1984. Soil amendments at planting. Jour. Environmental Hort. 2(1):27-30.

13. Davidson, Harold. 1968. Instructions for planting trees and shrubs. Coop. Ext. Serv. Bulletin 592, Michigan State University, East Lansing.

14. Feustel, I.C. and H.O. Byers. 1936. The comparative moisture-absorbing and moisture-retaining capacities of peat soil mixtures. U.S.D.A. Technical Bulletin 532, 1-25.

15. Flemer, W. 1972. To plant a tree in the city or suburb. Garden Jour. of the New York Bot. Garden, 22:117-118.

16. Gartner, J.B., D.C. Saupe, J.E. Klett and T.R. Yocom. 1970. Hardwood bark as a medium for container growing. Amer. Nurseryman. 131:11, 40, 42-44.

17. Gartner, J. B. M.M. Meyer, and D.C. Saupe. 1971. Hardwood bark as a growing media for container-grown ornamentals. Forest Prod. Jour. 21:25-29.

18. Hensley, D.L. and C.F. Fackler. 1984. Do water-holding compounds help in transplanting? Amer. Nurseryman 159(3):93.

19. Hummel, R.L. and Charles R. Johnson. 1985. Amended backfills: their cost and effect on transplant growth and survival. Jour. Environmental Hort. 3:76-79.

20. Ingram, D.L. and Will Burbage. 1985. Effects of antitranspirants and a water-absorbing polymer on the establishment of transplanted live oaks. SNA Nursery Res. Conf. Proc. 30:114-115.

21. Ingram, D.L., R.J. Black, and C.R. Johnson. 1980. Effect of backfill composition and fertilization on the establishment of container-grown plants in the landscape. SNA Nursery Res. Conf. Proc. 25:68-71.

22. Ingram, D.L., R.J. Black and C.R. Johnson. 1981. Effect of back fill composition and fertilization on establishment of container-grown plants in the landscape. Proc. Fla. State Hort. Soc. 94:198-200.

23. Ingram, D.L. and T.H. Yeager. 1987. Effects of irrigation frequency and a water-absorbing polymer amendment on ligustrum

growth and moisture retention by a container medium. Jour. Environmental Hort. 5:19-21.

24.   Jacobs, H.L. 1938. Shifting small trees and shrubs.   The Arboriculturist 4:5-12.

25.   Munday, Vivian and G.E. Smith. 1979. Landscape establishment of container-grown azaleas in three different media.   Ornamentals South 1(7):12-14.

26.   Paul, J.L., D.C. Bowman, and R.Y. Evans. 1990.   Fertilizer salts reduce hydration of polyacrylamide gels and affect physical properties of gel-amended container media.   Jour. Amer. Soc. Hort. Sci. 115:382-386.

27.   Pellet, Harold. 1971. Effect of soil amendments on growth of landscape plants. Amer. Nurseryman, 134:12, 103-106.

28.   Pirone, P.P. 1959. Planting and transplanting trees and shrubs. Flower Grower, 46:68-73.

29.   Salter, P.J. and J.B. Williams. 1968. Effects of additions of farmyard manure and peat on the moisture characteristics of a sandy loam soil and on crop yields. Jour. Hort. Sci. 43:263-273.

30.   Schulte, Joseph R. and Carl E. Whitcomb. 1975. Effects of soil amendments and fertilizer levels on the establishment of silver maple. Jour. of Arboriculture 1:192-195.

31.   Taylor, K.C. and R.C. Halfacre. 1986.   The effect of hydraphilic polymer on media water retention and nutrient availability to *Ligustrum lucidum.* HortSci. 21:1159-1161.

32.   Thompson, A.R. 1954. Transplanting trees and other woody plants.   Tree Preservation Bulletin #1.   U.S. Nat'l Park Serv., Washington, D.C.

33.   Tomlinson, J.D. and T.E. Bilderback. 1985.   The effects of moisture extenders, gentomite and irrigation frequency on a pine bark medium. SNA Nursery Res. Conf. Proc. 30:114-115.

34. Townsend, L.R. 1973. Effects of soil amendments on the growth and productivity of the highbush blueberry. Can. Jour. Plant Sci. 53:571-577.

35. Whitcomb, Carl E. 1975. Effects of soil amendments on growth of silver maple trees in the landscape. SNA Nursery Res. Conf. Proc. 20:49-50.

36. Whitcomb, Carl E., Robert L. Byrnes, Joseph R. Schulte and James D. Ward. 1976. What is a $5.00 planting hole? Amer. Nurseryman 144(5):111-115.

37. William, J.F. and G.J. Keever. 1990. Water absorption of hydrophylic polymers (hydrogels) reduced by media amendments. Jour. Environ. Hort. 8:113-114.

38. Wright, R.D. and D.C. Milbocker. 1978. Influence of container media and transplanting technique on establishment of container-grown rhododendron 'Hershey Red' in landscape plantings. Nursery Res. Jour. 5:1-7.

CHAPTER 7

GYPSUM AND CHANGES IN SOIL STRUCTURE

Gypsum and High Sodium - - - - - - - - - 136

Gypsum and Low Sodium - - - - - - - - - 137

Alternatives - - - - - - - - - - - - - 138

Gypsum and Changes in Soil Structure

In many areas there is a misconception that adding gypsum (calcium sulfate) to heavy clay soils will improve the tilth, structure and permeability. This may or may not be true, depending on the nature of the soil and the chemicals in the soil.

Gypsum and High Sodium. Gypsum is calcium sulfate. Gypsum **will** improve soil tilth, structure and permeability **only** when the soil has a high level of **sodium** present. When gypsum is added to a soil containing substantial sodium, the calcium and sulfate separate. Calcium has two electrical charges and is a stronger element than sodium with only one electrical charge and will replace the sodium on the clay particles of the soil. The sodium is then free to react with the sulfate to form sodium sulfate which is very water soluble. The sodium sulfate then leaches downward in the soil and out of the root zone. Since the sodium has only one electrical charge and the calcium that replaced it has two, the calcium has the capacity to attach several clay particles together, thereby creating soil aggregates. These soil aggregates make the soil more friable and granular with an increased water infiltration and percolation rate.

The amount of gypsum necessary to improve the structure of high sodium soils depends on the purity of the gypsum, exchange capacity of the soil and the amount of sodium present. Application rates vary from about 1 to 10 tons per acre or more (Table 7.1). Apply no more than about four tons per acre at one application (about 200 pounds per 1000 square feet). Finely ground gypsum (#100 sieve) will react more quickly with the soil than more coarse-textured gypsum (#8 sieve). Since gypsum is only slowly soluble in water, the finer the particles, the more rapid the reaction with the soil. Gypsum incorporated into the soil two to four inches deep will have the greatest effect. Incorporating gypsum deeper simply dilutes the chemical and since the sodium accumulates primarily near the soil surface, there is generally no need for deep incorporation.

Gypsum may also be beneficial to plant growth on some acid soils where sulfur and/or calcium are deficient. This situation is much less common but may occur. In general, this may occur under conditions of acid soils, moderate to high rainfall, and the long-term use of acid-forming nitrogen fertilizers such as urea (46-0-0), ammonium nitrate (33-0-0), or sulfur-coated urea. If a soil test reveals both low sulfur and low calcium, then applying calcium sulfate (gypsum) will aid plant health. The rate would depend on the severity of the need and soil texture. A higher rate would be required on a heavy clay soil than on a sandy loam, for example. In most acid soils, both calcium and magnesium are needed, thus dolomite (calcium and magnesium carbonate) should be used instead of gypsum. Also gypsum is a neutral salt, meaning that it does not change the pH of the soil. On the other hand, dolomite does raise the pH of the soil which on acid soils may be needed.

Table 7.1. Approximate gypsum requirements of soils high in sodium (tons of gypsum per acre).

Texture	Exchangeable sodium (%)			
	15	20	30	40
Coarse	2	3	5	7
Medium	3	5	8	11
Fine	4	6	10	14

Gypsum and Low Sodium. Gypsum **will not** improve soil tilth, structure and permeability unless excess sodium is present. In most areas of heavy clay soils, sodium is not the problem. Consequently adding gypsum simply adds additional calcium and sulfur to the soil. In many cases, the soils contain more than enough calcium so adding the gypsum makes the overall nutrient availability less favorable. Calcium levels in most soils, above a minimum level, create restrictions to the growth of woody plants by tying up micronutrients. Soil pH should be considered in the overall soil management, however, soil pH in the range from 4.5 to 6.5 is very favorable and should not be raised unless calcium levels are extremely low. For example, if a soil test shows a pH of 4.5 and a low calcium level (below 600 pounds of available calcium per acre) then calcium carbonate (lime) should be added to raise the soil pH to about 5.5 and raise the level of calcium up to 600 to 1000 pounds per acre. On the other hand, if magnesium is also low, dolomite (calcium and magnesium carbonate with about 20% calcium and 10% magnesium) should be used to raise the pH and increase levels of both elements. However, if the level of calcium in the soil is low and the soil pH is already 5.5 to 6.0, then **do not** add calcium carbonate or dolomite as the availability

137

of the micronutrients, especially iron, manganese and copper will be decreased. In this case, add gypsum to supply calcium. Gypsum will have little or no change on soil pH.

Since gypsum is a neutral salt, that is, for every acid-forming fraction (sulfate) there is a basic-forming fraction (calcium), no change in soil pH occurs. Magnesium sulfate is another example of a useful neutral salt that has little, if any, effect on soil pH while increasing the level of a useful element.

Alternatives. If heavy clay soils are the problem, and they do not contain excess sodium, the only practical solution is the addition of some structural material to improve soil tilth and structure. Adding organic matter will improve soil tilth, texture and permeability, but only for relatively short periods of time. For example, adding peat moss will aid the structure of a heavy clay in Oklahoma for little more than one year before the organic matter is decomposed by microorganisms. Adding sand, calcined clay, pea gravel or other non-organic structurably stable material, will help **only** if enough is added to reach the threshold point. The threshold point is that amount of sand required to hold all of the clay particles apart. If 10% sand is added to a heavy clay, the tilth, texture and porosity of the clay soil **is not** changed sufficiently to influence porosity. This is because as long as there are enough clay particles to completely surround the sand granules, you have simply made concrete. However, at some point, perhaps 25% to 30% sand, when there is no longer enough clay particles to surround each sand granule, the soil tilth, texture and permeability will be decidedly and **permanently** changed. (See the chapter on plants in containers for further information and procedures for determining the threshold point for improving soils) No two soils are the same, therefore, there are no broad general recommendations for the amount of sand required to reach the threshold level and permanently change the soil.

Another factor to consider is the depth of the soil to be changed. If only the top three to four inches need to be changed, the quantity of sand required will be one-half the quantity needed to change the soil to a depth of six to eight inches. Also keep in mind that if the top three to four inches of soil are made more permeable by adding sand, what will happen to the water after it percolates to the bottom of the amended soil. If the water simply accumulates at this point, little, if anything, has been accomplished. Consider the entire soil drainage profile before adding soil amendments. There are few, worthwhile, short-term and

138

inexpensive solutions to soil drainage problems.   Adding organic matter generally provides no permanent benefit.   Adding enough sand can provide permanent changes in soil texture and permeability.

CHAPTER 8

ESTABLISHMENT OF CONTAINER-GROWN PLANTS

Water Movement in Soils - - - - - - - - - 141

Soil Amendments May Create Problems - - - 146

Root Growth Out From Containers - - - - - 147

Topdress for Better Establishment Success 150

Disturb the Roots at Planting? - - - - - 152

Cuttings Vs. Seedlings - - - - - - - - - 154

Disadvantages of Containers - - - - - - - 155

Advantages of Containers - - - - - - - - 156

Literature Cited - - - - - - - - - - - - 159

Establishment of Container-Grown Plants

Plants grown in containers, if handled properly, have 100% of the roots retained at transplanting. In theory this should mean minimal plant stress since none of the roots are either disturbed or lost. Unfortunately the water-air relationships in a container growth medium and the restrictions imposed by the limited root volume make container-grown plants less than ideal, especially when planted during late spring or summer when the rate of water loss from the top is high and the soil may be dry.

Water Movement in Soils. One of the basic principles of soil physics is that **water will move from a coarse-textured material (or soil) to a fine-textured material (or soil) but it will not move from a fine-textured material to a coarse-textured material until it is saturated.** This is due to capillarity, the adhesive forces (attraction of water to the surfaces of soil particles) and cohesive forces (the attraction of water for water). This is why it is possible to fill a glass with water above the top of the rim). Because of the perched water table in the bottom of every container*, the mixture of materials or growth medium in the container **cannot** be soil. Water drains through normal field soils via capillary action and percolation, and the greater the porosity and depth of the soil, the more rapid the movement of water downward. Even in heavy soils, if the soil depth is several feet, the movement of water occurs at a moderate rate. **On the other hand, once the container is removed and the plant is planted into the landscape, the water retention of the container growth medium abruptly changes. Since the growth medium in the container is more coarse in texture than the surrounding soil in the landscape- -any surrounding soil--water is quickly drawn away from the container growth medium and the plant suffers from drought, even though the surrounding soil may be adequately moist to support plant growth.**

*Perched water table defined: In the landscape, nearly all soils have a water table at some depth. A perched water table is one abnormally high or "perched" above the normal water table. The abrupt textural difference between the mix in the container and the open drain hole prevents the water from exiting. Water will flow out of the drain holes in the bottom of the container only when the weight of the water above is sufficient to force out the water at the bottom against the adhesive and cohesive forces that hold the water in the mix. Even after part of the water exits, considerable water will remain in the bottom of the container. As soon as the weight of the water on top is no longer enough to force water out the bottom, drainage stops. The saturated zone in the bottom of the container is called a perched water table.

The situation becomes even more complicated when the alternative condition occurs. If an abundance of moisture is applied to the surface of the container growth medium following planting, root suffocation is likely to occur, especially when soils have a moderate to high clay content (Figure 8.1). Since the container growth medium is more coarse in texture (has larger pores or openings) than the surrounding soil, water percolates into the container growth medium more quickly than the surrounding soil and may create a "bath-tub" effect, whereby the roots may be suffocated if a) watering persists for sufficient time or b) if the soil is sufficiently heavy to restrict relatively rapid water movement. If enough water is applied often enough, the roots will likely be suffocated, even in soils with good drainage characteristics (see Figures 6.5 and 6.6 in Chapter 6 on soil amendments).

Figure 8.1. The newly planted container-grown tree is wilting but the surrounding clay soil is quite moist. Inspection of the original container growth medium shows it to be very dry. Since tree roots have not yet grown into the surrounding clay the water in the clay is not available to the tree. All water used by the leaves must come from the original container growth medium. In addition, the clay quickly draws water out of the growth medium since the clay is much finer in texture. The practical management procedure is to apply a modest amount of water to just wet the container mix, but do it frequently. The opposite complication can also occur. When a rainy period occurs, water will percolate into the container growth medium much more quickly than the surrounding soil creating a bath tub effect which may cause root suffocation.

The difference in rate of percolation between container growth medium and surrounding soil is easily demonstrated using two containers with similar volumes of water. Pour the water from one container directly onto the surface of the container growth medium of a tree or shrub that has been recently planted into the soil. A few feet away pour water from the other container onto the soil surface. The rapid percolation of water into the container growth medium shows why plants grown in containers and planted into soil are **much more** likely to suffer from over watering and root suffocation when watered by hand as opposed to sprinklers or natural rainfall (Figure 8.2). An exception would be where the surface of the soil slopes to the area of the container or where a depression occurs around the container growth medium such that surface water from irrigation or rainfall drains into the porous mix.

Irrigating with one-half inch of water will wet the container growth medium to a greater depth than the surrounding soil. This is due to the much lower water holding capacity of the container growth medium per unit volume. The practical consideration is that, **if** the soil surrounding a newly planted container-grown plant is moist, a relatively small amount of water needs to be applied frequently to keep the container mix moist and support root activity and plant growth. This is because one needs only to wet the container mix. On the other hand, if both the surrounding soil and the container mix are dry, a much larger quantity of water is needed since the water will be quickly drawn away from the container mix by the finer textured dry soil. But once the surrounding soil becomes thoroughly wetted, subsequent quantities of water can be reduced, but not the frequency since the surrounding soil will continue to draw water away from the container mix, although at a somewhat slower rate depending on the texture of the soil, dryness, and other conditions.

Roots of plants grown in containers do not have to extend vast distances in order to establish the plant in the new site. Once roots from the container growth medium extend out into the surrounding soil and can draw water and nutrients from a volume of soil equal to or greater than the volume of mix in the container, the plant can be treated as though it is established. For example, if the volume of growth medium in a #2 (two-gallon or seven-liter) container is approximately 400 cubic inches, plant roots need only to extend about one-inch from the sides and bottom to have contacted 400 cubic inches of soil. Once this point in root growth out from the container growth medium is reached, the

144

moisture level in the container growth medium is no longer of major importance. Since roots absorb water and nutrients almost exclusively at the root tips, and the actively growing root tips are now mostly in the surrounding soil, the roots connecting these root tips and the plant stem serve only as plumbing to transport materials back and forth. The porous container growth medium can become quite dry with little or no adverse effects on the plant or its roots.

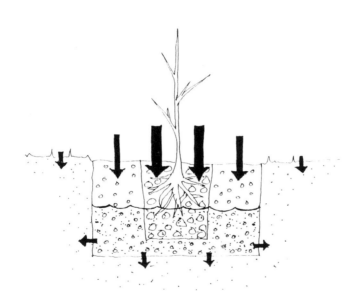

Figure 8.2.   The rate of water percolation into the container mix and the loosened soil around the root mass will be much greater than the surrounding undisturbed soil.   If the soil is well drained, no complication occurs, but if the soil is heavy and drains poorly, a "bath tub" effect can occur.   Keep in mind that because of the limited water holding capacity of the container mix, once it has been removed from the container, light frequent waterings will be required to keep it from drying out.   The same volume of water per square inch of surface area will wet the container mix to a greater depth than the surrounding soil.

Soil Amendments May Create Problems. The principles discussed above emphasize why it is important **not** to amend the soil around the plant **unless** the entire soil area where the plant will develop roots over the next several years is amended. If the soil is amended around the container growth medium, two moisture/water relationship barriers are established as opposed to one (Figure 8.3). When the soil around the plant is amended, the roots are forced to grow out into an amended zone and then later grow from that amended zone into the surrounding soil. The principles of water movement and the capillary attraction of the surrounding soil on the amended soil is the same as the soil has on the container growth medium directly when no soil amendments are used. In short, amending a limited area around a newly transplanted tree or shrub is nearly always detrimental or at best of no benefit. On the other hand, in some situations, amending a very large area relative to the size of the plant and soil conditions may be beneficial. See the chapter on soil amendments for a more thorough discussion and specific research results.

Figure 8.3. Roots of this container-grown shrub (six-inch container) grew into the amended soil and stopped at the amended soil/soil interface of the 18-inch diameter planting hole. Roots from the same plants without the soil amendments were not restricted and extended further out into the surrounding soil.

Root Growth Out From Containers. Roots of plants grown in containers do not retain or remember the circular design of most containers. Consequently, following transplanting roots grow into the surrounding soil relative to their position in the container growth medium at planting time. Therefore, the ideal root system in a container would have active root tips oriented in all directions at time of transplanting into the landscape. This would anchor the plant most securely and provide the greatest volume of water from the surrounding soil. Unfortunately, most container-grown plants have roots mostly on one side, especially when the plants have been spaced so that the sun hits one side of the container (Figure 8.4).

Only a few minutes of direct sun on the side of a container will kill roots, so be especially careful when moving plants onto or around a landscape job before planting. If part of the roots on one side of the container were killed in the nursery, then during handling and holding on the landscape site the container gets positioned so that part, or all, of the healthy roots are killed by heat, the plant has virtually no chance of surviving in the landscape.

The key factor to remember is that the more rapidly roots grow from the soil-less container growth medium into the surrounding soil, the more rapid the establishment and the less the stress. Many plants grown by wholesale nurseries in containers are fertilized through the irrigation system and no provision is made for fertilization once the plants leave the nursery. Rapid root growth into the surrounding soil following transplanting is very important due to the rapid water loss from the container growth medium. Costello and Paul (2) concluded that the rapid moisture loss from the container growth medium following transplanting was the result of drainage to the surrounding field soil. They observed that moisture tension increased more rapidly in the growth medium following transplanting than in the surrounding field soil or in the growth medium of the plants that remained in the containers.

Figure 8.4. Plant roots are quickly killed by excess heat when containers are exposed to direct sun (above). The plant on the left was in a container with one side exposed to the sun, whereas, the two on the right were shaded. This shumard oak was grown in a #3 (10-liter) container that had one side exposed to the sun (below). Following transplanting, living roots existed only on one side of the container, therefore, the plant was unsupported on the other side. Container-grown plants like this are much more subject to drought stress and being blown over than plants with a more or less radial root system which provides equal support in all directions.

Topdress for Better Establishment Success. To determine if topdressing with a slow-release fertilizer during holding prior to planting in the landscape would influence the number of roots developed following transplanting, the following study was conducted (1). Mojave pyracantha (*Pyracantha* X 'Mojave') and pfitzer juniper (*Juniperus chinensis* 'Pfitzeriana') in one-gallon containers were obtained from a wholesale nursery that used liquid fertilizer (nitrogen and potassium) injected through the irrigation system. The plants were two years old. The growth medium was 70% pine bark and 30% sand. The plants were received on March 10 and held without further fertilization until April 21, when the plants were treated with either 0, 1/3 or 1/2 ounce of Osmocote 18-6-12 per container as a topdress. After five weeks the plants were shifted from one-gallon to three-gallon containers. However, the medium in the three-gallon containers was a 3-1-1 by volume mix of ground pine bark, peat and sand with no nutrients added. This was done to try to more clearly determine the effects of the topdress fertilizer on the root growth following transplanting. After three weeks in the three-gallon containers the plants were removed and the number of roots that had grown from the original root ball were counted.

The average number of roots growing from the pyracantha root ball were 164, 187 and 189 for the 0, 1/3- and 1/2-ounce Osmocote treatments, respectively. The fertilized pyracantha had 13% more roots compared to the untreated control.

The average number of roots growing from the juniper root ball were 13, 17, and 18 for the 0, 1/3- and 1/2-ounce Osmocote treatment, respectively. The fertilized juniper had 25% more roots compared to the untreated control.

Studies of this type emphasize the importance of nutrition to root development of container-grown plants immediately following transplanting (Figure 8.5). Allowing container-grown plants to remain without fertilizer for even short periods of time reduces the number of roots that develop into the surrounding soil following transplanting. Since newly planted container-grown nursery stock dries very quickly following planting, rapid root growth following planting greatly reduces plant moisture stress and increases survival (Figure 8.6).

Figure 8.5. These two Japanese honeysuckle (**Lonicera japonica**) came from the same parent. The plant above received a more favorable fertilizer regime in the small container prior to planting into the landscape than the one below. They were planted into a landscape situation and dug three weeks later. The condition of the plant, that cannot be seen can have a tremendous effect on root growth.

Figure 8.6. Internal energy stress cannot be detected by observing external plant parts. This juniper has received no fertilizer for six months, yet the top looks good. However, when planted, root growth into the surrounding soil will be slower than if proper fertility had been maintained.

Disturb the Roots at Planting? There is considerable disagreement among nurserymen and landscapers with regard to the handling of the root system of container-grown plants at planting time. Many feel that the root system must be cut or in some way disturbed in order to prevent the continued formation of circling roots and to encourage good root development into the soil at the planting site (3). Fulmer and Jones (5) reported that container-grown dwarf burford holly developed a better root system following transplanting when the roots were disturbed.

To study this further, Appleton and Whitcomb (1) selected root-bound plants of Mojave pyracantha, (*Pyracantha* X 'Mojave') and rotunda holly (*Ilex cornuta* 'Rotunda') which were obtained from a commercial nursery and transplanted from one-gallon containers to three-gallon containers using four treatments:

1) repotted, no root disturbance;
2) vertical slits the length of the root ball, 1/2-inch deep, two locations;
3) vertical slits the length of the root ball, 1/2-inch deep, four locations;
4) two vertical slits 1/2-inch deep and the bottom of the root mass pulled apart.

Several large, circling roots were cut on plants of both species. The plants had been grown in a mix of 90% bark and 10% sand. The mix in the three-gallon container was 3-1-1 pine bark, peat, and sand with 14 pounds Osmocote 17-7-12, six pounds dolomite and 1.5 pounds of Micromax per cubic yard. The repotted plants were allowed to grow four weeks, then evaluated for new root growth. The treatments were evaluated by removing the three-gallon containers and counting the root tips extending from the surface of the original container medium.

The rate of root elongation and new root growth was far greater for the pyracantha than for the holly. However, there were no differences in number of roots developed as a result of the root ball treatments. This suggests that if aeration in the back-fill soil is not limiting, the short-term root growth of container-grown plants, even when root bound, is not increased by cutting or disturbing the root ball prior to transplanting. When large roots are cut, the development of secondary branch roots is fairly slow, probably somewhat like the development of roots on a cutting. The root tips lost due to the vertical cuts on the root ball may be similar to the few root tips produced at the ends of the larger cut roots (Figure 8.7). This may explain the absence of treatment effects. Perhaps the best safeguard is to cut the sides of the root ball of container-grown nursery stock **if any doubt exists** regarding the possibility of circling/girdling roots. The greater short-term stress can be handled better than long-term complications from root-bound plants.

Figure 8.7. If the root system of this oak had been disturbed at planting, fewer roots would have grown into the surrounding soil in the same period of time since many of the root tips that extended to establish this plant would have been damaged. On the other hand, if the tree had been "root-bound" some long-term benefit might result if the tree survived the transplanting stage.

Cuttings Vs. Seedlings.   There is a distinct difference in the root systems of shrubs propagated from cuttings and trees grown from seed when placed in containers.   Plants propagated from cuttings characteristically have a multitude of roots of similar size and age originating from the base of the cutting.   Because there are many roots of similar size and age, there is a limited tendency for one root to become dominant and suppress the activity of others.   On the other hand, plants grown from seed have a primary or tap root which results from the radical or primary root at germination.   Even when this primary root is removed, it quickly recovers and re-establishes dominance over the remaining roots (6).   Tree seedlings that are lifted from flats and the primary root cut during the transplanting process into large containers grow at very different rates.   The plants that grow rapidly have developed a fibrous root system without redevelopment

154

of a primary root. However, plants that grow slowly have re-established a dominant primary root which suppresses secondary root growth (6).

Two eucalyptus species were subjected to four root treatments prior to transplanting from polyethylene bags. When plants were dug after 2.5 years, it was observed that the combination of vertical slicing and removal of the lower one inch of the root ball increased the number of vertical roots and largely eliminated root curling with both species. Shoot growth was restricted for several months, suggesting a loss of active root tips for a time and the need for careful watering (4, 6).

Disadvantages of Containers. Disadvantages of container-grown plants are:

a) Frequent but light watering is required during establishment due to the soil-growth medium textural difference (Figure 8.8).

b) Root wrapping/distortion occurs due to container design and/or leaving the plants in the container too long. Root-bound container-grown plants should be avoided as there is no practical way to return these plants to vigorous growth. This is a far more serious problem with trees than with most shrubs which develop secondary root branches more readily as a result of root restrictions (Figure 8.9).

c) Root growth may be from only from one side of the container (Figure 8.4). This is a frequent problem with plants in containers that have been exposed to direct sun. Roots of most species are killed in a few minutes in the summer by excess heating of the side wall of the container. Containers that are handled several times from wholesaler to final planting in the landscape may, unfortunately, have 50% to 80% of their roots killed before planting.

d) Roots sometimes grow out of the drain holes and into the soil below. Once this occurs, the plant should be rejected as it will perform poorly, if at all, following planting (Figure 8.10)

Figure 8.8. Plants container-grown and recently planted in the field or landscape require frequent watering to aid establishment and growth. Be careful not to suffocate the root system by excess water.

Advantages of Containers. Advantages of container-grown plants are:
   a) retention of 100% of the roots, if handled properly,
   b) lightweight relative to plants dug B & B,
   c) ease of handling and transporting,
   d) harvest and shipping is nearly independent of weather conditions.
   e) little or no mess in handling; this is especially advantageous for retail customers.
   f) if handled properly and carefully, may be planted any time of year in the South and the entire growing season in the North. However, there are some distinct "best" times for planting which minimize maintenance. See the chapter on spring vs. fall planting.

Figure 8.9. The tree above shows one girdling root. However, when it was dug, several circling roots were observed. This tree should not have been grown in a round container when small. There is no practical means to save a tree with such a poor root system.

Figure 8.10.   Roots grew out of the container and into the soil below.   This plant now has few functioning root tips inside the container and will perform poorly or die once planted into the landscape.

The production of plants in containers has been a boon for the nursery business in general and especially for the retail garden centers.   Like most techniques, it is not without its complications.   If done properly and timely it offers substantial benefits but one of the most difficult points to communicate is the fact that it is a useful tool only as long as the plant remains there for a limited period of time.   At some point every plant in a container must be sold, shifted into a larger size, or thrown away.

Literature Cited

1. Appleton, Bonnie L. and Carl E. Whitcomb. 1984. Establishment of container-grown ornamentals. SNA Nursery Res. Conf. Proc. 31:106-108.

2. Costello, L. and J.L. Paul. 1975. Moisture relation in transplanted container plants. HortSci. 10:371-372.

3. Deneke, F.J. 1984. Blueprint for spring tree planting. Amer. Forests 90(4):13-15.

4. Ellyard, Roger K. 1984. Effect of root pruning at planting on subsequent root development of two species of eucalyptus. Jour. of Arboriculture 10:214-218.

5. Fulmer, J.P. and E.V. Jones. 1974. The effect of four transplant treatments on root growth of container-grown *Ilex cornuta* 'Burford Nana'. SNA Nursery Res. Conf. Proc. 19:27.

6. Harris, R.W. 1971. Root pruning improves nursery tree quality. Jour. Amer. Soc. Hort. Sci. 96:105-108.

7. Whitcomb, Carl E. 1988. *Plant Production in Containers. Lacebark Publications*, Stillwater, Ok.

CHAPTER 9

SPRING VS. FALL PLANTING

Fall Planting for Container Stock- - - - 161

Research Findings I - - - - - - - - - - 161

Research Findings II - - - - - - - - - - 166

Literature Cited - - - - - - - - - - - - 170

Spring vs. Fall Planting

Fall Planting for Container Stock. There is a distinct advantage to fall planting of container-grown nursery stock in hardiness zones 6 and southward. Further north, the timing of fall planting is more critical but the concept still has merit. Knowledge of plant root and top functions relative to the growing season suggests fall planting may have advantages over spring planting (Table 9.1). Container-grown plants planted into the landscape in the fall are developing roots in the soil whenever conditions are favorable. This is far better than losing roots above ground while waiting for spring planting.

Table 9.1. Contrasting spring vs. fall conditions supports fall planting of container-grown nursery stock, where the root system is not disturbed at time of planting.

	Spring	Fall
Day length	increasing	decreasing
Air temperature	warm-increasing	cool-decreasing
Soil temperature	cool/cold	warm
Soil moisture	good to excessive	fair-good
Soil oxygen level	low to moderate	moderate to good
Leaf water loss	new leaves-high	old leaves-low
Stored energy level in the plant	low, after spring flush	very high

---

Research Findings I. Fall planting of container-grown nursery stock can provide a tremendous advantage over spring planting for some species (1). For example, eighteen two-year-old plants of each of the following species were planted on November 6 and 7 in a field of clay loam soil:

Chinese pistache, *Pistacia chinensis*
Japanese black pine, *Pinus thunbergi*
cluster pine, *Pinus pinaster*
bur oak, *Quercus macrocarpa*
dwarf burford holly, *Ilex cornuta* 'Burford Dwarf'
pfitzer juniper, *Juniperus chinensis* 'Pfitzeriana'
sawtooth oak, *Quercus acutissima*

At the same time, 12 plants of similar size and quality were heavily mulched with ground pine bark in their original containers and held for spring planting. Container sizes were one-gallon for the pfitzer juniper, dwarf burford holly, Chinese pistache and Japanese black pine; and three-gallon for the cluster pine, bur oak and sawtooth oak. The growth medium for all species had been a 2:1:1 mix of ground pine bark, peat moss and sand.

No soil amendments or fertilizers were used in the planting holes and all plants were watered in three times by hand. Rainfall was very limited during the winter period with only 4.2 inches occurring between November 6 and March 19 when one-third of the fall-planted trees and shrubs were dug.

The winter period during this study had minimum temperatures of minus three degrees Fahrenheit on two occasions. However, it was a mild winter by central Oklahoma standards, and the soil did not freeze below about three inches.

On March 19, six plants of each species that had been fall-planted were selected at random to evaluate root growth during the dormant period. There were no leaves present on the deciduous species when planted and at the time of evaluation, no new top growth had begun. All species had developed some new roots during the dormant period (Figure 9.1). Sawtooth oak, bur oak, cluster pine, Japanese black pine and pfitzer juniper developed the most roots with some roots extending as far as ten to twelve inches beyond the original face of the container ball. Fewer roots were observed on the Chinese pistache (a tree known for its growth during hot, dry weather) and dwarf burford holly. One interesting factor observed was that **all roots extending beyond the original container ball were not "new roots" but were extensions of roots that were in the container at the time of planting the previous fall.** That is, new roots in the surrounding soil could be followed back to the container and around, or into, the container ball. New roots had branched very little, although tremendous quantities of root hairs were present. This shows that roots of container-grown plants in soilless mixes will readily grow into the surrounding soil during the fall and winter period whenever soil temperatures are sufficiently warm. It also suggests that the new roots growing around the container when it was planted were not fixed in that position, as has been previously theorized and readily grew into the surrounding soil (1, 2). Root growth was aided by the **absence** of soil amendments. Whitcomb et al. (5) and Schulte and Whitcomb (4) reported that when soil amendments were used in the back fill when planting trees or shrubs, the root growth beyond the amended back fill soil was restricted.

162

Following excavation of 1/3 of the fall-planted plants in the spring, the 12 plants of each species that were mulched-in over the winter were planted in the same field. All plants were fertilized with one pound 10-20-0 per 25 square feet (175 pounds of nitrogen per acre).

On October 21, six spring- and six fall-transplants were selected at random, dug and evaluated for further root growth after one full growing season. Top growth, stem caliper and number of branches, were taken from all 12 replications. All plants were dug at approximately the same depth with a backhoe with a 24-inch wide bucket. In all cases, many roots were still in the shape of the original container, providing an easy separation point for roots in the container from those developed in the surrounding soil, hereafter referred to for brevity, as old roots and new roots.

Figure 9.1. Typical root growth of bur oak that had been grown in a container. Photo taken March 19, following planting November 7. The broken black line is the edge of the original container ball. No leaves were present at time of planting and bud swell had not yet occurred in the spring when this photo was taken.

163

After one growing season (seven months after spring planting and 11 months after fall planting), Japanese black pine, bur oak and sawtooth oak had more new roots, old roots, total roots, top weight, stem caliper and height when fall-planted, than when spring-planted (Figure 9.2). Stem caliper and height of bur oak was strikingly favored by fall planting (Figure 9.3). Pfitzer junipers had slightly more roots when planted in the spring, however, top weight was greater when fall-planted. Cluster pine and Chinese pistache responded similarly to the juniper, in that there was no advantage to fall planting for these species, but there was no damage or injury.

All plants of all species survived fall planting except the dwarf burford holly. Survival of the dwarf burford holly in this study was poor. Of the 18 planted in the fall, nine died during the winter. In addition, in the open field with no supplemental irrigation during the summertime, several of the fall- and spring-planted dwarf burford holly died prior to termination of step two of the experiment in the fall of the following year. The location of this study was such that a portable irrigation system could not be utilized and only hand watering was possible. In an adjacent field with similar soil, 45 of 47 fall-planted dwarf burford holly survived in a separate experiment using plants from the same uniformly grown container material. The difference was due to about one inch of water applied by irrigation sprinklers on two occasions following planting of this container material. Thus the contrast in survival at the two locations was probably due to soil moisture and not the winter conditions or planting time.

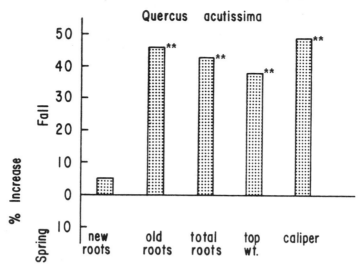

Figure 9.2. Comparison of fall vs spring planting expressed as percent increase for sawtooth oak (**Quercus acutissima**). Japanese black pine and bur oak responded similarly. Had more roots developed as a result of spring planting, the bar would have been below the 0 line.

Figure 9.3. Bur oak stem caliper, fall-planted (left) and spring-planted (right). The fall-planted trees had better developed root systems for support the following summer and experienced less stress which especially favored stem caliper increase which occurs mostly in the fall.

Research Findings II. In another fall vs spring planting study, only top growth at the end of one growing season was evaluated and no complex root examinations were done (7).

Uniform plants of river birch (*Betula nigra*), deodar cedar (*Cedrus deodara*), shumard oak (*Quercus shumardi*), mugo pine (*Pinus mugo*) and pyracantha (*Pyracantha* X 'Mojave') in two-gallon containers were planted in the field on October 28. Plants of identical size were held in an unheated polyethylene-covered greenhouse and planted on April 16. Plants were evaluated on November 20 for survival, height, stem caliper and in some cases, the number of branches. The summer had been quite hot and dry and the plants received **no** supplemental irrigation following planting. Spring rains were accomodating through June 28, but no meaningful rainfall occurred again until September 28 in north central Oklahoma where the study was done.

The results can best be summarized by two photos (Figures 9.4 and 9.5). Every river birch, deodar cedar and shumard oak survived, regardless of treatment, although growth differences were sizeable. The only pyracantha that died were from those planted in the spring. All mugo pine eventually died. However, the sequence of death supported the concept of fall planting. In late July a few of the spring-planted mugo pines began to show severe moisture stress. By August 10, all spring-planted mugo pines were dead. At that time, all of the fall-planted mugo pines looked thrifty. By August 24, several of the fall-planted mugo pines began to show severe moisture stress and all were dead by the September 15 evaluation date.

These data suggest that with most species, there is a decided advantage in terms of root growth, top growth, and, in some cases, stem caliper, in planting in the fall versus the spring. Species such as juniper, cluster pine and Chinese pistache are very heat-tolerant and this probably explains why there was no particular advantage to fall planting. Growth of some species was strikingly greater when fall-planted as opposed to planting in the spring (Figure 9.3).

Figure 9.4. River birch planted in the spring (left and right) and planted in the fall (center). All plants survived the summer with no irrigation, however, the growth and visual appearance of the trees clearly emphasize the benefit of fall planting.

Most plants could be developing roots during the winter in the field or landscape if fall-planted as opposed to being held in some type of overwintering apparatus. In overwintering plants grown in containers, the small root tips are first to be injured, yet are most critical to plant establishment. In addition, overwintering apparatus is expensive and difficult to construct and maintain.

It is important to re-emphasize that these plants were all grown in containers prior to planting in the field. In addition, the roots that developed during the wintertime were extensions of roots that were already present in the container at the time of planting and thus grew out into the surrounding soil. **A great deal depends on the condition of the plant. Fall planting of container-grown nursery stock that is root bound would no doubt be less than satisfactory! It is critical that some roots extend from the container mix into the surrounding soil before the onslaught of severe winter weather.**

The difficult definition then becomes, "When is fall?" Fall comes much earlier in Chicago than Mobile and it is difficult to define it as to a specific series of dates. A good rule of thumb is that fall is that first morning when you go outside and immediately go back in for a jacket. In hardiness zone 9 and lower, (further north in the U.S.A.) the progressively shorter days following the June equinox send an increasingly stronger signal to plants **not** to produce top growth and to prepare for winter. The first cool morning in September or October when air temperatures drop to the lower 40 degrees (F) or 30 degrees further signals the plant that winter is approaching.

The highest level of energy occurs in a plant in the fall. The top has ceased to grow and the leaves are sending reserves down to the stems and roots. The combination of downward transfer of energy which enhances root growth with warm soil conditions, good soil aeration, and all of the other positive factors in the fall should be used to advantage whenever possible (see Table 9.1).

Do not procrastinate. It is much better to install landscape plants early and have even better root establishment than to put it off and wonder or lose plants due to dehydration during the winter. The lowest humidity and in turn the most drying condition for evergreens and buds on deciduous plants occurs in the winter.

With bare root plants and, to some degree, balled and burlapped plants, initiation of new roots must come from the cut ends of older, larger roots. This process is dependent on a chemical signal from the terminal buds. Richardson (3) reported that after silver maple had been dug bare root, no new roots developed until the buds expanded in the spring. This has been observed by the author many times. Because of this factor, **bare root trees and shrubs should not be planted in the fall.** With balled and burlapped trees and shrubs, it is a tough call. If the plants have a good fibrous root system and as a result there are many root tips inside the root ball poised to extend into the surrounding soil, it will work well. On the other hand, if there are few, if any, root tips in the root ball and all new root growth is dependent upon the new roots that grow from the cut root ends, fall planting is questionable or at least less beneficial.

The prime reason roots of container-grown plants developed readily into the surrounding field was due to the high energy level in the plant and the fact that the roots were not disturbed. The high energy level was aided by a slow-release fertilizer system in the growth medium in the container (4). In addition, the **absence** of soil amendments incorporated into the back fill around the trees or shrubs enhanced lateral root development (4, 5).

Figure 9.5. Pyracantha planted in the spring (left) and fall (right). The spring-planted shrub on the left is dead, the fall-planted one has dense foliage at the end of the summer drought and showed no symptoms of moisture stress.

It is important to note that these studies were done with trees and shrubs started in the spring so they were in prime condition in the fall or the following spring. If plants were prime for planting in the fall or spring and held over until the next fall, to compare spring vs. fall establishment, the fall planting would be poor, not because of the conditions in the fall but because of the severe root bound condition of the plants. Chapter 2 has more informa-tion on root-bound conditions of container-grown plants.

Mulching of the soil surface adjacent to the newly fall-planted tree or shrub, to retard the cooling of the soil and assist moisture and temperature relationships will stimulate further development of roots during the fall and early winter period.

Literature Cited

1.   Dickinson, Sancho and Carl E. Whitcomb. 1977. The effects of spring vs. fall planting on establishment of landscape plants. Nursery Res. Jour. 4:9-19.

2.   McGuire, John J. 1972. Growing ornamental plants in containers: a handbook for the nurseryman. Univ. of Rhode Island Ext. Bulletin. 197. 39 pages.

3.   Reisch, K.W. 1957. Propagating plants directly in containers by means of hardwood cuttings. Proc. Int. Plant Prop. Soc. 7:78-81.

4.   Richardson S.D. 1953. Root growth of *Acer pseudoplatanus*, L. in relation to grass cover and nitrogen deficiency. Meded. Landbouw. Wageningen. 53:75-07.

5.   Schulte, Joseph R. and Carl E. Whitcomb. 1975. Effects of soil amendments and fertilizer levels on the establishment of silver maple. Jour. of Arboriculture. 1:192-195.

6.   Whitcomb, Carl E., Robert L. Byrnes, Joseph R. Schulte and James D. Ward. 1976. What is a $5 planting hole? Amer. Nurseryman 144(2):14, 22.

7.   Whitcomb, Carl E. 1984. Another look at fall planting. Okla. Agri. Exp. Sta. Res. Rept. P-855:28-29.

CHAPTER 10

THE RESTRICTED PLANTING HOLE

Keys to Success - - - - - - - - - - - - - - 172

The Restricted Planting Hole

The question often arises regarding the best techniques for planting in median strips, cut outs in sidewalks and parking lots or similar areas where root space is very restricted. In many cases trees and shrubs are planted with little or no prior planning or preparation of the site. In cases where the soils are poor, compacted or poorly drained, plant performance generally equals the planning and preparation effort. Even under the best of conditions, life will be short in this restricted space, however, there are several factors that can improve plant performance and extend their functional life.

Keys to Success. Considering the following factors can greatly increase the likelihood of success:

a. Get the largest planting spaces possible under the circumstances. It is better to have five large planting spaces than 10 small ones.

b. Plant only those species that show tolerance for such sites in the geographic area.

c. Provide drainage, both surface and internal if soils do not drain well. See the chapter, The Planting Hole, for details. Aeration is crucial to root health. Poor drainage is the number one cause of problems in these areas, especially where surface water flows into the restricted planting hole (Figure 10.1)

d. If soils are poor, excavate and replace with good soils. However, keep in mind the drainage factor. Excavating subsoil clay and filling with a sandy loam simply creates a "bath tub" unless drainage from the bottom of the amended soil is provided (Figure 10.2).

e. Make the planting hole as large as possible. For example, 4 x 6 feet is much better than 4 x 4 feet and 6 x 6 feet would be even better. These conditions are much like a container; a plant in a 15 gallon container will grow better than one in a 12 or 10 gallon. Every little bit helps.

f. Insulate the soil mass from the surrounding mass of pavement. Asphalt (tarmac) and concrete absorb vast quantities of heat in summer. Since the soil beneath these surfaces is generally moist, heat is readily conducted to adjacent planting beds or tree pits. The optimum temperature for root functions of most species is between 70 and 80 degrees F. Surfaces of pavings may reach temperatures in excess of 150 degrees F. To be effective the insulation should extend three to four feet deep and to remain effective in the soil it must be a closed cell material that will not allow water movement into or through (Figure 10.3).

g. When adding insulation around restricted planting holes, wrap the insulation in six-mil polyethylene when the paving is asphalt (tarmac) or make the barrier of plastic complete to prevent any root contact with the soil under the paving. **Do not** place plastic across the bottom of the planting hole. The reason for this is the widespread practice of treating the soil surface with Hyvar (bromacil) or Pramitol, soil sterilant herbicides. The herbicides are used to prevent weeds from pushing through the paving. However, since both of these herbicides are readily root-absorbed, any roots that contact the treated soil are likely to absorb enough chemical to damage or kill the tree or shrub. In many cases there is sufficient soil aeration for roots to survive a short distance under the paving. Where the soil is not treated, the additional soil volume is beneficial to the plant(s). When the soil is treated the plants often begin to show symptoms of herbicide injury as it reaches sufficient size to be effective in the landscape (Figure 10.4). Roots will not grow through six-mil polyethylene unless there is a weak or torn area. The barrier depth required to be effective has not been studied, but probably varies with soil conditions, drainage and the species involved. Three to four feet would probably be sufficient in most cases.

The small tree in Figure 10.5 would be aided even more by the use of insulation to reduce heat transfer from the paving.

Figure 10.1.   In this case water flows from upper right and upper left toward the tree in the restricted planting hole.   Good internal drainage must be present or the tree will suffocate since the normal soil aeration is partially restricted by the brick on sand.   Be very cautious about using herbicides in this area.   Only pre-emergent herbicides with very low water solubility should be used.   Roundup can be applied to control existing weeds.   Under NO circumstances should soil sterilant-type herbicides or brush killers of any kind, Trimec, or any herbicide containing Banvel/Dicamba be used.   Trees in limited spaces are very vulnerable to deicing salts.   When snow or ice is piled up around the tree, the chemicals are concentrated.   All of these factors combine to limit the life expectancy of such trees to a modest number of years.

Figure 10.2. One year before the excavation and photo, a soil core four inches in diameter and 24 inches deep was made and backfilled with good soil containing a slow-release fertilizer. Note the tremendous root development in the fill just below and to the left of the tree trunk as opposed to the surrounding soil. The smaller the soil volume available for plant growth, the more important it becomes to insure that roots can utilize all of the space available. The soil on the site was nearly 100% sand, yet the surface was sufficiently compacted so as to limit root growth. In many situations, simply digging out the existing soil to loosen and aerate, then replace the soil and plant is of great benefit to the plants

Figure 10.3. Installing rigid closed-cell urethane or styrofoam in a trench will reduce lateral heat transfer in the soil. In most cases, the insulation must be two inches thick (urethane) or three to four inches thick (styrofoam) and three to four feet deep to be effective.

Figure 10.4. Leaves from a hedge that was planted at right angles to a parking area where Hyvar (bromacil) had been used beneath the asphalt. The normal leaves (left) were typical except for the last two plants near the paving which had enough roots in the treated soil to cause severe herbicide injury (right). A plastic barrier at the edge of the paving could have prevented this problem.

Figure 10.5. The tree in this restricted planting hole has been mulched to reduce soil temperatures and can receive supplemental water. However, it would have benefited from perimeter insulation to prevent lateral movement of heat from the pavement into the root zone and prevent roots from extending beneath the pavement which may have been treated with an herbicide.

    h.   Provide for supplemental irrigation whenever possible. In many plantings of this type, the top of the plant experiences a near-desert environment and loses large quantities of water. On the other hand, if internal drainage is not provided, over zealous irrigation can be counter-productive by stimulating a shallower root system in hotter soils which will decrease root/moisture support for the top. Keep in mind that the chemical composition of the irrigation water will influence the soil chemistry over time and may require special soil treatments.

i. Mulch whenever possible or plant ground cover plants with limited competitive/restrictive effects on the tree species involved. Keeping the root system cool greatly enhances its ability to support the top (Figure 10.5). Mulch also allows for stem growth which is sometimes restricted by rigid materials (Figure 10.6)

Plants placed in restricted planting holes often live short lives (Figure 10.7). The decision for planting trees in restricted planting holes must be made on the basis of visual environmental benefits vs. economics. No doubt, trees in urban areas add shade, comfort and appearance factors, but their life will be short and maintenance high.

Figure 10.6.   The stem growth of this tree is being restricted by the bricks placed in the planting hole cut out.   Brick on sand work fine to provide a smooth surface for pedestrians, but maintenance is required.   Soon the bricks being elevated by the growth of the tree will become a hazard.

Figure 10.7. The trees in this urban planting are surviving in very restricted spaces. The blank in the center of the circular brick pattern is where a tree used to be. However, the people in the background would certainly attest to the shade and appearance value of the remaining trees.

Soil conditions have a great influence on how trees perform in restricted spaces. Heavy clays are not always undesirable if drainage is provided. In some cases, the soils provide an unseen benefit that allows trees to survive and grow in unique locations (Figure 10.8). Because this tree is doing well, people often think trees will flourish in restricted planting holes everywhere. Such is not the case. Each site is unique and must be carefully evaluated.

Figure 10.8. These Bradford pears grew too large for the street planting spaces. They are being removed and replanted in the city parks and other areas during the dormant period. Callery pears are one of the most tolerant species to restricted spaces due to the ability of the roots to function with limited aeration. Lacebark elm and live oak are also amazingly tolerant. More attention should be given to selection of the species rather than "This form or foliage color would be nice"!

CHAPTER 11

ROOT STIMULATORS

Supporting Research - - - - - - - - - - 183

Literature Cited - - - - - - - - - - - 188

Root Stimulators

Various products are sold as root promoters or root stimulators for nursery and landscape use. These are, no doubt, the outgrowths of research reports showing that auxins applied to the base of bare root nursery stock do stimulate additional root formation.

Supporting Research. As early as 1938, Romberg and Smith (9) used auxin impregnated toothpicks to stimulate the initiation of new roots at transplanting. Since that time the technique has been used successfully many times (1, 3, 4, 7). Recently, Magley and Struve reported that three- to six-inch caliper pin oaks dug either bare root or with a 44-inch tree spade produced more roots from cut root ends when auxin-treated toothpicks were inserted (5). They noted that with the auxin-treated trees, great numbers of new roots developed at the points of toothpick insertion. These roots were longer and of greater diameter than those produced by the untreated roots. The problem with the technique is the time and cumbersome steps involved in inserting the toothpicks in the ends of cut roots of trees dug either bare root or balled-in-burlap (B & B).

A spray or dip application of auxin solutions would be more practical and easier to apply. Lee, Moser and Hess used a 20-second dip of 2000 parts per million (ppm) of IBA (indolebutyric acid) on scarlet and pin oaks and found increased root produced (3). Cut root ends of northern red oak trees dug with a tree spade were sprayed with 3000 ppm IBA or NAA (naphthalene acetic acid) before planting (5). IBA stimulated more roots than no treatment. Large roots sprayed with IBA produced 45 roots while untended roots of similar size only produced 13.

IBA root dips are somewhat more effective than sprays of the same concentration. While dips may be practical for small plants, sprays are more practical for large trees either bare root, B & B or dug with tree spades (8).

The consistent benefits of either dips or sprays using 3000 ppm of IBA show that chemical stimulation of new roots is practical. However, several products are marketed, primarily through retail stores, that are said to stimulate new root production when added to water during the watering process following planting.

Root stimulators are products which are promoted to hasten both plant root growth and establishment of newly planted trees and shrubs. Commercially available root stimulators are generally low analysis liquid nitrogen-phosphorus-potassium fertilizers with trace amounts of IBA and/or other chemicals. The IBA traces range from four to 30 ppm. However, when the solution is mixed with water at the recommended rate, the concentration is much lower. IBA is a well known root promoting substance widely used in plant propagation, but there is little information regarding the fate of IBA when applied to field soil. The average cost of actual nitrogen per ton in root stimulator is many times more expensive when compared to conventional sources of nitrogen with the same analysis. Does a commercial root stimulator of such extravagant expense justify itself in plant response?

In order to answer that question, asexually produced spreading euonymus (*Euonymus kiautschovica* 'Manhattan') and wateri pyracantha (*Pyracantha coccinea* 'Wateri') in four-inch containers and bare root pin oak (*Quercus palustris*) seedlings were selected for uniformity and planted in a sandy loam soil (9). Treatments were as follows:

   a) control: no root stimulator,
   b) root stimulator at the manufacturer's recommended rate,
   c) root stimulator four times the recommended rate.

All treatments were replicated 18 times with all three species. The asexually propagated woody shrubs were chosen as test plants to avoid the variability associated with using seedling trees. When there is a great difference in plant response, even without treatments, the response to treatment becomes difficult to identify with certainty. Uniform planting holes were prepared, plants were placed in the holes and the treatment added. After the solution soaked in, more soil was added around each plant. Treatments were applied as directed on the label. Thereafter, sufficient rainfall distribution continued through July 20. After that date, plants were watered with drip irrigation.

No consistent visual benefit could be measured from either of the root stimulator treatments, and most plants treated with the four-fold rate were stunted. On June 15, observations of root development were made by excavating five replications of both test species. Only slight differences in root growth could be detected between the root stimulator treatments and the untreated control with the untreated control slightly superior. Six of the 18 plants of all species receiving the four-fold concentration of root stimulator were dead. Final evaluations of the remaining 12 replications were done on August 2. The root stimulator used in this study did not improve stem caliper, top growth, root weight, nor top weight of euonymus (Figure 11.1), pyracantha (Figure 11.2), or pin oak.

Figure 11.1. Top and root growth of euonymus following treating with a commercial root stimulator. The control plant (C) had more roots and about the same top growth as the recommended rate (R) and much more than the high rate (R4).

The commercial root stimulator used in this study was not effective in aiding plant establishment and growth (9). The reason for the lack of response at the recommended rate or detrimental effect of the four-fold rate is not understood, but is probably related to soil absorption of the chemicals. The concentration of IBA (auxin) is far below the rates routinely used to treat cuttings during mist propagation. Even at much higher rates the IBA would probably not be injurious to plant roots. Studies by several researchers has shown that IBA treatments to scarlet oaks and other species are effective in stimulating roots at planting time (1, 2, 3, 4, 5, 6, 8). The fertilizer concentration in the root stimulator solution is very low and unlikely to cause injury or stunting even at much higher rates. Thus the stunting by the four-fold rate is puzzling but very real.

185

Figure 11.2. Effects of a commercial root stimulator on plant growth. Above, pyracantha at recommended rate (left), four-fold recommended rate (center) and control (right). Below, control (left) recommended rate (center) and four-fold recommended rate (right). No benefit to root growth could be detected from the root stimulator.

A recent study of a root stimulator compared the commercial product which contained IBA, thiamine and fertilizer with an untreated control and each of the three components separately (11). The product and each of the components were used at three rates. They found that plants treated with IBA alone, or thiamine

186

alone, at any of the three rates had no better top or root growth, number of branches, or leaf color than the untreated controls. Positive effects on leaf color, number of branches, and top and root growth were obtained when fertilizer or fertilizer with IBA or thiamine were applied to the plants. **They concluded that the only benefit was from the fertilizer** (11). Additional work is needed to determine why the commercial products studied were not effective and what, if anything, can be done to create a safe and effective product for the future.

At this point, the use of commercial root stimulators appears to be a **travel-at-your-own-risk** situation. On the other hand, spraying cut root ends with 3000 ppm IBA is a practical, and in some cases, perhaps, economical treatment.

If a dip is used on seedlings and bare root liners, they should be washed thoroughly **before** dipping in the IBA solution. The reason for this is that the silt/clay particles in the water will probably tie up the IBA very quickly and render it ineffective. We now know that even small amounts of silt in water can tie up large quantities of Roundup herbicide and render it ineffective. There is also a great deal of evidence to show that water sources that contain substantial levels of calcium, sodium, etc. (hard water) can reduce the effectiveness of some insecticide and fungicide sprays. In all likelihood the same situation will occur with IBA.

In that same light, if the cut ends of roots of balled-in-burlap or tree spade-dug trees are to be treated, they should be washed off to remove the typical coating of soil before treating.

I see these techniques as crutches to try to overcome problems in the production system. In the long run, it would be much better to grow the plants in such a way so that such cumbersome and erratic performing treatments are not needed.

187

Literature Cited

1. Farmer, R.E. 1975. Dormancy and root regeneration of northern red oak. Can. Jour. Forest Res. 5:176-185.

2. Hartwig, R.C. and M.M. Larson. 1980. Hormone root soak can increase initial growth of planted hardwood stock. Tree Planters Notes 31:29-33.

3. Lee, C.I., B.C. Moser and C.E. Hess. 1974. Root regeneration of transplanted pin and scarlet oak. New Horizons, Hort. Res. Institute, Washington, D.C. 1:10-13.

4. Looney, N.E. and D.L. McIntosh. 1968. Stimulation of pear rooting by pre-plant treatment of nursery stock with IBA. Proc. Amer. Soc. Hort. Science 92:150-154.

5. Lumis, Glen P. 1982. Stimulating root regeneration of landscape-size red oak with auxin root sprays. Jour. of Arboriculture 8:325-328.

6. Magley, S.B. and D.K. Struve. 1983. Effects of three transplant methods on survival, growth and root regeneration of caliper pin oaks. Jour. Environmental Hort. 1:59-62.

7. Maki, T.E. and H. Marshall. 1945. Effects of soaking with indolebutyric acid on root development and survival of tree seedlings. Bot. Gazette 107:268-276.

8. Moser, B.C. 1978. Research on root regeneration. New Horizons, Hort. Res. Institute, Washington, D.C. 5:18-24.

9. Reavis, Rick and Carl E. Whitcomb. 1979. Do root stimulators really work? Okla. Agri. Exp. Sta. Res. Rept. P-791:63-65.

10. Romberg, L.D. and C.L. Smith. 1938. Effects of indole-butyric acid in the rooting of transplanted pecan trees. Proc. Amer. Soc. Hort. Sci. 36:161-170.

11. Williams, Donald B. and T.E. Daly. 1986. Effects of IBA, thiamine and fertilizer on the growth of 'Manhattan' euonymus in containers. Proc. Nurs. Res. Conf. 31:75-77.

CHAPTER 12

TOP PRUNING AT PLANTING

No Support for an Old Practice - - - - - - 190

Experiments and Answers - - - - - - - - 190

Related Research - - - - - - - - - - - 195

Top-Root Relationships - - - - - - - - - 195

What Makes Roots Grow? - - - - - - - - - 195

Research Continues - - - - - - - - - - - 196

Summary - - - - - - - - - - - - - - - - 197

Literature Cited - - - - - - - - - - - 198

Top Pruning at Planting

No Support for an Old Practice. One of the widely held beliefs regarding bare root nursery stock was the necessity of cutting back the top at, or prior to, time of planting. This was probably based on the idea that since most of the plant's roots have been lost, the top of the plant must be reduced in order to maintain a root-to-top balance. This is **not true** when balled-in-burlap, bare root trees or shrubs are dug, stored and planted properly.

The practice was questioned one spring when a large number of trees of five different species were planted for a weed control study. The plan was to come back after planting and watering and cut back the tops of all species. The entire planting was complete, except for cutting back two species, when Mother Nature decided to water the plants well and water and water. Over four weeks passed before the newly tilled field dried sufficiently to allow access to prune the tops of the remaining trees. However, by that time the trees that had not been pruned were beginning their spring flush of growth. Since all trees of both unpruned species were growing, the decision was made to leave them alone. On the other hand, the three species that had been top-pruned were slower to begin growth, and plant losses were greater than with the unpruned species. Was the difference in survival a difference between the species, or was it related to the pruning treatment? Observations such as this are an excellent basis for further research, but no firm conclusions can be drawn from such experiences without further study.

Experiments and Answers. The first experiment (13) to study the question was set up in the spring of 1978 to evaluate effects of top pruning and fertilizing at planting time on six bare root deciduous species: pin oak (*Quercus palustris*), redbud (*Cercis canadensis*), Bradford pear (*Pyrus calleryana* 'Bradford'), Hopa flowering crab (*Malus* spp. 'Hopa'), Summit green ash (*Fraxinus pennsylvanica* 'Summit'), and Kwanzan cherry (*Prunus serrulata* 'Kwanzan'). All plants were six to eight feet tall, dormant, bare root stock when planted on March 16, 1978. Treatments were removal of 0%, 15%, 30% or 45% of the plant height before the spring flush. Trees were either not fertilized immediately following planting or were fertilized with four pounds of nitrogen per 1000 square feet using a 10-20-0 analysis dry fertilizer (1742 pounds per acre) applied to the soil surface following planting. All treatments were replicated 12 times for greater accuracy since all trees were either seedlings with considerable genetic variation or grafted onto seedling rootstocks. All trees were planted in a sandy loam soil and watered thoroughly following planting. Spring rains were accommodating, but after June 20, no further measurable rain fell during the summer. Drought stress was allowed to progress sufficiently to defoliate some trees before any supplemental irrigating was done.

The second study was started on March 20, 1979 to expand the study to other species and to compare the findings with the previous study. Treatments were 0%, 15%, 30% and 45% removal of the crown of the dormant bare root trees before the spring flush. However, no fertilizer treatments were used. The five tree species were: red delicious apple (*Malus domestica* 'Red Delicious'), Kifer pear (*Pyrus communis* 'Kifer'), dwarf Alberta peach (*Prunus persica* 'Alberta'), Stuart pecan (*Carya illinoensis* 'Stuart'), and Arizona ash (*Fraxinus velutina*). All trees were the same size as in the first experiment, were planted in rows adjacent to the first study, and were watered thoroughly following planting. This experiment was also replicated 12 times.

Pruning or fertilizer treatments had no effect on initiation of growth in the spring or survival of any of the tree species planted in 1978. Out of 288 trees of the six species planted, 242 or 84% survived. Numbers of basal suckers on Bradford pear and crabapple increased significantly when tops were pruned back 30% or 45% (Figure 12.1). Pruning in excess of 15% reduced the visual quality (natural form and branch development) of all species.

All species planted in 1978 made similar flushes of growth during the spring of 1979 regardless of pruning treatments. This suggests that all trees had recovered from the initial transplant disturbance and assumed normal growth. Except for some unnatural branch development from the severe pruning treatments, all plants were similar in size and vigor at the end of two growing seasons (Figure 12.2). Fertilizing at planting time had no effect on tree growth the first growing season and was only detectable as darker foliage color the second season. This was not surprising in this instance since the fertility of the field soil was high. The fact that no detrimental effect of the fertilizer could be detected is important in light of the widespread recommendation that no fertilizer be added at planting time. In good soils such as those used in this study, adding fertilizer at planting has little impact on top growth the first season since the first flush of growth following transplanting is controlled mostly by conditions experienced by the plant the previous summer and fall when the

191

buds were formed. However, it is important to remember that fertilizing at or shortly after planting is important to the bud development the first summer and fall after transplanting which will be seen with the spring flush of growth one year after planting. To express it another way, **the flush of growth of a bare root or balled-in-burlap tree planted in the spring mostly reflects the conditions in the nursery the previous summer and fall, whereas, the flush of growth one year after spring planting reflects the conditions of the new site.** Do no make the false assumption that just because plants look good the first growing season following planting that all is well. It is the second spring flush of growth that tells a more accurate story.

Figure 12.1. Hopa crabapple trees with 0%, 15%, 30% or 45% of the top removed immediately after planting. Note the suckers on the 30% and 45% pruning treatments. Pruning or fertilizer treatments had no effect on initiation of growth or survival of any of the six species tested.

Figure 12.2. Apple trees two years after top pruning treatments. Beginning in the lower left corner of the photo, every group of four trees down the row represent one of each of the four pruning treatments. Without the aid of the suckers at the base and some unusual branching, it is difficult to tell the pruned from the unpruned trees.

In the second study, pruning treatments had no effect on survival of any of the five species planted in 1979. Pecans broke buds slightly earlier when pruned 15% compared to no pruning. Plants pruned 30% or 45% developed slightly more branches as a result of more bud breaks compared to the unpruned trees. At the end of the growing season, all leaves were stripped from the dwarf Alberta peach and Kifer pear and counted and weighed fresh. Number of leaves and weight of leaves per tree were similar regardless of the pruning treatment. The fact that all treatments had similar quantities of leaves at the end of the first growing season suggests a rapid recovery of the leaf canopy from the severe pruning treatments, mostly from suckers and water sprouts.

There was no advantage to pruning at planting time, and pruning more than 15% of the top was detrimental to the structural development of branches and natural form of the species (Figure 12.3). These studies emphasize that only corrective pruning at planting time should be practiced since excessive pruning reduces visual plant quality, increases suckers on some species, and does not aid in establishment or survival.

There is the temptation to conclude that these findings apply only to small plants and that larger specimens would respond differently. It did not work out that way as larger trees showed the same response--for details see Chapter 16 on transplanting large trees.

Figure 12.3. All Arizona ash pruned at planting time developed double leaders. In contrast, trees unpruned developed a strong central leader and excellent side branches.

Related Research. Other research has also shown that shoot-pruning decreased root growth (7). Plant dry weight, which is the result of energy from the leaves, of young peach trees was reduced by all top-pruning treatments, and the more severe the top-pruning, the greater the reduction (12).

In spite of all the data, Flemer (5) notes that, "hundreds of years of experience have shown that trimming at transplanting time increases both survival and subsequent growth." The experimental results do not agree with Flemer's broad statement. Conditions do change and perhaps the improvements in nutrition, weed control, and other factors affecting plant health as well as storage and handling conditions are the difference between the recommendations of nurserymen over the years and the recent research findings. Flemer (5) wrote that "a few small specimens of very easily transplanted species in very favorable conditions" were used in the study by Shoup, Reavis and Whitcomb (13). In fact, a total of 816 trees over three growing seasons using 11 species under Oklahoma's stressful summer conditions were studied. Overall the findings of Evans and Klett (2, 3, 4) on Colorado's arid eastern slope were very similar to the findings of Shoup, Reavis and Whitcomb (13).

Top-Root Relationships. A detailed study was conducted of the initiation of new roots in the spring from pin oak, silver maple and honeylocust trees planted bare root in late winter (15). With every specimen of each species, new root growth from the cut ends of old roots did not occur until the buds began to swell. Of the 24 trees of each species studied, there were no exceptions. After the first few observations, the extent of new root growth could be predicted by the extent of bud expansion. Very small roots could be observed at the time of the slightest swelling of the buds, but not before bud swell. This shows that new root growth of bare root trees is directly related to bud expansion. **Any reduction of the combined growth regulator concentration from all expanding buds reduces the strength of the chemical signal received by the roots and subsequent root growth**

What Makes Roots Grow? Initial root development of newly planted bare root trees is supported by energy (carbohydrates) stored within the stem and root tissues. As soon as top growth begins, however, total energy within the plant rapidly decreases (10, 14). When a portion of the top of the plant is removed, the leaf surface area in the spring and the capacity to replace energy used in the initial flush of growth are also reduced. Apparently the moisture stress from leaving the entire plant top intact is offset by the more rapid development of a supporting root system. This is not surprising when one remembers that in most areas, the spring is humid and rainfall is generally frequent enough to minimize moisture stress. On the other hand, by early July in most of the USA east of the Rocky Mountains, high temperatures, dehydrating winds and drought conditions may occur. The greater the root development of the plant **before** the onset of summer stress conditions, the more likely the survival and good growth the following spring.

These studies support the hypothesis that **one of the most important factors in transplanting is the internal condition of the plant when it is dug.** All the lavish precautions such as soil amendments, "root stimulators", top-pruning, and other practices are unlikely to help an unthrifty plant, and a thrifty plant does not need it. For further information on pruning at time of transplanting, see the chapter on transplanting large trees.

Research Continued. Recently the research has been carried further (2, 3, 4). Dormant bare root Newport plum (*Prunus cerasifera* 'Newport') and Sargent's crabapple (*Malus sargenti*) were planted in 10-gallon paper mache containers with a medium of clay loam soil, peat and sand (2-1-1 by volume). Selective pruning treatments were approximately 8%, 56% and 68% for the crabapple and 0% and random thinning from 21% to 78% for the plum. The terminal shoot (leader) was left undisturbed in all cases. The experiments were terminated after about three months when all plants had set terminal buds and leaf expansion was complete. With the crabapple they found leaf weights were 31% less when 50% or more of the top had been pruned at planting compared to no top-pruning. Newport plum had similar leaf weights regardless of top-pruning treatments. Pruning at planting time had no effect on root production of either species. Newport plum developed more shoots on top-pruned trees such that total leaf production was not changed.

Hummel and Johnson (8, 9) studied sweetgum trees in Florida. They concluded that removal of 20% to 50% of the tops of the trees by heading back (top pruning) at transplant time did not improve growth or establishment. In addition, severe pruning, 30% and 50% top removal, stunted plant growth. They also noted that top pruning had an undesirable influence on the overall natural growth form of the tree.

Ranney, Bassuk, and Whillow (11) studied the effects of top pruning and antitranspirants on transplanting cherry trees. They observed that the reduction in leaf area as a result of top pruning paralleled a reduction in root growth. Chandler (1) cut back pear seedlings 0% or 50% at planting. He concluded that pruning had no detectable effect on establishment and survival. By the end of the second growing season the height of the trees was 80.7 inches for the pruned trees and 83.8 inches for the unpruned trees.

Summary. Arbitrary top-pruning has no place in modern horticulture (see chapter 21, Transplanting Large Trees for further evidence). However, top-pruning to aid branch development and structure is a valid consideration. Branches that are to become the main scaffolds for the tree should be spaced vertically on the trunk as well as around the trunk (Figure 12.4). Wide angles between the major branches and the vertical axis of the tree are stronger and are not likely to need bracing or cabling.

When considering the branch and crown development of a young tree, allow for the natural form. It is unwise to prune a young elm to look like a sweet gum or pin oak or vice versa. Natural branch and crown development of the tree will proceed normally and will be structurally sound with little or no interference by man. Only the occasional crossing branches or branches that are too close for the development of a strong primary stem and crown should be removed. "If you don't want an elm to grow and look like an elm, then don't plant an elm" is a quote from a long-forgotten source that deserves remembering.

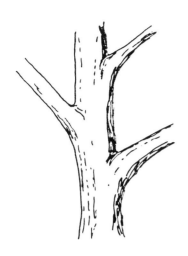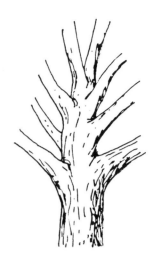

Figure 12.4. Branches should be selected that are spaced vertically on the trunk as well as around the trunk. In most cases, more desirable branch development occurs on unpruned trees (left), whereas, top pruned trees tend to form dense clusters of branches (right).

Literature Cited

1. Chandler, Craig K. 1990. Comparison of pruned and unpruned pear seedlings for survival and growth. HortSci. 25:123.

2. Evans, Philip and James E. Klett. 1984. The effects of dormant pruning on leaf, shoot and root production from bare root *Malus sargenti*. Jour. of Arboriculture 10:298-299.

3. Evans, Philip and James E. Klett. 1985. Pruning at planting may not enhance growth. Amer. Nurseryman 145:53-59.

4. Evans, Philip and James E. Klett. 1985. The effects of dormant branch thinning on total leaf, shoot and root production from bare root *Prunus cerasifera* 'Newport'. Jour. of Arbor. 11:149-151.

5. Flemer, William III. 1982. Successful transplanting is easy. Jour. of Arboriculture 8:234-240.

6. Fordham, R. 1972. Observations on the growth of roots and shoots of tea (*Camellia sinensis*) in southern Malawi. Jour. Hort. Science 47:221-229.

7. Head, G.C. 1967. Effects of seasonal changes in shoot growth on the amount of unsuberized roots on apple and plum trees. Jour. Hort. Science 42:169-180.

8. Hummel, Rita L. and C.R. Johnson. 1987. Does pruning at transplanting improve sweetgum growth? Amer. Nurseryman. 165(3):99-105.

9. Hummel, Rita L. and C.F. Johnson. 1986. Influence of pruning at transplant time on growth and establishment of *Liquidambar styraciflua* L., sweet gum. Jour. Environ. Hort. 4:83-86.

10. Kramer, P.J. and T.T. Kozlowski. 1960. Physiology of trees. McGraw-Hill Book Co., New York. 642 pages.

11. Ranney, T.G., N.L. Bassuk, and T.H. Whitlow. 1989. Effect of transplanting practices on growth and water relations of 'Colt' cherry trees during reestablishment. Jour. Environ. Hort. 7:41-45.

12. Rom, Curt R. and David C. Ferree. 1985. Time and severity of summer pruning influences on young peach tree net photosynthesis, transpiration and dry weight distribution. Jour. Amer. Soc. Hort. Sci. 110:455-461.

13. Shoup, Steve, Rick Reavis and Carl E. Whitcomb. 1981. Effects of pruning and fertilizers on establishment of bare root deciduous trees. Jour. of Arboriculture 7:155-157.

14. Siminovitch, D., C.M. Wilson and D.R. Briggs. 1953. Studies of the living bark of the black locust in relation to its frost hardiness. V. Seasonal transonal transformations and variations in the carbohydrate: starch-sucrose interconversions. Plant Physiology 28:383-400.

15. Whitcomb, Carl E. 1969. Effects of root competition between trees and turfgrass. Ph.D. dissertation, Iowa State University, Ames, Iowa.

CHAPTER 13

MULCHES

Many Benefits from an Old Practice - - -   201

Traits of an Effective Mulch - - - - - -   201

Mulch Over Plastic - - - - - - - - - - -   202

Plant Response to Mulching - - - - - - -   204

Weed Barrier Fabrics   - - - - - - - - -   211

Summary - - - - - - - - - - - - - - - -   214

Literature Cited - - - - - - - - - - - -   216

Mulches

Many Benefits from an Old Practice. The old adage, "all things in moderation" certainly holds true for mulches. In general, mulches are very beneficial, however, there are exceptions, especially when used in excess. A mulch could be described as any protective covering over the surface of the soil. The natural organic matter on the soil surface of the forest or woodland is an excellent example of a very favorable mulch (Figure 13.1). It is loose and well-aerated, breaks down slowly and buffers the soil from rapid changes in temperature and moisture. On the other hand, a mulch that packs and seals over the soil surface can be very detrimental to plant health by blocking the necessary exchange of carbon dioxide out of, and oxygen into, the soil.

Figure 13.1. A good mulch is loose, well aerated, breaks down slowly and buffers the soil against changes in temperature and moisture. This natural litter beneath oaks is a good example. Excess mulch can be harmful.

Traits of an Effective Mulch. If the texture of the mulch is more coarse than the soil below, the rate of water loss from the soil surface is decreased. Following rainfall or irrigation, the small

201

amount of water held in the mulch occurs as a thin layer over the particle surfaces. As evaporation takes place, this water layer dries **without** drawing water from the moist soil below, since the fine-textured soil has a greater affinity for water than the coarse-textured mulch. Water loss from the soil surface through the mulch, does occur but this is slowed greatly since the water vapor must now diffuse through the pores of the mulch into the atmosphere. The diffusion process is slowed by the irregular shapes of the air spaces in the mulch. In general, the smaller the air spaces, the slower the rate of diffusion of water through the mulch; however, if the mulch becomes compacted or the pores become so small that they approach the texture of the soil, the mulch will attract water from the soil and no longer provide a buffer against water loss. With very fine-textured and/or compacted mulches, the very important exchanges of gases between soil and atmosphere becomes restricted.

During a 40-day period in California, mulched and unmulched trees were compared. Six irrigations were required for unmulched trees, while the mulched trees required only two irrigations to maintain soil moisture levels favorable for plant growth (3). Since the amount of irrigation water required can be greatly reduced by mulches, the problems associated with salt buildup in the soil can also be minimized. As irrigation water is used in plant growth or evaporated, all dissolved salts in that water are left behind in the soil. Even with water containing only a few parts per million of salts (calcium, magnesium, sodium or bicarbonates are generally the most troublesome salts in irrigation water) after numerous irrigations over several years, the soil chemistry can be substantially changed.

Mulch Over Plastic. During the 1960s and early '70s the use of polyethylene plastic film beneath mulches was widely used. The idea was based on two points: 1) the plastic beneath the mulch would retard weed growth and 2) the plastic would separate organic mulches from the soil surface and the microorganism population that causes the natural decomposition of organic matter in contact with the soil, thus the organic mulch would last longer. The oversight, of course, was the blockage of the natural gaseous exchange in the soil which is critical to maintaining a healthy root system. Some argued that by cutting slits approximately six inches long in each square foot of plastic problems were prevented.

A long-term study was conducted to determine the effects of mulches on plant health and placing plastic beneath mulches (9).

Plots eight feet wide and 24 feet long were established, each containing one of the following species:

dwarf burford holly (*Ilex cornuta* 'Burford dwarf') drought sensitive;

sawtooth oak (*Quercus acutissima*), moderately drought-tolerant; and

pfitzer juniper (*Juniperus chinensis* 'Pfitzeriana') and

Chinese pistache (*Pistache chinensis*) drought-tolerant.

The treatments were:

1) no mulch,

2) bark mulch two inches deep and

3) black plastic beneath bark mulch.

With each of the three mulch treatments, three fertilizer levels were maintained:

1) no fertilizer applied,

2) 1 1/2 pounds nitrogen per 1000 square feet per month during the growing season, and

3) three pounds of nitrogen per 1000 square feet. Fertilizer applications were made April through August (five applications) to the clay loam soil (Figure 13.2). The study was initiated on October 30 and was terminated after three years.

Soil samples 2 inches in diameter and 2 1/2 inches deep were taken during dry periods from each of the plots in the study.

During the first summer dry period, the plastic plus bark mulch plots had 6.5% moisture when sampled, followed by the bark mulch plots with 4.4%. The least moisture was in those plots not mulched, 1.1%. The experimental area was irrigated twice during the first summer to assure plant survival.

Many weeds were removed by hoeing the plots without mulch. A few weeds were removed by hand from the bark mulch plots and plastic plus bark mulch plots.

Figure 13.2. The study was begun in the fall with container-grown plants. The plots were irrigated the first year using overhead sprinklers. Kentucky 31 fescue was used as grass borders between plots that were 8 by 24 feet.

Plant Response to Mulching. After 10 months all plants were evaluated for growth response. No discernible response to the application of fertilizer was detected where no mulch was present. Where the plastic plus bark mulch or bark mulch was present, a growth increase of 30% and 21%, respectively, was detected due to application of fertilizer on the Chinese pistache (Figure 13.3).

Figure 13.3. Growth response of Chinese pistache to fertilizer and mulches the first year. A typical plant in the mulched plot with high fertility (left, M) and the same fertility level with no mulch (right, B). This benefit from mulching was a bit surprising since Chinese pistache is a very drought-tolerant species.

Pfitzer junipers, generally considered a drought-tolerant plant, increased in size 23% by the presence of either mulch treatment but did not respond to the fertilizer. Even though the plots were irrigated twice during the summer months and one rain occurred, none of the plants benefited from the additional fertilizer with no mulch.

Tops of some of the Chinese pistache trees died during the second winter. When plastic was present beneath the bark mulch, 40% of the trees were killed at the low fertilizer level, 60% were killed at the medium level, and 80% were killed at the high level (Figure 13.4). Where bark was used alone as mulch, no injury could be detected on trees at the low and medium fertility levels but 40% of the trees were killed at the high fertility level. No injury could be detected on any tree at any fertility level with no mulch.

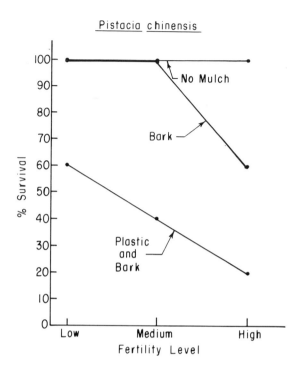

Figure 13.4. Effects of mulches and fertilizer levels on percent survival of Chinese pistache trees the second winter.

The reason for the increased damage when the plastic was present beneath the bark was due to the much shallower root system. Root development was restricted by the plastic due to decreased soil aeration. Thus a high percentage of the more shallow root system remained frozen longer during the winter and the top injury was due to dehydration of the stem and buds.

No injury from any treatments could be detected in sawtooth oaks. The oaks grew similarly whether mulch alone or black plastic plus mulch was used and both treatments were superior to no mulch. Likewise, both fertilizer levels gave equal response and both were better than no fertilizer.

Pfitzer junipers were about the same size whether mulched or not mulched. However, both fertilizer levels substantially increased top growth.

During the third growing season, the Chinese pistache trees all re-sprouted from the root crown, but because of the multiple

206

stems and erratic growth, further evaluation was difficult. As a result of the injury, pistache trees were 13% taller and had 15% greater stem caliper when they were not mulched as compared to bark mulch alone. Many trees in the unmulched plots were over 10 feet tall with two-inch or greater caliper stems after three growing seasons. Pistache response to fertilizer was slight with only a seven percent growth increase due to the high rate at the end of the third growing season.

Pfitzer junipers were 20% larger when not mulched as compared to either mulch treatment. Likewise, top growth was 20% greater when the high fertilizer level was used.

Sawtooth oaks were 10% larger when mulch or mulch plus black plastic was used compared to no mulch. Higher fertilizer response was greatest where mulches were present. There was a 31% increase in both height and stem caliper when compared to low fertilizer and no mulch.

Burford holly grew best with high fertility and mulch alone (Figure 13.5). This combination yielded plants 8% larger than plastic and mulch and 20% larger than no mulch. High fertilizer levels gave an overall plant size 34% greater than low-level fertilizer.

All plants were dug during late winter after the third growing season and observations on root development were noted. All species had many fine fibrous roots in the interface between the plastic beneath the mulch and the soil surface (Figure 13.6). A few roots were found growing into the pine bark mulch where no plastic was present between the soil and the mulch. Most roots were 2 to 3 inches (5 to 8 cm.) or more below the soil surface in the unmulched plots. Although a distinct difference in the location of fine, fibrous roots was observed, all plants had some larger roots penetrating to a depth of 12 inches (30 cm.) or more. These larger roots had few branches, especially with the mulch plus plastic treatment. No difference in root development due to fertilizer levels could be detected.

Figure 13.5. After three growing seasons most plants had made considerable growth. The arrows note missing holly plants that died in low fertility, unmulched plots during the second summer when no irrigation was provided. During the same summer drought, holly plants in the mulched plots remained attractive with no symptoms of moisture stress.

All four species benefited from the mulch the first year. Burford holly and sawtooth oak continued to benefit from the mulch through the third growing season. After three growing seasons, the largest Chinese pistache and juniper were in plots where no mulch was present. This emphasizes the need for mulches to assist plant establishment, particularly the first growing season, but also shows that growth of drought-tolerant species may not be assisted by mulching for long periods. Once the plant is "established", continued coddling, especially on tough drought-resistant species, may restrict growth. Black plastic beneath the mulch made little difference in weed problems and provided no additional benefit to the plants compared to mulch alone (9).

Figure 13.6. Many fine roots were observed in the interface between plastic and soil on all species when the plastic was pulled back. These shallow roots provide poor anchorage for the tree plus when drought conditions do occur, the soil water reserve available to the plants is small.

Species such as burford holly and sawtooth oak respond to improved moisture conditions but also need adequate aeration to the root system. In geographic areas of heavy soils, high rainfall, or where irrigation is practiced, the detrimental effect of the plastic would probably be greater due to the lower aeration levels in the soil. The aeration level in the soil is probably less critical the first season, but as the roots develop and the soil settles with time, a greater deficiency occurs.

Little fertilizer response was detected the first growing season and only a moderate response during the second. However, by the third growing season the plants had developed sufficient root systems so as to be less drought-sensitive and better able to absorb and utilize the higher fertilizer levels. **This should not be interpreted to mean that newly planted trees or shrubs should not be fertilized, but rather that the fertilizer level the first year should be lower and that visually detectable benefits to fertilization may not be seen for several years.**

209

Wood chip and bark mulches around landscape trees is gaining in popularity. Wood chips from power line clearance and other sources are often readily available.

The effects of wood chip mulch on tree growth on two soil types were studied in South Carolina (4). Mulches were four inches deep over an area 16 feet in diameter around each treated tree. Root distribution was modified under the mulch on both soils. Fine roots were present in the mulch/soil interface and often into the base of the organic mulch. This is not an unnatural location for roots. In a natural forest setting, many small roots are in the soil surface layers (6). Moisture levels were always higher under the mulch and soil temperatures were lower. No differences in populations of *Pythium* spp. or *Fusarium* spp. disease organisms or nematodes between mulched and unmulched plots were found. Fraedrich and Ham (4) concluded that the improved growth of the mulched trees was moisture related. Zahner (10) concluded that 80% to 90% of the variation in tree diameter growth is related to moisture availability.

Mulching can reduce weed problems and complement the overall landscape appearance. Placing black plastic beneath the mulch not only restricts root depth, but does little to aid weed control around plantings (Figure 13.7).

Figure 13.7. Mulches can complement landscape appearance and aid weed control (above). However, when black plastic is placed beneath the mulch, root depth is restricted and plants are more susceptible to drought and wind-throw. In addition, black plastic provides little increase in weed control over the mulch alone. This lacebark elm (below) blew over during a thunderstorm. Close inspection revealed black plastic beneath a rock mulch. When the tree blew over the surface roots were pulled loose from just beneath the plastic on the left side and the plastic was torn. The tree died after a few months.

Weed barrier fabrics. In recent years an array of "weed barrier" fabrics have been marketed. Two of the most comprehensive studies in this area were done by Derr and Appleton (3), and Appleton, Derr, and Ross (1). Derr and Appleton (3) used six polypropylene landscape fabrics in comparison with black plastic, mulches, and herbicides. They found that large crabgrass roots were able to penetrate all fabrics with no apparent differences in penetration

211

among the fabrics. Yellow nutsedge shoots were able to penetrate all of the fabrics, with no difference in shoot number between any fabric and the untreated controls.

Large crabgrass plants penetrated the fabrics, either by sending shoots up or by sending roots down through the fabrics, and developed into large plants. Although fewer plants were present in the fabric-covered plots, shoot fresh weight was generally similar to the untreated controls, demonstrating the rapid growth that can occur after fabric penetration.

When no mulch was added to the plots, less time was required for hand-weeding the fabric-covered plots than for the untreated or the Surflan (oryzalin) treatments but this would not be visually acceptable in the landscape.

Weeds were able to germinate below the Exxon and Typar fabrics when they were not covered by mulch, since sunlight was able to penetrate these fabrics. The Duon fabric, when uncovered, exhibited considerable breakdown during the growing season. Little deterioration was present in the DeWitt, Visqueen, and black plastic materials one year after establishment.

All fabric manufacturers recommend that mulch be put on top of the fabrics. With fabrics that lack ultra-violet light inhibitors, this mulch layer is important to prevent photo-decomposition that leads to fabric deterioration and subsequent weed seed germination. With fabrics that are either white in color or light-weight, light passes through the fabrics and weeds grow beneath them, again showing the necessity of the mulch layer.

The problem with covering the fabrics with mulch is the **increased** weed growth that frequently occurs. In this study weed weights and weeding by hand times were greater for the mulch-covered fabrics than for the unmulched fabrics. Weed seeds either blew in or were carried in by irrigation water, or may have been contaminants of the mulch itself. Annual weeds were able to germinate and develop in the mulch layer above the fabrics. Once the weeds penetrated the fabrics, rapid growth occurred, showing the need for timely weeding by hand or herbicide application.

They (3) concluded that the new landscape fabrics have both positive and negative attributes. Certain landscape fabrics can effectively reduce annual broadleaf and grassy weed growth; however, most are far less effective against perennial weeds which are capable of growing through several inches of mulch, and then thrive in the absence of annual weed competition. Even when fabrics are used, some hand weeding or herbicide application will still be necessary.

In the second study, Appleton, Derr, and Ross (1) used a landscape site with a well drained, fertile loam soil covered with a heavy stand of bermudagrass. Roundup was applied twice to kill all existing vegetation. Three each of Japanese holly (*Ilex crenata* 'Roundleaf') and azaleas (*Rhododendron obtusum* 'Orange Beauty') and one red maple (*Acer rubrum*) were planted into each plot. No supplemental irrigation was provided.

Once planted, plots were covered with one of eight soil coverings, then half of all plots were covered with mulch. The soil coverings were: bare ground; the herbicide Surflan at 2 pounds per acre; black plastic (polyethylene); the landscape fabrics Typar (gray spunbonded), Duon (gray spunbonded), DeWitt (black woven), and Exxon (white spunbonded); and the landscape film VisQueen (black embossed). VisQueen film is polyethylene; all other landscape fabrics used are polypropylene.

The partially composted, chipped hardwood and softwood bark, and wood mulch was applied three inches deep and replenished to that depth after the first year.

Natural weed growth was allowed to establish. The time required to weed each plot by hand and weed weights were recorded. After the summer weeding, weeds were allowed to regrow.

When mulched, there were no significant differences in morning or afternoon soil temperatures among the five landscape fabrics/film during any season. When unmulched, differences occurred among all the soil coverings for both morning and afternoon soil temperatures during all seasons.

Mulching bare ground buffered temperature fluctuations, increasing fall and winter morning and afternoon soil temperatures, and decreasing spring afternoon and summer morning and afternoon temperatures. When mulched, there were no differences in soil moisture among the eight soil coverings during any season. Though the manufacturers' technical data for the various fabrics show differences in water flow rates, these differences did not alter the soil moisture content under any of the fabrics when they were covered with mulch. Also, independent testing has shown little effect on water flow rates with single layers of fabric (5).

Light passing through the Exxon and Typar supported weed growth beneath them, and large numbers of weeds grew in the bare soil plots. Mulching helped increase plant growth with most soil coverings.

Roots of all species were found growing on the soil surface in the mulch, herbicide plus mulch, plastic, plastic plus mulch, and all fabric/film plus mulch treatments. This was not surprising because not only are most tree and shrub roots naturally shallow, but also because roots were probably responding either to a limited oxygen supply or to the moist, yet well aerated conditions created by the mulches on top of the soil.

In addition, roots of all species were found growing in the mulch layer in mulch alone and herbicide plus mulch treatments. Red maple and Japanese holly roots grew into, through, and often on top of certain of the fabric/film coverings. The greatest amount of penetration was observed for Duon, Typar, and VisQueen.

Runs of voles were more prevalent under plastic and the fabrics/film than under the bare ground, herbicide, only mulch coverings. Since voles are vegetarians, their increased presence under the fabrics could potentially increase tree and shrub injury via their feeding on roots. Field vole nesting under polyethylene mulches caused severe damage of root collar bark which was gnawed and, in some cases, caused small trees to fall.

These studies (1, 3) do not support the general use of weed barrier fabrics. In some situations some benefits were derived (7, 9). When the fabrics were anchored in place some improvement in erosion control was gained although organic mulches tend to wash off the fabrics with a slick surface. Weed barrier fabrics are not a substitute for mulches and add substantially to the cost of landscape installations. Proceed with caution is probably the best advice.

Summary. When using wood chip mulch, there are several key factors to remember:

a) Aged wood chips are superior to fresh wood chips. Some toxic materials exist in fresh hard wood chips from some tree species. Once composted for a few months, the problem appears to be reduced or eliminated. There is no complication with using fresh pine bark or bark from other coniferous trees.

b) If the soil surface is compacted **before** placement of the mulch, the normal freeze-thaw loosening of that compaction will be reduced. If the soil is compacted, aerify the soil before adding the mulch.

c) Mulch a sizable area around newly planted or existing trees whenever possible since tree roots extend horizontally well beyond the widely recognized drip line.

d) Do not make the mulch so deep that the soil beneath the mulch seldom, if ever, dries out. This can be a serious problem in areas with a high water table and heavy soils, especially during rainy periods.   Retention of soil moisture is beneficial only if soil aeration is sufficient to support root activity.   In general, the more sandy and porous the soil, the greater depth of mulch without becoming counter-productive.

e) Do not place mulch more than a few inches deep around the stem of the tree or shrub. An extremely deep mulch of fine texture around the basal stem may cause the death of the bark near the soil line and kill the tree. Very deep mulch may encourage rodents which may damage plant stems.

f) Mulches of wood chips or other organic materials that decompose may temporarily tie up a substantial portion of the nitrogen applied to the plants. In time, the nitrogen bound by the decomposing mulch will be released, but in the short run, additional nitrogen may be required to support vigorous growth of new plantings.

g) Porous fabric used beneath mulches can aid in erosion control and may reduce the rate of decomposition of a mulch and soil compaction from any foot traffic on the mulch. However, their expense is substantial yet their benefits are modest or, in some cases, nonexistent when compared with an organic mulch used alone.

Literature Cited

1.   Appleton, Bonnie L., J.F. Derr, and B.B. Ross. 1990. The effect of various landscape weed control measures on soil moisture and temperature and tree root growth. Jour. Arboriculture 16:264-268.

2.   Billeaud, L.A. and J.M. Azjicek. 1989. Influence of mulches on weed control, soil pH, soil nitrogen content, and growth of *Ligustrum japonicum.* Jour. Environ. Hort. 7:155-157.

3.   Derr, J.F. and Bonnie L. Appleton. 1989. Weed control with landscape fabrics. Jour. Environ. Hort. 7:129-133.

4.   Fraedrich, S.W. and D.L. Ham. 1982. Wood chip mulching around maples: effect on tree growth and soil characteristics.   Jour. of Arboriculture 8:85-89.

5.   High Performance Textiles. 1988. Geotextiles in soil. Elsevier Science Publishers 8(8) 10-12.

6.   Kramer, Paul J. and T.T. Kozlowski. 1979. Physiology of woody plants. Academic Press, New York.

7.   Powell, M.A., W.A. Skrock, T.E. Builderback. 1989. Landscape mulch evaluation: A three-year study.   Proc. SNA Nursery Research Conf. 34:274-276.

8.   Richards, S.J. 1965. Porous black mulch for ornamental plantings. Calif. Agriculture. Dec. 12-14.

9.   Whitcomb, Carl E. 1980. Effects of black plastic and mulches on growth and survival of landscape plants.   Jour. of Arboriculture 6:10-12.

10.   Zahner, R. 1968. Water deficits and growth of trees.   Pages 191-254 in "Water deficits and plant growth". Vol. 2. Kozlowski, T.T. ed., Academic Press, New York.

CHAPTER 14

ESTABLISHING AZALEAS AND OTHER SENSITIVE SPECIES

Peat as a Soil Amendment - - - - - - - - - 218

Research to the Rescue - - - - - - - - - 218

Understanding the Effects of Peat - - - 219

Excessive Drainage - - - - - - - - - - - 222

Soil Tests - - - - - - - - - - - - - - - 224

Fertilizing Azaleas and Other
          Salt-Sensitive Species - - - 228

Research Results - - - - - - - - - - - - 228

Literature Cited - - - - - - - - - - - - 232

Establishing Azaleas and Other Sensitive Species

Azaleas and rhododendrons are spectacular plants. Unfortunately, in many areas few plants survive more than a few years and are treated nearly as annuals. These areas include all of the states of the Great Plains, the adjacent states to the east and parts of Florida. Many landscape sites in this geographic area have alkaline soils, either naturally or due to residues remaining from construction and/or from irrigation water containing substantial quantities of bicarbonates, calcium, or sodium.

Peat as a Soil Amendment. Several cultural practices have been used in attempts to grow azaleas successfully. The practice of adding peat or other organic matter to the planting hole has been suggested by vast numbers of people and publications for years. In the late 1960s Whitcomb and students showed that soil amendments, including peat and pine bark, did not aid the establishment or growth of several woody plants (not including azaleas) on sandy soils of Florida (13). Further studies on clay and clay loam soils in Oklahoma showed similar results (10, 12). Research in Georgia, Tennessee and New Jersey confirmed these findings (6, 7, 8, 9, 11). On acid soils of Georgia, peat did not aid azaleas (1, 2, 3, 4, 5). (For further information see the chapter on soil amendments).

Establishment of azaleas and rhododendrons in the landscape remains a problem, especially in areas of marginal adaptation for these unique plants. Nonetheless, many people in the nursery and landscape industries, testify as to the observed benefit of adding peat to the soil when planting azaleas. These observations proved to be real in our research in Oklahoma but could not be explained relative to the data available. Most peats are very acid in reaction and therefore reduce the pH of the soil when incorporated into the planting hole. Thus the question arose: is the benefit observed from adding peat due to an alteration in soil texture and water holding/aeration characteristics, or is it simply the lowering of soil pH and releasing the micronutrients from the native soil? If soil acidification is the primary benefit, then adding sulfur and/or micronutrients to the soil should provide similar benefits.

Research to the Rescue. An experiment was set up beneath the shade of large pecan trees in north central Oklahoma on a sandy clay loam soil with the following treatments with all possible combinations:

1) with or without peat added to the planting hole at the rate of about 1/3 of the planting hole volume,
2) planting on grade or on raised beds of the same sandy clay loam soil,
3) with or without granular sulfur added to the planting hole at six pounds per 100 square feet over a four-square-foot area,
4) with or without Micromax micronutrients added to the planting hole at rate of four ounces incorporated per four square feet of surface area.

The 16 treatment combinations were replicated six times. Osmocote 18-6-12 was applied to all plants at the rate of 1/2 pound per four square feet and shallowly incorporated. This formulation will last six to nine months in the landscape. No mulch was applied in order to avoid confusion between mulch effects and soil treatment effects. Test plants were 'Hinodegiri' azaleas grown in one-gallon containers. Weed control was from Treflan 5% granules at 2.5 pounds active ingredient per acre unincorporated. Watering was from one gallon per hour drip emitters, one per plant, with watering as needed during the summer. Plant performance evaluations were made during the next three years, using a visual rating where 1 = very dark green, 4 = mild chlorosis, 7 = severe chlorosis, and 10 = dead plant. Flower counts and measurements of plant size were also recorded.

Understanding the Effects of Peat. If no peat was incorporated at planting time, a visual benefit resulted from the incorporation of both sulfur and Micromax micronutrients resulting in an excellent grade of 2.8 (Table 14.1). However, if peat was incorporated at planting time, the visual grade was 2.5 with no visual benefit from adding sulfur or Micromax micronutrients during the first two years. By contrast, if neither peat, sulfur, nor Micromax micronutrients were added, the visual grade was a poor 8.2 at soil grade or 7.5 on the raised bed. Interestingly, there was no benefit from adding peat and either sulfur or micronutrients in combination during the first two years, but there was no detrimental effect and the visual grade was excellent at 1.7 (Figure 14.1). The combination of sulfur and micronutrients plus peat began to provide a benefit at the end of the second growing season as the peat was completely decomposed and the alkalinity of the soil increased due to the calcium in the irrigation water.

Figure 14.1.   Azaleas with no peat, sulfur, or Micromax died by the end of the first growing season (lower left), whereas, those with peat (upper left), peat and micronutrients (lower right), or only micronutrients (upper right) grew at a moderate rate for the first two years).

By the spring of the third year, plants originally planted with peat, sulfur and micronutrients were visually superior and in some replications, they were the only plants alive (Figure 14.2).

Figure 14.2. At the beginning of the third growing season most of the living plants, thrifty in appearance, had received either peat plus sulfur plus micronutrients or sulfur plus micronutrients (above). The remnants of the three dead plants in the photo were planted either with nothing added or with only peat or only micronutrients. The thrifty plants produced many more flowers (right) than the unthrifty plants with varying degrees of chlorosis (left).

Eight of the 12 plants without any soil amendment, sulfur, or micronutrients died within one year, whereas, none of the plants died with peat or sulfur or Micromax micronutrients added either alone or in combination.

Table 14.1. Effects of peat, sulfur and micronutrients on growth of azaleas in the landscape. Values are averages of four soil samples per treatment two years expressed as parts/million.

Treatment	pH	Fe	Mn	Cu	Z	S	Ca	Mg	Plant Visual Grade
-P-S-MM	5.6	60	33	1.4	1.6	27	1439	190	8.2
-P-S+MM	5.0	93	46	8.7	4.9	56	1240	157	6.8
-P+S-MM	4.2	105	45	1.4	1.1	305	934	115	7.5
-P+S+MM	4.1	133	49	5.9	3.2	136	777	80	2.8
+P-S-MM	5.1	64	49	1.1	1.3	62	1409	178	2.5
+P-S+MM	5.0	85	46	5.0	4.4	37	1274	166	1.7
+P+S-MM	4.1	96	54	1.3	1.2	166	1013	98	2.0
+P+S+MM	3.9	132	55	4.9	2.8	193	931	85	1.7
Control soil (before planting)	6.2	42	15	1.1	1.3	14	1856	256	---

---

P = Canadian peat moss @1/3 of the planting hole volume
S = Elemental sulfur granules 96% S @ 6 lbs./100 sq. ft.
MM = Micromax micronutrient fertilizer @ 4 oz./4 sq. ft. or 6 lbs/100 sq. ft. of bed surface area, - = none added, + = added.
Note: a low visual grade is best.

Excessive Drainage. The benefit observed by incorporating peat when planting azaleas is from the acidification of the soil since similar benefits to the plant were obtained by incorporating both sulfur and micronutrients. This is further supported by the **detrimental** effect of incorporating peat in the raised bed where the visual grade was poorer with an average of 4.8 as opposed to the plants in the ground bed with a visual grade of 2.5. In this case the sandy clay loam had sufficient internal drainage, to provide for good root growth and function. When the peat was added to the raised bed, drainage was further hastened and the plants experienced greater moisture stress. On the other hand, with a heavy, poorly drained soil, the raised bed or the raised bed with the peat would be beneficial.

Soil samples taken after 18 months showed that over 90% of the peat had decomposed. Because of the rapid decomposition of peat, the azaleas must survive in the native soil provided after two growing seasons in Oklahoma. Where good soil drainage does not exist, raised beds are probably the practical answer.

The absence of the peat after two growing seasons further emphasizes the importance of treating the soil with sulfur and/or micronutrients to insure availability of micronutrients to the plants over a much longer time (Figure 14.3). The length of time such soil treatments remain effective are dependent on the nature of the soil and the quality of the irrigation water. The liberal use of organic or inorganic mulches to moderate moisture and temperature conditions in the plants root zone may further extend the effective time of the soil treatments, especially if the mulches are acid in reaction. For example, redwood and most pine bark are acid and will aid the maintenance of soil acidity, whereas, if the mulches are alkaline, as is the bark from most hardwood trees, the effective time will be shortened.

Figure 14.3. These azaleas were planted into a soil with moderate levels of calcium and the irrigation water contained 40 parts per million calcium. The peat incorporated at planting, aided their growth for the first growing season, however, with the beginning of the second growing season, the new growth was chlorotic, whereas, the old leaves were dark green. This coincided with the decomposition of most of the peat.

Soil Tests. Soil tests from the various peat, sulfur and Micromax micronutrient treatments relate rather clearly with the visual appearance of the azaleas. In general, wherever levels of sulfur, iron, and manganese were up; calcium, and to a lesser extent, magnesium were down and appearance of the plants was excellent (Table 14.1 and Figure 14.2). The combination of sulfur and Micromax micronutrients did not increase levels of sulfur, iron and manganese above the level when either one of these treatments was used alone, which was surprising. This is probably due to the greater downward movement of these elements in the soil. The higher levels of iron and manganese in a deeper soil profile may provide assistance to the plant in the future.

It remains somewhat unclear whether the primary benefit to the azaleas from the soil treatments is due to the increased availability of sulfur, iron and manganese, the decreased availability of calcium, or both. Regardless of why it happens, the positive benefit in growing these plants in the landscape is reflected in improved foliage color, growth rate, number of flower buds (Figure 14.2) and a substantial increase in root growth. Root growth is dependent on the availability of proper levels and proportions of all the essential nutrient elements to the leaves so that there is an abundance of soluble carbohydrates (energy) available for translocation downward to the roots. Since the roots are the last portion of the plant to receive energy from the leaves, any factor that restricts the capacity of the leaves to manufacture energy shows in restricted root growth before any other plant part is affected. This has been graphically shown in studies of how nutritional conditions and light intensity restrict root growth before other plant parts are affected. (See the chapter on light intensity for details). In this case the influence of nutritional conditions on root growth in containers is identical to the effects on root growth in the landscape (Figure 14.4). However, be aware that information from many studies conducted in containers **cannot** be applied to landscape conditions.

The other point in this complex study worth noting is the pH of the soil. The original soil was 6.2 which many would consider acidic enough to grow azaleas. However, when asked (by way of the experimental procedure in the research) the plants emphatically said "NO". In this site there was over 1856 ppm calcium or roughtly 4000 pounds per acre. Only about 600 to 900 pounds per acre is needed for good plant growth with most species as long as aluminum toxicity does not become a problem in conjunction with very acid soils. The best plants by all evaluation criteria were those where the soil was near a pH of 4.0 and the level of calcium was roughly 1000 ppm (2000 pounds per acre). In areas with soils more alkaline than this site it may require substantially more sulfur and several years to get the soil pH and calcium levels down to the point where azaleas, rhododendrons, blueberries, kalmia, and other ericaceous/acid-loving plants can be grown. The changes in soil chemistry occur slowly and the heavier the soil (read, more silt and clay content) the longer time required.

The other key factor is the calcium, sodium, and bicarbonate level in the irrigation water. If there are 70 ppm calcium in the water, nearly 200 pounds are applied per acre every time the equivalent of 12 inches of water is used for irrigation. Even when peat, sulfur, and micronutrients are added to the soil and a pH of 4.0 is achieved, further applications of sulfur will be required at some point in the future in order to maintain that level. If this critical point is ignored. the plants will slowly decline over time.

It is also important to note that soil pH could be 6.2 on one site and the calcium could be 600 ppm, whereas, in the study just covered, at the same pH the calcium level was 1856 ppm. This is why the levels of specific elements should be checked and monitored rather than relying only on soil pH. The pH reveals only the proportion of acids to bases, NOTHING more. There can be considerable bases in the soil, but if the acids are greater, the pH will be low without giving a clue as to the level of the bases.

Studies of this nature are good for finding combinations of factors that work. They do not, unfortunately, give detail on ideal levels of the factors involved. For example, the benefit of granular sulfur may have been increased or decreased at a higher or lower rate. The six pounds per 100 square feet rate was chosen because it was effective in reducing the iron chlorosis of pin oaks growing in an alkaline heavy clay soil. Further studies with sulfur alone and in combination with micronutrients should be done on several soil types.

CA MG

Figure 14.4.   Azaleas grown in containers with varying levels of calcium and magnesium. The poorest plants (left) received what is widely used by wholesale container nurseries as the "optimum level" of calcium and magnesium in the soil mix, whereas, the best plants (right) received no calcium or magnesium other than that dissolved in the water supply.   The tops of all plants were dark green.   The only clue to a calcium restriction of growth came when the levels were lowered.   The functional capacity of the top (above) is even more graphically reflected in the size of the root system (below).

Fertilizing Azaleas and Other Salt-Sensitive Species. Most azalea cultivars are well known to be sensitive to fertilizer salts. Water soluble chemical fertilizers beneficial to other woody plants and grasses may injure or kill azaleas, particularly if moisture stress occurs shortly thereafter.

Osmocote is a plastic resin-coated fertilizer that absorbs water, thus creating a miniature water balloon that slowly releases fertilizer depending on coating thickness, moisture and temperature. Osmocote 19-6-12 or 14-14-14 has a very thin coating and should be used on salt-sensitive plants only with care, while Osmocote 18-6-12 has an intermediate coating thickness and Osmocote 17-7-12 or 24-5-9 are comprised of three coating thicknesses (for example, 17-7-12 is about 20% thin coating, 40% intermediate coating and 40% heavy coating). Because of the combinations of coatings, the 17-7-12 or 24-5-9 Osmocote formulations release fertilizer over a longer time than 18-6-12 with only the intermediate coating, however, shortly after applying either 17-7-12 or 24-5-9, the fertilizer salt level will be higher than with the 18-6-12 formulation because of the relatively quick release of the 20% of fertilizer with the thin coating. With most crop plants, this quick release is beneficial, but with very salt-sensitive species such as azalea, rhododendron and blueberries, it may be detrimental.

Slow-release fertilizers based on sulfur-coating urea, phosphorus or potassium sources provide not only a slow-release of nitrogen-phosphorus-potassium but sulfur and soil acidification as well. Nutrient-release from sulfur-coated fertilizers is less dependent on temperature and more dependent on coating thickness and moisture. If increased sulfur availability is a key factor in growing azaleas in the landscape, then using sulfur-coated fertilizers should prove beneficial (but proceed with caution, read on). Water soluble dry chemical fertilizers must be used in very low doses fairly frequently in order to encourage good growth of salt sensitive species. Because of the very soluble nature of the chemicals, fertilizer burn is very common. Unfortunately, fertilizer damage to roots may go undetected and simply show up as greater injury from drought or heat or just poor plant performance overall.

Research Results. To determine the safest and most effective fertilizer for azaleas and other salt-sensitive species in the landscape a study was conducted beneath the broken shade of large pecan trees. Fertilizer treatments were applied to plants at the existing soil level in a sandy clay loam soil with moderate internal drainage. No peat or other organic matter was added, however, all plants received granular elemental sulfur at six pounds per 100 square feet incorporated at planting time. The test plants were 'Hinodegiri' azaleas from one-gallon containers. Fertilizer treatments were replicated 12 times and applied annually to the soil surface.

Treatments were:

Osmocote 18-6-12 at 1/8 or 1/4 pound per plant

Osmocote 17-7-12 at 1/4 or 1/2 pound per plant

Osmocote 24-5-9 at 1/4 or 1/2 pound per plant

Sulfur-coated urea 20-4-6 at 1/8 or 1/4 pound per plant

Control 10-20-10 at one ounce per plant (0.05 pound of nitrogen per 100 square feet twice per year)

All treatments were distributed over a four square foot area around the individual plants. Drip irrigation was used as needed. Plants were evaluated spring, mid-summer and late fall for three years using a visual chlorosis rating from 1 to 10 where 1 = no chlorosis, dark green, 4 = mild chlorosis, 7 = severe chlorosis and 10 = dead plant.

Azaleas fertilized with Osmocote 18-6-12 at the 1/8 pound rate had excellent visual ratings of about 1.2, whereas, at the 1/4 pound rate, the visual rating was 3.6 and 1.4 for the chemical fertilizer control. Osmocote 17-7-12 and 24-5-9 and sulfur-coated urea 20-4-6 at the 1/4 lb. rate all were less satisfactory (7.7, 5.8 and 5.8 respectively) (Table 14.2) while most plants were killed by the high rates of these three fertilizer formulations.

The acceptable performance of Osmocote 18-6-12 at the 1/4 pound rate (visual grade 3.6) vs the poor performance of the Osmocote 17-7-12 and 24-5-9 at the same rate (7.7, 5.8) confirm the greater salt level of the longer lasting products for the first one to four weeks following fertilizing which resulted in plant root injury.

The erroneous assumption is frequently made that if Osmocote 18-6-12, which has a six- to nine-month release at 70 degrees F, is a good slow-release fertilizer for azaleas in the landscape then 17-7-12 or 24-5-9 which have 12- to 14-month release rates at 70 degrees F should be even better. It should also be noted that all of the Sierra Blend formulations of Osmocote (18-6-10 or 17-7-10) contain a small fraction of uncoated, soluble fertilizer and **should not** be used on azaleas in the landscape unless a substantial nitrogen deficiency exists **and** soil moisture will be closely monitored for the following three to four weeks and application rates are low.

The chemical fertilizer control had a good visual rating of 1.4 as compared to the 1.2 for the 1/8 pound rate of the Osmocote 18-6-12. It should be noted, however, that the water-soluble 10-20-10 must be applied at low rates to avoid salt injury and **the length of the spring flush of growth was 80% greater with the Osmocote 18-6-12.**

These data emphasize that 1/8 pound of Osmocote 18-6-12 per four square feet per year is a safe and effective slow-release fertilizer for azaleas in the landscape. The effects of Osmocote 18-6-12 were probably enhanced by the sulfur added at the beginning of the study to lower the soil pH and increase the availability of micronutrients. On the other hand, adding sulfur to the soil probably minimized the benefits of the sulfur from the sulfur-coated slow-release fertilizer, at least in the short term. In any case, the sulfur-coated fertilizer failed to provide good plant color and growth. At the same rates the Osmocote 18-6-12 provided superior plant color and growth.

Osmocote 18-6-12 is an excellent and safe slow-release fertilizer in the landscape for plants sensitive to fertilizer salts. A rate of about five to eight pounds per 100 square feet of bed area once a year will provide an adequate supply of nitrogen, phosphorus and potassium to maintain good plant growth and color. Even though Osmocote is an expensive fertilizer in comparison to dry chemical fertilizers suitable for general lawn use, the labor saved, and superior plant color and growth with complete safety from fertilizer burn easily justify the additional expense.

Table 14.2. Effects of slow-release fertilizers on the visual color rating of azaleas in a landscape planting in Oklahoma.
- -

Visual Rating
    Osmocote 18-6-12
        1/8 lb./4 sq. ft. or 5 lbs./100 sq. ft.   1.2 *
        1/4 lb./4 sq. ft. or 10 lbs./100 sq. ft.   3.6

    Osmocote 17-7-12
        1/4 lb./4 sq. ft. or 10 lbs./100 sq. ft.   7.7
        1/2 lb./4 sq. ft. or 20 lbs./100 sq. ft.   9.6

    Osmocote 24-5-9
        1/4 lb./4 sq. ft. or 10 lbs./100 sq. ft.   5.8
        1/2 lb./4 sq. ft. or 20 lbs./100 sq. ft.   10.0

    Sulfur-coated urea
        1/4 lb./4 sq. ft. or 10 lbs./100 sq. ft.   5.8
        1/2 lb./4 sq. ft. or 20 lbs./100 sq. ft.   10.0

    Control (2 applications of 10-20-10 dry
        fertilizer at 0.05 lbs./100 sq. ft./yr.   1.4
- -
*Visual rating scale of chlorosis where 1 = dark green plant, no chlorosis and 10 = very chlorotic plant.

_____

Note that the control and the 1/8 pound of Osmocote 18-6-12 were similar in visual color rating but the plants with the Osmocote made five times as much growth. In general as the top grows, so does the root system.

Literature Cited

1. Corley, W.L. 1978. Backfill tests in the Georgia Piedmont. SNA Nursery Res. Conf. Proc. 23:60-63.

2. Corley, W.L. 1979. Backfill tests in the Georgia Piedmont II. SNA Nursery Res. Conf. Proc. 24:79-80.

3. Corley, W.L. 1980. Backfill tests in the Georgia Piedmont III. SNA Nursery Res. Conf. Proc. 25:79-81.

4. Corley, W.L. 1980. Rhododendron backfill tests in the Georgia piedmont. SNA Nursery Res. Conf. proc. 25:82-83.

5. Corley, W.L. 1984. Soil Amendments at planting. Jour. Environmental Hort. 2(1):27-30.

6. Hummel, R.L. and Charles R. Johnson. 1985. Amended backfills: their cost and effect on transplant growth and survival. Jour. Environmental Hort. 3:76-79.

7. Ingram, D.L., R.J. Black and C.R. Johnson. 1980. Effect of backfill composition and fertilization on the establishment of container-grown plants in the landscape. SNA Nursery Res. Conf. Proc. 25:68-71.

CHAPTER 15

TRANSPLANTING WITH TREE SPADES

Advantages and Disadvantages - - - - - - 234

Pulling Trees - - - - - - - - - - - - - 235

Comparing Transplanting Techniques - - - 235

Further Techniques Explored - - - - - - 240

Literature Cited - - - - - - - - - - - 249

Transplanting with Tree Spades

Advantages and Disadvantages. Digging and planting landscape trees with tree spades is likely to increase in the future due to demand for an immediate landscape effect at a tolerable installation cost. Despite disadvantages such as the need for a special equipment operator, the inability to use tree spades in unfavorable weather or where underground utilities exist, or where buildings, paving or vegetation reduce mobility (1), some advantages and the immediate landscape effect encourage their use. Tree spade-dug and -planted trees have been promoted for year-round planting (1) and can reduce manpower and save time under some conditions (6). Cool (1) conducted a 10-year study in Michigan of bare root vs tree spade-dug and transplanted trees. Mortality of bare root trees was 28% while mortality of trees dug and transplanted with a tree spade was only about 1%. Even though the expense of operating a tree spade is much greater than planting bare root trees, he concluded that 1.5 tree spade trees could be planted for the same cost as one bare root tree when survival was considered. In other instances, tree spades allow use of larger trees that can better withstand mechanical abuse and vandalism along streets (8) and may be less expensive in the long run (1, 6).

When tree transplanting fails, profits decrease for the grower and the landscape contractor (3). All production and preplanting efficiencies then are in vain. In tree digging and planting, many factors must be considered (6, 8): time of year, climate, exposure, production site, landscape site, soil types, digging-to-planting time span, post-planting care, and tree species.

Watson and Himelick (9) stated that up to 98% of the root system can be lost when a tree is dug with a tree spade. Such injury also permits pathogen entry. Therefore, efforts to minimize the loss of roots and reducing shock and recovery period should be made (5). Although more roots may be retained by a properly dug bare root tree than with balled-in-burlap or tree spade-dug trees (3, 7) they sustain more damage to the important small shallow feeder roots and with large trees, show less growth one year after transplanting than with tree spade-dug trees (8).

When roots are cut during digging, new roots develop from the point where the older roots were severed. These new roots grow and branch (4). One of the key soil characteristics important for new root development is soil aeration (9).

234

A frequent criticism of the tree spade is that holes dug to receive the tree are not quite the same shape or size as the ball dug with the tree spade, thus, various gaps or voids exist between the two soil masses following transplanting. These air spaces are thought to restrict root development since roots seldom extend through large air spaces. An additional concern lies with the glazing of the sides of the tree spade-dug hole and the face of the soil ball dug with the tree spade. Soil glazing may be sufficient to retard root penetration and development into the surrounding soil in some instances and restrict normal moisture movement in the soil following planting and watering. The relative shape and size of the tree spade-dug ball is also frequently a concern among landscape contractors. Balls of earth from tree spades are narrower and deeper than conventional hand-dug balls and may contain a smaller proportion of the fine roots.

Pulling Trees. An additional technique which contrasts with both the tree spade and hand digging is the procedure of pulling the tree from the ground using a pin and clevis through the trunk. At first, this technique seems undesirable, but with close inspection, it has merit. Root tips which survive the harvesting procedure and those which develop quickly following transplanting probably play the greatest role in insuring survival of the tree. With either the tree spade or hand digging, a sizable portion of the root tips are lost and the number and extent of larger roots which are most responsible for developing new root tips are greatly reduced. If the soil is moist when the tree is pulled, many of the small roots as well as most of the larger roots will be retained. It is important to prevent drying of the root mass once it is removed from the soil, and replanting should be done as soon as possible. With a pulled tree, the quantity of functioning roots and the potential for development of new roots at the new site appears greater than with a tree spade or conventional B & B.

Comparing Transplanting Techniques. In order to determine the merits of the various transplanting methods for trees, Preaus and Whitcomb (7) compared the following digging/planting treatments:
   1) tree spade-dug tree planted into tree spade-dug hole,
   2) tree spade-dug tree planted into hole dug by a backhoe,
   3) hand-dug balled-in-burlap (B & B) tree planted into hole dug by backhoe,
   4) trees pulled from moist soil via pin and clevis and planted into hole dug by backhoe.

Tree species used were:

lacebark or true Chinese elm (*Ulmus parvifolia*) two years old, 5 1/2 to 6 feet tall with 2 1/2- to 3 1/2-inch stems near the soil line;

Japanese black pine (*Pinus thunbergiana*) four years old, 5 to 6 feet tall with 2- to 3-inch stems near the soil line. Both species had been grown during the seedling establishment period in bottomless containers which destroys the tap root and stimulates a very fibrous root system.

summit green ash (*Fraxinus pennsylvanica* 'Summit') were two years old and about five feet tall when obtained from a commercial nursery and four years old and 9 to 11 feet tall with 3- to 3 1/2-inch stems near the soil line when this study began.

All trees were grown in a heavy clay loam soil and were transplanted to a site of similar soil type about one-fourth mile away. All transplanting was done during late March while all trees were dormant. Each treatment was replicated six times for each treatment and species. The tree spade used was a Vermeer T-20 mounted on the three-point hitch assembly of a 40-horsepower tractor.

All trees were planted and watered thoroughly the same day they were dug. Spring and summer rains provided good soil moisture until early August. Soils became very dry during late August and September but no supplemental watering was done.

Several assumptions were made in order to calculate transplant costs:

1) Equipment cost was based on 1/10 of 1% of the value of the machine used in each operation.

2) Labor cost was based on $5.00 per hour per man.

3) Overhead costs were calculated by multiplying the cost of labor per treatment by 30%.

Based on the assumptions made and time required, the following transplanting costs were determined:

Lifted/Hole preparation	elm	pine	ash	average
Tree spade/tree spade	$4.38	$4.65	$3.55	$4.19
Tree spade/backhoe	3.71	3.68	4.28	3.89
B&B/backhoe	9.67	9.16	7.28	8.70
Pulled/backhoe	4.85	5.52	did not work	5.18

236

Since all trees were transported only about one-fourth mile, transport time did not become a major factor. However, in most landscape situations, transport time would become a very important consideration, especially if the tree spade was driven several miles between sites. Transport distance may also influence the performance of trees pulled from the soil with many exposed roots, unless additional measures were taken to prevent root desiccation.

On September 23, a visual grade was taken for the lacebark elm and Japanese black pine (1 = best appearance and 4 = poorest appearance) and length of current season's flush was measured on the Japanese black pine and summit green ash.

Visual grade of lacebark elm and Japanese black pine was highest (indicating more stressed appearance) when the trees had been transplanted by a tree spade and planted into a tree spade-dug hole, treatment 1 (Table 15.1). Appearance of lacebark elm trees, transplanted with treatment 2 (tree spade into a backhoe hole), treatment 3 (B & B into a backhoe hole) or treatment 4 (pull method into a hand-dug hole) were similar, and all were significantly better than treatment 1 (tree spade into tree spade hole), Figure 15.1.

Table 15.1. Effects of transplanting method on visual grade or length of new growth of trees after one growing season.

	Treatments			
	(1)	(2)	(3)	(4)
	Tree spade/	Tree spade/	B & B/	Pull method/
	Tree spade	backhoe	backhoe	backhoe
Tree species	hole	hole	hole	hole
Visual Grade*				
Lacebark elm	3.5	2.2	1.8	2.4
Japanese black pine	3.5	2.0	1.7	2.0
Average New Growth (inches)				
Japanese black pine	6.0	9.6	11.0	10.1
Summit green ash	2.6	2.3	6.2	--

*Visual grade based on 1 = best appearance and 4 = most stressed appearance.

237

Japanese black pine grew most when transplanted with treatments 2, 3, or 4, and the length of the current season's flush was significantly shorter when trees were transplanted with treatment 1 (Table 15.1). In addition to a shorter flush of growth, Japanese black pine dug with a tree spade and planted into a tree spade-dug hole (Treatment 1) also had an overall unthrifty appearance (Figure 15.2).

Summit green ash grew best when transplanted with treatment 3 (B & B) as compared to either tree spade treatments (Table 15.1). The difference in the summit green ash appearance and length of new growth when compared to other test species may be related to the manner in which the trees were grown prior to initial planting in the field. Air root-pruning during the seedling stage greatly increases the quantity of fine fibrous roots as compared to trees grown in conventional ground beds. In the limited volume of soil in the tree spade ball, more roots on the elm and pine were transferred to the new site compared to the ash. Likewise, air root-pruning probably increased the success of the pull method with the elm and pine.

It is interesting to contrast treatments 1 and 2. The success of the tree spade-dug tree in the larger planting hole, (treatment 2) suggests that glazing of the tree spade-dug ball is not a problem. When loose backfill can be placed in intimate contact with the face of the ball following transplanting, the new roots produced readily grow **out** through the glazed surface. On the other hand, when a tree spade-dug tree is placed in a tree spade-dug hole, air spaces are likely to occur in numerous positions around the ball. In addition, both the face of the ball and the face of the hole may be glazed, depending on soil type and moisture conditions. Root penetration into the face of a glazed surface is probably much more difficult than root emergence through the back of a glazed surface.

Figure 15.1.   Lacebark elm foliage density and relative leaf size with tree spade-dug tree in a tree spade-dug hole (left) and typical response of other treatments, (right) in September after transplanting in March.

The fact that the conventional balled-in-burlap technique was not superior to the tree spade and backhoe hole combination suggests that digging machines can be used with a similar degree of success as with B & B, if the seedlings are root-pruned initially.   The pull method deserves more attention, particularly when transplanting large trees.   This may be a way to retain more roots capable of aiding re-establishment without the awesome weight encountered with very large soil balls.

Figure 15.2. Japanese black pine foliage density and length of current season's flush of growth with tree spade-dug tree into a tree spade-dug hole (left) and typical response of other three treatments (right) in September after transplanting in March.

Further Techniques Explored. Because it is expensive to dig large tree-planting holes by hand, improvements in tree spade-dug holes are being sought. Tree spades compact and glaze the hole walls by their pressure as the blades are inserted into the soil. It is impractical to manually roughen or disturb the face of the tree spade-dug hole. Even if the soil is roughened to break any glaze of the face of the tree spade-dug hole, new roots would still be forced to grow into undisturbed soil which is relatively low in oxygen. One proposed improvement is to hand-dig a tree spade-dug hole at least two feet larger in diameter to provide well-aerated backfill near the surface (6).

Bridel, Appleton and Whitcomb (2) designed a tree transplant study to determine if the planting/filling process around tree spade-planted trees could be improved. The study was conducted using Japanese black pine (*Pinus thunbergiana*) and 'Hopa' flowering crabapple (*Malus* X 'Hopa') and four treatments:

1) tree spade-dug tree planted into a tree spade-dug hole, with normal efforts made to water-in soil around the root ball;

2) tree spade-dug tree planted into a tree spade-dug hole with approximately one cubic foot of soil added to the bottom of the hole and made into a mud slurry. The volume of the mud slurry was enough to fill the air spaces around the root ball from the bottom of the hole to the soil surface, thus preventing any air pockets (Figure 15.3);

3) tree spade-dug tree planted into a tree spade-dug hole with a ring of soil approximately eight inches deep and eight inches wide removed from around the top of the tree spade-dug hole. This soil was then used to backfill and water-in around the tree, thereby reducing or eliminating the air space in the upper eight inches of soil and any glazing in the surface eight inches of soil where the tree roots are most concentrated and active;

4) tree spade-dug tree planted into a hole approximately four feet by four feet by 30 inches deep, dug with a backhoe. The tree spade-dug tree was held in the hole by the blades as the soil was backfilled. When all backfill soil was in place, the blades were removed and the tree was watered-in (Figure 15.4).

Figure 15.3. About one cubic foot of mud slurry was made in the bottom of the hole for treatment 2. The volume of mud was adjusted so that when the tree spade-dug tree was inserted into the hole the thick mud would just reach the soil surface.

241

The tree spade used was a 30-inch Vermeer. The crabapples were 12 feet tall with two-inch stem diameters; the Japanese black pine were six feet tall with two-inch stem diameters. Both tree species had been grown on a clay loam soil. The planting site was an unproductive; very heavy clay with shallow topsoil. All trees were watered well following transplanting and numerous rains occurred until mid June. No further watering was done. Trees were evaluated by measuring 10 new shoots per tree after three months.

For both species, shoot growth was best for treatment 4, the tree spade-dug tree in the backhoe-dug hole (Table 15.2).

By mid August, the flowering crabapples were visually evaluated for summer heat and drought tolerance using a 1 to 10 rating where 1 = small leaves and much stress while 10 = large leaves and little, if any, stress. Again treatment 4 was best (Figure 15.5, Table 15.2).

Figure 15.4. The tree spade was positioned over the backhoe-dug hole, then the spade was lowered and soil back-filled around the blades before the blades were removed. The backfilling was mostly done by a second tractor with a box blade.

242

Little benefit was seen from treatments 2 and 3, the mud slurry and loosened top ring of soil, compared to treatment 4, backhoe-dug hole. It appears that loosening the soil surrounding the transplanting root mass is the most practical means of reducing the stress of transplanting trees. This benefit is probably due almost exclusively to improving soil aeration. The reduced soil density allows more rapid root growth from the root ball into the surrounding soil.

Table 15.2. Average length of 10 new shoots of Japanese black pine and Hopa flowering crabapples, for each of four transplanting treatments.

	Treatment			
Tree Species	Tree spade dug hole (1)	Tree spade dug hole with mud slurry (2)	Tree spade dug hole with loose soil rim (3)	Backhoe dug hole (4)
Crabapple avg. shoot length	11.8 cm. (4.6 in.)	8.6 cm. (3.4 in.)	13.5 cm. (5.3 in.)	20.3* cm. (8 in.)
Crabapple visual rating^	2.6	3.5	3.7	9.4
Pine--avg. shoot length	1.5 cm. (0.6 in.)	3.1 cm. (1.2 in.)	5.4 cm. (2.1 in.)	11.7 cm. (4.6 in.)

*Averages in horizontal line followed by the same l
^Visual ratings from 1 to 10 where 1 = very poor appearance and 10 = excellent appearance.

When a tree is transplanted, new root growth occurs at the cut ends (Figure 15.6). In the case of a tree spade-dug tree planted into a tree spade-dug hole, the new roots are forced to develop either into the narrow space or loose soil caused by the imperfect fit of the two cone-shaped masses of soil or into the undisturbed soil on the planting site. In either case, the aeration and general conditions for the production of new roots are poor. By contrast, when a tree spade-dug tree is planted into a larger hole and the backfill soil is loosened and aerated, a much more favorable environment exists for new root development. This difference in the rapid production of new roots may not make the difference of life or death, however, it can make the difference between trees with severe stress and trees with only moderate stress. The overall landscape contribution of the two trees for the first two, three, or four years following transplanting is vastly different and well worth the extra expense. Figures 15.7 and 15.8 give some insights as to the effectiveness and operation of a tree spade. A key phrase to remember is that it is not how much real estate you move, but rather, what's in the real estate. This is true with any size plant but increases as the plant size goes up.

One technique that works extremely well is to start with liners with fibrous root systems then grow the trees for two to three years in fabric containers to stimulate further root branching and improve energy reserves in the roots. During the dormant period the trees are dug, fabric is removed using a "can opener" (see Chapter 2 for details) and replanted at a spacing that allows the trees to reach 4-, 5-, 6-inch stem caliper or larger without restriction of branch growth. When the trees are dug with a tree spade, many times more roots are present in the soil volume compared to trees grown conventionally. This means fewer losses to the contractor and greater satisfaction to the customer. In addition, the trees experience much less stress and are, therefore, much less susceptible to various secondary pathogens or pests. There clearly is a natural immunity system in plants and the healthier the plant and the lower the stress, the better it works.

Figure 15.5. The tree on the left was typical of the crabapples transplanted into the large holes dug by the backhoe. Even though the trees were not given any supplemental water during the summer, foliage was dense, dark green and no internal leaves were turning yellow or beginning to drop as of late August. No measurable rain had occurred for seven weeks prior to these photos. The tree on the right was typical of plant response to the other treatments. Of the 18 trees in the three poorer treatments, only two had died. However, all appeared unthrifty and had very small leaves. These findings emphasize the importance of loosening a large volume of soil when planting to reduce transplanting stress.

245

Figure 15.6. Development of new roots following transplanting occurs almost exclusively at the cut ends. Consequently, roots of trees dug with a tree spade and planted into a tree spade-dug hole are forced to develop into undisturbed soil. This is more difficult for coarse new roots from large cut roots than for small roots growing through the soil naturally. Oxygen plays a key role in the initiation of new roots from the cut ends. Once the new roots are formed, they are somewhat less dependent on oxygen.

Figure 15.7.   Moving trees with tree spades requires a machine with enough weight and hydraulic power to insert the three or four blades into the soil to cut the roots and retain a soil ball with the tree (above).   In this case, one blade has been moved to show the relationship of the other three.   In some cases, trees of considerable size are planted into restricted planting holes to create an instant landscape effect (below).   How successful these trees will be will not be known for at least one year and possibly two.

Figure 15.8. After making a hole to receive the tree, the tree spade with the tree is moved into position (above). The landscape effect is substantial, but in this case the tree was not properly positioned before the blades were removed and the tree is leaning (below). Because the top is large and provides for substantial wind leverage, the tree should be staked or secured with guy wires for most of the first growing season.

Literature Cited

1. Cool, R.A. 1976. Tree spade vs bare root planting. Jour. of Arboriculture 2:92-95.

2. Bridel, Robert, B.L. Appleton, and Carl E. Whitcomb. 1983. Planting techniques for tree spade-dug trees. Jour. of Arboriculture 9:282-284.

3. Flemer, W. 1982. Successful transplanting is easy. Jour. of Arboriculture 8:234-235.

4. Furuta, T. 1982. Influences on root determine transplanting success. Amer. Nurseryman 156(7):65-69.

5. Hamilton, D.F. and S.D. Verkade. 1982. The development and care of a healthy root system. Amer. Nurseryman 156(6):73-80.

6. Himelick, E.B. 1981. Mechanical tree digging and planting with a tree spade. In: Tree and shrub transplanting manual. pp. 29-32.

7. Preaus, K.B. and Carl E. Whitcomb. 1980. Transplanting landscape trees. Jour. of Arboriculture 6:221-223.

8. Vanstone, D.E. and W.G. Ronald. 1981. Comparison of bare root versus tree spade transplanting of boulevard trees. Jour. of Arboriculture 7:271-274.

9. Watson, G.W. and E.B. Himelick. 1982. Root distribution of nursery trees and its relationship to transplanting success. Jour. of Arboriculture 8:225-229.

CHAPTER 16

TRANSPLANTING LARGE TREES

Clues from Smaller Trees - - - - - - - 251

Tree Size Vs. Stress - - - - - - - - - 251

A Transplant Study with Large Trees - 258

Moving Large Trees - - - - - - - - - - 262

Literature Cited - - - - - - - - - - - 270

Transplanting Large Trees

The demand for large trees following construction and grading continues to increase. In many instances, two- to three-inch diameter trees are not of acceptable size to the client. On the other hand, landscape contractors and nurserymen have consistently observed that large trees transplanted conventionally or by tree spades generally perform poorly for several years before either recovery or death. This is a discussion of some of the factors involved.

Clues from Smaller Trees. Tree spade transplanting studies showed that when tree spade-dug trees were planted in a larger hole, they grew much better than when tree spade-dug trees were planted in a hole dug by the same tree spade (3). The superior growth of the trees following transplanting was due to the aerated soil around the root ball, thus providing a better environment for the initiation and rapid extension of new roots. Several techniques to fill the void between a tree spade dug-tree and a tree spade-dug hole have been studied (1). It was found that tree growth in the larger planting hole was superior in all cases.

Both of these studies showed that a well aerated soil around the root ball of a tree following transplanting can assist rapid root develoment and subsequent growth and appearance. However, this benefit can only partially compensate for stress incurred at time of transplanting, especially the stress incurred when transplanting large trees.

Tree Size Vs. Stress. In order to better understand the stress incurred by large trees following transplanting, a study was conducted with southern magnolia (*Magnolia grandiflora*) (7). The trees ranged in size from one- to five-inch stem diameter measured 4 1/2 feet above the soil. The diameter and length of each limb on each tree was measured and grouped according to size in 1/2-inch increments. By multiplying the stem diameter (rounded off to the nearest 1/2 inch) of each 1/2-inch increment times pi (3.1416) the circumference of the stem was obtained. By multiplying this value times the number of linear inches of each 1/2-inch size class, an estimate of the total stem surface area of living cells was obtained. For example, a one-inch diameter tree that had 68 linear inches of stem one inch in diameter and 236 linear inches of stem 1/2 to 1 inch in diameter would have 1 x 3.1416 x 68 = 213 square inches of stem surface area on the one-inch diameter branches and 0.5 x 3.1416 x 236 = 370.5 for a total of 584 square inches of branch surface area. In this study, all branches below 1/2 inch in diameter were not considered. Ten trees in each 1/2-inch size class (based on trunk diameter) were measured for a total of 90 trees.

Most of the cells in a woody tree or shrub are dead. However, the cambium and adjacent zones of cell division constitute a layer of very active living cells surrounding all stems and roots of all dicots (most woody landscape plants except the palms). On either side of the cambium is a zone of young and active living cells: on the inside, xylem cells; and on the outside, phloem cells.

Regardless of the thickness of this layer of living cells, when the branch surface area is plotted proportionately to the size of a particular kind of tree, one begins to gain an appreciation for why the larger the tree the greater the stress following transplanting. As the stem diameter of a tree increases from one to three inches, the stem surface area of living cells increases from 580 to 5,200 square inches (Figure 16.1). This is nearly a ten-fold increase in the surface area of living cells. When the stem diameter of a tree increases from about three inches to five inches, a further five-fold increase in surface area of living cells results. Compare the mass of living cells in a tree one inch and five inches in diameter and the difference is over 40 times greater.

These findings are striking. However, consider that there is a priority of distribution of carbohydrates (energy) within a woody plant; essentially flowers, fruits, leaves, stems and roots. In other words, if flowers and developing fruits are present on a tree they will preferentially receive carbohydrates at the expense of other plant parts (2). On the other hand, if no flowers or fruits are present, the leaves utilize the carbohydrates manufactured with any excess being translocated to the stem. If there are sufficient carbohydrates manufactured by the leaves to meet the needs of all leaves and stems, some are translocated to the root system (Figure 16.2). More and Halevy (2) observed that in a rose plant in full sun, 82% of the carbohydrates produced went to young shoots, 13% went to other above-ground plant parts, and only 4.3% went to the root system.

Research by Gordon and Larson (15, 16) showed that with red pine, which holds needles for two years, the one-year-old needles were the prime supplier of energy for current shoot development and growth of the terminal bud, whereas, the two-year-old needles were the prime supplier of energy for the roots. When a nutrient deficiency of nitrogen, phosphorus, potassium, or magnesium develops or drought occurs, the older leaves are lost first so the roots are most affected. This phenomenon probably holds true for all woody plants.

Roots are the key factor in plant vigor. If the energy carbohydrate production by the leaves is restricted for any reason, root growth is restricted before any other plant part. It seems ironic that root growth is restricted by a lack of energy from the leaves when the top of the plant is deficient in nutrient elements that can only be supplied by the roots. In short, the plant hastens its own demise by failing to provide energy to that part (roots) that could best help overcome a nutrient element deficiency by expanding into additional soil.

On the other hand, if the energy manufactured by the leaves is sufficient to meet all requirements of the above-ground parts and the living cells in the stem, the roots receive appreciable quantities of energy from the leaves and grow vigorously. With vigorous root growth, more soil is contacted to supply water and nutrients and add stability to the plant's physical location (keeps trees upright) and growth is further accelerated.

Roots cannot maintain water and nutrient absorption capacilities and grow without energy from the leaves. In short, **as the root system goes, so goes the plant!** Also remember that increased plant stress, for any reason, means an increased likelihood of disease and insect problems and conversely, reduced stress means increased resistance to problems.

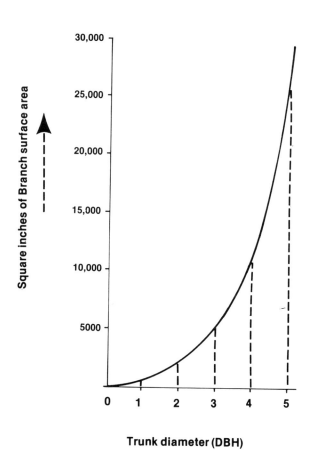

Figure 16.1. The square inches of branch surface area (an estimate of living cells) increases dramatically as trunk diameter of the tree increases. Respiration of all living cells in the top of a tree must be maintained before any appreciable energy can be translocated to the root system.

254

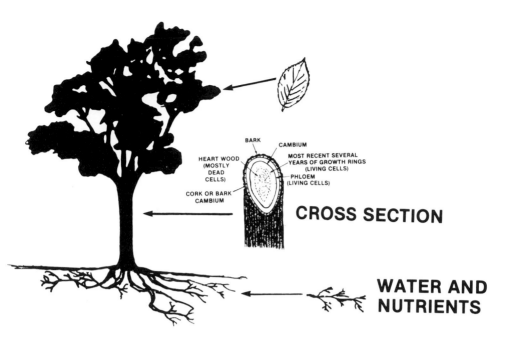

Labels in figure:
BARK
CAMBIUM
HEART WOOD (MOSTLY DEAD CELLS)
MOST RECENT SEVERAL YEARS OF GROWTH RINGS (LIVING CELLS)
PHLOEM (LIVING CELLS)
CORK OR BARK CAMBIUM
CROSS SECTION
WATER AND NUTRIENTS

Figure 16.2. Movement of absorbed water and nutrients is up to the leaves via mostly living cells in the xylem and back down from the leaves via living cells in the phloem. If there is insufficient energy to meet the needs of all tissues, the plant parts most removed (stem and roots) will be the ones that suffer most.

When one considers a three- to five-inch tree recently transplanted with a substantial reduction in roots, the problem becomes more clear (Figures 16.1 and 16.2). Unless leaves and/or stored carbohydrates in the stems have the capacity to meet the needs of all leaves and all living cells in the stems, the roots receive little or none for the initiation of new roots. Thus new root growth is dependent on stored reserves and growth regulators in the roots. A good balanced nutritional program for the tree **prior** to transplanting will build the stored reserves in the stems and roots. If only a few new roots are initiated following transplanting, the leaves become stressed for water and nutrients, and thus soluble carbohydrates (energy) and growth regulating chemical production is greatly restricted. This further restricts root growth which, in turn, places a greater stress on the leaves and thus the sequence of events that may ultimately lead to the death of the tree (Figure 16.3). On the other hand, the carbohydrate needs of the living leaf, stem and root tissues remain more or less constant.

This emphasizes the importance of energy (stored carbohydrate reserves) in the stems and roots prior to transplanting. The larger the tree the more critical are the stored reserves and the demand for stored reserves immediately following transplanting.

It is important to emphasize the value of well-aerated soil around the root ball following transplanting to encourage rapid root growth (1, 3). A larger planting hole at time of transplanting will probably not increase the survival of trees with low carbohydrate reserves. However, it will assist new root development of trees with adequate carbohydrate resources and reduce stress.

A theoretical analysis of the stress imposed on large trees at time of transplanting and the length of time necessary for recovery has been done (6). The model showed that when a small tree was transplanted, the length of time necessary before the root development on the new site was sufficient to support normal resumption of top growth was much less than when a large tree was transplanted, and the length of time for recovery was much greater. The model fits well with general observations of real situations over many years. The key item lacking from the model, however, is an allowance for the tremendous mass of living cells in the larger trees that must be sustained by energy from the leaves before energy can be translocated to the root system. It is this massive number of living cells, the complex array of growth-regulating compounds and the energy requirements of these cells that are primarily responsible for the poor performance of most transplanted large trees.

Because so much of this mass of living cells is present in the main stem and branches of a large tree (in excess of 60%), pruning the top of the tree has virtually no effect on reducing the total energy demand. Removing all small branches in the top of a five-inch caliper tree, short of destroying the primary branch structure and thus the appearance of the tree, would only reduce the living cell mass by two to four percent. This is why top-pruning of trees provides little or no benefit in most cases. The energy manufacturing and growth regulating chemical production is reduced by top-pruning without any appreciable reduction in energy demand.

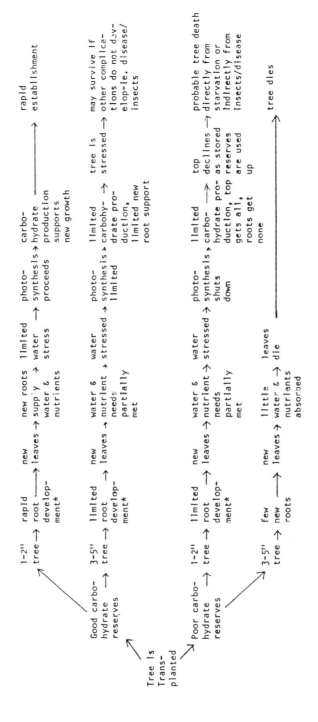

Figure 16.3. Probable sequence of events following transplanting of trees with or without good carbohydrate reserves and of small or large size.

*assuming a well aerated soil with good moisture and a reasonable supply of nutrients.

A Transplant Study With Large Trees. To examine this further, Whitcomb, Gray and Cavanaugh (8) designed a study to determine if top-pruning following transplanting would assist the establishment of large trees and if the methods of preparing the planting hole affect tree response to pruning. Since pruning reduced the quantity of living cells in the tree crown only slightly but substantially decreased the number of leaves available for growth regulator and energy production, the question was, will the benefits of a lower above-ground demand for water outweigh the loss of energy production because of fewer leaves?

Four-year-old seedlings of London planetree (*Platanus acerifolia*) with 3 1/2- to 4 1/2-inch stem diameters were grown especially for the study. The trees were grown in a clay loam soil and were transplanted into a similar but poorer soil.

The treatments were:

A. None, 20%, or 40% top pruning after transplanting.

B. Planting hole preparations:

    a. A tree spade-dug tree, planted into a tree spade-dug hole and watered in well to fill in the gap between ball and hole sidewall.

    b. A tree spade-dug tree, planted into a backhoe-dug hole approximately three times the diameter of the tree spade-dug ball but the same depth.

The tree spade used was a 30-inch Vermeer, four-blade trailer-mount type. The trees were transplanted during February. The six treatments in the study were replicated six times for a total of 36 trees. The tops of the trees were pruned prior to spring bud break (Figure 16.4). Drip irrigation with two one-gallon per hour emitters per tree, was provided to prevent moisture stress the first season.

At the end of the first growing season, a substantial difference in the number of suckers at the base of the trees could be observed. Trees planted into the tree spade-dug hole with 40% top-pruning had the most suckers (34) followed by 20% pruning (30) and no top-pruning (26). Trees planted into the larger holes had substantially fewer suckers, regardless of top-pruning treatment (14, 40%; 12, 20%; and 10, no top-pruning, Table 16.1 and Figure 16.5).

Figure 16.4. Appearance of tree crowns following no pruning vs. 40% pruning at the beginning of the study.

Sucker growth at the base of a tree is the result of dormant shoot buds on the stem. These dormant buds create the multitude of stems which form on stumps of living trees when cut down. In the case of cutting a living tree, the entire top of the tree **and** the complex of chemical growth regulators from the terminal buds are removed. Consequently, without the continuing supply of the chemicals from the top of the tree, the dormant buds begin to grow. A similar situation occurs when a tree is pruned at transplanting and/or experiences enough stress during the transplanting process that the chemical supply of growth regulating compounds from the leaves is reduced to the point that the dormant buds in the stem begin to grow. **Suckers are the result of reduced activity (stress) in the top of the tree.**

Table 16.1. Effects of top pruning and planting procedure on growth and quality of London planetrees.

	Tree spade-tree/ tree spade hole			Tree spade-tree/ larger planting hole		
Top-Pruned	0	20%	40%	0	20%	40%
Basal suckers, average/tree after one growing season	26	30	34	10	12	14
Length of terminal growth (inches) 1st season	4.6	3.1	3.9	9.8	6.5	6.6
2nd season	19	18.5	15.8	25.0	20.6	21.6
Total (2 years)	23.6	21.6	19.9	34.8	27.1	28.2
Overall Visual Quality	6.8*	5.2	5.6	9.0	9.0	8.0

*based on a rating scale where 1 = top dieback and poor growth, 4 = sparse foliage but no dieback, 7 = good foliage, 10 = excellent foliage and growth.

Figure 16.5. Heavy sucker development occurred on the trunks of trees pruned 40%, especially when planted into the tree spade-dug hole.

During the second growing season following transplanting, four trees died back 60% to 80%. All were trees with 20% or 40% top-pruning which had been planted into tree spade-dug holes.

Trees planted in the larger planting holes, regardless of top-pruning, had the greatest terminal growth for both the first and second growing seasons (Table 16.1). Among the three top-pruning treatments and trees in the larger planting holes, the trees with no top branches removed at time of transplanting had the greatest growth both seasons and overall for both seasons (Table 16.1). An overall visual rating at the end of the second growing season, however, showed little difference among the three top-pruning treatments as long as the larger planting hole was used. On the other hand, with the tree spade-dug hole, the trees with no top pruning had higher visual quality than those with 20% or 40% top-pruning (Figure 16.6).

All of the trees planted into the larger hole regardless of top pruning were attractive, effective landscape trees the second season following transplanting.

Figure 16.6. After two growing seasons following transplanting, the trees with no top-pruning (left) were fuller, larger and more attractive than those that had been top-pruned at planting time (two trees on the right), especially when planted into a tree spade-dug hole.

Moving Large Trees. Large trees present three major complications to the nurseryman; the large mass of living tissue in the crown that must be maintained, the volume or space requirement of the top, and the weight of the root ball. The large mass of living cells has been covered in an earlier section of this chapter, Tree Size Vs. Stress. It is mentioned here as a further reminder of its importance. **It must be considered.**

The volume or space requirement of the crown of a large tree sometimes prevents it from being moved. Limbs can be tied or confined only to some degree. Limbs of river birch and elm can be compressed a great deal without damage. On the other hand, honeylocust (*Gleditsia triacanthos*) limbs are quite stiff and can be flexed only slightly. Young trees that still have the tall triangle-form are easiest to move and, in general, have the greatest likelihood of success. Trees with multiple stems and/or strong horizontal branches often prove challenging.

Moist soils weigh from 100 to 140 pounds per cubic foot. Since the root ball must be kept moist, any additional watering can add more pounds to the load. For example, the London planetree (*Platanus acerifolia*) in Figure 16.7 has a stem diameter of nearly nine inches and is about 28 feet tall. The root ball is about eight feet in diameter and 30 inches deep. The Florida sand weighs about 120 pounds per cubic foot (moist), so the root ball weights about 15,000 pounds plus the weight of the tree. The ball was partially dug with a backhoe and finished by hand. The soil was wrapped in burlap and secured with four- by six-inch fencing prior to lifting.

Figure 16.7. The root ball was partially dug with a backhoe after the limbs were tied to prevent damage. The remaining ball shaping was done by hand. It was wrapped in burlap then wrapped in four-inch by six-inch mesh fencing. At intervals, the wires were twisted to draw the wire as tight as possible around the soil mass. Note the width and position of the nylon straps. The straps must be just below the center line of the root ball to prevent slippage.

In order to keep the tree in a semi-upright condition while lifting and loading, the tree was tied to the lifting straps using a broad nylon strap around the trunk (Figure 16.8) The placement of the cable and strap is very important. If the strap is placed too high in the tree, the load on the stem may be too great and breakage or damage many result. If the strap is too low, relative to the height and weight of the top of the tree compared to the soil ball, upon lifting, the entire tree and ball may become horizontal. Since it is not possible to weigh the top of the tree or the soil ball prior to lifting, experience and estimates are the only guidelines.

264

As for lifting the soil ball, the broader the strap(s) and webbing, the greater the distribution of the load and the less the root ball is disturbed. Since a root ball greater than eight feet in diameter requires special width and weight permits, few large root balls are dug. This means that in proportion to the root balls used on smaller trees, the root balls are quite small. Thus all possible precautions to protect the root ball must be taken. **If in doubt, use heavier equipment.** Once lifting begins, quite often it is not possible to stop and reposition or re-hook. Lifting in the nursery can be precarious since soils are soft and outriggers that provide the principal support for lifting can sink. Watch out for areas where large trees have been previously dug that may appear firm until the lift begins.

The tree shown in Figure 16.9 was to be moved only a few miles, with no overhead power lines, street lights, bridges or overpasses to confront the movers. Prior to digging a large tree, the route should be mapped out carefully and checked and rechecked. The size and volume of the top of a sizable tree is easy to under estimate prior to loading. An eight-foot ball placed on a truck bed four feet off the ground will clear most lines and tree limbs since any major street has a vertical clearance of at least 12 feet. When the tree is placed on a truck, the limbs against the truck bed may prevent the main stem of the tree from approaching horizontal, leaving it many feet in the air. If a tree has a multiple stem, position of the lifting cable must be positioned carefully to allow for the best hauling position in addition to the lifting position. Excess horizontal width can be worked around more easily than excess height. **Always watch for power lines and always assume they are hot. Limbs on living trees contain water and are conductors of electricity.**

Figure 16.8. The tree being lifted for loading. Note the position of the nylon straps around the ball and the strap around the tree stem and padding to prevent injury. In this case, the strap around the stem was slightly too high which prevented the tree from leaning enough. The result was that getting the tree positioned on the truck was difficult. On the other hand, when lifting the tree for planting, this position would be desirable since it would help in positioning the tree upright, while still allowing for the root ball.

In summary:

a) Digging a bigger (wider) planting hole greatly reduces plant stress.

b) Pruning the tops of larger trees at time of trans-planting does not aid survival or tree appearance, even of large trees.

c) Top-pruning in conjunction with planting trees into tree spade-dug holes was the poorest treatment.

d) Pruning tops in conjunction with a larger planting hole caused fewer suckers but provided no detectable benefit to the tree.

e) For best results, leave the top of the tree alone, except to remove structure weaknesses or broken, damaged limbs.

f) Since moisture stress of the top is a major factor that influences leaf function, one technique that can be very beneficial is to install a mist head or sprinkler in the top of the tree (Figure 16.10). This may be operated intermittently during late morning until early evening to reduce moisture stress on the new leaves. However, be careful to not over water the soil around the tree so that new root growth will be restricted due to poor soil aeration. The key is to humidify and moisten the leaves, much like the misting of cuttings. Excess water leaches chemicals from the leaves and may do more harm than good. Likewise, if the water used has substantial sodium, boron, bicarbonates or chlorides, the leaf injury from the chemicals may offset the benefits provided by misting.

Figure 16.9. This tree was moved only a short distance and did not have to go under power lines or other obstacles. It is very easy to under estimate the volume and space required by a tree prior to harvest and loading.

Figure 16.10.   Placing a mist or sprinkler head in the top of a large tree following transplanting can sometimes be helpful.   Be careful to not over water the soil.   At intervals, moisten the leaves, but do not soak the leaves and soil.

Literature Cited

1. Bridel, Robert, Carl E. Whitcomb and B.L. Appleton. 1983. Planting techniques for tree spade dug trees. Jour. of Arboriculture 9:282-284.

2. Bridel, Robert and Carl E. Whitcomb. 1981. Improving performance of trees dug and planted with a tree spade. Okla. Agri. Sta. Res. Rept. P-818:14-15.

3. More, Yoram and A.H. Halevy. 1980. Promotion of sink activity of developing rose shoots by light. Plant Physiology 66:990-995.

4. Preaus, Kenneth and Carl E. Whitcomb. 1980. Transplanting Landscape Trees. Jour. of Arboriculture 6:221-223.

5. Shoup, Steve, Rick Reavis and Carl E. Whitcomb. 1981. Effects of pruning and fertilizer on establishment of bare root deciduous trees. Jour. of Arboriculture 7:155-157.

6. Watson, Gary. 1985. Tree size affects root regeneration and top growth after transplanting. Jour. of Arboriculture 11:37-40.

7. Whitcomb, Carl E. 1983. Why large trees are difficult to transplant. Jour. of Arboriculture 9:57-59.

8. Whitcomb, Carl E., Charlie Gray and Billy Cavanaugh. 1985. Methods of transplanting large trees. Okla. Agri. Exp. Sta. Res. Rept. P-872:17-21.

CHAPTER 17

STAKING LANDSCAPE TREES

Stakes = Problems - - - - - - - - - - - - 272

Literature Cited - - - - - - - - - - - - - 283

Staking Landscape Trees

Stakes = Problems. In general, trees recently transplanted should not be staked unless absolutely necessary and then the stake should be attached as low as possible. The arbitrary staking of all trees planted is a waste of time and effort on many landscape sites and does sufficient damage to more than offset any benefits.

On the other hand, on windy sites with heavy soils, trees with relatively tall tops proportionate to the size and quality of the root ball may need to be staked for a few months. If the site is sufficiently windy so that the root ball moves regularly, staking is necessary to prevent young roots from being disturbed as they attempt to grow into the surrounding soil.

Some trees, especially container-grown trees, may need support to hold the top of the tree upright (Figure 17.1). Trees grown with excess levels of nitrogen and close spacing of containers so that few side branches develop, may need the assistance of a stake for several years following planting (Figure 17.2). Nursery stock in this condition should not be accepted on any landscape job and should not be accepted by any serious garden center operator or nurseryman. Growing trees in this manner shows a complete disregard for the ultimate customer by the wholesale producer. By simply reducing the nitrogen level and providing more space between the young trees the same species can be grown without the need of a stake both in the nursery and after transplanting into the landscape.

A staked tree will:
- a) grow taller than an unstaked tree (1, 2, 8, 9),
- b) grow less in trunk diameter near the ground but more near the top support tie (4, 8),
- c) produce a trunk with little or no taper (1),
- d) develop a smaller root system (1, 4),
- e) have increased wind resistance, compared to trees of equal height but not staked, because of the proportion and distribution of the entire crown (5, 6), and
- f) be subject to more stress per cross-sectional area of the stem at the point of top support (6). All of these factors work against the proper development and structural soundness of a tree.

Figure 17.1. There are some situations even staking will not help. This container-grown tree was staked for several years. However, due to poor root development from the sides of the root ball, the tree was poorly anchored. When the stakes were finally removed, the tree leaned considerably. In an effort to "assist" the tree, the contractor added additional soil thinking it would help. Shortly after this photo was taken the tree blew over and had to be replaced. The basic problem was that the container-grown tree was root-bound. See the discussion and figures in Chapter 2 for further information on this very common problem.

Figure 17.2. This young tree was staked in a container prior to planting. The stem would not support the top without staking in the landscape (above). The stakes were too tall and damaged the major branches in several places (below). In addition, the stakes were too large relative to the size of the tree and allowed no flexing to aid stem growth. The absence of any lower side branches also reduced the rate of stem growth.

274

A tree stem must be free to move or flex for proper development. Neel (8) and Leiser et al. (4) studied extensively the effects of staking young trees and found trees grown with stakes in the nursery to be taller and have smaller diameter stems. When these trees were planted into the landscape, staking during production resulted in more stress per unit cross-sectional area of the stem either at the soil line if not staked when transplanted (Figure 17.3) or at the point of the top tie to the stake. When Neel and Harris (9) mechanically moved the tops of sweet gum trees for 30 seconds daily in a greenhouse, they found that the trees that had been moved were 30% shorter than trees not moved and had larger diameter stems. They concluded that if you must stake a tree, use a flexible stake (like a one-half inch concrete reinforcing rod) for only partial support of the top and allow for some natural movement of the stem (Figure 17.4).

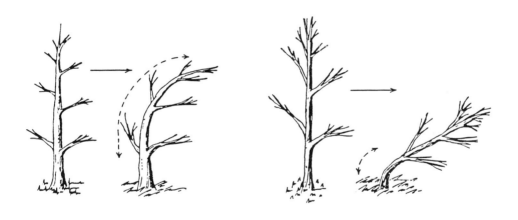

Figure 17.3. A tree grown without staking in the nursery and with lower limbs in place, develops good stem taper. When wind stress occurs, the entire stem flexes (left). Staked trees with little taper experience more stress at the soil line when planted and not staked or when the stakes are removed (right).

275

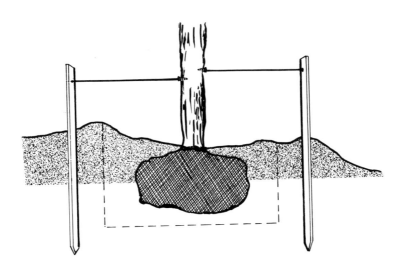

Figure 17.4. Be sure stakes are located outside of the soil disturbed during planting for greater strength and to avoid root damage. Use a flexible stake and attach it as low as is practical for the size of tree and site condition.

The most beneficial aspect of staking trees probably lies not in the support of the top of the tree, but rather in the protection the stakes provide against lawn mower blight (Figure 17.5). Unfortunately stakes provide little protection for the various "weed eater" devices. Only a tough but expandable trunk protector will prevent damage to young trees from the high-speed string (Figure 17.6)

Figure 17.5. Lawn mower blight is a serious problem for young trees. The young magnolia (above) has a slim chance of reaching maturity due to the severe stem injury caused by a mower (below).

Figure 17.6. "Weed eaters" can quickly damage the stems of young trees (above). Only a tough, expandable trunk protector will prevent injury (below).

Attachment of stakes to trees may be accomplished by an assortment of ties, wires, water hoses or combinations of these devices (Figure 17.7). If the tree is to be staked for three to six months, the various ties around the stems may be acceptable. However, on especially windy sites and/or where the stakes are likely to remain for a year or more, eyescrews are the preferred method of attachment (Figure 17.8). Critics of this technique immediately bring up the injury to the stem. However, the stem is damaged in only a very small area compared to the rubbing-girdling effect of a hose or wire which may damage 60% or more of the bark around the stem. Do not remove the eyescrews after the stakes and wires are removed. As the tree grows the eyescrews will be callused over and eventually disappear entirely with no consequence to the tree. Removal of the eyescrew leaves an open wound with a greater likelihood of entrance of decay organisms. A healthy tree will quickly compartmentalize the area around the eyescrew and prevent spread of any decay organisms.

A healthy tree planted without soil amendments, so that soil density is not changed, into an area with proper water and drainage relationships and proper fertilization, will need staking for only a few months (1, 3, 7). In a study on a windy knoll in Stillwater, Oklahoma with large trees and a very poor heavy clay soil on the site, the stakes were removed from the trees three months after bud break with no damage or loss of trees in spite of several severe winds shortly after removal of the stakes (10). These trees had 3.5- to 4-inch diameters at the base, were 12 to 14 feet tall, and were moved with 30-inch tree spade-dug root balls. In spite of the size of the tops and the small root balls and stressful planting sites, staking was needed for only a brief time.

279

Figure 17.7. In this case, old water hose reduces the pressure of the wire on the stem. If the tree is staked for only a few months, this may be satisfactory.

In cases of trees moved during the dormant period where bud swell in the spring occurs at the new site, rates of root growth following bud swell will be several inches per week. The key factor to consider is the length of time since bud swell, not simply the length of time in months. By contrast, a tree moved in late spring, after bud swell, may need to be staked for a full year. Since the spring chemical signal from the buds has passed, the tree will be severely stressed for the remainder of the growing season in most cases. A good burst of new root production into the surrounding soil may not occur until bud swell the following spring. This tree should be staked using eyescrews to attach the ties to the stem, because of the length of time involved. Wire ties on trees staked for any length of time can only mean trouble (Figure 17.9) and in many cases staking is not necessary (Figure 17.10).

Figure 17.8. Eyescrews of appropriate size may be used on small trees (above) or large trees (below). Do not remove the eyescrews, thus avoiding an open wound. The tree will grow over the eyescrew with minor disruption of tissues.

Figure 17.9. Stem girdling by a wire used to stake a tree. In this case even if water hose or other material had been used around the wire, considerable damage would have occurred. Eyescrews are superior overall.

Figure 17.10. In situations like this, one is tempted to say, "its the thought that counts", however, many young trees would be better off if they were never staked.

Literature Cited

1. Harris, R.W. 1984. Effects of pruning and staking on landscape trees. Jour. Environmental Hort. 2:140-142.

2. Harris, R.W., A.T. Leiser and W.B. Davis. 1976. Staking landscape plants. Univ. of Calif. Agri. Sci. leaflet #256.

3. Kelly, R.J., B.C. Moser. 1983. Root regeneration of *Liriodendron tulipifera* in response to auxin, stem pruning and environmental conditions. Jour. Amer. Soc. Hort. Sci. 180:1085-1090.

4. Leiser, A.T., R.W. Harris, P.L. Neel, D. Long, N.W. Stice and R.G. Maire. 1972. Staking and pruning influences trunk development of young trees. Jour. Amer. Soc. Hort. Sci. 97:498-503.

5. Leiser, A.T. and J.O. Kemper. 1968. A theoretical analysis of a critical height of staking landscape trees. Proc. Amer. Soc. Hort. Sci. 92:712-720.

6. Leiser, A.T. and J.O. Kemper. 1973. Analysis of stress distribution in the sapling tree trunk. Jour. Amer. Soc. Hort. Sci. 98:164-170.

7. Magley, S.B. and D.K. Struve. 1983. Effects of three transplant methods on survival, growth and root regeneration of caliper pin oaks. Jour. Environmental Hort. 1:59-62.

8. Neel, P.L. 1971. Experimental manipulation of trunk growth in young trees. Arborists News 36(3):25-31.

9. Neel, P.L. and R.W. Harris. 1971. Motion induced inhibition of elongation and induction of dormancy in *Liquidambar*. Science 173:58-59.

10. Whitcomb, Carl E., Charlie Gray and Billy Cavanaugh. 1985. Methods of transplanting large trees. Okla. State Univ. Nursery Res. Rept. P-828:17-21.

CHAPTER 18

COMPETITION BETWEEN WOODY PLANTS AND GRASSES

The Competitiveness of Grass - - - - - - 285

Trees Can Restrict Grass - - - - - - - - 288

Grass-Shrub Competition - - - - - - - - 289

Bermudagrass Competition - - - - - - - 289

Allelopathy or Chemical Growth Factors - 293

Literature Cited - - - - - - - - - - - - 295

Competition Between Woody Plants and Grasses

The urban landscape environment is very complex.   Studies show that grasses are very competitive with woody plant materials. In contrast with classical agriculture where large areas of a single crop are grown, the man-managed landscape is a consortium of woody plants, generally unpruned or lightly pruned, growing in a grass sod that is frequently and severely pruned (17, 18, 19, 20, 23).   In the southern states the warm season grasses are best characterized as very aggressive with strong development in full sun despite the severe pruning.

The Competitiveness of Grass. Competition from adjacent plants especially grasses, plays a subtle but certain role in the success of most plantings.   A newly transplanted tree or shrub always experiences some stress.   Since stress in a plant is impossible to measure, it is difficult to know when the degree of stress approaches the breaking point.   Some plants never resume growth following transplanting while many others resume growth only to die at some point during the first few weeks or months.   Others die after a year or more.

After excavating vast numbers of plants during the depression era, Weaver concluded that roots of grasses invade nearly 100% of the soil mass while woody plants rarely invade more than 5% (15, 16).   One need only to look at the extensive fibrous root system of any grass to gain a healthy respect for its competitive effect on adjacent plants.

Grass roots differ from woody plants in form, length of life and manner of development. Grass roots are very fibrous, whereas, woody plants have a primary woody root system with secondary fibrous roots.   Grass roots generally live no more than a year, whereas, the primary woody roots of trees and shrubs live for many years (15, 16).

The competition between grasses and woody plants intensifies whenever moisture, nutrients, or any other factor affecting growth becomes limiting.   Contrary to the widespread misconception that tree roots grow to great depths in the soil, the roots of most woody trees and shrubs grow in the upper 8 to 12 inches of soil along with the roots of any grasses in the area.   The roots of grasses and woody plants are constantly intermingling and competing for soil moisture and nutrients (3).

The closer grasses are cut, the shallower the root system (Figure 18.1) (6, 8, 11, 12, 13, 25).   It seems that closely mowed lawns would be only moderately competitive with woody plants compared to the same grasses not mowed. This is true, but the restrictive nature of the mowed grass is still a major factor affecting the establishment of woody plants.

There have been many reports of materials from one plant affecting the growth of an adjacent plant. Roots of walnut trees (*Juglans nigra*) produce juglone which has been reported to kill tomatoes, potatoes, alfalfa and apple trees (9, 14). The restriction in root growth of Kentucky bluegrass by established roots of silver maple (*Acer saccharinum*) and honeylocust (*Gleditsia triacanthos*) may be due to direct competition as well as biochemical inhibition (allelopathy) since the restriction in growth of the grass occurred even when water and nutrients were not limiting (17).

Figure 18.1.   There is a distinct relationship between top and root development of any plant.   As the tops of the red fescue was mowed shorter, the root system was restricted.   This is true for **all** *grasses.   Closely cut grass is more subject to drought and other stress factors compared to grass cut at a greater height or unclipped.   One of the most practical and economical ways to improve turf health is to raise the height of cut.   Interestingly, top pruning of any plant reduces root development.*

Trees Can Restrict Grass. Work by Whitcomb and Roberts showed that the established roots of silver maple restricted the depth of rooting of Kentucky bluegrass through some unknown mechanism (23). Therefore, the bluegrass became far more susceptible to drought when grown in conjunction with trees. On the other hand, in plots free of tree roots, the depth of rooting of the Kentucky bluegrass was six to eight inches.

The existence of inhibitors produced by one plant and released into the soil only to influence another plant have been known for sometime. Bonner (2) studied such inhibitors extensively. Garb (5) felt that plant growth inhibitors were probably far more widespread and important than is generally realized and that one of the most striking characteristics was the wide gap between concentrations that inhibit growth of sensitive plants and concentrations that actually kill those plants.

At first, it would seem that some trees have the capacity to greatly restrict the root growth and, in turn, the health and vigor of grasses. This is true **if** the tree roots are established in the soil when the grass is seeded or sodded. On the other hand, established sod of most grasses has the capacity to greatly restrict the growth of most woody plants.

Early attempts to establish trees in sod revealed the detrimental effect of grasses. For example, Armstrong and Pratt (1) observed that grasses restricted the growth of European larch (*Larix europa*) and European ash (*Fraxinus excelsior*) and caused the loss of many terminal buds, reduced leaf size, hastened early leaf drop the first growing season, and resulted in even more pronounced detrimental effects the second growing season. Richardson (10) studied the effects of ryegrass (*Lolium perenne*) on the sycamore maple (*Acer pseudoplatanus*) under two levels of nitrogen fertilizers. Roots of the maple were restricted by the ryegrass in growth rate, length of time tree roots actively grew during the growing season, root hair density, rooting depth, and lateral root spread of the tree. When nitrogen become limiting, roots of the maple tree were restricted, whereas, the ryegrass roots increased in rate of elongation. Similar results with magnolia and zelcova trees growing in fescue sod have been reported (7).

The detrimental effect of established Kentucky bluegrass on the growth of roots of newly planted silver maple (*Acer saccharinum*), honeylocust (*Gleditsia triacanthos*), and pin oak (*Quercus palustris*) trees has been studied (17, 22). Root growth of all trees were reduced from 40% to 70%, depending on the species, compared to roots growing in the same soil where grass was not present.

Further studies using the connecting pot technique (24) showed that if tree roots and grass roots invaded the same soil volume at the same time, the tree roots generally had a greater restricting effect on the grass roots (20).

Grass-Shrub Competition. The competitive effects of four southern turfgrasses have been studied (4). St. Augustine, centipede, Argentine bahia and bermudagrass were grown in conjunction with pittosporum (*Pittosporum tobira*), lantana (*Lantana camara*), pyracantha (*Pyracantha koidzumi*) and Chinese juniper (*Juniperus chinensis* 'Humphreys Pride') shrubs. Grasses were sodded up to the stem of the plant, or a circular area 18 to 36 inches in diameter was kept free of vegetation. The grasses were mowed and fertilized regularly and the entire area was irrigated as needed, similar to a well-managed landscape.

At the end of one year, differences in grass/shrub reactions were pronounced. The largest shrubs of all species were always in conjunction with St. Augustine grass. Top weight of pyracantha was nearly three times greater when grown in conjunction with St. Augustine as compared to bermudagrass or centipede grass; bahia grass was intermediate. Both the 18- and 36-inch clearing around the shrubs assisted growth of tops and roots of shrubs. However, in this one-year study, there was no advantage to the larger clearing and a slight detrimental effect to the pyracantha. This was probably due to the upright growth of the pyracantha exposing the soil surface to excess heating, whereas, the other shrub species had spreading growth habits and shaded the soil. Clearly bermudagrass was the most restrictive to the growth of the four shrubs.

Bermudagrass Competition. The response of four woody plants to competition with bermudagrass has also been studied (22). A dense sod of U-3 bermudagrass was established on a moderately fertile clay loam soil. Woody plants were planted in the sod using three clearing and three fertility treatments. Cleared areas were maintained by spraying Roundup herbicide during the growing season on the grass.

Clearing treatments:
a) A 60-inch square around the plant was kept free of grasses and weeds.

b) A 30-inch square around the plant was kept free of grasses and weeds.

c) No clearing, bermudagrass was allowed to grow up to the stem of the plant following planting.

Fertility treatments:

a) Base fertility only, approximately one pound nitrogen per 1000 square feet was broadcast over the entire area twice during growing season.

b) An additional two pounds of nitrogen per 1000 square feet applied spring and fall to an area five feet by five feet square around the plants.

c) An additional four pounds of nitrogen per 1000 square feet applied spring and fall to an area five feet by five feet square around the plants.

During October, uniform one-gallon container stock of the following species were planted: dwarf burford holly (*Ilex cornuta* 'Burford Nana'), hetzi Chinese juniper (*Juniperus chinensis* 'Hetzi') and Japanese black pine (*Pinus thunbergiana*) and golden vicary privet (*Ligustrum vicaryi*).

Only slight differences in plant response to reducing the bermudagrass competition could be seen during the spring and early summer. However, by the end of the first growing season, the rapidly growing vicary privet had 100% increase in the number of branches per plant with either cleared area as compared to close competition with the bermudagrass (Figure 18.2 and Table 18.1). Plants were only slightly larger where extra fertilizer had been applied and most plants were about the same height. On July 19, (after 17 months) dwarf burford holly were given a visual grade rating from 1 (poorest) to 10 (best). The high fertilizer treatment and the 60-inch square area free of bermudagrass around each plant averaged 7.6, whereas, the high fertilizer and 30-inch square averaged 6.6. Plants with no clearing of bermudagrass averaged 1.3 regardless of the fertilizer treatment. The average plant responses for all fertilizer levels are given in Table 18.1.

Japanese black pine had 11% greater stem caliper, 7% greater height and 31% greater branch number where bermudagrass was kept away from the young trees compared to no clearing (Figure 18.3 and Table 18.1). Increasing fertilizer from the maintenance level for the bermudagrass to the high rate increased height 10%, caliper 11%, but had no effect on number of branches.

Figure 18.2. Size of golden vicary privet with additional fertilizer and 60-inch clearing (lower left), additional fertilizer and 30-inch clearing (upper right), no additional fertilizer and no clearing (upper left), and additional fertilizer and no clearing (lower right) about 16 months after planting.

Pfitzer junipers were 33% larger with 38% more branches where either clearing was maintained. Fertilizer only slightly increased juniper growth, with or without the bermudagrass competition.

All four species responded to removal of bermudagrass from around the plants (Table 18.1). These results are similar to those observed earlier. Applying additional fertilizer around the plants did not increase the ability of the tree or shrub to compete with the bermudagrass where no clearing was provided. Nitrogen fertilization was effective in increasing growth of magnolia trees which had fescue sod growing to their trunks (7, 10).

Table 18.1.   Effects of maintaining a bermudagrass-free area
around landscape plants, on plant growth and visual quality.

_____

Bermudagrass-Plant

| | Bermudagrass-Plant Relationship | | |
	60 in. sq. clearing	30 in. sq. clearing	no clearing
Japanese black pine			
2nd year growth flush (in.)	19.2	18.0	9.4
Overall plant height (in.)	64.0	60.0	21.0
Visual grade*	7.4	7.3	4.4
Hetzi Chinese juniper			
growth spread (in.)	72.5	70.2	57.1
Visual grade*	9.5	8.8	4.5
Golden vicary privet			
Visual grade	8.1	5.5	2.2
Dwarf burford holly			
Visual grade	6.5	3.3	1.3

*Based on a 1 (poorest) to 10 (best) rating of overall landscape
appearance.   Values are the averages of ratings of all fertilizer
levels.

_____

Figure 18.3. Growth of Japanese black pine after two growing seasons with additional fertilizer and 60-inch clearing (left) and with no additional fertilizer and no clearing (right).

Allelopathy or Chemical Growth Factors. Allelopathy (the production of a chemical compound by one plant which is toxic to another plant) may be involved in many tree-turf relationships (2, 5). Since additional fertilizer did not assist the woody plants when the bermudagrass was present and since moisture stress was never severe during the study, allelopathy may have been involved. The subtle but certain restriction of growth of woody plants by bermudagrass, even though the grass is severely and frequently pruned, encourages such a hypothesis. There was little advantage to 60-inch over 30-inch cleared areas during the first two years, except with the privet and holly. However, as the trees and shrubs grew larger and roots progressed laterally, the larger cleared areas proved beneficial.

Keeping a cleared area free of grass at least 30 inches square is one additional way to aid the establishment and growth of newly planted trees and shrubs. Under stress conditions, removal of grass competition may make the difference between survival and death of some trees and shrubs.

If woody plants survive the initial confrontation with the grass, slowly they gain the upper hand. At some point, trees become the dominant landscape plants, making the management of turfgrasses nearby increasingly difficult (Figure 18.4). For additional information on this aspect, see the Chapter 32, When Trees Compete With Turfgrass.

Figure 18.4. Trees become the dominant landscape elements making the production of turfgrass increasingly difficult. In this case, the large elm severely restricts the growth of grass. However, the newly planted tree (see arrow in the foreground) is being restricted by the fierce competition from the grass.

Literature Cited

1. Armstrong, S.F. and E.R. Pratt. 1915. On the harmful effects of certain grasses around the roots of young forest trees. Quart. Jour. Forestry. 9:225-230.

2. Bonner, J. 1950. The role of toxic substances in the interaction of higher plants. Bot. Review 16:51-65.

3. Daniel W. H. and E. C. Robert. 1966. Turfgrass management in the U.S. Advances in Agronomy 18:229-236.

4. Dean, S.G. and Carl E. Whitcomb. 1970. Effects of four warm season turfgrasses on growth and development of four shrub species maintained at three levels of competition. HortSci. 5:336-337.

5. Garb. Solomon. 1961. Differential growth inhibitors produced by plants. Bot. Review 27:422-443.

6. Graber, L. F. 1931. Food reserves in relation to other factors limiting the growth of grasses. Plant Physiol. 6:43-72.

7. Harris, R. W. 1966. Influence of turfgrass on young landscape trees. Proc. Int. Hort. Cong. 17:80.

8. Harrison, Carter M. 1934. Response of Kentucky bluegrass to variations in temperature, light, cutting and fertilizing. Plant Physiol. 9:83-106.

9. Massey. A.B. 1925. Antagonism of the walnut in certain plant association. Phytopath. 15:773-784.

10. Richardson, S.D. 1953. Root growth of *Acer pseudoplatanus* in relation to grass cover and nitrogen deficiency. Mededlingen van de Landbouwhogeschool te Wageningen/Nederland. 53:75-97.

11. Roberts, E.C. 1958. The grass plant--feeding and cutting. Golf Course Reporter 25(3):5-8.

12. Roberts, E.C. and E.J. Bredakis. 1960. What, why and how: turfgrass root development. Golf Course Reporter 28(8):12-24.

13. Schmidt, R.E. and R.E. Blaser. 1969. Effect of temperature,

light and nitrogen on growth of Tifgreen bermudagrass. Crop Sci. 9:8-9.

14. Schneiderhan, F.J. 1927. The black walnut as a cause of the death of apple trees. Phytopath. 17:529-541.

15. Weaver, J.E. 1919. The ecological relations of roots. Carnegie Inst. Pub. 286. Washington, D.C.

16. Weaver, J.E. 1925. Investigation of the root habits of plants. Amer. Jour. Bot. 12:502-509.

17. Whitcomb, Carl E. 1969. Ph.D. Dissertation, Iowa State University, Ames, Iowa.

18. Whitcomb, Carl E. 1971. Maximizing tree growth. Horticulture 69:44, 45, 52.

19. Whitcomb, Carl E. Speeding up slow-growing trees. The Golf Superintendent 39:20-22.

20. Whitcomb, Carl E. 1972. Influence of tree root competition on growth response of four cool season turfgrasses. Agron. Jour. 64:355-359.

21. Whitcomb, Carl E. 1973. Establishing trees and turfgrass together. The Golf Supt. 41:28-29.

22. Whitcomb, Carl E. 1981. Response of woody landscape plants to bermudagrass competition and fertility. Jour. of Arboriculture 7:191-194.

23. Whitcomb, Carl E. and E.C. Roberts. 1973. Competition between established tree roots and newly seeded Kentucky bluegrass. Agron. Jour. 65:126-129.

24. Whitcomb, Carl E., E.C. Roberts and Roger Q. Landers. 1969. A connecting pot technique for root competition investigations between woody plants or between woody and herbaceous plants. Ecology 50:326-329.

25. Youngner, V.B. 1959. Environmental factors affecting bermuda-grass growth and dormancy. Calif. Turfgrass Culture 4:19-20.

CHAPTER 19

COMPETITION BETWEEN WOODY PLANTS AND GROUND COVERS

A Study of Tolerance and Suppression - - 298

Literature Cited - - - - - - - - - - - 309

Competition Between Woody Plants and Ground Covers

A Study of Tolerance and Suppression. With the exception of some general observations, there have been few studies to determine if there are beneficial relationships that could be exploited between specific ground covers and trees. In addition to determining what ground cover will grow best beneath a particular tree species, it seems plausible that some ground covers might aid in the establishment and growth of a tree if the two were planted at the same time.

In a study with cottonwood (*Populus deltoides*) and silver maple (*Acer saccharinum*) the interactions between trees and three ground covers were studied (2). Bare root trees six to eight feet tall (2 to 2.7 meters) with at least four roots were obtained in order to use the connecting pot technique developed by Whitcomb et al. (6)

Trees were planted in five-gallon containers with four root tips extending outside the container and into the drainholes of one-gallon plastic containers. Ground covers were planted into three of the four smaller containers. The remaining small container was kept free of ground covers and weeds and was used as a control. Additional small containers were planted to ground covers without the presence of tree roots to also serve as controls (Figure 19.1).

The ground covers were dwarf bamboo (*Sasa pigmaea*), liriope (*Liriope muscari*), and English ivy (*Hedera helix*). The growth of the ground covers was evaluated by measuring length of new growth and top and root weights when the study was terminated after seven months. The competition effect on the trees was evaluated by weight of root development in the small containers with or without ground covers.

Roots of cottonwood trees reduced English ivy top and root weights by 44% and 60% and liriope top and root weights by 38% and 32%. By contrast, dwarf bamboo top weight was not affected but root weight was reduced 20% by presence of cottonwood roots.

Figure 19.1. Arrangement of trees (in large containers) and ground covers in small containers. In the lower right two containers of liriope can be observed. The more dense foliage has no tree root competition (right) while foliage of the liriope, competing with silver maple is more sparse.

Roots of silver maple trees had no effect on top and root weight of English ivy or liriope, however, liriope tuber production increased 28% when the silver maple roots were present. By contrast, dwarf bamboo top and root weight and number of rhizomes were reduced 0%, 43%, and 50%, respectively, when silver maple roots were present.

The contrasting roles of the two tree species is intriguing. Both tree species are vigorous growers with fibrous root systems, yet cottonwood roots depressed the growth of English ivy and liriope but had no effect on dwarf bamboo while silver maple reduced the growth of dwarf bamboo but had no effect on English ivy and liriope.

It is interesting to note the effect of the ground covers on root development of the trees. Cottonwood root development was reduced 32% by English ivy, 19% by liriope and 24% by dwarf bamboo, while silver maple roots were reduced 64%, 49%, and 0% by the English ivy, liriope and dwarf bamboo, respectively (Table 19.1). The fact that both cottonwood roots and ground cover development were reduced to varying degrees by the presence of the other, suggests a difference between the compatibility and competitiveness of some species. This is further supported by the dramatic reduction of silver maple root weight by the English ivy while English ivy growth was not affected by the silver maple. The reverse occurred with the dwarf bamboo in that the silver maple suppressed the dwarf bamboo, but the bamboo did not restrict root development of the silver maple.

Table 19.1. Root growth of trees with and without ground covers.

	No competition	English ivy	Liriope	Dwarf bamboo
Cottonwood	35 grams	23 grams	28 grams	26 grams
% reduced		-32%	-19%	-24%
Silver maple	77 grams	27 grams	40 grams	72 grams
% reduced		-65%	-40%	-5%

Based on the results obtained, Shoup and Whitcomb (1, 3, 4) conducted a more elaborate study in an attempt to better understand the relationship between trees and ground covers. The trees in this study were selected for their varying types of root systems, (i.e., fibrous vs coarsely structured), shade density and landscape popularity. Ground covers were chosen on their abilities to withstand shade, their classification (both monocots and dicots), type of root systems and landscape popularity.

By first establishing the ground covers in two-gallon containers, then transplanting a single, air root-pruned tree seedling into the same two-gallon container, the effects of an established ground cover on the growth and development of newly planted trees could be measured. Likewise, effects of trees on ground covers were obtained by comparing the growth response of a ground cover without competition and a ground cover grown with a particular tree.

Ten ground covers and six tree species were selected for this study. The species selected represent a wide range of adaptable landscape plants (Table 19.2).

Table 19.2. Ground covers.
----

1. Cynodon dactylon   Common bermudagrass
2. Euonymus fortunei 'Coloratus'   Evergreen euonymus
3. Festuca rubra   Red fescue
4. Hedera helix   English ivy
5. Liriope muscari   Liriope
6. Ophiopogon japonicus   Mondograss
7. Pachysandra terminalis   Japanese spurge
8. Sasa pigmaea   Dwarf bamboo
9. Vinca major   Periwinkle
10. Vinca minor   Common periwinkle

                        Trees

1. Acer saccharum 'Caddo'   Caddo sugar maple
2. Cercis chinensis   Chinese redbud
3. Pinus thunbergiana   Japanese black pine
4. Populus deltoides   Cottonwood
5. Taxodium distichum   Bald cypress
6. Ulmus parvifolia   Lacebark elm

The connecting-pot technique was modified to allow use of tree seedlings grown in bottomless milk cartons to eliminate variation experienced with field-dug bare root trees (5, 6). The milk carton seedlings were started February 1, on expanded metal benches in a greenhouse to allow them to reach a transplantable size by early June. The milk cartons measured 2 3/4 inches square by 5 inches deep for a total volume of 37.8 cubic inches.

Ground covers (with the exception of bermudagrass and fescue) were propagated asexually from cuttings or divisions between December 20, and January 15.

The ground covers were allowed to grow and establish for one month before the tree seedlings were planted directly into the same two-gallon containers. In order to avoid any disturbance to the root system of the ground covers or the trees, an aluminum can (approximately the same shape and volume as the tree seedling containers) was placed directly in the center of the two-gallon container when the ground covers were planted. Therefore, on June 20 when the tree seedlings were transplanted, the can was removed and the tree seedling was slipped into the unoccupied space.

Six different tree species were used in combinations with ten different ground covers along with two controls: a) trees without competition, and b) ground covers without competition, for a total of 62 treatments.

Environmental factors such as light, water, nutrients and available growing space were held constant among all plants. The study was conducted under a 22% shade structure. Pots were spaced on 1 1/2-foot centers to reduce plant-to-plant shading.

Before making recommendations as to types of ground covers and trees that are compatible in a landscape, it is necessary to compare both sides of the relationship (i.e., effects of tree on ground cover and effects of ground cover on tree). Since trees are long-term elements in a landscape and play a major role in creating and modifying the immediate environment, the growth of the tree should receive a higher priority than the growth of the ground cover. Height of trees and top weights of ground covers were judged the growth characteristic most useful in reflecting plant responses.

Cottonwood was by far the most severe competitor of the six tree species used. Height of cottonwood was actually stimulated when grown in the presence of most ground covers. However, considering effects of trees on ground covers, it becomes apparent that the stimulated height of cottonwood was at the expense of ground cover top weight (Figure 19.2). This is similar to a parasitic type relationship, where individuals of one species benefit (cottonwoods), while individuals of another species (ground covers) are harmed. Other trees ranked according to their general degree of competitiveness were lacebark elm, bald cypress, redbud, maple and pine.

Pine seemed compatible with most ground covers used. Pachysandra, combined with pine, actually grew 53% better than pachysandra grown alone. However, looking at effects of ground covers on height of pine, this additional growth of pachysandra was at the expense of pine height, which was reduced by 24% over pines grown alone.

Figure 19.2. Growth of vinca minor with pine (left), with cottonwood (center), and alone (right). Pine and vinca minor were especially compatible.

303

Ground covers as a group had only a slight restriction on tree performance. Instead, relations seemed to be more species specific. For example, Japanese black pine and lacebark elm were reduced in height 47% and 36%, respectively, by bermudagrass. Maple top weights and heights were only moderately reduced by bermudagrass, however, the root system was only a fraction of the control (Figure 19.3). Cottonwood was slightly restricted (13%), but redbud was actually taller when bermudagrass was present.

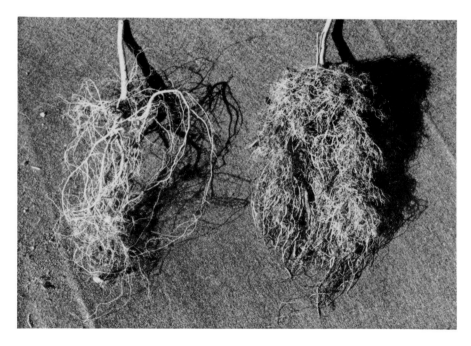

Figure 19.3   Roots of sugar maple with bermudagrass competition (left) and no competition (right).

The effects of liriope on height of tree seems to show another species-specific relationship. The elm and cottonwood were virtually unaffected by the presence of liriope. However, redbud and pine were restricted 49% and 39%, respectively. Looking at the opposite side of the effects, liriope top weight was restricted by 23% and 60% when combined with redbud or cottonwood. However, pines actually promoted a slight (6%) increase in liriope top weight. Also fescue was severely restricted by elm and cottonwood, but not by pine (Figure 19.4).

Figure 19.4. Growth of Kentucky 31 fescue with pine (left), alone (second from left), elm (second from right) and cottonwood (right). Fescue grew very little after elm and cottonwood seedlings were placed in the large containers.

Since trees are much more likely to be the established plant in a landscape, recommendations from this study are for ground covers that appear to be most compatible with the six tree species used (Table 19.3). Growth of some of the ground covers was restricted; however, density and visual quality remained acceptable.

Some of the results were confusing and hard to understand. For example, how could Chinese redbud withstand competition from bermudagrass when all other tree species used were restricted, some of which were much more vigorous growers (elm, cypress, cottonwood)? Is it related to the fact that redbuds, being a member of the legume family, are able to fix nitrogen in the nodules of their root system? The competition between redbud and bermudagrass for nitrogen might be reduced or could the large leaf surface area of the redbud have restricted sufficient amounts of light to have reduced the vigor of the sun-loving bermudagrass? A further example is cottonwood, which severely restricted growth of all ground covers except pachysandra. Why was pachysandra able to compete reasonably well with cottonwood when all other ground covers failed?

This study obviously raised more questions than it answered, but, there must be a beginning point if relationships between trees and ground covers, the two most functional elements in a landscape, are to ever be understood and utilized. The tree-ground cover relationships in Tables 19.3 and 19.4 should be considered as suggestions only. Remember these studies were short-term and confined to containers. These species may react somewhat differently in a landscape setting.

Table 19.3. Summary of the effects of trees on ground covers.

Compatible   Non-compatible

Bermudagrass
1. Pine   1. Cottonwood
2. Cypress   2. Elm
                              3. Maple
                              4. Redbud

Fescue
1. Pine   1. Cottonwood
2. Maple   2. Elm
3. Redbud   3. Cypress

Dwarf bamboo
1. Pine   1. Cottonwood
                              2. Elm
                              3. Cypress
                              4. Maple

Vinca minor
1. Pine   1. Cottonwood
                              2. Elm
                              3. Cypress
                              4. Redbud

Vinca major
1. Pine   1. Cottonwood
2. Redbud   2. Elm
3. Maple   3. Cypress

English ivy
1. Pine   1. Cottonwood
2. Redbud   2. Maple
3. Cypress   3. Elm

Euonymus
1. Maple   1. Cottonwood
2. Pine   2. Elm
3. Redbud
4. Cypress

Liriope
1. Maple   1. Cottonwood
2. Pine   2. Redbud
3. Cypress   3. Elm

Table 19.3 (continued)

Compatible	Non-compatible
Pachysandra	
1. Pine	
2. Elm	
3. Cypress	
4. Redbud	
5. Maple	
Mondograss	
1. Pine	1. Cottonwood
2. Maple	2. Cypress
	3. Elm
	4. Redbud

Table 19.4. Ground cover recommendations for specific trees.

Compatible	Non-compatible
Bald cypress	
1. English ivy	1. Dwarf bamboo
2. Pachysandra	2. Bermudagrass
Lacebark elm	
1. English ivy	1. Bermudagrass
2. Pachysandra	2. Liriope
3. Euonymus	
Japanese black pine	
1. Vinca major	1. Bermudagrass
2. English ivy	2. Liriope
3. Pachysandra	
4. Euonymus	
Cottonwood	
1. Pachysandra	1. Bermudagrass
	2. Liriope
	3. English ivy
	4. Fescue
Maple	
1. Euonymus	1. Bermudagrass
2. Pachysandra	2. Liriope
Redbud	
1. Fescue	1. Liriope
2. Vinca major	2. Vinca minor
3. Bermudagrass	
4. Dwarf bamboo	

Literature Cited

1. Shoup, Steve and Carl E. Whitcomb. 1980. Interactions between trees and ground covers. Okla. Agri. Exp. Sta. Res. Rept. P-803:24-25.

2. Shoup, Steve and Carl E. Whitcomb. 1981. Interactions between trees and ground covers. Jour. of Arboriculture. 7:186-187.

3.   Shoup, Steve and Carl E. Whitcomb. 1981. Trees and ground covers. Okla. Agri. Exp. Sta. Res. Rept. P-818:56-59.

4. Shoup, Steve and Carl E. Whitcomb. 1981. Relationships between landscape trees and ground covers.   Nursery Res. Conf. Proc. 26:262-263.

5.   Whitcomb, Carl E. 1969. Effects of root competition between trees and turf grasses.   Ph.D. dissertation, Iowa State University, Ames, Iowa.

6.   Whitcomb, Carl E., Eliot C. Roberts and Roger Q. Landers. 1969. A connecting pot technique for root competition investigations between woody plants or between woody and herbaceous plants. Ecology 50:326-329.

CHAPTER 20

WEED CONTROL

The Basics - - - - - - - - - - - - - - - 311

Pre-Emergent Herbicides - - - - - - - 315

Post-Emergent Herbicides - - - - - - - 326

Complications with Roundup - - - - - - 331

Root-absorbed Roundup - - - - - - - - 331

Grass Specific Herbicides - - - - - - 334

Chemicals to Avoid - - - - - - - - - 334

Soil Sterilization - - - - - - - - - 334

Charcoal and Herbicide Damage - - - - 340

Studying the Problem - - - - - - - - 340

Incorporation of Charcoal Helps - - - 343

Literature Cited - - - - - - - - - - - 346

Weed Control

The Basics. Weed control is very important. Since most weeds are very aggressive, they compete for the water and nutrients that would otherwise be used by landscape plants and can suppress growth of most trees and shrubs. Weeds have been defined in many ways, but perhaps the most functional definition of a weed is "a thoroughly successful plant". In that sense, weeds are capable of utilizing and responding to the cultural conditions more than most landscape plants. Grassy weeds have a far more fibrous root system and thus are more severe competitors than broadleaf weeds (Figure 20.1). Wilburn and Rauch (20) found that growth of pyracantha and juniper plants in containers were restricted by 24% in the presence of bittercress (*Cardamine* spp.), pigweed (*Amaranthus retroflexus*), and curled dock (*Rumex crispus*). Later Fretz (6) found that one redroot pigweed could reduce the growth of a Japanese holly by as much as 44%. These findings emphasize the importance of weed control if maximum plant growth and quality are to be obtained.

When professional nurserymen and landscape personnel are asked their principle method of weed control, they generally reply, "herbicides". However, herbicides **should not** be the principle emphasis of a weed control program. Mulches and other weed suppressing techniques should be the first line of defense. Weeds are thoroughly successful plants and can tolerate growing conditions that would be unsuitable for most landscape plants (Figure 20.2). Because of their success in adverse conditions, they become very aggressive in an array of locations. These locations often serve as the principle sources of weed seed to be blown by the wind, carried by birds, rain or irrigation water or if those weed seeds fall into surface water systems, additional spread of weeds can occur through irrigation systems.

Within the arsenal of weed control methods, pre-emergent herbicides (those applied prior to weed seed germination), post-emergent herbicides (those that kill existing plants) and soil sterilants (those chemicals that eliminate all vegetation from a particular site) should be considered in combination with other management practices in and around the landscape site. Certainly the safest and most effective of these three herbicide approaches is the use of pre-emergent herbicides. There are, however, some herbicides such as Ronstar (oxidiazon) and Goal (oxyfluorfen), that are principally pre-emergent in nature but also have some post-emergent properties in that they will also kill very small

311

weeds of some species, even after the seed has germinated (20) (Figure 20.3). This can be particularly advantageous since one can wait until small weeds are noticed before making the next application of herbicides without having to go to the additional labor and expense of hand pulling the weeds. There is, however, the additional risk of foliar damage to the landscape plants in the area when using herbicides with post-emergent property. Damage is less likely with most pre-emergent herbicides with no post-emergent activity (2, 3, 5, 23). In bed and mulch areas, combinations of pre- and post-emergent herbicides can be very useful. For example, tank mixtures of Treflan and Roundup where Roundup kills the current weeds and Treflan prevents further weed seed from germinating.

Figure 20.1. Grassy weeds develop aggressive root systems, even when small. A young goosegrass (**Eleusine indica**) seedling has become established in a container and looks relatively innocent (above), however, even before the top of the plant reaches a menacing size, the root system is very extensive and is a very aggressive competitor for water, nutrients and oxygen (below).

313

Figure 20.2. A tear in the polyethylene cover of a nursery holding area provides an entry for weeds. Soon these plants will produce seeds to spread throughout the nursery.

Figure 20.3. Weeds, mostly prostrate spurge (**Euphorbia supina**), were 1/4 to 1/2 inch tall when Ronstar was applied. Treated with Ronstar (left), and untreated (right) five weeks later.

314

Currently, the safest and most effective pre-emergent herbicides for landscape use are: Treflan (trifluralin), Ronstar (oxidiazon), Goal (oxyfluorfen), Surflan (oryzalin), Princep (simazine), Devrinol (napropamide), Casoron (dichlobenil), Gallery and Snapshot. These are not registered for use on all plant materials, only certain species. Always check the label to be certain the herbicide is registered and cleared for use on the particular crop plant in question. This may not always be possible in that a particular planting may contain 20 species, four of which are not labeled. Under these practical circumstances, it is proceed at your own risk, since no liability can be implied or assumed by the manufacturer when the herbicide is used on species not listed on the label. It is important to conduct trials of the herbicide(s) considered, on all species of plants being grown.

Herbicides vary in their phytotoxicity or potential to damage plants depending on air temperature, watering practices, nature of the soil, perhaps nutrient levels and other factors. Therefore, there are probably plants with an adequate tolerance to an herbicide that because of some question under some particular circumstance, have been left off the registration label. Under your circumstances, the tolerance of the crop to a specific herbicide may be sufficiently different that you may wish to assume the liability for using that herbicide. Regardless of the rules, procedures, and regulations dealing with the applications of herbicides, discretion of the individual manager must prevail in practical situations. It is illogical to assume that because a few species are not on the label the herbicide should not be used. Somewhere the judgement and responsibility must lie with the individual as to whether or not the potential of injury from the herbicide outweighs the difficulty of otherwise using less efficient herbicides or other methods of controlling weeds.

Pre-Emergent Herbicides. Pre-emergent herbicides are generally available and most safely applied as either wettable powders (WP), emulsifiable concentrates (EC), or as granular formulations (G). Whether a particular herbicide is available as a WP or EC generally depends on the chemistry of the compound involved and the necessary processes in manufacturing. Be cautious when using herbicides marked E.C. or emulsifiable concentrate. In numerous cases it has been found that the pre-emergent herbicide does not cause injury to the crop plant. However, the benzine or other organic chemical carriers and solvents that comprise part of the liquid may cause foliage injury. On the other hand, if the same herbicide is applied as a wettable powder, which does not contain the organic solvent, injury is less likely to occur.

Because of the difficulty of uniformly applying a very precise rate of herbicide around or among plants with spray equipment, several herbicides are available in the granular form. The granular formulations are more expensive since additional manufacturing effort is required, as opposed to the EC or WP form, but in many cases are worth the expense.

Granular herbicides are on some type of carrier or granule such as calcined clay, sand, ground corn cobs, vermiculite or other materials. The granule is simply a mechanism for carrying the herbicide onto the surface of the soil in a convenient manner. Granular herbicides are typically 2%, 4% or 5% active chemical on the carrier granule. Ronstar, for example, is commonly available as a 2% granule, thus for every 100 pounds of herbicide granules, there are two pounds of actual Ronstar herbicide. The importance of getting the right rate of herbicide applied at the right time cannot be over-emphasized and is essential for successful pre-emergent weed control. Be cautious of herbicides where the granule consists of 6%, 8% or 10% concentration. In those cases, there will be an insufficient number of granules to allow even dispersal of the herbicide over the soil surface.

In research studies, it has been shown that high concentration granules frequently miss spots allowing weeds to escape (23). The function of the herbicide granule is to carry one herbicide in a convenient mechanism onto the soil surface, then with one or more irrigation(s) or rainfall, release the herbicide on the surface of the soil. When the herbicide concentration is low and the granules are many, each granule releases a small amount of herbicide onto a specific area, however, when the concentration increases and the herbicide granules are fewer, voids or skips are more likely to occur. It is true that the major cost of granular herbicides is the shipping and handling, however, the relative cost of the chemical and the granular formulation proportionate to the value of the weed control and labor requirement of cultivating, pulling weeds by hand, or applying post-emergent chemicals, more than justifies this slight increase in expense.

Numerous devices have been developed to aid in the dispersal of granular herbicides. Probably the most widely used procedure is the cyclone or whirlybird-type spreader. This is an apparatus normally on two wheels with a handle or carried around the neck

316

and shoulders of the applicator, or attached to the back of a small tractor and holds a few pounds of the herbicide (Figure 20.4). A small gate or opening in the bottom of the hopper containing the herbicide can be adjusted to allow a flow of the dry granules onto a spinning propeller-type apparatus either hand- or motor-powered which spins. The herbicide granules contact ribs or branches on the propeller apparatus and are thrown either to the left or to the right, depending on the design of the equipment.

Figure 20.4. When a cyclone or whirlybird-type spreader is used to spread granular herbicides over small plants in containers or in narrow rows, 1/2 the application rate should be applied from one side of a row or block of plants and 1/2 from the other side. This provides a more uniform distribution and prevents blank spots caused by the plant canopy. In other nursery and landscape situations, this split application procedure is not necessary.

Three key factors are important in calibrating an apparatus of this type:

    1) the size of the opening releasing the herbicide onto the spinning plate,

    2) the speed at which the plate is being turned, particularly if it is being cranked by hand and

    3) the forward speed of the individual or machine applying the herbicide.

An additional technique that helps in uniform dispersal of the herbicide is to split applications. Once the horizontal spread of the herbicide granule is determined with a particular speed of the hand crank of the apparatus, calculate the rate of application of 1/2 of the desired rate. The approach is to apply 1/2 of the rate of the herbicide in one direction and apply the other 1/2 over the same landscape bed, field row, or blocks of plants in containers in the other direction. Cyclone or whirlybird herbicide applicators are not uniform in distribution of granules from near the operator to the farthest point of horizontal spread. Therefore, when an area is covered on the left side for example, the plants nearest the operator will receive a lower rate. However, when this is reversed and a second one-half rate application is made over the same bed area or block of plants, the plants that previously got the light rate, now get the heavy rate and vice versa. This helps compensate for the unevenness of distribution from the spreader and also compensates for some deflection of the granules by the top of the plants. Deflection of granules by plants that are relatively tall or bushy, must be considered.

In calibrating the granular herbicide spreader, it is important to train a very conscientious employee, since the rate of herbicide applied and the accuracy of the distribution is very important. Using a hand spreader, it is helpful in calibrating and likewise in the routine distribution of granular herbicides, to sing or think of a favorite marching song. Unimportant as this may seem at the moment, it allows the person to establish a particular rhythm in turning the hand crank which propels the horizontal distribution of the granules and provides a repeatable pace or walking speed. Lullabies work poorly, whereas marches are especially effective. With a small tractor, use the same gear and engine speed each time to assure a consistent forward and pto (power take off) speed.

One effective procedure for calibrating a granular herbicide spreader, either hand- or machine-powered, is as follows:
   a) Weigh a known amount of herbicide, for example, one-half pound.
   b) Place this in the hopper of the spreader.
   c) Guess what may be an appropriate opening or setting of the discharge gate at the bottom of the applicator.
   d) Proceed with the normal walk and hand crank speed of the applicator or at an appropriate tractor speed with the gate open, over a parking lot, driveway or other open area

318

where distribution of the herbicide granules can be observed.

e) Measure the length and width of the herbicide coverage.

f) Determine the rate of herbicide per unit area of surface.

g) If the herbicide rate is too high, reduce the opening of the gate at the bottom of the hopper, put in another one-half pound (any known amount) of herbicide and repeat the procedure. On the other hand, if the rate is too low, increase the opening of the hopper and proceed to a second trial. Several tries may be required before the proper rate of herbicide distribution is reached. Remember that if you choose the split application procedure, 1/2 would be applied on one side of a planting and 1/2 on the other, so the discharge rate would also be 1/2.

The same technique can be used for calibrating other spray applicators. Additional information on sprayer calibration is readily available from county agents and sprayer manufacturers.

Granular herbicides should be applied only when the foliage is dry (Figure 20.5). If moisture droplets, either from irrigation, rainfall, dew or gutation, are present on the leaves at the time the herbicide granules are applied, some release of the herbicide may begin. The most desired procedure is to apply granular herbicides when the foliage is dry and just prior to a normal irrigation or rainfall. With rainfall or the normal quantity of overhead watering, the granule may be dislodged or the herbicide will be leached from the granule and thus carried onto the soil, preventing plant injury. This is especially true with granular herbicides applied to crops such as yucca, liriope or other plant species that have foliage in rosettes or dense whirls that may catch and trap granules (Figure 20.6). In some cases, it may be necessary to avoid using granular herbicides on these species and use a spray instead.

Figure 20.5.   When leaf surfaces are dry, the herbicide granules may stick but are quickly washed off by irrigation water.   On the other hand, if water is present on the leaf, the granules may release a portion of the herbicide and cause plant damage.

Figure 20.6. *Entrapment of granules of Ronstar, Goal, Rout or Ornamental Herbicide I or II by the whirl of yucca leaves will cause injury. Use the EC or flowable formulation or an herbicide that does not cause leaf burn such as Treflan 5G over plants that may trap or hold granules.*

Pre-emergent compounds such as Treflan can be applied to some woody landscape plants two times during the growing season (Figure 20.7), if necessary, with little, if any, detrimental effect. Probst (17) reported no buildup of Treflan in the soil occurs with time. Treflan treatments of five pounds active ingredient per acre (aia) gave increases in top weights of 150%, 50%, 50% and 120% over no herbicide controls and increases in root weights of 130%, 40%, 40% and 100% over controls for variegated pittosporum, green pittosporum, ligustrum, and juniper, respectively, grown in containers. In no case did the highest rate of Treflan suppress top or root growth of test shrubs below that of the hand-weeded control, nor was visual damage noted on any test plant. The rate of Treflan per acre would be 1.5 to 2.5 pounds for field soils. Treflan is a safe and effective herbicide for weed control in containers and most field nursery and landscape situations when applied properly (14, 24, 27).

Figure 20.7. Fine, fibrous roots are more susceptible to herbicide injury than larger roots, yet the fine, fibrous roots play the major role in water and nutrient absorption. If root injury from pre-emergent herbicides is suspected, check the fine roots.

Unfortunately, the weed population in any given area is constantly shifting and with the use of herbicides, the shift is accelerated (5). For example, if an herbicide controls all weeds except prostrate spurge, in a short time prostrate spurge goes from a very minor weed to a major problem. With the elimination of competition from other weeds, the weed(s) missed by the herbicide produce more seeds and become more aggressive (Figure 20.8).

The activity of pre-emergent herbicides is affected by media raised beds or planters or field soil type (4, 13). Moles and Whitcomb (15) showed that as long as ground pine bark was a component in a container growth medium, Ronstar did not leach even after repeated heavy waterings. However, if only peat and sand were used, Ronstar continued to leach downward with successive waterings.

Figure 20.8.   Above, the pre-emergent herbicide controlled all weeds except two pigweeds.   If these are allowed to go to seed, next year there will be more pigweed to contend with, assuming the same herbicide is used.   Below, this plot was treated with an herbicide that controlled nearly all weeds except prostrate spurge.   After two seasons, a minor weed became a major problem. These examples are from field nurseries, however, the same conditions occur in the landscape.

323

The Ronstar was "tied up" on the bark in some manner which provides a "slow-release" mechanism. This slow-release mechanism increases the safety factor for the crop plant by retarding downward leaching of the herbicide, plus, it appears to prolong effectiveness of the herbicide, thus extending the weed control. This observation of long-term weed control has been reported by Weatherspoon and Curry (21, 22) and others (15, 19, 26). **This mechanism works equally well with mulches in plant beds.**

As organic matter and/or clay content of a soil increases, the rate of pre-emergent herbicide must increase in order to obtain weed control similar to a sandy loam soil. This is related to the greater surface area and chemical attachment sites as a result of the organic matter or clay. The reverse is also true.

It is impossible for someone to predict precisely how an herbicide will perform under the conditions of a specific landscape.

In general, as the water solubility of a pre-emergent herbicide increases, so does its susceptibility to downward movement by water. When dealing with an array of species, such as in a nursery, use only pre-emergent herbicides very insoluble in water (generally less than 1 ppm). Plants are compatible with herbicides either by being tolerant to the herbicide, or by avoiding herbicide/root contact. A good example of plant tolerance of an herbicide exists in the case of junipers, taxus and most species of pine and the pre-emergent herbicide, Princep (simazine). With these species, Princep can be used at a rate that would stunt or kill sensitive woody species such as crapemyrtle, hibiscus, flowering quince, lilac, forsythia and many other species, yet these conifers are not adversely affected and weed control is likely to be good. The bad news is that if the conifers are the only plants considered and a susceptible species is growing in the same area, there may be plant damage.

The other option is to use an herbicide that is very insoluble such as Treflan, Ronstar or Goal, whereby the herbicide stays at or near the soil surface and **away** from the roots. In addition, these herbicides are generally more quickly broken down by microorganisms, thus little, if any, residue remains in the soil after one season.

To demonstrate the importance of this, the author has used Goal and Treflan among crapemyrtle which are very sensitive to herbicides. When the Goal or Treflan was rototilled or cultivated into the soil, plant stunting occurred. However, when the herbicides were left on the soil surface, the plants grew just as well as the untreated control plots where weeds were controlled by frequent sprays of the contact herbicide, cocodylic acid. Keep in mind that on 20 acres of landscape, there may be 50 or more species of plants, whereas, if the entire field was planted to cotton, corn or peanuts, only one species is involved and an herbicide specific for that crop could be used.

When the cultural practices stimulate vigorous plant growth which in turn quickly shades the surface of the soil, the herbicide may not have to be used a second time during the growing season or only twice instead of three times, depending on the species and circumstances. Any cultural practice that can increase plant vigor and reduce total herbicide usage and labor required to distribute herbicides or spray or pull weeds, is money in the bank.

In general, avoid incorporating pre-emergent herbicides. When pre-emergent herbicides are incorporated, two distinct complications occur: 1) the herbicides are introduced deeper into the soil, thus increasing the root/herbicide contact and 2) the rate of herbicide at the soil surface is decreased or diluted. Since most weed seed require light to germinate, it stands to reason that the greatest herbicide concentration should be at the soil surface. Likewise, since virtually all herbicides are likely to have some adverse affect on the roots of crop plants if direct contact is made, keep the herbicide and root system separated as much as possible.

Why do some companies suggest that their herbicides be incorporated? In the case of a product like Treflan, it is because the chemical is subject to decomposition by light and is also volatile when sprayed on warm surfaces. On the other hand, since Treflan is very insoluble in water, by applying it to the soil either in early spring or in the fall when the soils are cool and just before a rain which does a good job of shallow incorporation, light decomposition and volatilization can be minimized, while leaving the herbicide at or near the soil surface and away from the root zone. In short, incorporation is used as a crutch and should be avoided. Mulches protect the pre-emergent herbicides from light and heat, thus no incorporation is necessary.

HERBICIDES MUST BE APPLIED AT PRECISE RATES AT ALL TIMES. TOO LITTLE WILL PROVIDE POOR WEED CONTROL, WHEREAS, TOO MUCH MAY CAUSE SLIGHT TO SEVERE DAMAGE OR STUNTING. DON'T TAKE CHANCES, ALWAYS TEST A NEW HERBICIDE ON A SMALL PLOT OF ALL PLANTS GROWN BEFORE TREATING LARGE NUMBERS OF PLANTS.

Post-Emergent Herbicides. In general, post-emergent herbicides kill the growing plant (generally anything green), as opposed to pre-emergent herbicides that kill the germinating seed or seedling. Post-emergent herbicides are most effective when used to control weeds not controlled by pre-emergent herbicides and perennial weeds.

Several post-emergent herbicides are available:

a. Cacodylic acid (sold as Dilic, Phytar 560, Ansar and other names) is an arsenic base herbicide that kills any green plant vegetation. It is useful for controlling **annual** weeds when the air temperature is above 55 degrees F, however, it is not effective in controlling perennial weeds since even though the top of the weed will be killed, it will quickly re-grow from the crown, rhizome or root system. The toxicity or LD-50 is 830 mg./kg. or moderately toxic (the lower the number, the greater the toxicity) (see the listing of toxicities of several herbicides and other chemicals commonly used in the appendix).

b. Paraquat, also sold as Gramoxone, is one of the most toxic herbicides available and has an LD-50 of 150. Paraquat kills any green vegetation very quickly and at any air temperature, whereas, some other post-emergent herbicides are less effective during cool weather. However, because the toxicity is high and Paraquat is suspected of accumulating in the body, **it is not recommended for use.**

c. Roundup (glyphosate) is a very effective post-emergent herbicide effective on most annual and perennial weeds. It has an LD-50 of about 5,000. Roundup is non-selective, with a few exceptions and is readily absorbed by any green plant part, especially on sunny days. Unlike cacodylic acid, which leaves a residue of arsenic in the soil, Roundup breaks down to carbon dioxide and water.

In order to obtain the most effective results from Roundup, remember the following steps (8, 25):

1. Good coverage of the weed with the spray is essential.

Good coverage and rate of Roundup are related. Good weed control will result from poor coverage and a high rate or good coverage and a low rate.

2. Roundup must be translocated to the roots of perennial weeds in order to be effective. If the weed is rapidly growing, little downward translocation is occurring and control may be poor. However, when most plants are maturing or flowering (no longer making rapid vegetative growth), translocation of carbohydrates from the leaves downward is occurring and Roundup will be most

effective. Likewise, if the weed is under drought stress, control will probably be poor.

3. Spray dry foliage on a sunny day to be most effective. However, the plant may not show any symptoms of injury for 3 to 6 days or longer. By contrast, Paraquat generally causes browning in 24 to 48 hours.

4. The lower the volume of water carrier with the Roundup, in general, the more effective it will be. It's the concentrated chemical that does the job, not the water and if so much water is used that some of the spray runs off the foliage of the weed and carries the Roundup with it, money is wasted.

5. Roundup is an acid and will react with galvanized and mild steel and release hydrogen gas which is explosive. In addition, the Roundup is modified to ferrous glyphosate which has no effect on weeds. Use only spray tanks of plastic, fiberglass, aluminum or stainless steel.

6. Fall applications are much more effective than spring applications on problem perennial weeds such as Johnsongrass, bermudagrass, nutsedge and field bindweed, than spring applications because of the strong downward translocation.

7. Some species of the rose family: pyracantha, rose, peach, pear, flowering quince, etc.; also bald cypress and forsythia are very sensitive to Roundup at very low rates.

8. Rodeo is Roundup without the surfactant and is labeled for aquatic weeds. It is very effective on cattails and other weeds around the edges of water reservoirs and in moist or seepy areas.

9. As soon as an area is sprayed with Roundup to kill perennial weeds or a mix of annual and perennial weeds, provision should be made for the re-growth of weeds from seeds that are present on the site. As soon as the existing vegetation is killed and exposes the soil surface, more weed seeds will germinate (Figure 20.9). In some areas, a pre-emergent herbicide may be mixed with the Roundup or applied later to control the germinating weed seeds. Check with a Monsanto representative for pre-emergent herbicides that are compatible with Roundup.

Figure 20.9. The grassy weeds in the rows were sprayed with Roundup. With the death of the grassy weeds and exposure of the soil surface, other weed seed will germinate. In order to be most effective, a good pre-emergent herbicide should be mixed with the Roundup. Where vegetation exists on the soil surface, a Roundup/Treflan mix works well since the dead weeds reduce the light decomposition and volatility of the Treflan. This works especially well in landscape situations.

In a few situations, Roundup can be used over the top or around a few landscape plants. Junipers, pines and yucca appear to be tolerant **as long as new growth is not present** (Figure 20.10).

Care must be used when spraying Roundup around many young trees and shrubs. Nick the stem of many woody plants and the inner bark is green. Even though the stem may be brown or gray, if the bark has not yet developed the corky outer bark layer, it will absorb Roundup.

One of the unique things is that Roundup absorbed by the stem of a young tree in August will not show up as damage until the following spring (Figure 20.11). Because of the delay, the injury is frequently blamed on other factors.

328

Figure 20.10. When junipers are not making active top growth, Roundup can be used around them with only moderate risk. In this case, the juniper was overgrown with bermudagrass and there was no practical way to treat the weed without getting Roundup on the shrub (above). By waiting until late summer when the juniper had ceased top growth, Roundup was sprayed over the top, killing the bermudagrass with no juniper injury (below).

A simple spray nozzle shield can be made with any round one-gallon plastic container (Figure 20.12) Simply cut off the bottom of the container at a slight angle and cut a slit downward roughly two inches in what was the top of the bottle. Cut a piece of old water or heater hose about two inches long, then split this lengthwise to use as a bushing around the brass portion of the sprayer roughly eight to ten inches up from the nozzle. Use a radiator hose clamp to secure the plastic container onto the spray nozzle shaft and adjust up or down until the fan spray just contacts the inside of the container. With this unit, weeds adjacent to the stem of a sensitive species can be sprayed safely. It also allows spraying to be done on windy days when otherwise it would not be practical.

Figure 20.11. Roundup injury to crapemyrtle. The plants received some Roundup when weeds were sprayed around the base in July, August, or September. This abnormal and dwarf growth appeared the following spring. Depending on the dosage, the plant will either die or slowly recover.

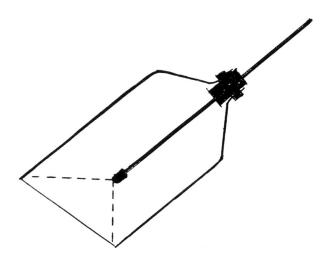

Figure 20.12. A round one-gallon container can be modified to make a very inexpensive, yet effective shield for spraying Roundup and other post-emergent herbicides.

Complications with Roundup. Roundup is quickly adsorbed by soils. Even microscopic clay particles in water used to mix the spray solution can reduce the effectiveness. Likewise, spraying weeds covered with even a thin layer of dust will generally give disappointing results. Roundup effectiveness can be reduced by "hard" water and if sprays are mixed and then stored for a few days. Once spray is mixed, it should be used the same day.

Root-absorbed Roundup. During 1981, a block of seedling shumard oak were grown in a field with areas heavily infested with nutsedge (nutgrass). The trees were planted in April and the soil surface treated with Treflan for pre-emergent weed control. Drip irrigation was used and fertilizer was banded along the rows. By late summer the nutsedge in some parts of the rows was a solid sod. Roundup at the rate of five tablespoons per gallon of water (four quarts per acre) was applied to the nutsedge in late September using a hand sprayer and nozzle shield made from a plastic bottle. None of the chemical contacted the foliage or

331

stems of the trees. The nutsedge tops were killed within a week, but no injury could be detected on the oak trees prior to normal leaf drop in late October. The following spring, trees in areas that had been heavily infested with nutsedge and sprayed with Roundup had distorted leaves and made little growth the entire season even though fertility was good and drip irrigation continued. The trees did not leaf out in the spring of 1983.

During early October 1984, a dense area of honeyvine milkweed surrounded a group of two- to three-inch caliper pin oak trees on 12-foot centers. Previous treatments of this weed with Roundup at two to three tablespoons per gallon of water (two to three quarts per acre) caused moderate top dieback, but recovery the following season showed little, if any control. The honeyvine milkweed was sprayed on October 10, 1985, using Roundup at five tablespoons per gallon (four quarts per acre) using a boom sprayer on a tractor. Since the leaf surface is very glossy, a surfactant (Rhom & Haas Ag 98) was added to improve leaf wetting. Trees in all areas sprayed were seven to eight feet tall and lower branches had been removed to about three feet. The trees had been planted from five-gallon containers, two years earlier and drip-irrigated to aid establishment. No spray contacted the stems or leaves of the trees.

Leaf emergence of the trees in April 1985 was normal. However, by early June, considerable leaf injury (yellowing and death of leaf margins and some leaf distortion) was readily visible (Figure 20.13). By mid July trees in the areas where the honeyvine milkweed had been sprayed with Roundup were completely defoliated and twig dieback was visible. Trees the same age and under similar growing conditions where annual grasses and some common bermudagrass had been sprayed with the same Roundup surfactant combination at the same time did not show any injury. This is consistent with results of repeated use of Roundup to control bermudagrass in both field nurseries and landscape situations.

Figure 20.13. Injury of pin oak leaves where Roundup had been sprayed on the soil surface the previous fall to control honeyvine milkweed. This is similar to injury observed where high rates of Roundup have been used to control nutsedge adjacent to trees in nursery or landscape situations.

Nutsedge has a sizable storage organ beneath the soil surface. Honeyvine milkweed has a very extensive root system. Since roots of all plants are growing in the aerated soil near the surface, perhaps the Roundup could have been translocated from the foliage of both weed species into the soil and after the death and decomposition of the weeds, the chemical was absorbed by roots of the trees. Bermudagrass, on the other hand, has a strong rhizome near the soil surface in addition to the stolons aboveground and may not carry the Roundup into the soil in the same way or to the same depth as the other two weeds.

The likelihood of this happening seems remote, yet the trees were dead only in the areas where nutsedge and milkweed were treated with Roundup. At this point **additional caution** appears justified when using Roundup on perennial weeds with extensive roots or storage organs near woody landscape plants.

Grass Specific Herbicides. Poast and Fusilade 2000 are relatively new post-emergent herbicides that are very specific for grasses and can be safely sprayed around many woody plants. Check the label carefully to be sure your plants are listed as safe before spraying. Since grassy weeds are far more competitive and restricting of woody plant growth than broadleaf weeds, these chemicals are useful in landscape management. However, the key to success with both of these products is to apply the chemical while the grassy weeds are **small**. Once crabgrass gets six inches tall control will be slower and less acceptable. These are not substitutes for Roundup, but rather alternatives for controlling grassy weeds among landscape plants.

Over-the-top applications of Poast and Fusilade 2000 have given good grassy weed control in conjunction with an array of species of woody and broadleaf herbaceous plants with little or no injury. Check the label for species tolerant to either of these products as it is extensive.

Chemicals to avoid. Never, never, never use banvel, Dicamba, Picloram, Tordon, or commerically blended products that contain these chemicals around desirable plants in the landscape. Examples are Weedmaster, Mondak, Graslan, Spike, Tordon, Grazon. Trimec contains 40% 2, 4-D compounds plus 2.75% Dicamba and is used extensively on turf for control of broadleaf weeds. It sould be avoided in areas even remotely near desirable trees or shrubs. Grazon is a range/pasture herbicide that contains 24% picloram (a strong 2, 4-D relative) and is death on woody plants, even in very low doses by spray drift. Both the Dicamba (banvel) and Picloram (tordon) are very soluble in water and are adsorbed by soils very little, if at all. Thus, whenever water moves these chemicals can move. On one occasion, Grazon was sprayed on a pasture area according to the label. However, across the fence about 150 feet were desirable trees. The site was such that a rock layer existed about two feet deep below the sprayed area and surfaced near the drip line of the trees. The chemical moved downward then horizontal at the surface of the rock layer and killed the desirable trees. **The only safe way to use these compounds is to leave them at the chemical supply house.**

Soil Sterilization. Some landscape nurseries and contractors choose to hold plants on gravel, sea shells, or similar materials treated with herbicides. Unfortunately, most of the herbicides that are registered for soil sterilization (Karmex, simazine,

Hyvar, and Pramitol) are readily absorbed by roots. When plants are set on a gravel surface for a long period of time, some roots may grow out of the drain holes of containers or from the B & B soil mass (Figure 20.14). Since these herbicides are moderately water soluble, over a period of time with irrigation and rainfall, the herbicide leaches down and roots of weeds can survive in a shallow zone at the soil surface (Figure 20.15).

As with most herbicides, soil sterilants rarely control every weed species. As with weeds controlled by pre-emergent herbicides, the weed population on any soil area treated with soil sterilants is constantly shifting. Any weed that can tolerate the herbicide is freed from competition with other weeds and produces more seed than before and the species spreads. The spread may be slow at first but as the population builds, it can present a major weed control problem (Figure 20.16). It generally requires a shift to another herbicide or some other cultural practice that makes growing conditions less favorable to that particular weed species. In some cases where soil sterilant herbicides are used around parking lots or storage areas, the problem may be such that plastic or ground cover cloth will be required for several growing seasons in order to eliminate the problem weed. If plastic is used, do not forget about the importance of surface drainage.

*Figure 20.14. Above, a leaf of rose-of-sharon or althea (**Hibiscus syriacus**) injured by Karmex absorbed when roots grew out of a drain hole. Below, Persian lilac (**Syringa persica**) injured by simazine in the ground bed beneath the container.*

Figure 20.15. As the herbicides slowly decomposes or leaches downward, roots can survive outside of the container if left in place too long. This means greater work when lifting for shipping and more stress to the plant.

*Figure 20.16. A severe infestation of bittercress or flickweed (**Cardamine pennsylvanica**), among container nursery stock. The weed neither competes with, nor shades the plants, however, it does harbor insects, particularly aphids and mites and perhaps disease organisms and becomes a visual eyesore as well as providing a constant barrage of seed onto the surface of the growth medium since at maturity this species throws its seeds. In this case, simazine was used on the ground bed surface for many years. Slowly this species, which is tolerant to the herbicide, increased and became a major problem. It was controlled by shifting to Goal as a soil treatment at a high rate.*

In some cases, plants may be killed when the soil sterilant herbicides are applied adjacent to containers or B & B plants and rainfall or irrigation moves a sufficient quantity of the herbicide into the bottom of the container growth medium or root ball (Figure 20.17).

Figure 20.17. Mugo pine in three-gallon (11-liter) containers being held adjacent to a roadway treated with a soil sterilization rate of Hyvar X (bromacil). In this case, the containers were setting on ground cover cloth (polypropylene fabric) yet enough of the herbicide leached from the gravel into the base of the containers to kill most of the plants along the edge.

Roots of trees generally extend far beyond the outer branches. In some cases, if there are few other competing plants, roots of a tree may extend several times the distance from the trunk to the tip of the outermost branches. Because soil sterilant herbicides are generally absorbed readily by roots, especially roots of woody plants, desirable trees may be damaged (Figure 20.18).

If used carefully and with full knowledge of the destructive qualities they possess, soil sterilant-type herbicides can be safe and useful in some areas. Weeds of many species are spread by wind so weeds on ditch banks, around storage buildings and various other out-of-the-way locations can be a major source of weed seeds in the nursery or landscape. **PROCEED WITH CAUTION!**

Figure 20.18.   Herbicide damage to a tree that was part of the landscape around a nursery office building.   In this case, the soil sterilant, Pramitol (prometon) was applied to the soil surface before a parking lot was paved with asphalt (mecadum or bitumin), the next growing season the herbicide injury became severe and finally killed the tree.

Charcoal and Herbicide Damage.   Hyvar X (bromacil) is frequently used as a total vegetation control herbicide at high rates and has a half-life of more than one year (7).   There have been numerous reports of Hyvar X damage to landscape and street tree plantings.

Unsuspecting people have used Hyvar X to eliminate grass and weeds in gravel driveways or from cracks between bricks or stones in walkways or patios.   Frequently, this action damages or kills desired plants.

Hyvar X is also used to prevent weed seed germination under pavement in parking lots, sidewalks and so on.   Most pavings extend the herbicide's half-life because they reduce exposure to rain, sun and wind and reduce the oxygen level in the soil. Because microorganism activity is also reduced, the normal processes active in breaking the herbicide down are also reduced (18).

Studying the Problem.   Recommended rates of activated charcoal have not been effective in eliminating further herbicide injury to plants in heavy clay soils (1, 9, 11, 12, 16).   Shoup and Whitcomb investigated whether activated charcoal could deactivate Hyvar X if applied to soils at rates higher than normally recommended.

Another objective was to determine any potential detrimental effects to landscape plants from applying activated charcoal.

Twenty pounds active ingredient per acre of 80 percent wettable powder Hyvar X was applied to three- by six-foot plots. This is the labeled rate for complete vegetation control. Grosafe activated charcoal was applied at 0, 1, 3, and 5 pounds per 100 square feet and either left on the soil or incorporated with a rotary tiller to a depth of two inches (Figure 20.19).

Test plots were also set up to evaluate the effects of activated carbon, either incorporated or unincorporated. The experimental design was a randomized block with 16 treatments and six replications.

Hyvar X was applied to a clay loam soil with a boom sprayer on May 15, and watered in with one inch of water from overhead irrigation to reduce loss to the atmosphere.

Figure 20.19. Plot set-up of incorporated and unincor-porated charcoal. The black area is the highest rate used, which to to the applicator and when viewed following even distribution over the soil, appears to be a tremendous rate.

341

The activated carbon was applied three days later with a drop-type spreader, incorporated or left on the surface and watered-in during a two-week period with 1.5 inches from irrigation and rainfall.

One-gallon sweet mockorange (*Philadelphis coronarius*) shrubs were planted into each of the 96 test plots on June 1. Soil was removed from circular areas about 10 inches in diameter to a depth of three inches. The remaining soil removed from each planting hole was used to backfill during planting. Thus only backfill soil not contaminated with either Hyvar X or activated carbon was used. On September 21, the dead plants were removed and forsythia (*Forsythia* X intermedia) from one-gallon containers were planted with the same precautions used before. In this way, the residual activity of Hyvar X could be measured with and without the presence of activated charcoal. Because an increasing number of weeds were noticed in the test plots on June 4, 1981, the test plots were re-planted with wintercreeper (*Euonymus fortunei* 'Coloratus') from one-gallon containers.

Evaluations were made using a visual grade of 1 to 10 with 1 representing no damage and 10, a dead plant. Four people made the evaluations, and then results were averaged.

Hyvar X treatments killed all sweet mockorange within six weeks regardless of the rate of activated charcoal. However, the degrees of injury and rate of death suggest that incorporation of activated charcoal does provide some benefit.

After three weeks, the rate of one pound activated charcoal per 100 square feet was of little benefit in reducing injury, with or without incorporation. Where three or five pounds of charcoal had been incorporated, plants rated 4.1 and 2.4, respectively. However, when the same amounts were used but not incorporated, there was slightly more damage, resulting in ratings of 4.6 and 3.9.

Plots without Hyvar X and treated with activated charcoal exhibited no detrimental or beneficial effects from the charcoal.

After 35 days (on July 5), a second visual analysis was taken. All plants in plots treated with Hyvar X were dead. The higher rates of activated charcoal delayed reaction to the Hyvar X but did not prevent eventual death.

By late September, a few weed species (smooth crabgrass, pigweed and trumpet creeper) had established themselves in the plots treated with Hyvar X and three or five pounds of incorporated charcoal now planted to forsythia.

A visual rating of the forsythia on October 24 revealed herbicide damage on all plants in treated plots. The best ratings, 4.2, were found in plots where five pounds of charcoal had been incorporated. Forsythia is very sensitive to triazine herbicides.

By May 10, plants in plots treated with Hyvar X were dead or severely damaged. As before, damage was slower to develop in the plots with three and five pounds of incorporated activated charcoal.

Incorporation of Charcoal Helps. The comparison of incorporated and non-incorporated treatments is interesting (Figure 20.20). Less damage was seen on all plants at all rates of charcoal when it was incorporated than when it was not incorporated. This difference in probably due to an increase in oxygen in the soil. Microorganism activity, which breaks down the herbicide, and the contact between charcoal and herbicide both increase (18).

Figure 20.20. Forsythia treated with five pounds charcoal per 100 square feet, demonstrate how incorporating the charcoal (left) is better in delaying the effects of Hyvar X than not incorporating (right).

343

One month after planting the euonymus, a visual rating again showed all test plants in plots with Hyvar X were damaged compared to those in control plots. Ratings for the incorporated charcoal plots were 6.5, 5.2, 4.2, and 3.1 for charcoal rates of 0, 1, 3, and 5 pounds per 100 square feet, respectively. For the unincorporated charcoal plots, ratings were 9.0, 7.9, 6.2 and 4.1.

Activated charcoal has been used successfully on many less persistent herbicides than Hyvar X (9, 11, 12, 16). Although the incorporated charcoal reduced damage, injury to new plantings was severe more than one year later (Figure 20.21). Readily adsorbed residual herbicides (soil sterilants), such as Hyvar X (10), should be used only in non-productive areas where desirable plant roots are not present or are not likely to be planted.

Figure 20.21. After 14 months, all woody plants of the three species were dead in the treated plots and the study was terminated. It was interesting to note the weed growth where the charcoal had been incorporated (left and right), as opposed to where the charcoal had not been incorporated (center).

Hyvar X is also somewhat mobile in sheet erosion and should not be used for weed control in areas where runoff water could come into contact with desirable plants or surface water used for irrigation. Because no other readily available substance exists that might neutralize persistent herbicides, **using residual herbicides like Hyvar X in any areas where desirable plants exist or where vegetable, turf or landscape plants may be planted in the future is strongly discouraged.**

The activated charcoal rates used in this study were only partially effective in deactivating residual herbicides used for total vegetation control. The loss of a valuable landscape tree is a high price to pay to eliminate a few weeds from a driveway or patio. This study showed that on a heavy clay soil, activated charcoal at the rate of five pounds per 100 square feet was not effective as a short-term solution to injury caused by Hyvar X. Although high rates of incorporated charcoal reduced the rate of development of injury, all test plants eventually died in all plots treated with Hyvar X, even after one year.

Retail nurserymen and landscape contractors are frequently contacted regarding weed control in various landscapes. **Hyvar X and other soil sterilant herbicides such as Pramitol, Simazine and Karmex caused extensive damage or death and persist for several years.**

If charcoal is used to neutralize Hyvar X's effects, a rate of 7 to 10 pounds per 100 square feet or more may be necessary. Incorporation of the charcoal helps, but in most situations, this is not practical or would cause further damage. **The only sure prevention for injury induced by Hyvar X and other soil sterilant-type herbicides is to not use it on any site near landscape plants.**

Literature Cited

1. Ahrens, J.F. 1965. Detoxification of simazine and atrazine-treated soils with activated carbon. Proc. Northeast Weed Control Conf. 19:364-365.

2. Ahrens, J.F. 1966. Trials with dichlobenil and diphenimid for controlling weeds in container nursery stock. Proc. N.E. Weed Control Conf. 20:232-236.

3. Bingham, S.W. 1968. Influence of herbicides on Japanese holly and hand labor for weed control. Weeds 16:478-481.

4. Dean, S.G., Carl E. Whitcomb and C.A. Conover. 1970. Effects of media and container type on herbicidal activity in container-grown woody ornamentals. Proc. Fla. Sta. Hort. Soc. 83:502-507.

5. Fretz, Thomas A. 1972. Control of annual weeds in container-grown nursery stock. Jour. Amer. Soc. Hort. Sci. 97:667-669.

6. Fretz, Thomas A. 1972. Weed competition in container-grown *Ilex crenata* 'Convexa'. HortSci. 7:341.

7. Gardiner, J.S. et al. 1969. Synthesis and studies with 2-C14 labeled bromacil and terbacil. Jour. Agr. Food Chem. 17:980-986.

8. Goodale, Toby, Robert D. Hathaway, James D. Ward and Carl E. Whitcomb. 1977. Controlling common bermudagrass with hand applications of Roundup. Fla. Nurseryman 22(4):71-72.

9. Hasseltine, B.B. and W.H. Mitchell. 1976. Activated charcoal for turfgrass establishment. Proc. Northeast Weed Sci. Soc. 30:313-319.

10. Hilton, J.L., T.J. Monaco, D.E. Moreland and W.A. Gentner. 1964. Mode of action of substituted uracil herbicides. Weeds 12:129-131.

11. Jagschitz, J.A. 1979. Protecting turfgrass seedlings from chemical residue with activated charcoal. Proc. Northeast Weed Sci. Soc. 31:371-376.

12. Jagschitz, J.A. 1979. Charcoal's neutralizing powers. Golf Course Mgmt. 47(10):21-25.

13. Mason, D.D. and R.P. Upchurch. 1962. The influence of soil organic matter on the phytotoxicity of herbicides. Weeds 10:14-18.

14. Milbocker, Daniel C. and Henry Wilson. 1975. Dinitroanalines as nursery herbicides. Proc. SNA Nursery Res. Conf. 20:131-132.

15. Moles, Ann and Carl E. Whitcomb. 1976. Movement of Ronstar in containers as influenced by the growing media. Proc. SNA Nursery Res. Conf. 21:137.

16. Myers, H.G., W.L. Currey and D.E. Barnes. 1973. Deactivation of Kerb with sewage sludge, topdressing and activated charcoal. Proc. Fla. State Hort. Soc. 86:442-444.

17. Probst, G.W. 1967. Fate of trifluralin in soil and plants. Jour. Agri. and Food Chem. 15:592-599.

18. Torgeson, D.C. and M. Henry. 1967. Microbial degredation of bromacil. Proc. Northeast Weed Control Conf. 21:584.

19. Wadsworth, Grady L. 1975. Evaluation of eight herbicides in container nursery stock. Proc. Int. Plant Prop. Soc. 25:471-476.

20. Ward, James D., Toby Goodale and Carl E. Whitcomb. 1976. Control of prostrate spurge and other weeds in containers with a post-emergence applications of Ronstar. Okla. Agri. Exp. Sta. Nursery Res. Rept. P-741:61-62.

21. Weatherspoon, D.M. and W.L. Curry. 1975. Evaluation of Treflan, Lasso and Ronstar herbicides for use in woody ornamental nurseries. Proc. Fla. Sta. Hort. Soc. 88:535-540.

22. Weatherspoon, D.M. and W.L. Curry. 1976. Repeat applications of Treflan, Lasso and Ronstar applied separately and in combination on container ornamentals. Proc. SNA Nursery Res. Conf. 21:125-128.

23. Whitcomb, Carl E. 1976. Effects of herbicides on growth of container nursery stock. Nursery Res. Jour. 3(2):1-12.

24. Whitcomb, Carl E. 1977. A comparison of Ronstar, Lasso and Treflan for weed control in containers. Okla. Agri. Exp. Sta. Res. Rept. P-760:79-84.

25. Whitcomb, Carl E. 1978. Roundup--Effective for controlling perennial weeds. Amer. Nurseryman 147(7):11, 67-68.

26. Whitcomb, Carl E. and Carol Boyer. 1980. Activity of Ronstar (oxidiazon) in containers as affected by the growth media. Nursery Res. Jour. 6:14-18.

27. Whitcomb, Carl E. and Joel F. Butler. 1975. Performance of trifluralin, nitralin and oxyzalin in nursery containers. Jour. Amer. Soc. Hort. Sci. 100:225-229.

28. Wilburn, T.A. and R.D. Rauch. 1972. Weed competition in container-grown nursery stock. HortSci. 7:341.

CHAPTER 21

PLANTS IN LANDSCAPE CONTAINERS

Containers Are Different - - - - - - - - 350

Containers Without Bottoms - - - - - - - 351

Containers With Bottoms - - - - - - - - 359

Determining Drainable Pore Space - - - - 364

Drains and Drainage - - - - - - - - - - 365

Insulating the Root Zone - - - - - - - - 378

Literature Cited - - - - - - - - - - - - 381

Plants in Landscape Containers

Containers Are Different. Plant production in containers is relatively new and misconceptions abound. Whitcomb (8) details many aspects of these growth conditions in *Plant Production in Containers.* Many of the factors and conditions of growing plants in containers in greenhouses and nurseries apply to plants in the landscape. However, there are also some major differences. Only the key factors and those unique to containers in the landscape will be covered here.

Containers are unique and unnatural environments for plants. Because of the perched water table* and restricted root system, containers require changes and adjustments relative to growing plants in a landscape with natural soils.

Any container or structure that has a bottom (even though some do not look like containers) has a perched, abnormal water table. The deeper the container, the less critical this perched water table becomes. However, with shallow containers, especially those less than 24 to 30 inches in depth, attention to drainage/aeration factors as controlled by the porosity of the growth media ("soil" or substrate) means life or death to the plant. In containers less than 12 inches deep, normal field soils cannot be included as even part of the growth medium without dropping the aeration levels below the minimum for good root activity and plant growth. However, in containers of greater depth, soils may be used effectively **if** proper modifications and adjustments are made. This will be covered in detail later.

> * Perched water table defined: In the landscape, nearly all soils have a water table at some depth. As long as that water table is four or more feet below the surface, plant growth is generally not affected. A perched water table is one abnormally high or "perched" above the normal water table. This can happen in landscape soil situations such as in a fill where a clay layer is added and/or compacted and a lighter textured soil is placed above. Water will percolate down through the lighter soil, reach the clay layer and begin to accumulate, creating a perched water table. In a container, the same thing happens, only the abrupt textural difference is the bottom of the container. All water in the container is in various stages of contact either with particles in the soil mix or other water. These two forms of attraction of water for other surfaces are very strong

(adhesive: attraction of water for other surfaces and cohesive: the attraction of water to other water). Water will flow out of the drain holes in the bottom of the container **only** when the weight of the water above is sufficient to force out the water at the bottom of the container against the adhesive and cohesive forces. Even after part of the water exits, considerable water will remain in the bottom of the container. As soon as the weight of the water on top is no longer enough to force the water out at the bottom, drainage stops and considerable water is retained or perched at the bottom of the container (Figure 21.1). As is pointed out in further reading, if there is no bottom in the container, this restriction to water flow does not occur (Figures 21.2 and 21.3).

Containers Without Bottoms. Whenever possible, containers above ground should be constructed **without** bottoms. This can be the complete absence of a bottom or omission of as little as 30% of the bottom. When the bottom of a landscape container is partially or completely absent, good soil can be used in the container and good plant growth will result **without** the precise physical and chemical amendments required for containers **with** bottoms. The difference is due to the perched water table when a bottom is present.

*Figure 21.1.   Water exits the drain hole of a container only when the water above produces sufficient downward pressure to overcome the adhesive and cohesive forces that tend to retain the water. However, as soon as the weight of the water on top is no longer enough to force out the water at the bottom, drainage stops and considerable water is retained or perched at the bottom.   Note the dashed line across the container.   Below this line the mix is saturated while above the line, sufficient air has been drawn into the mix by the exiting water to allow active root growth.   In this case, a plastic container was cut and sealed against glass plates so the water movement could be seen and photographed.   A red dye was added to the water to enhance the contrast.   If a mix of finer texture is placed in this container, the perched water table will rise.   If a more coarse-textured mix is used, the perched water table will be lowered, **but** it will always be there.*

Figure 21.2. To demonstrate the water-retaining effect of the container bottom, metal containers were placed on a sandy soil with a conventional bottom in place (left) and with the bottom removed (right). The containers were filled with the same mix and shrubs planted. This photo was taken 24 hours after a watering. Note the dark color of the moist surface of the container with the bottom, whereas, the mix in the container without the bottom was already dry. Where the bottom was present, the water was blocked from exiting until sufficient water from above forced some of the water at the bottom out of the container. There was considerable water retained after drainage ceased. However, where the bottom was absent, the water percolated through the soil mix and into the sandy soil below with no restriction. The exit of water from the container without the bottom was further hastened by the coarse texture of the mix in the container relative to the finer texture of the sandy soil.

Figure 21.3. These three columns were 6, 12 and 18 inches deep and 6 inches in diameter and were all filled with the same growth medium or mix. Water was added to the container only 6 inches deep until water just began to exit the open wire mesh drain on the bottom. The saturated zone at the bottom was about 3.5 inches deep (see arrows on the container on the left). When the same amount of water was added to the 12- and 18-inch deep containers, the entire quantity of mix moistened by the water was also well aerated. This is because the water did not reach the bottom of the container. Note how far the quantity of water that the 6-inch deep container held, wetted the 12- and 18-inch deep containers (see arrows). The wetted mix is the same in the 12- and 18-inch deep containers because the water added was insufficient to reach the bottom. If more water had been added, the water would have begun to perch at the bottom of the 12-inch container while continuing to move down in the 18-inch. If enough water was added to cause a perched water table in both the 12- and 18-inch deep container, the depth of the perched or saturated zone in the bottom would be exactly the same as in the 6-inch deep container because it is the porosity of the mix that controls drainage.

Elevating good field soils, even heavy clay soils, above the existing soil grade will vastly improve drainage and soil aeration as long as there is no bottom in the container. Because most soils are **not** suitable for the shallow containers used widely in the container nursery and greenhouse industries, it is often assumed that only very sandy, porous soils can be used in any container, of any size or construction. This is **not** true when there is no bottom in a container. In fact, the reverse is true. For example, consider a container 30 inches deep without a bottom. (Diameter does not matter when considering soil, soil mixes or growth media in containers). The native soil is a good sandy loam that drains well. If this same soil is placed in the 30-inch deep container without a bottom, it will be **excessively** drained and the plants will often experience drought unless watering is frequent. Percolation of water through a soil is controlled by the distribution of particle sizes in the soil and the soil depth relative to the water table. When the depth of a normally well-drained sandy loam soil is increased by 30 inches (in the container), the drainage is greatly accelerated and water retention may be sufficiently limited to create droughty conditions. The drought conditions are often increased by the higher soil temperatures since the containers are above ground and are generally exposed to direct heating by sunlight or the surrounding air. Root zone temperatures in containers may be 10 to 30 degrees or more higher than the same soil a few feet away in a normal landscape situation. This dramatically increases the rate of evaporation. The fact that the soil volume is restricted means that the plant is more dependent on the available moisture in a very limited volume of soil compared to the landscape. Combined, these factors make water management much more precise than a few feet away outside the container.

A practical, partial solution to this situation would be to use a **heavier** soil with **more** clay **in the container without a bottom** to increase water retention. If a fertile clay loam soil is used, management for good plant growth becomes relatively easy (Figure 21.4).

Figure 21.4. This landscape container has only a partial bottom. As a result, a good clay loam soil was used as fill and plant growth and health is excellent with minimal maintenance. The light-colored wall of the container further aids in preventing heat buildup in summer which otherwise could injure roots which accumulate at the inner surface of the container. This raised planter was filled with a fertile but heavy clay soil and supports excellent plant growth because of the accelerated drainage as a result of the greater depth (below).

Consider another example where the normal soil on the landscape site is heavy clay which drains poorly. The tendency is to avoid further use of this soil at all costs. However, if the soil is otherwise fairly fertile and productive, elevating it in a container without a bottom will greatly improve the drainage/aeration characteristics. Good plant growth with minimal maintenance can result. Many heavy poorly drained soils are very productive soils if they are drained. They are not severely leached of nutrients and have excellent retention of added nutrients, especially nitrogen. Doubters should spend some time in Iowa where poorly drained, rich, black, heavy clay loam soils become extremely productive with the proper installation of drain tile.

Why the emphasis on soil? Because soil provides the excellent natural complex of nutrients and water adsorption and release unparalleled by any man-made soil mixes or container growth media. In 20 years of study, the author has yet to obtain the same quality of plant growth in any growth medium as that which occurs in only moderately good soils.

Water moves in soils by capillarity, the adhesive and cohesive forces. Gravity comes into play only under saturated conditions. Consequently, the omission or removal of only a portion of the bottom of an above-ground container will allow drainage as though the entire bottom is absent. The water moves down to the partial bottom; water in the soil above the area with no bottom drains through readily; the water in the soil above the bottom portions then moves horizontally and down as though no bottom were present in the entire container (Figure 21.5). Whenever possible, in new construction, removal of 30% or more of the bottoms of above-ground containers makes plant management much easier. **Under no circumstances should gravel be placed in the bottom**, since this abrupt change in soil texture causes a perched water table just as though the bottom were intact and made of plastic or concrete.

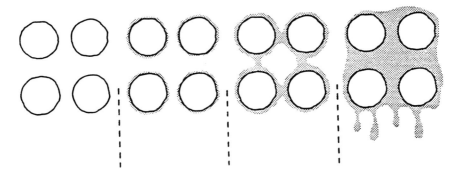

Figure 21.5. A productive soil or soil mix is approximately 25% air space and 25% water and 50% soil or mix particles. Water attaches to the surfaces of soil or soil mix particles (second from left) as the moisture level increases, air is only in the large spaces between particles (second from right). When the soil or soil mix is saturated, all air is excluded. The occasionally brief saturation of the soil or soil mix is not harmful as long as the excess water drains and the two center moisture-soil or soil mix conditions return.

Landscape containers **below** the surrounding soil grade can have problems just the reverse of above-ground containers. For example, if the surrounding soil is heavy clay and the below-grade container is filled with a good clay loam soil, drainage and aeration may be fair or poor, depending on the water table and/or distance above less permeable layers. If the soil placed in the container is of finer texture than the surrounding soil, water may drain into the container instead of away. When working with below-grade containers, proper drainage is a must and each situation must be evaluated independently. Interestingly, in many of these situations, having a bottom in a container may be an advantage (Figure 21.6).

Figure 21.6. The natural soil grade is at the top of the vertical wall. The planter/container is about five feet below the soil surface. If the retaining wall at the back is solid to the same depth as the container in the foreground, it can be treated as a container without a bottom. However, if the tall vertical wall extends only partially to the bottom of the foreground container, drainage characteristics can be radically changed.

Containers With Bottoms. When containers must have bottoms, the soil mix or growth medium must be designed carefully and the texture **must** be adjusted relative to the depth. A very common error in filling above-ground landscape containers with bottoms is to use soil mixes or growth media similar to those commonly used in greenhouses and container nurseries. These growth media are often 50 to 100 percent organic matter (peat, pine or hardwood bark, sawdust, etc.) Since the container depth in nurseries and greenhouses is very shallow, and the plants are in these containers for only a short time (rarely more than two years), the organic matter provides the drainage/aeration required and lasts long enough for the production of the crop. **However**, in landscape containers, plants remain in the same container for many years. (Note: Since most die within two to four years, this is not a true statement, but it is what is expected or desired.)

When organic matter is used in landscape containers, for the first one to two years all appears favorable. However, as the organic matter decomposes, the size of the structural particles becomes smaller and smaller which means a greater depth of water is retained above the bottom (the perched water table). Furthermore, as the organic matter decomposes, the volume of the growth medium decreases so the depth of the growth medium becomes less which also means a greater retention of water and a further decrease in aeration (Figure 21.7). This is further complicated by the fact that plant roots grow between the particles, in the air spaces, thus the longer the plant is in the same container, the more the roots infiltrate the spaces between particles and reduce aeration. Root growth is, of course, essential and the porosity of the container growth medium must be great enough to allow for good root growth and still retain adequate aeration. When aeration is marginal, root growth hastens the onslaught of plant stress by restricting aeration.

In order to maintain good plant health in above-ground containers, **permanent, non-organic** soil amendments must be used in order to avoid the decomposition, shrinkage and aeration problems. In containers 16 or more inches deep, soil may comprise a portion of the mix if weight is not a restricting factor as often occurs in roof gardens. When considering load (weight), remember that water is very heavy (62.43 pounds per cubic foot) and the mix must contain some water at all times to support plant life. In addition, the **maximum** load will occur during or just after a hard rain when extra water builds up temporarily before draining to the water table level which is controlled by the texture (porosity) of the mix and depth of the container.

Examples of non-organic soil amendments are: vermiculite, perlite, styrofoam beads, calcined or baked clays also called zeolite, clinolite, turface, oil dry and other trade names, sand and pea gravel.

Vermiculite holds water and nutrients well but easily compresses and packs, thus loses its capacity to aerify the soil and improve drainage.

Figure 21.7. The pines in this roof garden/parking complex are struggling from decomposition of the organic mix which has reduced aeration to the critical level. The ground cover junipers are still attractive, but eventually they will begin to decline from the same problem.

Perlite is less easily crushed but breakage and crushing can occur. It holds little water and nutrients, readily segregates during mixing and floats. It does aerify and improve drainage of soils if a sufficient volume is used. Perlite dust is very irritating to eyes and nose.

Styrofoam beads function similarly to perlite but hold no water. However, if only the physical separating of other particles is desired, they can be useful under some conditions. Dust is not a problem as with perlite.

An extremely common error is to assume that adding sand or gravel to soil will improve drainage. Sand or pea gravel are useful in aerating and improving drainage of soils and soil mixes **only** if used in sufficient quantity to exceed the threshold level. The point at which the volume of sand or gravel begins to increase drainage is called the threshold. (Figure 21.8). Remember that fine particles (cement) plus sand, gravel and water = concrete. The same thing is true when adding sand or gravel to soils. Until the volume of sand or gravel reaches the point where there are no longer enough fine particles (silt, clay and very fine sand granules) to surround the sand or gravel particles, little or no change in drainage and aeration will occur. Because no two soils are the same, even within a small area, a test to determine the threshold point should be done for each different soil used.

Sand and gravel are heavy and do little to reduce the container load (weight). Further, if large quantities of sand or gravel are mixed with a small volume of soil and placed in a container, the much smaller silt and clay particles will slowly erode to the bottom and the improved drainage conditions will be short lived. In addition, sand is extremely variable and must be evaluated for each site (Figure 21.9).

Calcined, fired or fixed clays are the best materials for general use in modifying soils for long term above-ground planters with bottoms. These materials are essentially finely ground bricks. They retain most of their original clay properties yet are structurally fixed so that the size of individual particles can be screened to various sizes as conditions require and the natural shrink-swell characteristics of clay soils are eliminated. The individual granules are most often used as large or larger than large sand granules yet retain the internal porosity to hold water and nutrients and are lighter in weight than sand or gravel.

As was described above, on the topic of adding sand or gravel to soil, adding small quantities of calcined clays or other materials **will not** improve the drainage and aeration until the threshold level is reached.

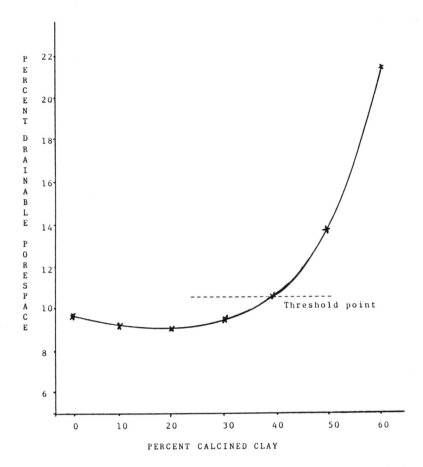

Figure 21.8. The threshold point, in this case, was reached when 40% calcined clay (by volume) was added to a clay loam soil. Drainable pore space was not changed by adding 10, 20 or 30% calcined clay to the soil. However, at about 40%, the drainable pore space increased from about 10% to 14%. No two soils will react the same way. These findings may serve as a beginning "guestimate", but only evaluations of the soil and soil amendments in question will provide accurate answers.

A mix or container growth medium could be constructed from vermiculite, perlite and calcined clays if load is very limited. However, using these materials is not practical in many conditions since nutrition and water management become nearly as critical and demanding as growing container nursery stock.

Figure 21.9. Sand is extremely variable. The coarse particles (left) are vastly different than the fine particles (right) yet both come from the same source as "concrete sand". To be effective as a soil amendment, sand should be of uniform particle size. The smaller the particles (right) the more the sand will pack or fit among the soil particles and may reduce drainage.

Determining Drainable Pore Space. In order to provide for good plant health in above-ground containers with bottoms, a drainable pore space test should be done for each depth of container involved. Thinwall six-inch PVC pipe works well for the purpose of simulating the depth of the container (Figure 21.3). (Remember diameter is not a factor). Always do at least three duplications for each depth/mix evaluated.

Cut the pieces of PVC pipe three to four inches taller than the depth of the soil column to be tested. Set each pipe on a piece of heavy wire mesh covered with several layers of ground cover cloth, weed barrier or other strong fabric that does not stretch (Figure 21.3). Place a plastic trash bag of sufficient depth inside each piece of pipe. Use the smallest diameter trash bag that will provide the depth required in order to avoid air pockets inside the pipe but outside the bag. Fill the pipe and bag with the soil mix to be tested. Unless the depth is quite shallow, add 10 to 12 inches of mix, then add a known quantity of water and tap the outside of the pipe to aid normal settling and avoid trapping air inside or outside of the plastic bag. Repeat adding soil mix and water until the pipe is filled to the desired depth and a very small amount of free water can be seen on the surface with lightweight mixes. Make sure that none of the materials are floating and giving a false reading. Record the quantity of water added.

After the pipes filled with soil have set 18 to 24 hours and additional measured amounts of water have been added and recorded as needed to saturate the soil mix with a small amount of free water seen on the surface of the mix, suspend the entire unit (pipe, soil mix, wire mesh and fabric) over a container of sufficient volume to hold 1/4 to 1/2 of the total volume of water added. Puncture the bottom of the plastic trash bag several times with a knife, sharp pencil or screw driver. Make sure all water drained is caught. Allow to drain for four to six hours before proceeding with the final step.

The total water added represents the volume of the total pore space within the soil mix column. The volume of water that drains out represents the volume of pores that are now filled with air. If the volume of water drained out is divided by the volume of water added, the resulting value will be the percent drainable pore space. Average the values from the three repeated tests for the best estimate of how the mix will perform. For good plant health in above-ground containers with bottoms, drainable pore space values of 12% to 15% are required (8).

If load is a consideration, weigh the columns soon after the test is completed. Calculate the volume of the pipe at the depth tested and determine the weight per cubic foot of soil mix. This is the best method of determining the actual load the container will provide on the structure.

By using a sandy loam soil of good fertility amended with materials to give an acceptable load, plant performance in above-ground containers can generally be assured for many years. Soil, even a sandy loam soil, provides good nutrient holding capacity and buffers the soil mix system against abrupt changes in nutrient and moisture status and aids plant health.

Drains and Drainage. Gravel in the bottom of containers does not improve drainage. In fact, by reducing the depth of the soil mix, the gravel complicates the drainage process. This is due to the perched water table **above** the gravel instead of at the bottom of the container as before. A key factor to remember in water relations in soils is: **water moves from a coarse-textured material to a fine-textured material readily.** However, **water will not move from a fine-textured material to a coarse-textured material until saturation occurs and the weight of the water above forces the water below into the coarser material.**

Since most containers have only one or two drains, once water percolates to the bottom, much of it must move horizontally to the nearest drain. If the soil mix is very porous (above 25% drainable pore space) and the container is small (less than three feet across) there is no benefit from providing a gravel layer in the bottom. However, where containers are wider and soil mixes have a drainable pore space of 10% to 15%, a thin gravel layer in the bottom of the container can aid removal of excess water. The gravel layer **does not** aid drainage of water through the vertical column of soil mix, but rather **reduces** the drainage by making the vertical columns shorter. The benefit arises from the more rapid horizontal movement of water that has percolated through the vertical column of soil mix to the free drains. There is no advantage to more than one to two inches of gravel and, unless the smaller particles of the soil mix are kept separate from the gravel, **no** benefit will result. A workable system is to place the gravel in the bottom of the container, then cover with one or more layers of soil separator or weed barrier synthetic fabric that will not decompose (Figures 21.10, 21.11, 21.12, 21.13, 21.14). The separator keeps the soil mix separate from the gravel so that water can move freely across the bottom of the container to the drain. The soil separator fabric also keeps the drains free of debris. Under these conditions, water percolates through the column of mix, through the fabric and into the gravel, then horizontally to the nearest drain.

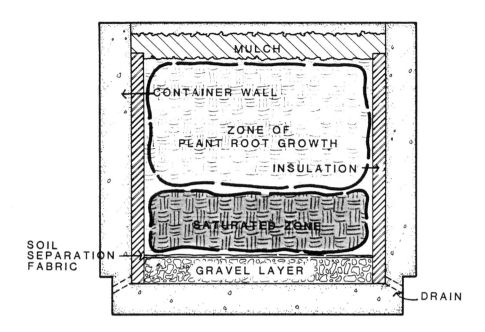

MULCH

CONTAINER WALL

ZONE OF
PLANT ROOT GROWTH

INSULATION

SATURATED ZONE

SOIL
SEPARATION
FABRIC

GRAVEL LAYER

DRAIN

Figure 21.10. A typical container cross section with insulation on the sides to protect the roots from both heat and cold. Mulch over the surface of the soil mix further insulates the root zone and aids in weed control as well as appearance. A weed barrier fabric beneath the mulch further improves weed control and makes organic mulches decompose more slowly since contact with the soil mix is reduced. Notice the saturated zone at the base of the soil mix and above the soil separator fabric and gravel. This saturated zone will always be present because of textural differences between the soil mix and the gravel and drain holes. A more porous soil mix will have a shallower saturated zone while a less porous soil mix will have a deeper saturated zone.

367

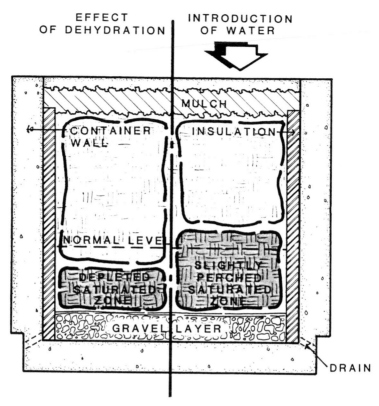

Figure 21.11. With rainfall or irrigation, water percolates downward through the soil mix until it reaches the surface of the water table and the surface of the water table begins to rise. If the soil mix is dry, such that there is no water table, the water will move downward to the upper surface of the gravel and begin to build or rise until the weight of the water at the top of the saturated zone is sufficient to force water out of the bottom. This saturated zone is the major moisture buffer that provides moisture for the plant between waterings.

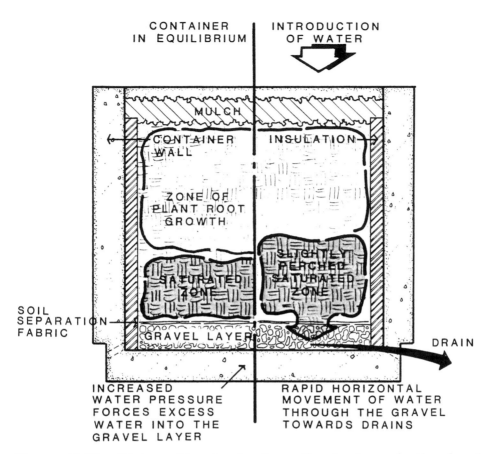

Figure 21.12. Water will saturate the soil mix to a depth whereby the weight of the water at the top of the saturated zone will exceed the capacity of the soil mix at the bottom of the saturated zone to retain the water, and drainage will begin. This can be easily demonstrated using a glass-fronted box. The surface of the saturated zone will rise to a high point just before water begins to enter the gravel, then drop down to a lower level once water begins to enter the gravel. Once water begins entering the gravel zone, the surface of the saturated zone will remain constant unless the gravel is too fine to allow drainage to occur as rapidly as water exits the soil mix or unless the drain holes become clogged. During a heavy rain, the rate of water percolation through the small pores in the vertical columns of the soil mix generally is the limiting factor controlling the rate of water movement through the container.

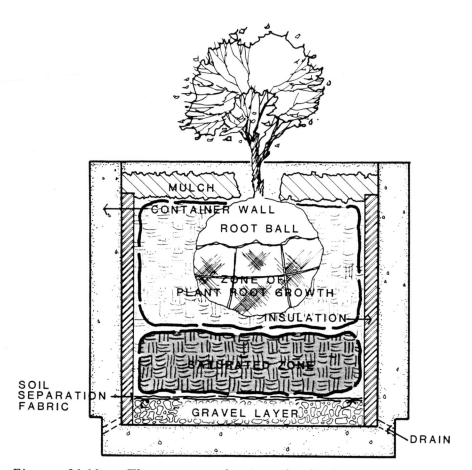

Figure 21.13.   The proper planting depth for container-grown or balled-in-burlap plants in the container is above the saturated zone.   If the plant's root system is placed too deep, all roots in the saturated zone will be suffocated.   Some roots just above the surface of the saturated zone may be killed or damaged by root rot organisms since most of these pathogens are favored by excess water and poor aeration.   In general, active new root growth requires more aeration than the functions of older roots, especially when plants are installed bare root or B & B.

370

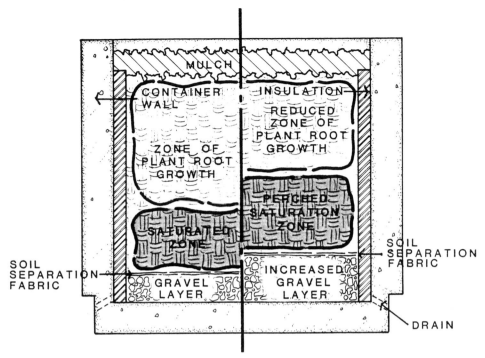

Figure 21.14. Increasing the depth of the gravel layer simply raises the saturated zone in the container and in turn reduces the volume of well-aerated soil mix suitable for root growth. Drainage is controlled by the texture of the mix, not by adding gravel.

The saturated zone at the bottom of the soil mix is not a liability unless it is excessively deep proportionate to the depth of the soil mix in the container. The saturated zone is part of the total water reservoir for the plant. As the soil mix dries near the surface, water from the saturated zone moves up by wicking action (capillarity). If the soil mix, container depth and drainage system complex are properly designed and synchronized, the saturated zone **aids** plant health by buffering the wet-dry cycles. Plants in containers are much more susceptible to water stress and associated pest problems such as mites than the same plant growing in the landscape. This is another reason why the soil mix should not be excessively drained. Four examples are presented as further information (Figures 21.15, 21.16, 21.17, 21.18, 21.19).

371

Figure 21.15. This entire garden is the roof of a parking garage. By careful selection of plants and proper development of a soil mix, proportionate to the texture of the soil and amendments used relative to the depth of the soil, an attractive, useful landscape was created. Maintenance is only slightly more complex than if the same plants were growing in native soil in a natural landscape.

Figure 21.16.   One technique that aids drainage and aeration when otherwise soil depth and drainage are unsatisfactory, is to create berms or mounds.   If the additional load can be tolerated by the structure, berms may allow trees to be grown that would otherwise perform poorly.   In this case, berms were created for the three oak trees which are growing well.

Figure 21.17.   The tree in the foreground is suffering stress due to the poor aeration of the soil mix used in these large containers with bottoms.   In this case, the drain has become plugged in the container in the foreground but has remained functional in the container with the attractive tree in the background.   The problem was primarily a result of improper installation of the drain system and not the soil mix.

374

Figure 21.18. Containers with bottoms in urban landscapes create a very unnatural environment for plants. The top of the tree experiences a near-desert environment due to the reflected light and heat, whereas, the root system is often experiencing a swamp-like condition if the soil mix/drainage complex is not properly designed and constructed. Few plants can tolerate these extremes of top and root conditions for prolonged periods. As plants become stressed they become more susceptible to diseases and pests. In this case, the stem split and canker is due to an organism that attacks only weakened trees.

Figure 21.19. Trees can survive for reasonable periods of time in containers if the drainage/water relations/nutrition complex is designed and managed carefully. However, the larger the container, the greater the success, especially if soil amended with stable ingredients is used to provide good drainage over the functional life of the plant. It is important to keep in mind that plants in containers or restricted planting spaces will never grow as large or live as long as their counterparts in good landscape soils with few or no root space restrictions. In addition, the plants in containers will be more subject to an array of pest, disease and stress problems.

The question frequently arises regarding the water relations in the soil ball of a balled-in-burlap tree or shrub. As long as the base of the soil ball is above the surface of the saturated zone and surrounded by a soil mix with good drainage characteristics relative to the depth of the container, plant establishment and growth will proceed favorably and without complications. However, should the soil ball extend to all sides of the container, the plant roots will quickly suffocate, even if an appropriate soil mix exists above or below (Figure 21.20). This occurs because of the difference in soil or soil mix texture and the depth of the drainage column. In general, more aeration is required for the development of new roots from the cut ends of roots dug B & B than for the extension and function of existing roots once the plant is established.

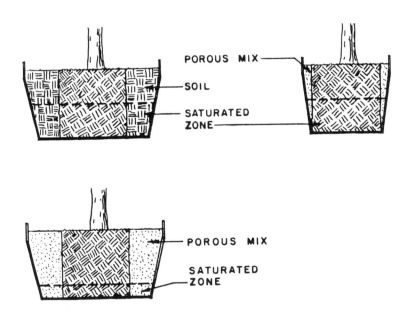

Figure 21.20. When a B & B root ball of field soil is placed in a container and a mix with appropriate porosity for the container depth is placed around the soil ball all is well (lower left). However, if soil is placed around the root ball (upper left) or if the root ball contacts the sides of the container, drainage will be poor and the root system will probably suffocate.

377

Insulating the Root Zone. Roots of plants are much less cold tolerant than the tops. For example, shore juniper (*Juniperus conferta*) fine roots will be killed at about 12 degrees F (-10 C), the larger roots at about -5 degrees F (-18 C) or more if the plant has experienced the appropriate cool nights and short days to induce cold hardiness. A Leyland pyracantha (*Pyracantha coccinea* 'Leylandi') that will survive temperatures of -15 degrees F or more (-30 C) will be killed if the root zone temperature drops below +15 degrees F (-10 C).

When the air temperature around a container drops below the temperature lethal to the plant's roots, and remains at or below that point long enough, the root zone will reach the same temperature. Wind greatly speeds up the rate of heat dissipation from the container and shortens the time required for the lethal temperature to be reached. It is not the freezing process, but rather the actual temperature that causes root death. The roots of the pyracantha mentioned above can be lowered to 17 degrees or 18 degrees F (-8 C) repeatedly with no injury. However, once the root temperature reaches about 15 degrees F (-10 C), death occurs.

The effect on plant growth of high soil temperatures in containers varies between plant families and probably between genera, species and cultivars. Some plants may be more sensitive to the maximum temperature, while others may be injured only if the temperature goes above a certain critical point and remains there for several hours (Figure 21.21).

Unfortunately, little information is available, but a few examples do exist. Loblolly pine (*Pinus taeda*) has been found to have maximum root growth between 70 and 80 degrees F (22 and 27 C), but growth was reduced by as much as 90% at 95 degrees F (35 C) (1) Roots of a number of conifers were killed in a few hours at 117 degrees F (46 C) (1, 5).

Peach roots grew most in soil temperatures between 65 and 70 degrees F (18 and 22 C). Root growth was reduced by 40% at 80 degrees F (27 C) and 97% at 90 to 95 degrees F (32 to 35 C) (2, 3). Shanks and Laurie (4) reported that roses in three-gallon containers had greatest fresh weights at soil temperatures between 52 and 62 degrees F (11 and 17 C) but were reduced by a third when grown at 72 degrees F (23 C).

*Figure 21.21.   Root development in the container growth medium:
the shaded side (left) and the side exposed to the sun (right).
Roots developed throughout the growth medium during spring but
died as the heat became more intense.   In a landscape container,
insulating the inside of the container can greatly aid plant
health.*

A pronounced difference was observed between two tropical fruits in their response to soil temperatures (7). Mexican avocado seedlings (*Persea americana*) were stunted by soil temperatures above 95 degrees F (35 C) while 1 1/2-year-old grafted 'Irwin' mangoes showed no difference in response to soil temperatures tested. Although these findings represent only a few of the many species grown in containers, they strongly support the conclusion that high soil temperature is a major limitation of plant growth in containers in mid summer.

Light-colored containers reflect heat and aid root health (6), however, insulation inside the container provides even greater temperature moderation. These factors in combination with selecting plants with the greatest tolerance to root temperature extremes are the only practical alternatives at the present time.

When plants are growing in field or landscape situations, the roots are protected from heat and cold by the insulating character of the soil. Even in severe climates where the soil freezes several feet deep, the actual temperature experienced by plant roots may not drop below 25 degrees F (-8 C) especially if snow cover is present during the severe cold periods.

Insulating the inside walls of above-ground containers can greatly reduce the rate at which heat is lost and the actual minimum temperature experienced by plant roots during severe cold spells. Also insulation buffers plant roots against extreme heat in summer. Even in relatively mild climates, one inch of urethane insulation around the inside parameter of containers will greatly aid plant health. Not only are the temperature extremes moderated to aid plant roots, water management is also easier due to reduced evaporation. In more northern climates, two inches or more of insulation may be necessary. If the container is raised so that air can move below, the bottom should be insulated as well. If the bottom of the container is in contact with the soil, it would appear that some heat transfer would result from the earth into the container, however, even when complete soil-container bottom contact occurs, little heat transfer occurs because of the insulating effect of the air spaces among the gravel in the bottom. By contrast, containers without bottoms and with good soil contact receive substantial warmth from the earth.

Literature Cited

1. Barney, C.W. 1947. A study of some factors affecting root growth of loblolly pine, *Pinus taeda.* PhD dissertation. Duke University School of Forestry.

2. Nightingale, G.E. 1935. Effects of temperature on growth, anatomy and metabolism of apple and peach roots. Bot. Gazette 96:581-639.

3. Rauch, Fred D. 1969. Root zone temperature studies. Miss. Farm Research.

4. Shanks, J.B. and A. Laurie. 1949. A progress report of some rose root studies. Proc. Amer. Soc. Hort. Sci. 53:473-488.

5. Shirley, H.L. 1936. Lethal high temperature for conifers and the cooling effect of transpiration. Jour. Ag. Res. 53:239-258.

6. Whitcomb, Carl E. 1980. The effects of containers and production bed color on root temperatures. The Amer. Nurseryman 136(11):11, 65-67.

7. Yusof, I.M., D.W. Buchanan and John F. Gerber. 1969. The response of mango and avocado to soil temperature. Jour. Amer. Soc. Hort. Sci. 94:619-621.

8. Whitcomb, Carl E. 1988. *Plant Production in Containers.* Lacebark Publications. Stillwater, Ok.

CHAPTER 22

PLANT NUTRITION, SOILS, AND FERTILIZERS

A General Summary of Fertilization
            Practices for Landscape Plants - 384

    Soil Test - - - - - - - - - - - 384

    Expressions of Soil Test Results - 388

    Build Reserves of Phosphorus
                    and Potassium - - 388

    Managing Nitrogen - - - - - - - - 389

Leaf Analysis - - - - - - - - - - - - - 391

Plant Nutrition and Fertilizers - - - - 392

Nutrient Absorption and
                Energy Distribution - - - 395

Sources of Nutrient Elements - - - - - 398

        Nitrogen - - - - - - - - - - 399

        Phosphorus - - - - - - - - - 399

        Potassium - - - - - - - - - - 400

        Calcium - - - - - - - - - - - 400

        Magnesium - - - - - - - - - - 401

        Sulfur - - - - - - - - - - - 401

        The Micronutrients - - - - - 402

Why a Fertilizer Burns - - - - - - - - 402

Nutrient Elements:
         Plant Response and Use - - -   404

         Nitrogen - - - - - - - - - - - - 404

         Phosphorus - - - - - - - - - - - 405

         Potassium - - - - - - - - - - - 408

         Sulfur - - - - - - - - - - - - - 408

         Calcium and Magnesium - - - - - 409

         The Micronutrients - - - - - - - 411

Relationships of Plant Nutrients - - - 416

Fertilizer Salts and Salt Index - - - - 419

Literature Cited - - - - - - - - - - - 423

383

Plant Nutrition, Soils and Fertilizers

A General Summary of Fertilization Practices for Landscape Plants. (For specific recommendations see chapters 24, 25 and 26). Good soil is an asset often unappreciated and overlooked in routine landscape management. In an array of studies of soil additives and amendments covering more than 20 years, there is nothing that can be added to a poor soil to make it a good soil. Adding organic matter and any deficient nutrient elements to a soil may substantially improve the productivity of the soil, however.

There are four basic steps in improving the productivity of soils.

1) **Soil Test**. Soil samples may be taken using a soil probe six to eight inches deep until approximately one pint of soil is accumulated from an area. Spade slices also work well (Figure 22.1). Remove any surface debris and insert a spade 6 to 8 inches deep. Force the spade forward creating an opening in the soil. Take another spade slice one-half to one inch down the face of the opening for the soil sample. Step on the soil that had been moved forward originally to close the opening. Three or four spade slices from an area should be taken and mixed together to give a representative sample. Dry the soil sample(s) at room temperature, then send to a laboratory with instructions for the desired analysis.

Most state universities and many private laboratories conduct tests of soil samples to determine the levels of available nutrients. The nutrient elements generally checked are:

nitrogen (sometimes expressed as nitrates, ammonia or organic matter level, since the breakdown of organic matter releases nitrogen for plant growth)

phosphorus,

potassium (sometimes called potash),

calcium, and

magnesium.

Rates may be expressed in pounds per acre or ppm (parts per million). To convert ppm to pounds per acre, multiply times two for most soils since there are approximately two million pounds of soil per acre six inches deep. Soil testing laboratories generally give the pH of the soil and on special request, check for the levels of sulfur, sodium, iron, manganese, copper and zinc. Levels of boron and molybdenum are determined by only a few laboratories.

*Note: Some labs do not evaluate nitrogen levels. Some labs give relative guidance figures for levels in the general range of low, medium , or high. These reference levels may or may not be useful in landscape management since most labs depend on classical agriculture for most of their work and growing trees, shrubs and turf in the landscape is substantially different from corn, wheat, cotton, or soybeans. Also, labs use different extracting agents to remove the elements from the soil. This can change the reading on the chart. For this reason it is best to stick with one laboratory unless major problems arise. Remember, the elements extracted from the soil by a particular chemical represent an attempted approximation of what a plant can extract from the soil. At best this is a rough approximation so consider it accordingly.

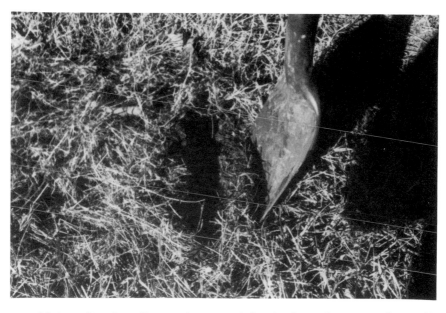

Figure 22.1. Spade slices six to eight inches deep work well for soil tests. Remove any surface debris and insert a spade six to eight inches deep. If the area is in an existing lawn or bed, insert the spade and push it forward to create an opening. Take another spade slice one-half to one inch thick down the face of the opening as the soil sample. Three or four spade slices should be taken and mixed together to represent an area. Simply step on the soil originally pushed forward to close the hole.

The pH of a soil is useful information. A high pH, above 7.0, generally reflects the presence of substantial quantities of calcium, magnesium, sodium, or bicarbonates since these elements are strong bases or alkali materials. On the other hand, a low pH, below 5.0, generally reflects a low to moderate level of calcium, magnesium, or sodium, **or** a moderate to high level of some acid-forming agent such as sulfur, sulfate, ammonium, or hydrogen.

For most woody landscape plants, in most soils, the "ideal" pH is in a range from 4.5 to 6.5, however, if the pH of your soil is higher or lower, there are generally practical adjustments that can be made. If your soil has a pH below 5.0, the soil test may reveal rather low levels of calcium and magnesium available for plant growth. Even if the levels of these two elements are not low, it is probably desirable to lime the soil to raise the pH to about 5.0 to 6.0 **but no more.** Lime is calcium carbonate and will raise the pH of the soil by adding calcium and carbonate. For an estimate of the quantity to add per acre, check with your county agricultural agent or state university. They should be knowledgeable of your specific soils. Otherwise, use the rough estimates in Table 22.1.

The primary reason for liming is to raise the soil pH. Even when adequate levels of calcium and magnesium are present, raising the pH will reduce the solubility of aluminum and manganese, since these are the major problems that accompany very acid soils. On the other hand, if the pH of the soil is above 6.5 to 7.0, it may be desirable to add elemental sulfur to lower the pH. Granular elemental sulfur is the most effective and safest material to use (Figure 3.2). **Do not use aluminum sulfate** since aluminum is toxic to most plants. Rates of granular sulfur should be from 30 to 60 pounds per 1000 square feet (600 to 2000 pounds per acre), depending on the pH and internal drainage characteristics of the soil. In order for moderate to high rates of sulfur to be effective, the internal drainage of the soil must be such that the calcium, magnesium or sodium displaced by the sulfur can be leached below the root zone of the crop plant. It is better to make several moderate applications of sulfur over a period of months instead of one heavy application. It is important to monitor soil changes over time.

Table 22.1. Approximate quantity of limestone needed to raise the pH of various soils. No two soils are the same and only a rough estimate can be offered here. In many, if not all cases, magnesium is needed as well as calcium, therefore dolomite, which contains magnesium, should be used as the lime source.

			Limestone, pounds per acre		
Current pH	Desired pH	Sand	Sandy loam	Silt loam	Clay loam
4.0	6.0	2000	4000	6000	8000
4.5	6.0	1500	3000	4500	6000
5.0	6.0	1000	2000	3000	4000
5.5	6.0	500	1000	2000	3000

Figure 22.2. Granular elemental sulfur is clean and easy to spread, whereas powdered sulfur can be a nightmare. Conventional rotary spreaders work well with most granules. Granular sulfur should be incorporated for best results.

2) Expressions of Soil Test Results. Soil test values should be adjusted to the following areas or general ranges:

pH: 4.5 to 6.5 with allowance for the species to be grown and the geographic area.

Nitrogen: 5 to 50 pounds per acre, depending on species involved, type of fertilizer used, desired growth rate of the plant and time of year.

Phosphorus: 60 to 120 pounds per acre. Levels above 150 pounds may suppress growth of some species.

Potassium: 150 to 300 pounds per acre.

Calcium: 600 to 2000 pounds per acre.

Magnesium: 200 to 1000 pounds per acre.

Iron: 40 to 150 parts per million (sometimes also expressed as milligrams per liter, which is the same)

Manganese: 15 to 40 ppm

Sulfur: 40 pounds per acre or more.

Copper: 3 to 8 ppm

Boron: 0.4 to 0.8 ppm

Zinc: 2 to 4 ppm

Plants may grow well with soil test values above or below these general ranges primarily due to the nature of the specific soil, soil test procedure used, and species involved. However, when problems occur or are suspected, adjusting soil nutrients to these levels will generally aid plant growth.

3) Build Reserves of Phosphorus and Potassium. Many soils are very deficient in phosphorus and unless the level of phosphorus is raised, plant growth will be poor, despite all other fertilizers added and cultural practices used. Unlike nitrogen, which moves readily in the soil, phosphorus **does not** move in any soil, even the pure sands of central Florida. Because of this, phosphorus applied to a soil is more effective when incorporated into the plant root zone, and once the level of phosphorus in the soil is raised to an adequate level, no additional phosphorus needs to be added for several years.

On the other hand, **excessive levels of phosphorus in the soils should be avoided.** Not only is phosphorus the most expensive fertilizer element, but if an excess is added to the soil, it will tie-up or make unavailable some of the micronutrients necessary for plant growth, and there is no practical way to remove excess phosphorus from a field soil.

For most landscape plants, a level of phosphorus expressed in pounds of available phosphorus (P_2O_5) per acre, should be between

60 and 120 pounds. No two soils are the same in terms of fixing phosphorus. For example, if a soil test shows 10 pounds of phosphorus per acre and 60 to 100 pounds is needed, adding 50 pounds of active phosphorus per acre (110 pounds of 0-46-0, triple superphosphate) will, in most cases, raise the level of available phosphorus for plant growth only to 25 to 50 pounds per acre. The reason for this is the fixing capacity of the soil for phosphorus. Consequently, on most soils add enough phosphorus to raise the level near the highest recommended level (100 pounds per acre). After fixing, the available level of phosphorus will be near the lower level (60 pounds per acre). Therefore, in the example of 10 pounds currently in the soil, add 90 pounds of actual phosphorus (about 200 pounds of 0-46-0, triple superphosphate or use 200 pounds of 18-46-0 to also provide nitrogen if nitrogen is also needed. After fixing in the soil, the level of phosphorus will be around 50 to 60 pounds per acre on most soils. To convert pounds per acre to pounds per 1000 square feet, divide by 43.5 since there are 43560 square feet per acre.

In established landscapes the only practical way to supplement phosphorus in the soil is by broadcasting dry granules on the surface. This is **not** a problem. Roots of all species of plants grow in the top few inches of soil where oxygen and other conditions for growth are most favorable. Tree roots are not at great depths in the soil. In fact, all trees have fine fibrous roots at or near the soil surface. These roots can absorb sufficient phosphorus to meet plant needs in nearly all cases. Potassium is most economically purchased as potassium chloride, KCl (58% to 62% K_2O). For maximum productivity, a field soil should contain between 150 and 300 pounds of available K20 per acre. Since potassium is not fixed to the same degree as phosphorus, if a soil test showed 80 pounds of available potassium, by adding 120 pounds of potassium (200 pounds of potassium chloride, 0-0-60, using a 200 pounds level as the target) the level of available potassium would be raised to the 150-pound level or above in most soils.

4) **Managing Nitrogen.** Nitrogen may be added infrequently using various slow-release forms such as sulfur-coated urea, Osmocote or ureaformaldehyde, or various organic sources, or frequently using soluble forms such as ammonium nitrate (33-0-0) or urea (46-0-0). Frequency and rate of nitrogen application are more influenced by soil porosity and leaching of the nitrogen below the root zone than by any other factor. Heavy clay or silt soils may require

limited nitrogen, whereas sandy soils require more frequent applications. The expense of slow-release nitrogen sources can easily be justified on sandy soils.

In the spring and fall, applications of urea (46-0-0) every six to eight weeks work well. However, during the summer, with greater soil temperatures, the frequency may need to be increased to every three to four weeks and the rate per application lowered, if maximum growth is to be achieved. Again, however, no two soils react and hold nitrogen the same. Therefore, some adjustments will be necessary on each soil and site. If the area is drip- or sprinkler-irrigated, the level applied during the summer will be higher than without irrigation. With most soils, 50 to 200 pounds of actual nitrogen per acre per year is necessary for good plant growth. A practical application in many geographic areas, for example, would be 20 to 50 pounds of nitrogen per acre in early spring just after leaves emerge, followed by another 20 to 50 pounds six to eight weeks later and the same rate again six to eight weeks later and again in early September if a soil test shows a nitrogen level below 20 to 30 pounds of available nitrogen per acre.

The use of slow-release fertilizer is relatively new. In clay loam and sandy clay loam soils, slow-release fertilizers have provided little benefit in Oklahoma when compared to dry chemical fertilizers. However, in sandy soils of Florida and elsewhere, the use of Osmocote or other slow-release fertilizer, either added to the planting hole or in a dibble hole on either side of the tree following planting or after the initial fertilizer application is depleted, has been effective. Check with your fertilizer distributor for specific rates in your area.

When using slow release fertilizers remember, the longer it lasts, the higher the rate in terms of pounds of material applied per unit area. It is easy to fall into the trap of not applying enough slow-release fertilizer to be effective. For example, if urea 46-0-0 is used as a quick release nitrogen source about two pounds of actual material is needed to provide one pound of nitrogen/1000 square feet. By contrast, if 17-7-12 Osmocote is used the release time is 12 to 14 months and a rate of six pounds is needed to provide one pound of nitrogen. **But** with the soluble fertilizer four or five applications are required during the growing season which would total 8 to 10 pounds of actual material (4 to 5 lbs. of N). To get the same level of nitrogen over the entire year, 25 to 30 pounds of Osmocote is needed/1000 square feet. This seems like an enormous rate until the lower analysis and extended release are considered.

A Word of Caution: soils are extremely variable, not only between geographic areas or states, but frequently within the same landscape. These recommendations should be considered as very general guidelines only. When nitrogen is deficient adding N in any form will be beneficial. However, excess nitrogen can be detrimental by stimulating excessive growth that is particularly 'soft'. Your soil may require more or less than the levels suggested here. Check with persons knowledgeable in your area for more specific fertilizer recommendations for your soil. On the other hand, **do fertilize, but not without knowing the specific needs of your soils.**

Leaf Analysis. Leaf analysis shows what the plant actually absorbed from the soil. However, there are some major factors to consider:

1) take a large enough sample of leaves to give a true picture of the nutritional conditions;
2) leaves recently reaching mature size are generally the preferred sampling point;
3) keep in mind that nitrogen, phosphorus, potassium and magnesium are mobile in the plant. These elements can be removed from old leaves and transferred to new leaves, giving a false reading of the quantity actually taken up by the plant. For example, if magnesium deficiency is suspected, take leaf samples from **old** leaves and **young** leaves about the time the last leaves of the season reach full size and analyze them separately. This procedure is also useful when toxicities of nutrient elements are suspected. For example, boron deficiency can best be detected by sampling new leaves, whereas excess boron accumulates in old leaves. On the other hand, calcium, sulfur and the micronutrients are not mobile in the plant and are more easily detected in an analysis of recently matured leaves.

With tree or shrub species, where desired nutrient ranges for leaf analysis have been established through extensive research and testing, this is a valuable diagnostic tool. However, for the many species for which no desired nutrient ranges have been established, a leaf analysis is like looking at a road map printed in an unfamiliar foreign language; it may be telling you where you want to go, but you generally won't be able to figure it out until an interpreter comes along. With most of the landscape plants, no interpretation exists.

In some instances, a clue to diagnosing plant problems can be obtained from leaf analysis of a healthy and a deficient specimen, especially if the two plants are relatively close together and growing in the same general soil conditions.

Even with this information, often a clear diagnosis of a problem cannot be made. For example, if the healthy plant has 500 ppm manganese and the unthrifty plant has 50, it is very tempting to conclude that manganese is needed. This is probably not the case since the level of manganese can vary over a wide range in many species with no apparent detrimental or beneficial effect. If the root system of the plant has been damaged by gophers, disease, a high water table that suffocated part of the roots, or other similar factors, leaf analysis may suggest very low levels of available nutrients when such is not the case. A final word of caution: do not draw hasty conclusions.

Plant Nutrition and Fertilizers. In order to grow healthy plants of excellent quality, a system must be maintained that keeps all factors near the ideal. Only under such favorable conditions can the nutritional program be most effective in maintaining growth and maximizing plant health. The nutritional factors presented in the next section assume reasonable growing conditions so that maximum response to nutrition can be obtained.

The meshing or synchronization of all nutritional elements in the proper rates and ratios can best be likened to a fine automobile: all the factors can be there (wheels, pistons, starter, carburetor, generator, etc.), but it only takes a malfunction of one of these components to stop the entire machine. Plant growth is not normally affected so abruptly. However, the greater the synchronization among the nutrient elements, the more strong and vigorous the growth of the plants. Strong growth with a proper balance among the nutrient elements reduces the likelihood of disease or insect problems. Figures 22.3, 22.4, 22.5, 22.6 dramatize the wooden barrel theory as it relates to plant nutrition and growth. The barrel can hold water (or the plant can manufacture sugars and starches) only to the level of the lowest stave (the wooden strips making up the barrel). As each stave is raised, the barrel can hold more, likewise, as the level of the most deficient element is raised, plant growth improves.

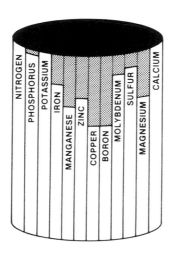

Figure 22.3. For many years, plants grown in the sandy soils of Florida suffered from numerous deficiencies of varying degrees. In this example, copper and boron were most deficient. Therefore those were the symptoms observed most, but the moderate deficiencies of manganese, magnesium and iron also played a role in restricting plant growth.

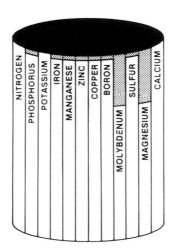

Figure 22.4. With improvements in micronutrient fertilizers, especially the balance or ratio between iron, manganese, zinc, copper, and boron, plant growth improved but restrictions remained. These restrictions were later diagnosed as deficiencies of both molybdenum and magnesium.

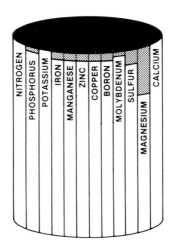

Figure 22.5. With improvements in the level of molybdenum, either alone or in micronutrient fertilizers, plant growth improved only to find magnesium deficiency symptoms more and more common.

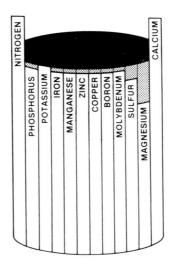

Figure 22.6. A common error in the management of nutrient elements is the excess of nitrogen and calcium. The excess nitrogen is added in an attempt to further stimulate growth. The excess calcium is added under the false information that the pH of the soil must be 6.8 to 7.0. The most common limiting factor of plant growth presently is the excess of these two elements and the deficiency of magnesium.

Nutrient Absorption and Energy Distribution. All plants have a distinct distribution system for the energy manufactured by the leaves (various carbohydrates, proteins and starches). In order to better understand the needs of the plant and the sequence of events involved, consider the following over-simplification of the nutrient absorption, food manufacture and distribution system:

A) Fertilizer is applied or is otherwise available to the root system.

B) **If** adequate moisture **and** aeration are available around the roots and temperature conditions are favorable, the roots will absorb the water and nutrients. Thus the translocation from the roots to the leaves begins (Figure 22.7). Remember that aeration is a key ingredient in this process. Without adequate aeration, the root system cannot carry on the necessary respiration, which is the energy-supplying process, necessary for water and nutrient absorption. Nutrient absorption mostly is an active process in that the plant must spend energy. It is not a passive or energy-free process as was once believed.

C) When the water and nutrients arrive in the leaves (or other green parts of the plant) most of the water is lost by the leaves, mainly through the stomates, as transpiration. A small portion must be retained in the plant to maintain cell turgidity and a very small fraction is utilized in the manufacture of energy (carbohydrates). The various nutrients are combined with carbon dioxide and water in the chloroplasts (green disc-like structures) in the leaves and capture the energy (sunlight) to form various simple sugars or carbohydrates that comprise the basic energy for all living cells in the plant.

D) The many cells within the leaves are closest and therefore have easy access to this energy. However, they do not necessarily have first priority.

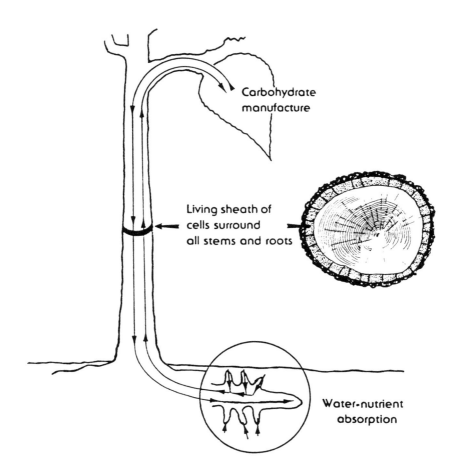

Figure 22.7. Root growth is a rather indirect, roundabout process. Nutrients and water are absorbed by the roots and transferred to the leaves where energy (carbohydrates) is manufactured. Roots can grow only if some of the energy is returned to the root tips. If there is a shortage, the roots are the first to suffer.

E) Within the plant, there is a distinct energy priority of distribution or "peck-order". In very broad general terms, it is: **flowers, fruits, leaves, stems, and roots**. In other words, if flowers or fruits are developing on the plant, they take precedence over the needs of other plant parts, especially if the plant is under stress. It has been well documented that trees under stress will frequently develop more flowers and fruits than trees with little or no stress. Likewise, it is not uncommon to observe the leaves on either side of a citrus or other fruit develop an off-color while the fruit is rapidly developing, whereas leaves further away from the fruit retain their normal green color. Once the fruit reaches maturity, these leaves will also return to their normal color. For ease of further discussion, assume no flowers or fruits are present, only leaves.

The quantity of energy manufactured determines the quantity available for distribution. If all is ideal, there is plenty of energy for all cells within the plant as well as some for storage within the stems and roots. However, what if there is not enough energy to go around? A restriction in energy production may be due to many factors. For example, too much or too little of any one or several of the essential nutrient elements, not enough or too much light, water, or carbon dioxide, or perhaps insect or disease injury or spray damage has affected the leaves and thereby reduced their functional capacity.

Regardless of why the leaves are restricted in their energy manufacturing capacity, if they are restricted, the priority distribution system dominates. The living cells in the leaves will retain the energy they need before transfer to the stems or roots begins. Likewise, when a leaf reaches the point where it cannot manufacture more energy than it needs, it will be dropped, in the case of most woody and many herbaceous plants. For example, if a leaf is shaded by other leaves or has been damaged by disease or suffers from a nutrient deficiency to where the energy manufactured does not exceed the energy required, it will be dropped. The break-even situation in which the amount of energy manufactured by the leaf just equals the amount used in respiration is referred to as the compensation point.

When energy manufactured by the leaves is restricted for any reason, the roots are first to be affected. For example, when azaleas were grown under varying levels of shade (15), 30% shade was ideal for growth of tops and roots. However, when plants were grown under 45% shade, the weight of the plant top was unaffected while the root weight was restricted. The same condition occurs when a nutrient deficiency or water stress develops.

Research by Gordon and Larson (6, 7) showed that with red pine, which holds needles for two years, the one-year-old needles were the prime supplier of energy for current shoot development and growth of the terminal bud, whereas the two-year-old needles were the prime supplier of energy for the roots. When a nutrient deficiency of nitrogen, phosphorus, potassium, or magnesium develops or drought occurs, the older leaves are lost first. Therefore, the roots are most affected. This phenomenon probably holds true for all woody plants.

F) Roots are the key factor in plant vigor. If the energy production by the leaves is restricted for any reason, root growth is restricted before any other plant part. It seems ironic that root growth is restricted by a lack of energy from the leaves when the top of the plant is deficient in nutrient elements that can only be supplied by the roots. In short, the plant hastens its own demise by failing to provide energy to that part (roots) that could best help overcome a nutrient element deficiency by expanding into additional soil.

On the other hand, if the energy manufactured by the leaves is sufficient to meet all requirements of the above-ground parts and the living cells in the stem, the roots receive appreciable quantities of energy from the leaves and grow vigorously. With vigorous root growth, more soil is contacted to supply water and nutrients and add stability to the plant's physical location (keeps trees upright) and growth is further accelerated.

Roots cannot maintain water and nutrient absorption capabilities and grow without energy from the leaves. In short, **as the root system goes, so goes the plant!** Also remember that increased plant stress, for any reason, means an increased likelihood of disease and insect problems and, conversely, reduced stress means increased resistance to problems.

Sources of Nutrient Elements. The discussion here will be on the various sources of nutrient elements, their solubility and how they are normally used. The following section will deal with various methods of fertilizer application and the plant response in various situations.

Nitrogen
Nitrogen is available in several soluble forms:
ammonium nitrate - 33% nitrogen
calcium nitrate - 15% nitrogen
potassium nitrate - 14% nitrogen, 44% potassium
monoammonium phosphate - 12% N, 48% phosphorus
diammonium phosphate - 21% nitrogen, 52% phosphorus
sodium nitrate - 16% nitrogen
ammonium sulfate - 20% nitrogen
urea - 46% nitrogen

Most liquid nitrogen fertilization is done with ammonium nitrate and potassium nitrate in a 2 to 1 up to a 5 to 1 ratio of the two nutrient elements, which provides both ammonium (NH_4) and nitrate (NO_3) nitrogen. Calcium nitrate is sometimes used as a foliar spray but seldom for soil applications, due to the much higher cost. Urea has the highest nitrogen concentration and is generally the least expensive of the granular sources. However, urea provides only ammonium nitrogen initially and under cool conditions, the conversion to nitrate is very slow. This may be an advantage or disadvantage depending on the immediate plant needs and the species involved.

Nitrogen is also available in several slow-release forms:
ureaformaldehyde - 38-0-0 sold as Blue Chip, Nitroform or Uramite in the U.S.A.
sulfur-coated urea - urea 46-0-0 is coated with molten sulfur which restricts water entrance into and out of the coated granule. In some cases the sulfur coating is further treated with a wax or resin to further slow the nutrient release. Final analysis is generally 32% to 40% nitrogen.

Osmocote - several formulations: 19-6-12, 18-6-12, 17-7-12, 24-5-9, 38-0-0 (coated urea), 16-38-0 (coated diammonium phosphate), and others. The thicker the resin coating, in general, the longer the fertilizer release.

IBDU (isobutylene diurea) - 30-0-0
various organic materials including sewage sludge and various animal manures.

Phosphorus.
Phosphorus is generally available in several forms:
diammonium phosphate, 21-52-0 and
monoammonium phosphate, 12-48-0 are water-soluble.

Slow-release sources of phosphorus include:
  single superphosphate, 0-20-0 which also includes 12% sulfur and 18% calcium as calcium sulfate.
  triple superphosphate, 0-46-0 which includes 12% calcium as calcium phosphate but almost no sulfur.
  magamp, 7-40-6, is magnesium ammonium phosphate.
Sierra Chemical Co. is using the Osmocote resin coating on diammonium phosphate, thereby creating an analysis of 16-38-0. The various coating thicknesses allow for varying release rates and provides a good slow-release source under conditions very subject to leaching. Sulfur coating of diammonium phosphate has also been successful.

Potassium.
  Potassium is widely available in three forms:
  potassium chloride (KCl), 0-0-60, is very soluble and has the **highest** salt level of any fertilizer material.
  potassium sulfate (K_2SO_4), 0-0-53, plus 18% sulfur, is very soluble.
  potassium nitrate (KNO_3), 13-0-44, is frequently used in liquid fertilizer systems in combination with ammonium nitrate.
Other sources of potassium include:
  sulfate of potash magnesia (K_2SO_4 $2MgSO_4$), 0-0-26 plus 15% sulfur and 10% magnesium, frequently sold as K-mag.
Sierra Chemical Co. used the Osmocote resin coating on potassium sulfate to create an analysis of 0-0-39 or 0-0-42, depending on the thickness of the coating and release rate.
sulfur-coating of potassium sulfate has also been accomplished to minimize release.

Calcium. Calcium is available in three principal forms but is also present in nearly all irrigation water. Calcium in the water supply is soluble and available for plant growth and must be considered in planning a nutrition program. In some cases, no calcium other than that in the water supply is needed and that can be in excess in some areas.
  calcium carbonate, lime, ($CaCO_3$), - 40% calcium
  calcium sulfate, gypsum, ($CaSO_4$), 29% calcium, 23% sulfur, is sometimes used, however, extra calcium without magnesium is generally undesirable.

dolomite, also referred to as dolomite lime. Analysis varies but generally 20% calcium and 9% to 10% magnesium from calcium carbonate and magnesium carbonate. Dolomite is a widely used source of calcium and magnesium but is more soluble than calcium carbonate alone.

calcium oxide (CaO), 70% calcium

some calcium is also available from single and triple superphosphate, 18% and 12%, respectively. Calcium nitrate is sometimes used in liquid fertilization programs and contains 22% to 37% calcium, depending on the source.

Magnesium. Magnesium is sometimes present in irrigation waters and should be considered in the nutritional program. However, there is generally only a small proportion of magnesium relative to calcium in the water. Sources include:

dolomite, calcium and magnesium carbonates (see under calcium).

magnesium sulfate, ($MgSO_4$), 10% magnesium, 20% sulfur, may be broadcast and incorporated or watered-in. It is very water soluble and may be injected into irrigation water, however, it is difficult to keep in suspension during cool weather.

magnesium oxide, (MgO), 58% magnesium. This is very insoluble (see Table 22.4) and, unless finely ground, may not supply enough soluble magnesium for crop growth unless the soil is acid, thus increasing the solubility. Martin-Marietta Corporation and Kaizer Chemicals produce a magnesium oxide, 120-mesh, that is helpful in preventing magnesium deficiencies in some situations.

sulfate of potash magnesia ($K_2SO_4\ 2MgSO_4$) is 10% magnesium, 15% sulfur and 26% potassium. It is soluble and may be used as a general incorporation into the soil (see Tables 22.3 and 22.4).

Sulfur. Sulfur is an impurity or associated element with several other nutrient elements. However as fertilizers become more refined, it may be necessary to add sulfur to the soil to maintain a sufficient supply. Sources of sulfur include:

ammonium sulfate,

sulfur coatings used on urea and other elements,

potassium sulfate,

sulfate of potash magnesia (also sold as K-mag),

calcium sulfate,

magnesium sulfate,

the various sulfate forms of micronutrients used in some micronutrient fertilizers, and

elemental sulfur, (S_2) which is generally 92 to 96% sulfur, may also be used. It is slowly oxidized to form sulfuric acid and therefore provides the sulfate (SO_4) needed for plant growth.

The Micronutrients. The micronutrients are available in several forms, but most common are the sulfates of iron, copper, zinc, and manganese, and sodium forms of boron and molybdenum. These are readily soluble in water. Oxide forms of iron, copper, zinc and manganese are also available, but are, in general, very insoluble and of minor importance.

Several of the micronutrients can exist in various valence states or levels of electrical charge. For example, iron and manganese are readily available with two or three electrical charges, ++ or +++. Both elements are primarily absorbed as the ++ form with little, if any, benefit to the plant from the +++ form. Because the electrical state of the micronutrient element is critical as are the rates and ratios among the micronutrients, be cautious when adding specific micronutrient sources to the soil. The safest and most practical approach is to lower the soil pH to release the natural complex of micronutrients in the soil, or use a manufactured micronutrient fertilizer that has been thoroughly researched and tested.

Micromax Micronutrients (Grace/Sierra Chemical Co.) is a unique formula or blend of the six micronutrients. In many cases it is best to apply the entire micronutrient complex rather than just one. For example, if iron is applied and the deficiency is more than just iron, the deficiency will not be corrected and may be made more severe.

Chelate forms of micronutrients are also available. These are much more expensive than sulfate forms and are useful primarily as foliar sprays where quick green up is desired. The benefits are, however, only short term. The key to solving micronutient problems is by modifying the soil environment and/or soil pH which addresses the cause instead of just the symptom. More on this in succeeding chapters.

Why a Fertilizer Burns. It is important to understand why a fertilizer burns. Soluble nitrogen fertilizers, if applied properly, can be just as effective as a slowly soluble nitrogen source in providing the plant with the nitrogen it requires **if** all of the factors are understood and considered. The risk of burn can be minimized if the factors that contribute to a burn are understood (8).

Fertilizers are salts. These salts are not unlike table salt (sodium chloride), except that they contain various plant nutrients. When a salt is added to water, the osmotic pressure of the solution is increased. Osmotic pressure is, in a sense, a measure of how tightly water is held in a solution. When a fertilizer, either as a solid or a liquid, is applied, the fertilizer salts must sooner or later enter and become a part of the soil solution before the nutrients can enter the roots and be used by the plant. The increase in the osmotic pressure of the soil solution associated with the application of a fertilizer may determine whether the plant will survive and thrive or suffer from moisture stress from excess fertilizer.

For a plant's root system to take in water, the water must pass through a root cell membrane. Water can pass through this membrane only when the osmotic pressure of the solution inside the cell is higher than the osmotic pressure of the solution outside the cell. Water moves from a solution with low osmotic pressure into a solution with higher osmotic pressure. If the osmotic pressure of the soil solution becomes higher than that of the solution inside the cell, water cannot enter the cell and, under severe conditions, may move out. This results in damage to, or death of, the cell. When root cells die, the whole plant may die. The end result is termed "fertilizer burn".

An understanding of the potential salt effect of the various fertilizer materials can help prevent possible fertilizer burn. Salt index values are a measure of a material's relative tendency to increase the osmotic pressure of the soil solution as compared to the increase caused by an equal weight of sodium nitrate (12). The salt index of sodium nitrate has been arbitrarily set at 100. The higher the salt index, the greater the potential of a material to increase the osmotic pressure of the soil solution outside the root, and thus the greater potential for burn (Table 22.3.)

The potential for burn is not totally dependent upon the salt index of the fertilizer material. The moisture status of the soil and the plant is also important. If the level of soil moisture is low, a fertilizer will have a greater effect on increasing the osmotic pressure of the soil solution. When a fertilizer is "watered in", the volume of the soil solution increases and thus the osmotic pressure is reduced. In well-drained soils, however,

403

heavy applications of water, while having the beneficial effect of reducing the osmotic pressure of the soil solution, may also have the harmful effect of leaching nutrients past the root system.

The water status of the plant is affected by both the air temperature and the humidity, which is the amount of water in the air surrounding the plant. These factors to a large degree affect the plant's water requirements. The plant requires more water as the air temperature increases and as the humidity decreases. As the osmotic pressure of the soil solution increases, less and less water is available to the plant. Watering-in a fertilizer material may increase the water available to the root system by decreasing the osmotic pressure of the soil solution, and may also aid in reducing the plant's water requirements by cooling the plant and increasing the humidity of the plant's micro-environment.

The key to using soluble fertilizers on sandy soils is to apply small quantities but frequently. On heavier soils the quantity applied per application can be increased and the frequency decreased but only within fairly narrow limits. Slow release fertilizers cost considerably more per unit of nitrogen or other fertilizer element but being able to apply more per application with much longer between applications and much less risk of fertilizer burn is frequently worth the expense.

Nutrient Elements: Plant Response and Use. Nitrogen. More nitrogen is required for plant growth than any other fertilizer element (5). In addition, nitrogen has the greatest effect on plant growth (10). This is both the good news and bad news. The good news is that additional nitrogen will generally stimulate additional plant growth (increase in size and especially height) up to some point which is controlled by other limiting factors such as light, water, temperature, etc. The bad news is that nitrogen is often misused or over-used at the overall expense of plant quality and health. There appears to be a favorable ratio among **all** the nutrient elements that provides not only good growth but ample internal storage of carbohydrates and other energy reserves as well. An excess or disproportionate level of nitrogen relative to one or all of the other essential elements will provide additional growth but the tissues will be weak, and, because the levels of stored energy (carbohydrates and other energy storage compounds) are low, resistance to disease, insects and environmental stress is also low.

404

The ideal level of nitrogen depends on many environmental factors, levels of the other essential nutrient elements as well as the basic growth potential of the particular species or cultivar (9). An African violet (*Saintpaulia* spp.) requires a very low level of nitrogen compared to a chrysanthemum or sweetgum (*Liquidambar* spp.).

Nitrogen requirements of the many species of plants are so varied under the vast array of environmental and cultural conditions that no specific level or generalization can be made at this point. The preferred nitrogen rate or level on a specific site with a specific crop at a particular stage of growth can only be determined on that site. Experimentation with several levels of nitrogen on the major plants grown at a nursery or present in a landscape is a wise investment. However, don't fall for the trap that bigger is always better. Excessive growth, due to excess nitrogen, especially at high temperatures, may be false prosperity, resulting in bigger plants but of poorer quality and a lowered resistance to problems.

Nitrogen is absorbed by plants both as nitrate (NO3) and ammonium (NH_4) (10). Once inside the plant, the nitrogen is transformed into the amine form (NH_2) and combines with soluble carbohydrates to form amino acids which are then translocated to the shoots in the xylem sap (2, 3, 4) and used in the formation of proteins. Most of the proteins are used in the protoplasm of new cells.

Phosphorus. Phosphorus may interact with other elements both directly and indirectly. Excess phosphorus may combine with calcium and several of the micronutrients to form insoluble compounds, thereby depriving the plant of these elements. Single superphosphate, 0-20-0, generally contains 20% P_2O_5 or 8.8% actual phosphorus plus 20% calcium as calcium sulfate and 12% sulfur. On the other hand, triple superphosphate, sometimes called concentrated superphosphate 0-46-0, generally contains 46% P_2O_5, or 20.2% actual phosphorus plus 14% calcium, but only 1.4% sulfur. Therefore, when either single or triple superphosphate is added to the soil, the calcium added should be considered in the overall nutritional program. **Excess phosphorus and calcium can suppress growth (14) (Figures 22.8 and 22.9).**

It is important to emphasize that slow-release sources of all elements must be evaluated carefully to determine not only the rate to be used but how much of the nutrient is released over what period of time.

Figure 22.8. Effects of no additional phosphorus other than that in Osmocote 17-7-12 (left), 4 pounds per cubic yard of 0-20-0 (left of center), and 1.5 pounds per cubic yard of 0-46-0, with or without gypsum (right) on growth of Fosters holly. Note the strong stem development and branching of the two plants on the left as opposed to the more shrubby growth of the plants on the right where excess calcium and phosphorus were present.

*Figure 22.9.   Osmocote 24-5-9, 12- to 14-month-release formulation was used in the mix with a constant rate of nitrogen but with phosphorus levels of 0.6, 1.2 and 1.8 pounds P_2O_5 per cubic yard. Note that the shore juniper (**Juniperus conferta**) is fuller and has many more branches at the 1.2 pound rate as opposed to either higher or lower levels of phosphorus . Even though this study was done in containers, the same effects can be observed in landscape soils.*

407

Potassium. Potassium may be applied either as potassium chloride or potassium sulfate, which are both very soluble. Slow-release fertilizer such as Osmocote 18-6-12, 17-7-12, 12-5-9, Scotts SREF 24-4-10, or others also works well on sandy soils.

The quantity of potassium required for excellent plant growth and quality is generally lower than the common levels used. There is no additional benefit in terms of increased cold tolerance or disease resistance from excessive levels of potassium, as has been proposed from time to time. In three different studies over a period of 11 years, plants with excessive levels of potassium were equally damaged by cold as plants with low levels of potassium. Only if the plant was severely deficient was cold hardiness affected.

In one of the studies reported under phosphorus, potassium and phosphorus combinations at various rates were studied (1). As long as a moderate level of potassium was supplied, and the other nutrient elements were at the proper levels, growth was excellent . **Excessive potassium can suppress growth.** This has occurred in several studies in both landscape soils as well as containers over several years, reducing the emphasis on potassium. Some of the potassium levels listed as ideal for tissue levels in various species are fiction. Some of these are based on potassium levels of plants grown in solution culture (hydroponics), which is quite different from practical plant production in the nursery or landscape.

Sulfur. Sulfur is an impurity in single superphosphate (0-20-0) amounting to about 12%, whereas triple superphosphate 0-46-0 contains less than 2% sulfur. Calcium sulfate (gypsum) and magnesium sulfate (Epsom salts) are also common sources of sulfur. In some cases the irrigation water contains dissolved calcium sulfate or other sources of sulfate in sufficient quantity to provide the plant's requirements.

The exact level of sulfur necessary for excellent plant growth when all other factors are at or near the ideal level is not well known. However, if a source of phosphorus without sulfur is used and dolomite is the calcium and magnesium source, sulfur deficiency symptoms may eventually appear in sandy soils. Under these conditions, broadcasting granular sulfur, (96% S) is an economical and effective source. Do not try to spread sulfur dust.

Calcium and Magnesium. Excess calcium can strongly interfere with magnesium nutrition in several ways as well as tie-up micronutrients (Figure 22.10). It should be noted that the reason the magnesium cation with two electrical charges is not as strong as the calcium with two electrical charges is probably due to the fact that water is always associated with the magnesium. This water of hydration prevents the magnesium from attaching as closely and, therefore, as strongly as the calcium.

Figure 22.10.   Excess calcium suppresses both top and root growth primarily by reducing the availability of magnesium and micronutrients.   The plant on the left was grown with a moderate level of calcium, whereas the one on the right was grown with a high rate of calcium.

Observations, experiments and experience have gradually increased awareness of the importance of water quality on calcium and magnesium levels and the growth of plants.

In one water quality study conducted in containers, shortly after the study began, calcium deficiency symptoms began to appear on the new growth of geraniums which had no dolomite in the soil mix and received only pure water. Geraniums grown to salable size with no dolomite and either pure water or water with 40 ppm (parts per million) calcium and 20 ppm magnesium showed calcium deficiency symptoms, while plants grown with the medium-hard water showed no deficiency symptoms. Geraniums grown with the medium-hard water and no dolomite were as attractive as any treatment in the study. Plants grown with the very hard water were somewhat less attractive. Geraniums grown with two pounds of dolomite per cubic yard developed calcium deficiencies with the two best quality water sources.

Geraniums grown with four pounds of dolomite per cubic yard were of similar quality regardless of the water quality used, except for the very hard water, which reduced flower size. Geraniums grown with eight pounds of dolomite per cubic yard were generally smaller and of poorer quality with all water sources showing the growth suppression of an excess (Figure 22.11).

Figure 22.11. Geraniums grown with pure water (all minerals removed) and eight pounds of dolomite per cubic yard (left) were full and attractive, whereas plants receiving the same level of dolomite but increasing quantities of calcium in the water supply were progressively restricted (left to right). This emphasizes how great the effect of dissolved minerals in the water supply can be. The same effect occurs in soils, only the symptoms are slower to appear because of the soil's buffering capacity.

Gardenias were more sensitive to the poor quality water used than were geraniums. In general, the gardenias grew poorly with the very hard water. On the other hand, they grew similarly with two or four pounds of dolomite and pure water or two pounds of dolomite and good quality water, or no dolomite and the moderately hard water. This shows that the soluble calcium and magnesium in the water is substituting for the calcium and magnesium normally provided by the dolomite.

It is difficult to determine precisely the quantities of calcium and magnesium a plant needs. If the irrigation water has even moderate quantities of soluble calcium and magnesium, the plant is being fertilized with these elements in the water just as is commonly done with nitrogen, and potassium injected into the irrigation system. Most of the calcium and magnesium in the water is adsorbed by the soil since they are readily exchanged cations (they have a positive electrical charge). The roots can exchange hydrogen for these ions as needed during the growth of the plant. Calcium levels continue to increase with time when calcium is present in the irrigation water because calcium can displace other elements such as potassium and magnesium.

Although the example above deals with plants in containers, similar changes in the soil occur from irrigation water. Since most soils are highly buffered (resistant to change), the changes occur over a period of years instead of months and, unfortunately, go undetected until plant problems arise.

Water quality is a major factor influencing the proper calcium and magnesium nutrition of plants. A good water quality test is an inexpensive investment. Remember that any time a change occurs in the water source, an additional water quality test should be done.

The Micronutrients. In most cases, micronutrients are sufficiently available and in reasonable proportions in good field soils that there is no benefit from adding them as fertilizers. There are exceptions, however, especially in the sandy soils of Florida and in the arid Southwest. Plant nutrition in containers is entirely a different story. In 1957, Matkin, Chandler and Baker (11) wrote, "Since micronutrients are required in such minute amounts by plants and are natural components of peat, soil, fertilizer, and water, it is improbable that a soil mix would develop micronutrient deficiencies." Since that time, many studies have been conducted to improve the physical and chemical aspects of container growth media and nutrition. In general, with each improvement in the conditions in the container (i.e. total pore space, air space, carbon:nitrogen ratio, and media structure and components), plant growth and quality improves. Likewise, with each advancement in the understanding of container nutrition,

411

plant growth has improved. These improvements in plant growth and quality have come in steps as successive limiting factors have been removed. There are probably many more limiting factors to be discovered and removed before maximum plant growth in containers can be achieved. The same holds true for field and landscape soils only the changes are more subtle and thus difficult to detect.

In 1969, it was shown that as nitrogen, phosphorus, and potassium rates increased, rates of Perk (a micronutrient fertilizer) also had to be increased to achieve maximum growth with the physical and cultural conditions imposed on the plants at that time (13) (Figure 22.12).

Deficiency symptoms of micronutrients are often difficult, if not impossible, to distinguish from toxicity symptoms. In addition, when the suspected deficient micronutrient element is provided to the plants and no response occurs, it may be because there were actually:

a) more than one deficient element,
b) already a toxicity of one or more elements,
c) a deficiency of one element and a toxicity of another, or
d) some other combination of deficiencies or toxicities.

The tendency is to assume a single deficiency. In reality, there may be several deficiencies or near-deficiencies but only the most severe deficiency is reflected in foliage symptoms on the plant.

One of the striking aspects of this research with micronutrients was the root growth response, especially with azaleas. When the "ideal" combination of micronutrients was provided in the container medium, the root growth was excellent, whereas, if one or more of the micronutrients was out of synchronization, root growth was limited (Figure 22.13). This occurred with the same mix, watering and other nutrient additives.

412

*Figure 22.12.   Effects of Perk micronutrients at rates of 0, 1, 2, 4, 6, 8 pounds per cubic yard (left to right) on wax leaf ligustrum (**Ligustrum japonicum**).   The bare stems on the tops of the plants are old flower stalks.   It is important to note that all of the leaves were of similar size, dark green and apparently healthy even though plant size was vastly different.   Just because no chlorosis is visible does not mean that a plant is making maximum growth.*

413

Figure 22.13.   The azaleas above were grown with the high rate of copper and boron and low manganese.   Azaleas grown with low iron (left), medium iron (center), and high iron (right) are shown. Leaf retention and color, flower numbers, and overall plant quality were increased by increased rates of iron, but only if manganese, boron and copper were at the correct level.   The azaleas below reflect the difference in both top and root development as a result of proper micronutrient nutrition when all other factors were held constant.

414

The reason for this improved root growth is the improved micronutrient formulation which greatly increases the capacity of the leaves to utilize other nutrients and manufacture energy (carbohydrates) for use in various aspects in plant growth. The greater the energy manufacturing capacity of the leaves, the greater the quantity of energy transferred to or stored in the stems or roots. Since root growth is dependent upon energy from the leaves, this increased leaf capacity is reflected in additional root growth, which in turn improves nutrient uptake and leaf energy manufacturing capacity, thus growth is accelerated. It also appears that as the total nutritional program is improved, the tolerance level of the plant to adversity increases.

Micromax is a unique formulation of water soluble micronutrients (16). It is not a slow-release formulation initially. However, when Micromax is incorporated into a soilless medium or soil, with the first wetting, the micronutrients react with the components of the mix and create a slow-release micronutrient fertilizer. The advantage of this process over other slow-release micronutrient products is that the threshold level of micronutrients in the growth medium or soil (whereby micronutrients are available for plant growth) is reached immediately. Micromax is recommended for incorporation only. This is because the fertilizer salts used in the manufacture of Micromax are soluble and, if allowed to remain on plant foliage for any period of time, may cause burning. In addition, some of the iron sulfate may oxidize if top-dressed, thereby altering the important ratio of iron to manganese and copper. However, Micromax has been successfully top-dressed on plants showing micronutrient deficiencies where contact with the stem or foliage is avoided, and where it is watered-in well and very soon. As work progresses, effects of micronutrient fertilizers on all aspects of plant growth become more clear. Preliminary studies with several species of shrubs and trees suggest that the micronutrient level in the parent plant, and/or increased plant growth and vigor associated with improved parent plant micronutrient nutrition, affects rooting of cuttings and subsequent growth. Micromax has, in some situations, provided increased plant growth and improved foliage color in landscape situations. **Unfortunately, defining the desired soil level of micronutrients is difficult, so proceed with caution.**

Relationships of Plant Nutrients. Plant growth is most vigorous and problem-free when all the nutrient elements and environmental conditions are synchronized. An excess of one nutrient element frequently influences the availability and absorption of other nutrients. There are several key element relationships that must be considered (Table 22.2). For example, the ratio of calcium to magnesium available for plant growth is important. If calcium is in excess, magnesium absorption is depressed or vice versa.

Table 22.2. Important Ratios of Nutrient Elements

Elements	Ratio
calcium to magnesium	2-1 to 6-1
nitrogen to sulfur	20-1

An excess of...	may cause a deficiency of...
nitrogen	potassium
potassium	calcium and/or magnesium
sodium	potassium, calcium, and magnesium
calcium	magnesium
magnesium	calcium
calcium	boron, iron, manganese, copper, zinc
iron	manganese
manganese	iron
iron	molybdenum
phosphorus	iron and/or manganese

When soluble sources of nitrogen are used, they must be applied frequently in order to maintain a reasonable level available for plant growth at all times. **Nitrogen, potassium and magnesium are the elements most readily leached.** Therefore, they are the most difficult to manage and require the greatest attention or monitoring. Phosphorus, calcium, magnesium, sulfur, and the micronutrients are best added to the soil at time of planting or bed preparation. The reason these elements can be incorporated is related to either their low solubility and low salt index, or their mechanism of binding with the soil.

The ideal quantity of any one nutrient element is probably not a specific level, but rather a range (Figure 22.14). In the case of soluble nitrogen fertilizer applications, maintaining the ideal range can be difficult. For example, when soluble nitrogen is applied, the maximum quantity is generally provided (short of root or top damage) so that the interval between applications can be longer. At the same time, unless nutrient levels are closely monitored, the level of nitrogen can drop below the ideal range before the next application. If a heavy rain occurs shortly after an application is made and the soil is sandy, the nitrogen is leached out, partially or entirely.

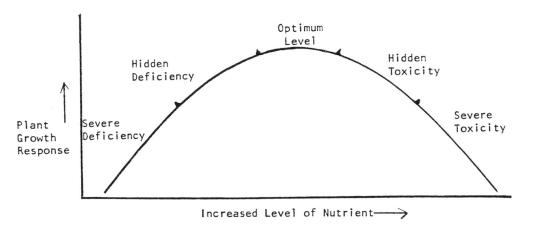

Figure 22.14. The optimum level of a plant nutrient is probably a limited range rather than a specific level. However, it should be noted that hidden deficiencies or toxicities occur long before either deficiency or toxicity symptoms appear. Just because there are no deficiency symptoms does not mean that all elements are near optimum.

Slow-release fertilizers are especially useful on salt-sensitive plants such as azaleas, rhododendrons and blueberries and salt sensitive annuals such as impatiens and petunias. When slow-release sources of elements are used, an important aspect is the rate of release per unit of time. For example, if 18-6-12 Osmocote releases the three nutrient elements over a period of six months, there will be a given quantity available for plant growth at any one time. On the other hand, if the Osmocote releases its nutrients over a period of four months instead of six, the quantity of nutrients available at any one time during the four-month period will be 33% greater. Consequently, knowing the

417

length of release time for a slow-release fertilizer in a given situation is very important in determining when to re-apply. The slow-release mechanism simply maintains the nutrient availability in the ideal range for a longer time between applications (Figure 22.15). Unfortunately, slow-release fertilizers are applied and forgotten. People often forget that they will supply nutrients for only some predetermined period of time under the specific environmental conditions. There is an easy way to determine if all the fertilizer has been released from the Osmocote granule. Simply break a capsule between the fingers and taste the liquid, if it is salty, fertilizer remains, but if it is not, all has been released. The failure to re-apply the slow-release fertilizer at the proper time is a management error. Unfortunately, slow-release fertilizers are often blamed for poor performance when it is really poor management.

Figure 22.15. Osmocote granules magnified several hundred times. Note the complete resin coating around the dry fertilizer granule. Because the fertilizer has an attraction for water, water is drawn into the resin-coated granule and creates a "water balloon" effect. When the fertilizer-salt concentration outside the "balloon" is lower than inside, the nutrient elements slowly move out. Because this movement is slow, a heavy rain leaches out only the small amount of fertilizer outside the "balloon" that has not been absorbed by the plant. The result is an effective slow-release delivery system for nitrogen and potassium, which are so readily leached.

Given all other factors are equal, slow-release sources of nutrients will provide for plants of equal or greater size and quality than dry chemical fertilizers.

Dry chemical fertilizers must be applied more frequently in order to effectively promote plant growth, thus increasing labor costs. Osmocote (Sierra Chemical Co., Milpitas, California) is a slow-release fertilizer containing nitrogen, phosphorus and potassium, produced by coating various water-soluble fertilizers with plastic resins. Isobutylidene diurea (IBDU) (Swift Agricultural Chemical Corp., Chicago, Illinois) is a synthetic organic nitrogen (31-0-0) containing 27.9% water-insoluble nitrogen. Variations in release rates are obtained through particle size and hardness and rainfall or irrigation water application. Sulfur-coated urea (SCU) is manufactured by Lesco (Lake Shore Industries) and others and contains 36% to 42% nitrogen. The O.M. Scotts Company has a modified sulfur-coated urea sold under the trade name SREF.

Fertilizer Salts and Salt Index. In areas where poor water quality is a problem in landscape management, slow-release fertilizers should be emphasized as an effective mechanism of nutrient delivery to the plant with virtually no salt effect to add to the salt from the water. If the soil has a limited water-holding capacity, the problem is further compounded. If a soil has a total salt reading of 500 parts per million at field capacity (the maximum water the soil will hold after watering), then later dries down to some point approaching the wilting point of the plant, the salt concentration will be much higher because the quantity of soluble salts remains the same while the water quantity has been reduced substantially. Therefore, the water-holding capacity of the soil and/or watering frequency has a great influence on the salt concentration experienced by the roots.

The total salt effect of a fertilizer is dependent upon the rate applied and the nature of the fertilizer. For example, if ammonium nitrate is applied, both the ammonium and the nitrate are used by the plant. On the other hand, if potassium chloride is applied, the potassium can be used but the chlorine is not. The same would be true of the sodium in sodium nitrate. These extra elements (chlorine and sodium) contribute to the total salt content of the soil while contributing nothing to plant growth. When water quality is good, unwanted elements are of little or no consequence. However, when water quality is poor or there is some other factor affecting the total salt level in the soil, these unnecessary elements carried along with the desired fertilizer element may be the proverbial straw that breaks the camel's back.

Table 22.3 shows the classical salt index of various fertilizers (12). In addition, there has been added a salt index per unit of fertilizer which gives a more accurate view of the salt effect of a fertilizer. For example, urea with a classical salt index of 75 appears moderately high. However, the salt index per unit of nitrogen is only 1.6, which is much lower than that of nitrogen from potassium nitrate which is 74 in the classical expression but 5.4 units of salt per unit of potassium. Assuming that both the potassium and nitrogen are needed for plant growth (in other words, the high potassium would not be in excess over and above plant needs) the values for potassium nitrate should be 13.8 + 46.6 = 60.4, divided into 74 = a salt index per unit of both nitrogen and potassium of 1.2.

In general, materials with classical salt indexes above 20 or on a unit of element above 0.5 should be added to a soil and incorporated per-plant or in moderate levels to the soil surface before rainfall or irrigation. On the other hand, the fertilizer materials with a very low salt index can be likened to hard candy. They very slowly dissolve and release a small portion of their contents. Dolomite, calcium carbonate, gypsum and single and triple superphosphates are the most widely used examples. These are naturally occurring slow-release fertilizers (dolomite, calcium carbonate and gypsum) or manufactured products with slow-release characteristics (single and triple superphosphates).

The solubilities of several commonly used fertilizer sources are listed in Table 22.3. In the case of the less soluble materials, assume the particle size is extremely small, a fine powder. Therefore, these values would be decreased if the particle size were increased. Using the hard candy analogy again, several small pieces of hard candy will dissolve faster than one large piece of equal size and weight, because the smaller the particles, the greater the surface area.

During the late '60s and '70s some of the research with agronomic crops grown in field soils suggested that the concern about the ratio of calcium to magnesium was unfounded. With fibrous rooted annual crops in field soils, where the plate-like or lattice structure of the clay colloids can adsorb many nutrients and the plant root system is unrestricted, this may be true. However, a point to keep in mind when considering plant establishment in the landscape is that **woody plant requirements**

are different: their root systems, in comparison, are very sparse and soil conditions are often marginal. Before the discussion of nutrition and fertilizers progresses, the reader is reminded that several materials provide more than one essential element, making it difficult to distinguish between the benefit of one or both, or the benefit from one and detrimental effect of the other during evaluation of plant responses. For example, single superphosphate contains 20% P_2O_5, or about 9% actual phosphorus, but it also contains about 20% calcium and 12% sulfur and numerous micronutrients in small quantities as impurities. If phosphorus and calcium are both low, the plant response may be from both elements. However, calcium is rarely lacking, so if single superphosphate is added, the phosphorus may be beneficial while the calcium is detrimental.

Dolomite is the major source of both calcium and magnesium. However, because it is a naturally occurring mineral, it also contains various impurities, especially micronutrients, depending on the specific source.

Proper plant nutrition is a constant challenge as the fertilizer elements interact with the soil, water, especially irrigation water, and other factors. It is a perpetual challenge to keep all 12 essential elements in the desire range. The payoff is that the healthier the plants, the fewer the problems.

Table 22.3. Chemical content and salt index of several fertilizer carriers (12).

Chemical	Analysis of fertilizer tested*	Salt index**	Salt index per unit of fertilizer element***
Nitrogen carriers:			
ammonium nitrate	35.0%	105	3.0
monoammonium phosphate	12.1	30	2.5
diammonium phosphate	21.2	34	1.6
ammonium sulfate	21.1	69	3.3
calcium nitrate	11.9	53	4.5
potassium nitrate	13.8	74	5.4
sodium nitrate	16.5	100	6.1
urea	46.6	75	1.6
Potassium carriers:			
potassium chloride	60.0	116	1.9
potassium nitrate	46.6	74	1.6
potassium sulfate	54.0	46	0.8
sulfate of potash- magnesia	21.9	43	2.0
Phosphorus carriers:			
monoammonium phosphate	61.7	30	0.5
diammonium phosphate	53.8	34	0.6
single superphosphate	20.0	8	0.4
triple superphosphate	46.0	10	0.2
Miscellaneous:			
calcium carbonate	56.0	5	0.09
dolomite	20.0	1	0.05
magnesium sulfate	16.0	44	2.7
gypsum	32.6	8	0.3

*Fertilizer analysis means % nitrogen in nitrogen carriers, % potassium oxide in potassium carriers, % magnesium oxide in magnesium carriers including dolomite, and % calcium oxide in calcium carbonate and gypsum.

**Salt index compared against equal weight of sodium nitrate, which was assigned a value of 100.

***Adjusted salt index per unit of fertilizer. (For example, divide salt index of 100 for sodium nitrate by 16.5, the number of fertilizer units, and the salt units per fertilizer unit is 6.1)

Table 22.4.   Solubilities of various nutrient elements.

Material	Solubility gm./100 gm. water
calcium carbonate (lime)	0.0014
calcium sulfate (gypsum)	0.209
calcium oxide	0.131
magnesium sulfate (Epsom salts)	26.0
magnesium oxide	0.00062
magnesium carbonate	0.176
potassium nitrate	13.3
potassium sulfate	12.0
potassium chloride	23.8
sulfate of potash magnesia	19.6
superphosphate, single and triple	0.0316 (about)
ammonium phosphates	22.7 or greater
ammonium sulfate	70.6
ammonium nitrate	118.3
calcium nitrate	121.2

Literature Cited

1.   Babcock, Frank E., Bonnie L. Appleton and Carl E. Whitcomb. 1982. Phosphorus nutrition of nursery stock. Okla. Agri. Exp. Sta. Res. Rept. P-829:44-48.

2.   Barnes, R.L. 1963. Nitrogen transport in the xylem of trees. Jour. of Forestry 61:50-51.

3.   Barner, R.L. 1963. Organic compounds in tree xylem sap. Forest Sci. 9:98-102.

4.   Bollard, E.G. 1957. Translocation of organic nitrogen in the xylem. Aust. Jour. Biol. Sci. 10:292-301.

5. Epstein, E. 1972. Mineral Nutrition of Plants: Principles and Perspectives. John Wiley & Sons, New York.

6. Gordon, J.C. and P.R. Larson. 1968. The seasonal course of photosynthesis, respiration and distribution of carbon in young *Pinus resinosa* trees as related to wood formation. Plant Physiol. 43:1617-1624.

7. Gordon, J.C. and P.R. Larson. 1970. Redistribution of C-labeled reserve food in young red pines during shoot elongation. Forest Sci. 16:14-20.

8. Knoop, W. 1976. Why a fertilizer burns. Weeds, Trees and Turf, 12:14-15.

9. Kramer, P.J. and T.T. Kozlowski. 1960. Physiology of Trees. McGraw Hill, New York.

10. Kramer, P.J. and T.T. Kozlowski. 1979. Physiology of Woody Plants. Academic Press. New York.

11. Matkin, O.A., P.A. Chandler and K.F. Baker. 1957. Components and development of mixes. In: The U.C. System for producing healthy container-grown plants. Calif. Agri. Exp. Sta. Manual 23.

12. Rader, L.F. Jr., L.M. White and C.W. Whitaker. 1943. The salt index--a measure of the effect of fertilizers on the concentration of the soil solution. Soil Science 12:201-218.

13. Whitcomb, Carl E. 1970. Response of four container-grown woody ornamentals to rates of Perk and Osmocote. The Florida Nurseryman 15:7, 36, 37.

14. Whitcomb, Carl E. 1988. Plant Production in Containers. Lacebark Publications. Stillwater, Ok. 640 pages.

15. Whitcomb, Carl E. and L.K. Euchner. 1979. Effects of shade levels on growth of container nursery stock. Nursery Res. Jour. 6:1-11.

16. Whitcomb, Carl E., Allan Storjohann and William D. Warde. 1981. Micromax--micronutrients for improved plant growth. Proc. Int. Plant Prop. Soc. 30:462-467.

CHAPTER 23

THE ESSENTIAL NUTRIENT ELEMENTS:
FUNCTION, DEFICIENCY AND TOXICITY

The Macro Elements - - - - - - - - - - - 426

    Nitrogen - - - - - - - - - - - - - 426

    Phosphorus - - - - - - - - - - - - 428

    Potassium - - - - - - - - - - - - - 430

    Magnesium - - - - - - - - - - - - - 432

    Sulfur - - - - - - - - - - - - - - 438

    Calcium - - - - - - - - - - - - - - 439

The Micro Elements - - - - - - - - - - - 440

    Iron - - - - - - - - - - - - - - - 440

    Manganese - - - - - - - - - - - - - 442

    Copper - - - - - - - - - - - - - - 444

    Zinc - - - - - - - - - - - - - - - 447

    Boron - - - - - - - - - - - - - - - 447

    Molybdenum - - - - - - - - - - - - 448

Literature Cited - - - - - - - - - - - 450

The Essential Nutrient Elements:
Function, Deficiency, and Toxicity

The 12 essential nutrient elements are generally referred to as macro (needed in relatively large quantities) and micro (needed in relatively small quantities). The macro-nutrients and their chemical symbols are: nitrogen (N), phosphorus (P), potassium (K), magnesium (Mg), sulfur (S), and calcium (Ca). The micronutrients are: iron (Fe), manganese (Mn), copper (Cu), boron (B), zinc (Zn), and molybdenum (Mo). All but three of the elements are absorbed as the elemental ion (the element without an accompanying element or group of elements). For example, you may apply potassium sulfate, K_2SO_4. However, if the potassium is absorbed, it is as K^+ not as K_2SO_4. The exceptions are: sulfur, which is absorbed as sulfate, $SO_4^=$; phosphorus, which is absorbed as phosphate, $PO_4^=$; and nitrogen, which may be absorbed either as nitrate, NO_3^- or ammonium, NH_4^+.

The elements carbon, hydrogen and oxygen, are also needed by plants. However, the carbon is obtained from carbon dioxide, CO_2, in the air and the oxygen and hydrogen from water. The following is a general discussion of each of the nutrient elements. When considering nutrient deficiency symptoms, keep in mind that a deficiency of one element rarely occurs, but varying degrees of deficiencies of several elements are more common. Quite often the symptoms of deficiencies we see are the most deficient element. See Figure 22.14 as a reminder of hidden deficiencies.

The Macro Elements. Nitrogen. Large quantities of nitrogen, generally from 1.5% to 4.0% on a dry weight basis, are required for rapid plant growth. When nitrogen is deficient, growth is generally slow and the lower leaves are pale or sometimes mottled because nitrogen is mobile in the plant and can be taken from older tissues and translocated to new growth. In rapid growing herbaceous and foliage plants, the lower leaves may become lighter green or yellow in color. On many woody plants, however, a nitrogen deficiency is reflected mostly as a reduced growth rate, and only under severe conditions do the lower or older leaves become pale green or yellow. In some instances, where a plant experiences an abrupt nitrogen deficiency and no new growth occurs, the entire plant will remain green, giving no clue to the problem. Only if bud break and new growth occurs will the classical lower leaf-yellowing symptom develop. Nitrogen can be supplied as nitrate such as calcium nitrate, $Ca(NO_3)_2$, from either ammonium or nitrate, as in ammonium nitrate, NH_4NO_3, or just from ammonium, as in diammonium phosphate (18-46-0). Nitrate, NO_3^-, has a negative charge and consequently is not attached as strongly to the soil as is ammonium. This means that the likelihood of leaching of nitrate from heavy rainfall or excess watering is greater. Ammonium, NH_4^+, has a positive charge and is held more strongly by the adsorptive capacity of the soil. Ammonium is usually converted to nitrate by bacterial action after a few days to a few weeks, depending on soil temperature and other factors. Once nitrogen is absorbed as either nitrate or ammonium, it is transformed in the plant to the amine form (NH_2) and combines with soluble carbohydrates to form amino acids and proteins.

Because nitrogen is required in large quantities by the plant and is so subject to loss by leaching, it is generally the most difficult nutrient element to manage. The management of nitrogen is very dependent on soil type and drainage. On very sandy soils, especially in areas of high rainfall and high temperatures such as Florida and some areas of the Gulf Coast, nitrogen is quickly converted from ammonium, which has a positive charge and is strongly held by the soil, to nitrate with a negative charge and is weakly held. This conversion factor, which is primarily dependent upon temperature, in conjunction with high rainfall and sandy soils that allow rapid percolation of water downward through the soils means frequent applications of nitrogen or the use of slow-release nitrogen sources. Where drip irrigation is used, nitrogen may be added to the water with each application to maintain a moderate but constant level of nitrogen available for plant growth. Slow-release fertilizers are also very useful on sandy soils. Osmocote (a plastic resin-coated fertilizer), sulfur-coated urea (where a molten sulfur-coating surrounds otherwise soluble urea nitrogen fertilizer making it slow-release), or compounds such as ureaformaldehyde and IBDU, which are only slowly soluble, are very useful under these conditions.

Where soils are clays, managing nitrogen is much easier, especially in cooler climates with moderate rainfall. For example, the heavy clay loam soils of eastern Iowa need only infrequent nitrogen applications for good plant growth. This is because of

    a) the adsorptive capacity of the soils,
    b) the limited percolation or leaching of water through the soil which leaches the nitrate nitrogen below the root zone,
    c) since the soils are generally cooler, the conversion of ammonium to nitrate is slower and,

d) the moderate rainfall which further limits leaching.

No two soils are the same and when coupled with climatic conditions, it can be easily seen that nitrogen management must be considered relative to each specific site. Add to this the unique aspects of various field soils and factors such as irrigation systems that may encourage more leaching, unusual soil depths, textures, and drainage systems and nitrogen management becomes much more complex. The important thing to remember is never allow the plant to become more than mildly nitrogen-deficient during spring growth. Because nitrogen has a profound effect on plant growth, it is sometimes used in excess. There is probably an ideal balance or proportion among all the nutrient elements required for plant growth. When an element is in excess or deficient, growth is restricted. However, excess nitrogen frequently stimulates additional soft, succulent growth that is slow to mature. These soft tissues are much more vulnerable to disease organisms than are tissues developed with a more favorable combination of all nutrients.

Another nitrogen-related management factor deals with shade and leaf color. Plants grown with moderate levels of nitrogen and under moderate shade levels are very dark green. This is frequently assumed to be a very good situation. However, this "false prosperity" is actually restricting growth and may make the plant more vulnerable to other problems. If the same plants are grown with a higher level of nitrogen and less shade, the leaves may appear slightly lighter green in color. However, the total energy production of the leaves and in turn the health and vigor of the root system will be improved and the plants can tolerate more stress.

Phosphorus. Phosphorus is tightly held in field soils, even those that are nearly 100% sand. Phosphorus is sometimes applied as phosphoric acid, H_2PO_4, or as mono- or diammonium phosphates as part of liquid fertilizer. More often, however, part or all of the phosphorus requirement of the plants can be met by incorporating either single or triple superphosphate (0-20-0 or 0-46-0) or diammonium phosphate (18-46-0) into the soil prior to planting. **Because these materials have a low salt index and are very slowly soluble, they can be safely incorporated without danger of a salt build-up or injury to developing roots of new plantings.** Soils with phosphorus levels of 60 to 100 pounds per acre (expressed as P_2O_5) will need no further phosphorus fertilizer for several years).

Phosphorus deficiency causes stunting long before the classical deficiency symptoms of reddening of the lower leaves (Figure 23.1). Plants mildly deficient in phosphorus have a dull appear-ance or lack of luster, especially on the older leaves. Because phosphorus is mobile in the plant, the older leaves show the symptoms first and most severely.

Phosphorus is used in the plant in several ways. However, the high energy organic complexes, ATP (adenosine triphosphate) and ADP (adenosine diphosphate), provide the energy for several chemical reactions within the plant. A phosphorus deficiency, even though very mild, will reduce this energy transfer system and slow growth functions of the plant. It is therefore very important to supply the proper amount of phosphorus. However, **excess phosphorus is equally detrimental to plant growth.** Excess phosphorus combines with calcium, iron and other micronutrients to form insoluble complexes of these elements. Thus, **excess phosphorus generally is observed as stunting and deficiencies of several micronutrients.** Phosphorus is normally found in plant tissues at only about one-tenth to one-eighth the level of nitrogen, comprising 0.14 percent to 0.32 percent of the dry weight of leaves.

Figure 23.1. Phosphorus deficiency on chrysanthemums. The leaf on the right is a normal leaf, whereas the leaf on the left has severe phosphorus deficiency symptoms. The darker areas on the upper portion of the leaf are reddish-purple, whereas the center and lower portions of the leaf are identical to the normal leaf.

Potassium. Leaves of healthy plants generally contain from one to four percent potassium. Potassium is very mobile in the plant tissues and is not bound into organic chemical complexes as are nitrogen and phosphorus. Simply dipping a leaf into a container of water a few times will remove 25 percent or more of the potassium. Potassium is leached from leaves during rains and probably is absorbed by the roots and recycled many times in the life of a large tree.

Deficiency symptoms always occur on older leaves due to the mobility of potassium within the plant. There is generally no chlorosis or leaf color change associated with potassium deficiency, but rather a death of the leaf margins (Figure 23.2). On some species, irregular spots or lesions develop on the leaves that, at first, look like a disease. These spots are most severe on the older leaves and may be various shades of tan, light brown, or gray, depending on the plant species. On one occasion in Hawaii, foliage plants grown in a soil of volcanic ash with some peat added had severe potassium deficiency symptoms that had been misdiagnosed as various diseases (Figure 23.3). The confusion was accentuated in this case because:

a) 3:1:2 nitrogen, phosphorus, potassium ratio fertilizer was used, thus the managers thought there was little likelihood of potassium deficiency, however, the rate was low,

b) it was supplemented with additional nitrogen through the irrigation system,

c) the volcanic ash soil has the capacity to bind large quantities of phosphorus and potassium,

d) when a plant becomes weakened from a severe deficiency, it is more susceptible to various diseases, and

e) as soon as the lesions form on the leaves, secondary organisms begin a further attack on the dead and damaged tissues, making it difficult to distinguish between the primary cause and the secondary effects.

Potassium may be added as potassium chloride, potassium sulfate or other sources. The needs of plants for potassium is difficult to define, in part because of the mobility and recycling of potassium. Usually 150 to 300 pounds of potassium (expressed as K_2O) is sufficient for good plant growth. When soils contained potassium at this level, adding potassium **restricted** plant growth in a series of studies over several years in central Oklahoma. As with most nutrient elements, more is not better. Add nutrients only when the soil test shows a need. Do not arbitrarily apply a 10-10-10 analysis fertilizer when only nitrogen is needed.

Figure 23.2. Potassium deficiency on southern magnolia (*Magnolia grandiflora*). Note that the margin of the leaf is dead and dark brown to dark gray, while the inner portion of the leaf appears normal except for a few small dark spots just in from the dead leaf margin.

Figure 23.3. Potassium deficiency on *Dracena fragrans*. In this case the symptoms appear only as spots on the leaves until the deficiency becomes severe, and the lower leaves begin to die along the margin and finally collapse entirely. The leaf spots are frequently misdiagnosed as various diseases and make these foliage plants unsalable.

431

Magnesium. Magnesium is a key element in the formation of chlorophyll and plays a vital role in several other plant processes. Magnesium is very mobile in the plant. Therefore, the symptoms develop first on the older leaves. However, **magnesium deficiency symptoms rarely develop the striking visual characteristics on woody plants as were noted for nitrogen, phosphorus and potassium, and the symptoms vary among species.** On most woody species, a slight yellowing of the outer margin of the older leaves is the extent of the visual symptoms. In most cases, the leaves drop before any further chlorosis develops (Figure 23.4). However, after some experience, the absence of older leaves on the plant and the more open appearance also become clues (Figure 23.5).

Magnesium deficiency on pittosporum *Pittosporum tobira* shrubs causes a slight yellowing of the margin of the older leaves near the center. As the deficiency becomes more severe the entire center portion of the leaf becomes chlorotic (Figure 23.6). *Podocarpus* spp. also show rather unusual magnesium deficiency symptoms. At first a faint loss of green color occurs in the center of the leaf followed by a progressive yellowing which eventually affects all but the tip of the leaf just prior to dropping (Figure 23.7).

Magnesium deficiency on flowering dogwood (*Cornus florida*) develops an interveinal chlorosis that is somewhat similar to iron and manganese deficiencies on this species, except the affected tissues remain light green to almost greenish white, whereas iron and manganese deficiencies cause a distinct yellowing and the symptoms are on older leaves as opposed to younger leaves. Magnesium deficiency on poinsettia also causes an interveinal chlorosis.

432

*Figure 23.4.   The slight chlorosis or yellowing near the tip of
the leaf is the only visual clue to magnesium deficiency on
Pyracantha coccinea (above) and **Ilex cornuta** 'Burfordi Nana'
(right two leaves).   The leaves drop soon after developing the
symptoms.   Therefore, there are few clues to magnesium deficiency.
The new leaves of the same holly (below, left) appear normal
because magnesium is mobile in the plant and is shifted from the
older leaves to the new growth.*

*Figure 23.5.   The faint yellowing of the outer narrow margin of a southern magnolia (**Magnolia grandiflora**) leaf is the only visual symptom of magnesium deficiency before the leaf drops (top).   A magnesium-deficient magnolia is barren of internal leaves as the result of the early leaf drop.*

434

*Figure 23.6. Magnesium deficiency on **Pittosporum tobira**. Note the slight yellowing of the sides of the leaf in the upper right hand section, whereas the entire center of the leaf to its left has yellowed. It is also important to observe that the young leaves in the lower portion of the photo are normal*

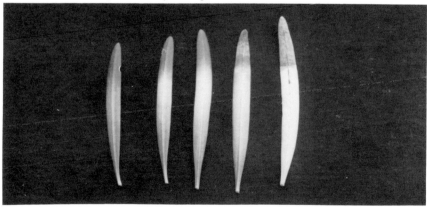

*Figure 23.7. **Podocarpus** spp. with magnesium deficiency progressing from the first visually detectable symptom on the left to the most severe symptom on the right. The earliest deficiency symptom is simply a reduction of the intensity of the green color in the center of the leaf.*

435

On some herbaceous plants, especially monocots such as dracenas and palms, the leaves are not dropped since no abscission (separation) layer is formed at the base of the leaf as on the dicots or woody plants. With these species, the leaves become more and more pale developing a yellow to yellow-green chlorosis, and finally tissues of the outer portion of the leaves begin to die.

With container-grown greenhouse and nursery stock, magnesium deficiency symptoms may be more dramatic and may appear very similar to severe iron deficiency. With the development of Micromax micronutrients, numerous cases of severe magnesium deficiency were misdiagnosed as iron deficiency, especially in some areas of Europe where little, if any, magnesium is normally added to the growth medium. When a mildly magnesium-deficient plant or seedling, that is also borderline deficient in one or more of the micronutrients, is planted in a growth medium with an abundance of micronutrients in the proper ratio, the magnesium deficiency abruptly becomes so severe that **all** leaves are affected, young and old alike. The leaf chlorosis symptoms in this case are nearly identical to iron deficiency and their appearance on young leaves makes diagnosis very deceptive. The answer becomes clear when a magnesium sulfate drench provides a response, whereas iron sprays have no effect.

Magnesium deficiency in plants is relatively slow to correct, compared to a deficiency of iron or manganese. Likewise, plants growing in containers are more responsive to supplemental magnesium than plants growing in the field or landscape. Once leaves have developed even mild magnesium deficiency, applying magnesium to the roots or spraying directly on the leaves is slow to provide a visual plant response. The new leaves continue to be green while the old leaves showing symptoms are unaffected. Only after the old leaves drop or are removed and sufficient new growth has occurred to provide a new plant canopy, are the symptoms eliminated (Figure 4.8).

Another factor of magnesium deficiency on woody plants lies in the energy supply and distribution from the leaves to various plant parts. Gordon and Larson (4) showed that the carbohydrates from the young leaves were directed principally to the new shoots and developing buds, whereas carbohydrates from the older leaves provided the primary source of energy for the roots. Taking this one step further, any deficiency that affects the older leaves, especially if the old leaves drop, will have a great effect on root activity. Since magnesium deficiency is slow to correct and probably affects the root system most, the best advice is to plan a nutrition program to **prevent** a magnesium deficiency from developing rather than to try to correct the deficiency once it becomes visually apparent. Nurseries and landscape managers that prune frequently and severely tend to create greater problems with magnesium than those that prune lightly. The reason is that with frequent pruning, much of the magnesium is removed in the new growth. Then, with further growth, the magnesium is translocated to the new growth from the older leaves, diluted even farther, and so on. The frequent pruning of hedges causes the same problem and is probably a major contributor to the open, leggy appearance of hedges over time. Also keep in mind that a nutrient deficiency generally causes stunting long before visual symptoms appear.

The elements covered: nitrogen, phosphorus, potassium, and magnesium are **mobile** in the plant. Therefore, deficiency symptoms generally appear **on the older leaves**.

The elements following: sulfur, calcium, iron, manganese, copper, boron, zinc, and molybdenum are **not mobile** in the plant. Therefore, deficiency symptoms generally appear **on the new growth**. However, toxicity symptoms, especially boron, may appear on the older leaves.

*Figure 23.8. Magnesium deficiency on schefflera (**Brassaia actinophylla**) causes an irregular blotching on older leaves. These leaves will never regain normal green color. Only after magnesium is supplied and enough growth has occurred to cover these leaves or the affected leaves are removed, will the symptoms disappear. By contrast, if this was iron or manganese deficiency, the leaves showing the symptoms would regain their normal color quickly after the deficient element was provided*

437

Sulfur. Sulfur deficiency appears similar to nitrogen deficiency except the symptoms appear on the new leaves instead of the old leaves. Leaves become pale and, with severe conditions, develop a yellowing with the veins remaining darker than the leaf tissues between the veins. Sulfur is absorbed as $SO_4^=$ instead of elemental sulfur. There appears to be a relationship or balance between nitrogen and sulfate of approximately 20 to 1. When single superphosphate 0-20-0, $(N-P_2O_5-K_2O)$ was readily available and widely used, the 8% to 10% sulfate was more than adequate for all plants. More recently, however, with the use of triple superphosphate (0-46-0) and diammonium phosphate (18-46-0) in most fertilizers little or no sulfate is carried as impurities. Granular elemental sulfur (92% sulfur) provides a good semi-slow release source for most uses. Sulfur deficiencies on plants grown in containers are relatively common (Figure 23.9). Once sulfur is applied as a topdress to the growth medium, the symptoms disappear within a few days.

Figure 23.9. Sulfur deficiency symptoms on geranium. The leaf on the left is from the newest growth and has the most severe symptoms while the leaf on the right is from the oldest part of the plant and shows only a slight off-color and loss of luster compared to a non-deficient plant. Nitrogen deficiency could appear very similar, except that the location of the symptom on the plant would be reversed because sulfur is not mobile in the plant, whereas nitrogen is very mobile.

438

Micronutrient products such as Micromax and Perk, that are based on sulfate forms of micronutrients, generally supply enough sulfate to meet the 20 to 1 ratio with the nitrogen supply. Likewise, if a liquid fertilizer program is used where potassium sulfate or ammonium sulfate is part of the fertilizer program, adequate sulfur will be provided. Sulfate toxicity is highly unlikely but large quantities of sulfate may create a very low pH in some soil. With the paranoia regarding pH, no one has studied the effect of excess sulfate on plant growth.

Calcium. Calcium is rarely deficient since some calcium source, generally calcium carbonate or dolomite (which is calcium and magnesium carbonate), is widely used to adjust the pH of soils. In addition, most soils contain sufficient calcium for plant growth even when soil pH is relatively low. However, as plant nutrition becomes more precise to further improve growth and health, specific calcium levels may be required for some species. The **excess** calcium added to raise the pH of soils may actually suppress plant growth in many instances. Because no visual symptoms occur from the excess calcium, or if chlorosis does occur, it is blamed on the high pH or micronutrient deficiencies and not the calcium. The high levels of calcium are generally ignored or thought to be acceptable. About 600 to 1000 pounds of available calcium per acre is sufficient for most plants. Likewise, the "ideal" pH for most woody plants is between 5.0 and 6.0. This is lower than many publications suggest. This is covered in greater detail elsewhere in this book.

Since most irrigation waters contain calcium, many plants are constantly being supplied with this element. Calcium is a strong cation and attaches readily to the exchange sites on the soil. This gradual accumulation of calcium slowly raises the pH of many irrigated soils.

Calcium is not mobile in plant tissues, therefore, if a deficiency develops, it will be noticeable first and most severely on the new growth (Figure 23.10). Applications of calcium will eliminate the deficiency symptom in a few days. On woody plants the terminal buds on the uppermost branches may die when calcium is severely deficient, with or without any chlorosis pattern. The older leaves may be brittle and will cup or curl upwards on some species.

439

Figure 23.10. This young geranium plant was grown in a mix of peat and perlite with no calcium added. Even under these conditions and no calcium in the water, the first leaves appeared normal. Then slowly the symptoms began to appear. The photo was taken looking down on the top of the plant. Note the dark older leaves and progressive symptoms with the newer leaves. Dolomite was applied to the surface of the medium and within four days, all symptoms had disappeared.

The Micro Elements.   Iron. Iron deficiency is common on many species grown in alkaline soils.   Iron deficiency is also common where high levels of calcium from calcium containing materials such as lime, dolomite, the water source, bicarbonates, or some component in the soil ties up the iron in insoluble compounds. High levels of phosphorus, either alone or in conjunction with calcium, may also tie up iron in insoluble complexes.

Iron is not mobile in the plant, therefore, symptoms are generally   most severe on new growth.   Iron deficiency first appears as pale green in the leaf tissues between the veins, then progresses to yellow-green to yellow (Figure 23.11).

440

*Figure 23.11.   Iron deficiency of Chinese hibiscus (**Hibiscus rosa-sinensis**).   Note that the veins in the leaf are darker while the areas of the leaf blade farthest from the veins are most affected.*

The symptoms are virtually identical to manganese deficiency symptoms on most species.   Iron and manganese react similarly to calcium and phosphorus or high pH situations.   In many cases what is diagnosed as an iron deficiency may be a manganese deficiency or even more likely, a moderate deficiency of both elements (Figure 23.12).

Iron is most noted for its presence in the chlorophyll of the leaves.   In the chloroplasts, iron plays a role in the synthesis of proteins. Iron also plays a role in the function of other enzymes.   Iron can be supplied to plants by foliar sprays, root zone treatments or quite often simply reducing the pH of the soil will release enough iron from the complexes with calcium to meet the plants' needs.

*Figure 23.12. Azaleas (**Rhododendron** X 'Hinodegiri'), grown with a low level of iron (left) and a low level of both iron and manganese (right). Interestingly, the overall size of the plants was about the same as plants with adequate levels of both elements. However, the number of flower buds were greatly reduced on the deficient plants.*

Manganese. Manganese is not mobile in the plant and reacts similarly to iron in many respects. It is also essential in the synthesis of chlorophyll and is similarly affected by calcium and phosphorus. Therefore, the deficiency symptoms of manganese and iron are virtually identical. Only the foolish or the very knowledgeable try to distinguish between visual iron and manganese deficiency symptoms on most species. There are, however, some distinct differences on some species. Mouse-ear disease on pecan is caused by a deficiency of manganese, but in this case, no chlorosis occurs, only the distortion of the leaflet from the normal pointed or oval shape to blunted end (Figure 23.13). *Ixora coccinea* is apparently a poor absorber of manganese so it is most often the deficient element causing the chlorosis of this otherwise very attractive shrub (Figure 23.14).

*Figure 23.13. A pecan (**Carya illinoinensis**) leaflet with manganese deficiency. Because of the deformity of the leaflet, which normally has a pointed tip, it has been dubbed mouse-ear disease. Because manganese availability is affected by soil temperatures, it is most common in early spring when soils are cold and may disappear with warmer weather. Generally no chlorosis is visible*

Manganese solubility is affected by the temperature of soils. As the temperature of soils decreases, so does manganese solubility. Therefore, deficiencies are most likely to occur during low soil temperatures. The ratio of manganese to iron is quite specific. An excess of either frequently causes a deficiency of the other.

*Figure 23.14.   Leaves of **Ixora coccinea** showing typical manganese deficiency. Deficient plants also flower poorly.*

Copper.   Copper plays a key role in several enzymatic systems. The most common deficiency symptom is the stunting of overall growth (Figure 23.15) followed by leaf stunting, a loss of leaf luster and leaf size, leaf distortion (Figure 23.16), and on some species, rosetting of buds on the branch terminal after the terminal bud has died (Figure 23.17).   There is generally no chlorosis or leaf discoloration symptoms associated with either copper deficiency or toxicity.   However, copper deficiency on roses (*Rosa* spp.) sometimes gives a general mottled or flecking pattern that appears like damage from a heavy population of mites (Figure 23.18).   Copper deficiency is most likely to occur on high organic soils and plants in landscape beds with high levels of organic matter.

Figure 23.15. Japanese holly (**Ilex crenata** 'Convexa') with copper deficiency (left), and a normal plant (right). Note the dull leaf surface on the deficient plant compared to the healthy plant.

Figure 23.16. Leaf distortion of waxleaf ligustrum (**Ligustrum japonicum**), caused by a mild copper deficiency. A normal leaf of this species is waxy, glossy green and smooth with no undulations on the leaf surface.

Figure 23.17. Severe copper deficiency on natal plum (**Carissa grandiflora** 'Boxwood Beauty'). Note the clustering of buds where the terminal bud should be and the very small leaves compared to the older normal leaves. In this case, a young plant was placed in a mix of Florida peat and sand with no micronutrients added. The result was an abrupt and very striking copper deficiency.

Figure 23.18. Copper deficiency on rose (**Rosa** spp.). Note the fine flecking pattern similar to damage from a severe infestation of mites.

Zinc. Zinc deficiency is common in pecans but uncommon with other species. Unlike iron, manganese and copper, as the soil pH changes, zinc solubility is affected slightly or not at all. Zinc toxicity is also rare.

Boron. Boron deficiency is not common, even in the synthetic or man-made "soil" mixes for containers. It is difficult to create a boron deficiency even when adding no boron but all other micronutrients at the normal rates and growing the plants for two growing seasons in the same growth medium. This is probably due to the minute amounts required and the fact that most irrigation water contains some boron. Dickey et al. (1) noted that boron deficiency symptoms caused an abnormal thickening of leaves and, in some cases, stems became shorter and abnormally thick and stiff and the terminal buds sometimes died or aborted.

On a few soils in California, plant growth responses have been associated with boron applications to the soil. Since few soil tests include boron, and because the requirement for boron is low, one should proceed with caution.

Boron toxicity, on the other hand, is much more common (2, 3). **Excess boron tends to accumulate in the older leaves** of a plant and causes a faint yellowing or chlorosis of the leaf margin followed by necrosis or death of the leaf tip and margins (5) (Figure 23.19). Boron toxicity is frequently caused by excess boron in irrigation waters or in micronutrient fertilizers. Improving the copper to boron ratio and iron to copper ratio may reduce injury. In one case, where a micronutrient fertilizer with high boron caused injury, adding another micronutrient fertilizer with high iron and copper eliminated the boron toxicity symptoms. However, this is not a recommended practice.

447

Figure 23.19. Boron toxicity on chrysanthemum. Note the faint yellowing of the leaf margin and death of the leaf tips of the older leaves. Old leaves may show severe toxicity symptoms while the new growth appears normal.

Molybdenum. Molybdenum is required in very small quantities in plants, but nonetheless is very essential. Molybdenum is required for the transformation of nitrate nitrogen into amino acids. Therefore one of the key symptoms of a molybdenum deficiency is a pale green color of the plant that at first appears as nitrogen deficiency. Deficiency symptoms generally appear on the youngest leaves, but may appear on older leaves as well. Molybdenum deficiency on chrysanthemums causes a lighter-than-normal green color at first, but as the deficiency progresses, leaves become pale green and lighter along the margins of the youngest leaves (Figure 23.20). The light margin color is white to cream, not yellow as in boron toxicity, and generally the tips or margins of the leaves do not die.

Molybdenum deficiency on Chinese hibiscus (*Hibiscus rosa-sinensis*) was, at one time, very common in Florida landscapes, especially on the very sandy and marl soils of south Florida. The deficiency, dubbed strap-leaf disease, caused the normally oval leaves to become narrow, rough-surfaced, thick and leathery.

Superphosphate and many sources of dolomite contain minute quantities of molybdenum as an impurity. As nutritional programs for phosphorus, calcium and magnesium become more precise, molybdenum deficiency may become more common.

Figure 23.20. Molybdenum deficiency on chrysanthemums. Note the pale color of the leaves and lack of sheen. Symptoms appear on some of the older leaves, but the younger leaves are most affected. The leaf margin becomes white or cream-colored, not yellow, as in boron toxicity.

Literature Cited

1.   Dickey, R.D., E.W. McElwee, C.A. Conover and J.H. Joiner. 1978. Container growing of woody ornamental nursery plants in Florida. Fla. Agri. Exp. Sta. Res. Bulletin 793.

2.   Eaton, F.M. 1944. Deficiency, toxicity and accumulation of boron in plants. Jour. Agri. Res. 69:237-277.

3.   Gilliam, C.H. and E.M. Smith. 1980. Sources and symptoms of boron toxicity in container-grown woody ornamentals.   Jour. of Arboriculture 6:209-212.

4.   Gordon, John C. and P.R. Larson. 1970. Redistribution of C-labeled reserve food in young red pines during shoot elongation. Forest Sci. 16:14-20.

5.   Kohl, H.C. and J.J. Oertli. 1961. Distribution of boron in leaves. Plant Physiol. 36:420-421.

CHAPTER 24

FERTILIZING LANDSCAPE TREES

Soil Test for Best Results - - - - - -   452

When and Where to Fertilize - - - - -   453

Where are the Roots? - - - - - - - - -   457

Summary - - - - - - - - - - - - - - -   458

Fertilizing Landscape Plants:
                        Three Examples- 461

Literature Cited - - - - - - - - - - -   463

Fertilizing Landscape Trees

Accurate and optimum fertilization can only be done with the aid of an accurate soil test and some knowledge of the soils and species involved. A soil test is a very inexpensive way to gain information about the levels and proportions of nutrient elements in the soil (see chapter 22). Soil tests over a period of years, in conjunction with good records of fertilizer application and plant response, can increase the accuracy of future treatments.

Soil Test for Best Results. The widespread practice of applying 10-20-10 or 10-10-5 or similar "complete" analysis fertilizer, without the aid of a soil test to see what is needed, is asking for problems. Excess phosphorus can suppress plant growth by making various micronutrients unavailable. In areas of Iowa and the Upper Midwest where soils were originally very deficient of phosphorus and have the capacity to bind large quantities, 18-46-0 or diammonium phosphate has been widely used. However, as a result of repeated applications without taking a soil test many landscapes have become low-grade phosphate mines. Unfortunately, there is no practical way to remove excess phosphorus from the soil and plant health suffers for many years.

In Oklahoma, 10-20-10 is widely recommended and used as a general fertilizer, yet few soils within the state need additional potassium. In controlled studies with field nursery stock, adding potassium (potash) above the level of about 300 pounds per acre suppressed growth.

If a soil test shows 60 to 100 pounds of phosphorus (P_2O_5) and 150 to 300 pounds of available potassium (K_2O), the only general fertilizer element needed is nitrogen. The rate of nitrogen depends on the plant growth rate desired, type of fertilizer used, type of soil, whether the area is irrigated, rainfall, time of year and other factors. In general, nitrogen rates will vary from 50 to 200 pounds per acre per year made in one application or spread over the growing season.

Most landscape plants have different requirements and the landscape manager's objective is different from the farmer striving for the maximum yield from a field of corn. Unfortunately, most fertilizer recommendations for landscape plants are based on research data from annual agricultural crops. Recommendations for liming and soil pH adjustment are the most radically different. Soil pH of 6.5 to 7.0 may be ideal for corn and wheat, but it is not optimum for most woody landscape plants.

A soil pH of 5.0 to 6.0 is more desirable. More acid soils (with a lower pH) should be limed while more basic soils (with a higher pH) should be treated with sulfur to slowly adjust the pH downward. Maintaining soil pH between 5.0 to 6.0 is the most practical way to insure the availability of all nutrient elements required for plant growth. For more information on sulfur treatments for acidification see the following chapter, Solving the Iron Chlorosis Problem.

There are situations where a single nutrient element other than nitrogen, phosphorus and potassium are required. Pecans in some areas of the southern Prairie States need additional zinc added to the soil. In North Florida, pecans generally respond to additional manganese. Many plants in Central and South Florida suffer magnesium deficiency. However, woody plants in mineral soils can generally best be treated by pH adjustments to insure that the complex of micronutrients that are present are available.

When and Where to Fertilize. Since the fine absorbing roots of established trees and shrubs are mostly near the soil surface, there is no advantage to applying fertilizer other than on the soil surface. There are many publications that suggest fertilizing established trees in holes 12 to 18 inches deep. This is analogous to putting the groceries in the basement when the kitchen is on the second floor. Not many of them get used! Liquid fertilizer applications are nearly as bad except that some of the liquid will rise by capillarity in the soil above the point of injection thus increasing availability to the roots.

The point is frequently raised that if phosphorus is needed and it is placed on the soil surface, it will not be available to the tree since it does not move in the soil. In new plantings and field soils it is best to incorporate phosphorus into the soil if a soil test shows it is needed. The benefit from incorporating phosphorus may be due to the greater aeration of the soil and root activity at greater depths in new plantings and field soils. However, with established trees and shrubs, a portion of the root system is at or near the soil surface so phosphorus absorption can occur (Figure 24.1). In addition, the activity of earthworms and insects shallowly incorporate the phosphorus over a period of years. If healthy roots are present in the surface soil, all of the nutrient needs can be absorbed from a very shallow layer. For example, in the chapter, Solving the Iron Chlorosis Problem, when the soil was treated with sulfur, the pH of the surface one inch of soil was lowered but the soil pH at the two- to three-inch

453

depth was raised. The lower pH near the soil surface provided enough available iron to the roots near the surface to improve plant growth even though the higher soil pH just below probably decreased the availability of iron.

Some argue that fertilizing on the soil surface means that grass or other ground covers get all of the nutrients. This is not true. Grass does have a very efficient and fibrous root system and does absorb a substantial portion of the fertilizer. However, since the roots of woody plants function in the same soil layer, they have an opportunity to absorb nutrients as well.

The best time to fertilize most existing woody landscape plants is in the fall. Consider the following contrast of conditions:

In the spring the air is getting warmer with the longer days but the soils are cold, generally wet and poorly aerated. With the spring flush of growth, root activity proceeds slowly since the bulk of the energy from the leaves goes to the new top growth. On the other hand, in the fall the soils are warm while the air is getting cooler and the length of the days, shorter. The soils are generally better aerated and when combined with greater energy levels in the stems and roots, root absorption of nutrients proceeds rapidly. This is covered in detail in the chapter Spring vs. Fall planting.

A great deal has been written regarding fall fertilization, growth continuing late in the season and increased winter injury. This is mostly false. With temperate zone plants the decreasing air temperatures and shorter days discourages new growth even with high levels of nitrogen. There are exceptions, however. For example, crapemyrtle (*Lagerstroemia indica*) is not photoperiod (length of the day) sensitive with respect to vegetative growth and if sufficient nitrogen and moisture are available and the temperatures remain warm, late fall growth may continue and winter injury may be greater than if less nitrogen were available. The semi-tropical plants in U.S.D.A. hardiness zones 8 and 9 fall into this same category as well. This factor is compounded by the fact that temperatures in October and November may be in the 80 degrees F range for several weeks with an abrupt drop well below the freezing point in a few hours or days.

Figure 24.1. (Above) Roots of a maple near the soil surface. Only a very thin layer of soil was removed to expose the roots. (Below) A tree root which grew out of the soil and through the turf before re-entering the soil.

In one study conducted at Gainesville, Florida, (3) ixora (*Ixora coccinea*) and sandanqua viburnum (*Viburnum suspensum*) were grown with various levels of nitrogen and potassium. When the temperature dropped below freezing, the tops of both species were damaged. There was no difference in the extent of injury between the fertilizer treatments on either species. However, the plants that had received the higher fertilizer treatments recovered from the cold injury more quickly than those from the low fertilizer treatments.

455

When lacebark elm (*Ulmus parvifolia*), Japanese black pine (*Pinus thunbergiana*), shumard oak (*Quercus shumardi*) and crapemyrtle (*Lagerstroemia indica*) were grown with three levels of fertilizer applied in the following sequences:

a. all in the spring,
b. all in the fall,
c. half in the spring and half in the fall and
d. in four applications applied in April, June, August and October, a clear best time to fertilize was observed (2).

The higher the fertilizer level the greater the growth (Figure 24.2). The biggest most attractive plants received at least part of the nitrogen fertilizer in the fall. The advantage of the half-spring, half-fall treatment or the four-times-per-growing-season treatment over applying all of the fertilizer in the fall was slight. One winter, the tops of all crapemyrtle were killed, but the most vigorous regrowth the following spring resulted from the high fertilizer level applied in the fall. None of the other three species showed any winter injury regardless of level of fertilizer or time of year during the three years of the study. For information on sources of fertilizer and the salt index, refer to Chapter 22.

Figure 24.2. Part of the field used in the fertilizer rate vs. time of year of application study. After one growing season, the three fertilizer levels could be detected on most plants. In this case the lacebark elm grew most at the high rate (H) and least at the low rate (L). However, there was no relationship between fertilizer rate and/or time of application and winter injury.

Where Are the Roots? Spread the fertilizer over the entire root zone of a tree. How extensive is the root system? Much greater than you think! For example, the author decided to determine the reaches of the root system of an isolated sugar maple (*Acer saccharum*). The tree was about eight inches in trunk diameter and had a branch spread of about 30 feet overall. The soil was a good silty clay loam. Soil samples were taken three feet out from the trunk and every two feet thereafter to a distance of 25 feet from the stem (10 feet beyond the outermost branches). Since the maple roots were reddish-tan and the grass roots were white, the tree roots could be easily identified upon examination. Many maple tree roots were present in the sample taken 25 feet from the trunk. Additional soil samples were taken out to a distance of 45 feet. Separation of roots and soil still showed many small maple roots 30 feet beyond the furthest branch tip.

There are many recommendations of X pounds of fertilizer per inch of trunk diameter. Unfortunately, most do not tell over what area the fertilizer should be spread. A more practical method is to fertilize the entire soil surface. For example, the lacebark elm in Figure 24.3 has roots throughout the front lawn of this home. Applying fertilizer over the entire front lawn provides nutrients for most of the tree roots, whereas, spreading fertilizer only inside the drip line would miss a great many.

Most landscape trees need mostly nitrogen fertilizer, but not excessive nitrogen. Only a soil test will tell the residual nitrogen in the soil and the levels of other nutrients. By maintaining records over several years of fertilizer applied and residual nitrogen, accurate fertilizer recommendations can be made.

Do not expect large trees to respond to fertilizers as quickly as young plants. Two, three or more years may be required before benefits of fertilizers can be seen or measured. Large trees are huge organisms and can have enormous leaf canopies. If a moderate level of fertilizer is applied, it may require considerable time and repeat applications before a response can be measured. if a large tree is growing slowly it cannot be given a "jump start" as can easily be seen on small plants. it is a bit like starting a locomotive from a standstill. With something so massive, considerable time is required before appreciable movement is attained. Short-term nutrition/fertilization studies miss the movement in succeeding years.

In most landscape situations there is no advantage to plant growth and health as a result of adding more than one pound of soluble nitrogen per 1000 square feet per application (43 pounds per acre). If part of the nitrogen is slow-release or where the soil is cool and urea, 46-0-0, is used a maximum of two pounds of nitrogen per 1000 square feet may be applied at one time. In areas of heavy rainfall and/or sandy soils, these rates of application may be repeated every two to four months if desired.

Fertilizer may not improve plant growth and health if some other factor is limiting. For example, if the soil is compacted and root function is poor, little fertilizer will be absorbed. Plant growth and health is the result of the synchronization of all the factors (Figure 24.4). Fertilizer is only one factor in the complex of plant requirements (1).

Summary.
A. Fertilize on the soil surface only.
B. If only one application is made per year, make it in the fall.

C. Spread the fertilizer over the entire lawn or landscape area to make sure all tree roots are contacted.
D. Do not apply more than one pound of soluble nitrogen per 1000 square feet per application, but make as many applications as necessary to achieve the desired result.

Figure 24.3. The lacebark elm above has roots far beyond the outermost branches. The restriction of the street in front and house to the back probably means the spread of the roots to the left and right is even greater than if the root barriers were not present. There is no practical way to "just" fertilize these large trees (below). The practical approach is to distribute fertilizer over the entire lawn area. These large trees have roots far beyond the outermost branches.

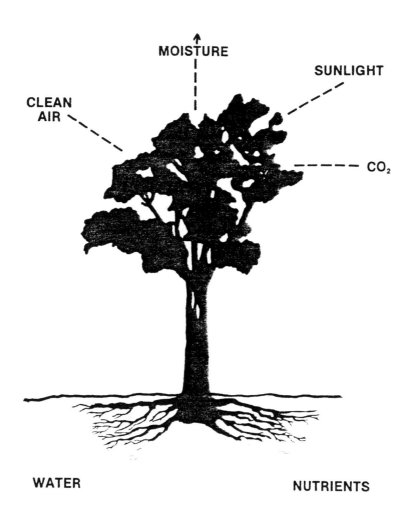

MOISTURE

SUNLIGHT

CLEAN
AIR

CO₂

WATER

NUTRIENTS

OXYGEN

Figure 24.4. Good plant growth and health is a result of many factors, not just fertilizer.

Fertilizing Landscape Plants: Three Examples. Example #1) Established trees and shrubs in a landscape setting where good plant health and moderate growth are the objective. Under these conditions, a key factor to consider would be the nature of the soil. Where soils are clay, clay loams, silt loams, or even moderately porous sandy loams, any one of the three types of fertilizers could be used, with price and personal preference being the major considerations. One pound of nitrogen per 1000 square feet (43 pounds per acre) applied both in spring and fall will work very well in most situations. Apply the fertilizer over the entire area to be sure all roots are contacted.

Research has shown little or no correlation between fall fertilization, even at fairly high rates with winter injury. In one study it was interesting to note that during one severe winter, the crapemyrtle were all killed to the soil line, regardless of fertilizer level or time of application. However, with the arrival of spring, the plants with the moderate or high levels of nitrogen **applied in the fall** recovered most quickly. Plants that received part of all of their nitrogen fertilizer in the fall were the largest and of highest visual quality of all four species, when evaluated after one, two, or three growing seasons. This is in direct contrast to the old and widely distributed recommendation that plants should not be fertilized in the fall. This recommendation probably resulted from studies done many years ago when sodium nitrate was the primary source of nitrogen. Sodium nitrate has a very high salt index (affinity for water), thus a moderate application in the fall may have sufficiently injured roots to have increased winter injury.

The same study(s) probably was the basis for the similarly erroneous recommendation that newly planted trees and shrubs **not** be fertilized the first growing season. By fertilizing in the fall, roots of woody plants are at their peak of activity since the energy level in the plant is at an all-time high for the year. Competition between trees and shrubs and grasses or other vegetation is always occurring. However, in the fall, the grasses and other plants are generally declining in their competitive ability so that the woody plants can be more or less preferentially fertilized. The nutrients absorbed during the fall and winter will provide greater support for the spring flush of new growth, since in spring, soils are cold and nutrient absorption is very slow.

Example #2) Azaleas, rhododendrons and other species sensitive to fertilizer salts and either just planted or just

461

established in the landscape. This is where natural organic and/or slow-release fertilizers are easily justifiable. Choosing between the natural organic and slow-release becomes a matter of personal preference, cost and duration of nutrient release at the specific site. Natural organics decompose and release nutrients much more rapidly in warmer climates. The slow-release fertilizers are also affected by the warmer conditions, however, in most cases, the effect is less than with natural organic fertilizers. Since azaleas and rhododendrons are very sensitive to micronutrient availability (especially iron, manganese and copper) the acid-forming and micronutrient fertilizers may provide a slight advantage. Dry chemical fertilizers may be used on these plants, but rates must be low and application frequent in order to maintain good plant growth without fertilizer burn. Mulches greatly assist these species since the effects of salts from any source (fertilizer, water, mulch) is greatly reduced when moisture availability is made more uniform. Since mulches also moderate temperatures somewhat, they extend the duration of release of both natural organic and slow-release fertilizers.

Example #3) Regardless of the size or shape, if there is a bottom in the planter (any material that stops the normal downward movement of water) it functions as a container. On the other hand, if there is no bottom, even if there are four sides above ground, it may be filled with good soil and treated as field soil. (For more information on containers, see the chapter on growing plants in containers). In order to provide adequate drainage and aeration for root growth in a container with a bottom, the "soil mix" must be much more porous than field soil. This means more rapid leaching of nitrogen and other nutrients, higher temperatures in summer and more frequent watering. All three of these factors are major justifications for the added expense of slow-release fertilizers. In general, slow-release fertilizers release plant nutrients far more accurately and over a longer period of time than natural organics.

Literature Cited

1.   Whitcomb, Carl E. 1985. *Know It & Grow It II: A Guide to the Identification and Use of Landscape Plants.*   Lacebark Publications, Stillwater, Ok.

2.   Whitcomb, Carl E. 1978.   Effects of spring vs. fall fertilization on the growth and cold tolerance of woody plants in the landscape. Okla. Agri. Exp. Sta. Res. Rept. P-777:11-12.

3.   Whitcomb, Carl E. 1988.   *Plant Production in Containers.* Lacebark Publications, Stillwater, Ok.

CHAPTER 25

PLANT STRESS AND LANDSCAPE PROBLEMS

Trees and Stress - - - - - - - - - - - - - 465

Gradual Changes in Soil pH - - - - - - - - 465

Soil Compaction - - - - - - - - - - - - - 467

Improper Nutrition - - - - - - - - - - - - 468

Water - - - - - - - - - - - - - - - - - - 470

Literature Cited - - - - - - - - - - - - - 473

Plant Stress and Landscape Problems

Trees and Stress. All plants are under varying degrees of stress at nearly all times. Moderate stress by a single factor for short periods probably is of little consequence to plant health and vigor. However, stress for prolonged periods or stress from several factors at the same time may reduce plant health and vigor sufficiently to cause permanent injury or encourage attack by disease or insects.

In natural stands of all vegetation, with or without insect and disease injury, cycles of stress and death of weaker plants occur regularly with little notice. In manmade or man-managed landscapes, however, the loss of any trees or shrubs is often viewed as failure of the manager in charge. In man's zeal to maintain the "perfect" landscape, the natural life cycle in plants is put aside. In many respects, trees are no different from people. As man has learned to prevent or cure various diseases, improve overall nutrition and health and maintain stress at reasonable levels, life expectancy has greatly increased. This does not mean that every person will live to reach the average age as averages include the extremes. The same is true of trees. An occasional tree may live only 20 years, whereas, the average for the species may be 50 years and a few live 80 years. The key to extending plant life is to emphasize plant health.

Unfortunately, as man's life expectancy has continually lengthened, the life expectancy of a tree, especially in the urban environment has **decreased**. Several factors are involved in the increased stress experienced by urban trees which directly or indirectly reduces the average life expectancy.

A tree dies because it starves to death. When the tree gets large enough so that the leaves cannot produce enough energy (sugars and starches) to meet the needs of all living cells, it dies. Various secondary factors may hasten the process but the basic cause remains the same. See Chapter 22 for more information on the energy production and redistribution process.

Gradual Changes in Soil pH. In many areas of the country, irrigation waters are alkaline, that is, they contain substantial quantities of bicarbonates, calcium, sodium, or magnesium (Figure 25.1). With each watering, a small amount is applied to the soil. Depending on the concentration in the water, symptoms of the problem may **not** appear for 5, 10 or 15 years. Unfortunately, slowly but surely, the levels of available micronutrients, especially iron, manganese, and copper, decrease (4). Long before visual symptoms of chlorosis (leaf yellowing) appear, the trees or shrubs begin to suffer stress from nutritional deficiencies which in turn means lower energy levels in the plants. Roots are the first to suffer from reduced energy levels since they are at the end of the energy distribution system within the plant. This by itself may not cause sufficient stress to create problems. However, in conjunction with a drought, soil compaction, a natural rise in the cyclic population of a leaf-damaging insect, disease, the application of an injurious herbicide to the root zone, or a combination of factors, this may lead directly to die back, other permanent injury, or death. Stress from one factor may cause sufficient weakening of the plant such that other insects or disease cause further injury or death.

Gradual decreases in soil pH may result from acid rain in heavily industrialized areas with fallout over a wide geographic range, depending on weather patterns and rainfall. As the soil becomes more acid, the culprit is primarily the increased solubility of aluminum which is quite toxic to plants. Aluminum solubility increases both at low or high pH. Where practical, treating the soil with calcium carbonate (lime) or calcium and magnesium carbonates (dolomite or dolomitic lime) to raise the pH provides substantial benefits to plant health. Remember, the only way to know the true soil conditions is with a soil test. See Chapter 26, for more details.

Acid rain does not cause direct injury to plant parts except in extreme cases. Sulfuric acid is commonly added to irrigation water high in bicarbonates to prevent staining of the foliage and/or sodium injury in plant nurseries. Water pH may be lowered to the low four range without leaf or bud injury. Adjustments in soil pH and the increased availa-bility of the deficient nutrients can make a great deal of change in the total energy output of the leaves. Changes in sandy soils are fairly rapid whereas clay soils are much slower to react. In either case overnight miracles do not occur, but slowly effective changes can be accomplished.

Figure 25.1. Water with substantial quantities of bicarbonates or calcium will often leave a white residue on plant foliage. Unfortunately, water with lower levels still cause plant problems, only more time is required and no visual clues are present.

Soil Compaction. Soil compaction is a major factor affecting plant health in many urban areas. Soil compaction can occur as a result of foot traffic by people (including small children), animals, or various vehicles. Soils vary greatly in their tendency to compact. In general, clay soils or soils with some clay or silt are more subject to compaction than sandy soils. However, nearly all sandy soils can be compacted sufficiently to restrict the activity of plant roots. As the absorptive capacity of plant roots decreases, nutrient stress occurs which, in turn, reduces leaf manufacture of energy (carbohydrates) and growth

467

regulating compounds which, in turn, further reduces root activity and so on. Soil compaction occurs primarily at or near the soil surface, since the soil near the surface spreads the load relative to the soil below. Loosening soil compaction near the surface occurs naturally by freezing and thawing action in colder climates. However, in areas where the soil does not freeze, mechanical aerifiers serve a similar function. Since the effective roots of all plants are in the top foot of soil, and compaction is at the surface, it is not necessary to aerify the soil more than one to two inches deep to aid plant health in many cases (Figure 25.2).

Improper Nutrition. Improper nutrition, especially the excess or imbalance of one or more nutrient elements relative to the others can cause plant stress. In some geographic areas the excessive use of a specific fertilizer formulation can lead to a severe nutrient imbalance. For example, in areas of the Upper Midwest, diammonium phosphate (18-46-0) is widely recommended because soils are naturally low in phosphorus. However, with the continual use of diammonium phosphate, many landscape areas become low-grade phosphate mines. Excess phosphorus, especially in combination with moderate to high levels of calcium leads to the formation of very insoluble calcium phosphates that tie up large quantities of iron and other micronutrients in the soil. Excessive levels of phosphorus are not only harmful to plant health, but unfortunately, there is no practical way to remove the excess phosphorus and thus aid recovery of existing plants once the problem is diagnosed. Similar problems can occur with most of the nutrient elements. Soil tests over a period of years, not only give indications of current nutrient needs, but developing problems as well.

Figure 25.2. Soil compaction occurs primarily at the soil surface. Simply cutting through the top inch of soil can achieve dramatic plant response. In this case a vertical mower sliced through the soil about one inch deep in two directions (above). Anyone for checkers?

Weeds can sometimes offer dramatic clues to soil compaction. Just out of the lower portion of the photo is an exit to a classroom building on the University of Florida campus (below). Note the flow pattern of foot traffic out of the building and around the plants. The weed is black medic and it is very intolerant of compacted soils.

469

Water. Water is probably the most common factor limiting plant growth. However, some lack of water during parts of the growing season is not necessarily bad, especially for woody plants. Consider this situation: the soil becomes drier, but in so doing, the depth at which sufficient aeration exists for active root growth also increases and roots extend to greater depths, absorbing nutrients and water that otherwise might not be available. With the beginning of moisture stress, top growth begins to slow, but the levels of energy (carbohydrates) in the plant increase. Since the volume of new tissue is slowing down the energy production can catch up. Since the root system receives substantial quantities of energy only when there is an abundance in the top, root growth is stimulated. This, in combination with the improved aeration of the soil due to the drying, **aids** overall plant health. Periodic moisture stress, for brief periods, is beneficial to plant health.

However, consider the alternative where moisture is rarely limiting. Plant growth progresses rapidly over a longer period of time, assuming some other nutrient or environmental condition is not limiting and the soil remains moist. The energy levels in the plant remain low for an extended period because most of the energy manufactured by the leaves is going to support new growth. The roots receive only limited supplies of energy in these conditions. Due to the constant moisture, aeration in many soils is poor to marginal which, in turn, restricts root functions. At some point, the top growth of the plant will be restricted by the capacity of the limited root system to absorb nutrients. Nutrient deficiency symptoms may develop in the leaves, even though there is an adequate supply in the soil. In this case, the top has simply outgrown the capacity of the roots, and moderate moisture stress would be helpful.

In a similar light, consider the golf course or grounds manager who wishes for an automatic irrigation system that will "solve all plant problems". Before the automatic irrigation system is installed, some moisture stress occurs when the landscape manager hopes for rain and delays irrigation until it reaches a certain critical point. This is good. Now consider the same site with the automatic irrigation system where water can be applied at anytime at the turn of a switch or worse yet, watering is determined by a time clock with no allowance for rainfall, temperature or stages of plant growth. Everything gets lots of water. Now consider the consequences:

a) reduced soil aeration,

b) reduced or eliminated wet/dry cycles,

c) **increased** soil compaction since wet soil compacts much more quickly than moderate or dry soils,

d) reduced root activity from excess water, poor aeration and low energy levels in the plants, and

e) overall the energy level in the plant is lower over a major portion of the growing season.

All of these factors contribute to plant stress and increased plant problems.

Over the years the author has seen a number of landscapes decline rapidly following installation of an automatic irrigation system that was used excessively without considering the consequences. The problem is, of course, not the irrigation system, but the lack of proper planning relative to its use. When an automatic irrigation system is in place, the most common reaction seems to be, "when in doubt, water", and the problems begin.

Although difficult to study and prove with certainty, there is no doubt that trees are predisposed to disease and insect problems by stress factors. Internal physiological processes (including energy levels) cannot be easily seen, measured or otherwise detected. Unfortunately, the reaction of a tree to stress may show only with the next flush of growth and even then may be only subtle, unnoticed even by many professionals. For example, pines that make only one flush each year show stress in the length of the current stem and length and diameter of the individual needles. However, unless plants with and without stress are adjacent or in a controlled experimental plot, the stress goes undetected because the changes are relatively small. A major error by many nurserymen, landscape architects and grounds managers is that if it made some growth in the spring and is green, then it must be fine. This may be far from the truth.

In carefully controlled experiments in containers, it can be demonstrated that just because a plant is dark green and growing, it is not necessarily at its peak of health. Figure 25.3 shows four holly plants that were grown with different levels of calcium and magnesium in the soil mix. All were dark green and **showed no visual deficiency symptoms**. However, the growth and health of the tops and roots were quite different. Conclusion: the healthier the top, the healthier and more vigorous the root system which, in turn, provides for more efficient water and nutrient absorption for the top and more energy for root functions, and so on!

471

*Figure 25.3. Growth of dwarf burford holly (**Ilex cornuta** 'Burford Nana') with four levels of calcium and magnesium. The tops showed no deficiency symptoms and leaves were identical size for all four plants (above), however the tops were very different in size. When the containers were removed a striking difference in root growth could be observed (below).*

472

Silverstein et al. (3) identified three chemicals (terpenes) from frass of Ips bark beetles in ponderosa pine. Weakened trees produced more of these chemicals than did healthy trees. The trees attacked by the Ips beetle consistently contained high quantities of these chemicals which were an attractant for the insect. Kozlowsky (1) noted in an excellent summary, "Tree Physiology and Forest Pests", that a physiological change in a tree is commonly a prerequisite to insect attack. The age at which trees are most likely to be attacked reflects very specific conditions which predispose them to invasion. In the abnormal and often unfavorable urban environment, the likelihood of some stress at all times is great. Furthermore, conditions can change more abruptly there than in the forest, thus accounting for the greater numbers and severity of problems.

Raupp, et al. (2) found that genera such as *Malus*, *Pyracantha, Cornus, Prunus*, and *Rosa* tend to be problem prone, while *Viburnum, Taxus* and *Forsythia* are relatively problem-free. The problem species may be less well adapted and/or planted in "high stress" locations as opposed to the problem-free species. Much remains to be learned in this area, but all factors point to an emphasis on plant health. Through plant selection, site selection, water and soil management on the site, nutrition, light intensity, and no doubt, many other factors plant health can be improved and problems reduced. The bottom line is certainly **the healthier the plant, the fewer the problems!**

Literature Cited

1. Kozlowski, T.T. 1969. Tree physiology and forest pests. Jour. of Forestry 26:118-123.

2. Raupp, M.J., J.A. Davidson, J.J. Homes and J.L. Hellman. 1985. The concept of key plants in integrated pest management for landscapes. Jour. of Arboriculture 11:317-322.

3. Silverstein, R.W., J.O. Rodin, and D.L. Wood. 1966. Sex attractants in frass produced by male *Ips confusus* in ponderosa pine. Science 154:509-510.

4. Whitcomb, Carl E. 1986. Solving the iron chlorosis problem. Jour. of Arboriculture 12:44-48.

CHAPTER 26

SOLVING THE IRON CHLOROSIS PROBLEM

Calcium Sources - - - - - - - - - - - 475

Treating the Symptoms - - - - - - - - 475

Treating the Cause - - - - - - - - - - 475

Determining What Happened - - - - - - 480

A Landscape Example - - - - - - - - - 483

Water Changes Soil Chemistry - - - - - 484

Summary - - - - - - - - - - - - - - - 487

A Technique for Solving
                Chlorosis Problems - 488

Literature Cited - - - - - - - - - - - 493

Solving the Iron Chlorosis Problem

Calcium Sources. Chlorosis of pin oaks and other species in the urban landscape is a frequent occurrence (2, 7, 8, 13, 14, 15). It is a continuing problem in most of the western and Prairie States due to the naturally alkaline soils (2, 5) but may be a problem anywhere construction has occurred and residues remain (4) or irrigation water is alkaline (16). In most areas of the U.S., domestic water contains substantial quantities of calcium, either naturally or as an additive during the water treatment process to precipitate clay and silt. When landscape plants are watered, calcium and other bases slowly accumulate, increasing the soil pH and reducing the availability of many of the micronutrients, especially iron and manganese. In many instances, a pin oak is planted and grows well for several years, only to begin showing signs of chlorosis about the time it reaches a functional size in the landscape. The tree is reflecting the gradual change in soil pH and micronutrient availability which goes undetected until **visual** symptoms appear.

Halverson et al. (4) found that the pH of water from rainfall was raised from 4.0 to 7.6 after it ran across concrete surfaces such as driveways and parking lots. In areas where clay soils exist and percolation of water and minerals through the soil is minimal and root systems are shallow due to poor soil aeration, chlorosis may develop more quickly (15, 16).

Treating the Symptoms. Most techniques to correct chlorosis have only short-term success because they treat the symptom instead of the cause. The symptom is leaf chlorosis, whereas, the cause is the reduced availability of micronutrients as a result of high soil pH and/or excess calcium. Fischbach and Webster (3) and Harrell et al. (5) noted that in some cases adding iron or manganese gave no response while in other cases it increased chlorosis. This is understandable since in some soils, the primary deficient element may be manganese (7, 13) and if additional iron is added, the iron-manganese ratio is widened, further decreasing manganese absorption. The reverse situation can also occur. Trunk injections create undesirable wounds (12) and provide only short-term benefits to the tree since they treat only the symptom (3, 5, 6, 9).

Treating the Cause. On the other hand, soil treatments to reduce pH and decrease calcium affect change more slowly but address the cause. A drastic improvement in the color of pin oaks growing in a heavy clay soil in Oklahoma resulted from treating with elemental sulfur (11). Messenger (8) observed a decline of soil pH for 1.5 years after treating with granular sulfur at rates of 60 to 100 pounds per 1000 square feet.

The following long-term study shows both the effectiveness and longevity from treating the soil with sulfur (17). On June 6, 1975, granular sulfur (96%) was applied to plots 20 inches wide by 18 feet long in a bermudagrass sod at rates of 0, 100 and 200 pounds per 1000 square feet of surface area. Granular sulfur was applied with a drop-type fertilizer spreader and watered-in using a low volume sprinkler.

Identical treatments were applied to individual pin oaks with 8- to 12-inch diameter trunks growing in the same area on the same date. Granular sulfur treatments to trees covered an area approximately twice the distance from the trunk to the drip line. A chlorosis rating was made of all trees before the study began and at intervals thereafter, using a 1-10 scale, where 1 = very chlorotic and 10 = no chlorosis.

Soil samples three inches deep and two inches in diameter were taken at intervals throughout the study. For simplicity, only the findings taken from plots after 0, 1, 3, 5 and 7 months and 10 years are shown. The soil was a heavy red clay which had been disturbed many times over the years by construction, therefore no specific soil classification is possible.

After seven months, soil pH had dropped from 8.2 to 7.8 with 10 pounds of sulfur and to 6.6 with 20 pounds per 100 square feet (Figure 26.1). Soluble salts increased from about 11 mili mohs to 55 or 63 with 10 or 20 pounds per square feet of sulfur (Figure 26.2). Soluble iron increased from 11 parts per million (ppm) to 46 or 65 ppm (Figure 26.3) while manganese increased from about 9 ppm to 30 and 45 ppm with 100 and 200 pounds of granular sulfur per 1000 square feet, respectively (Figure 26.4).

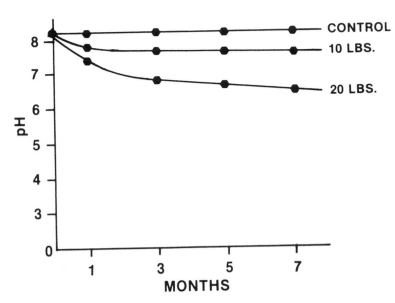

Figure 26.1. Effects of sulfur on pH of a clay soil. Rates are in pounds per 100 square feet.

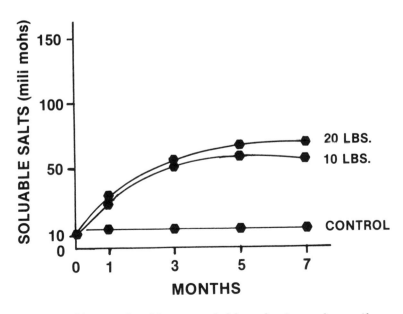

Figure 26.2. Effects of sulfur on soluble salts in a clay soil.

477

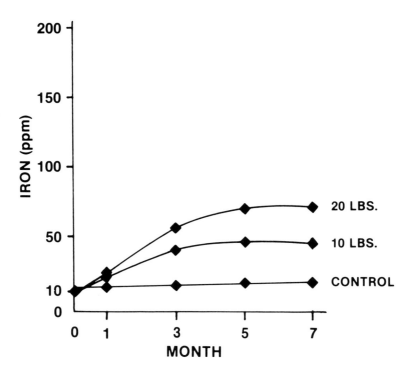

Figure 26.3.   Effects of sulfur on soluble iron in a clay soil. Multiple light applications would be equally effective to heavier applications if sensitive vegetation exists on the soil surface.

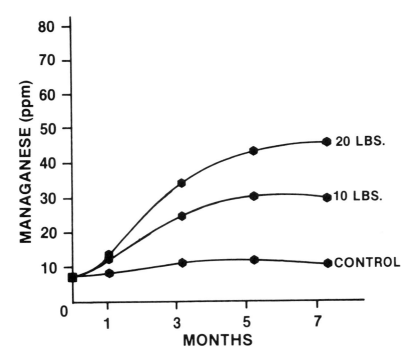

Figure 26.4.   Effects of sulfur on soluble manganese in a clay soil.

Trees with a severe chlorosis rating of 2.2 increased to 6.4 by the end of the growing season, and most had a rating of 8 or higher at the end of one year (where 10 is dark green). All trees treated with 10 or 20 pounds of granular sulfur per 100 square feet had an excellent visual rating near 10 after two growing seasons.

The bermudagrass turf was not injured by either rate of sulfur. However, most weeds in the sod were killed by the 20 lb. rate. This relates to the findings of Messenger (8) who observed injury to Kentucky bluegrass from granular sulfur at rates of 12 to 18 pounds per 100 square feet. Caution: Some grasses, groundcovers or shrubs may be affected by high rates of sulfur applied at one time. If in doubt, a similar soil treatment effect can be obtained by applying two pounds per 100 square feet at a frequency of about every two to three months.

Determining What Happened. The pin oak color improvement was much greater than expected since the soil pH remained high seven months after the 10-pound treatment. Subsequent soil samples were divided into sections from 0 to 1.5 inches deep and 1.5 to 3 inches deep. Note the difference in pH and nutrient availability from the two depths of soil samples taken on May 17, 1985 (Table 26.1). The soil pH at the 1.5 to 3 inches depth was still 7.6, whereas, the 0- to 1.5-inch depth was only 5.9. The sequence of events was probably as follows:

a) alkaline heavy clay soil exists;

b) granular sulfur was applied on the soil surface and watered-in;

c) sulfur reacts with soil, lowering pH at or near the soil surface which in turn releases calcium and other cations and increases soluble salts (see Figure 26.2);

d) as the calcium and other cations move downward in the soil, they re-attach to the clay colloid, giving an average pH reading of the entire 0 to 3-inch depth unusually high, since much of the calcium removed from the surface is still present in the lower portion of the sample,

e) however, since many tree roots are present in the upper few inches of soil, the tree responds favorably to the improved availability of micronutrients.

Soil samples after 10 years (May 17, 1985) show that the availability of iron, manganese and zinc all remained high in the soil as a result of the one application of granular sulfur (Table 26.1). The slight drop in pH and increase in available iron and manganese in the control treatment (no sulfur) after 10 years is probably due to the acidifying effect of urea (46-0-0) used as the nitrogen source for the past eight years.

Table 26.1. Effects of one application of 96% granular elemental sulfur at 10 pounds per 100 square feet on micronutrient availability in soil after 10 years.

			Parts Per Million Available		
		pH	Iron	Manganese	Zinc
		June 6, 1975			
	Sample Depth				
Treatment	0-3 inches	8.2	11.0	9.0	2.2
		May 17, 1985			
No	0-1.5 inches	7.9	23	13	3.0
sulfur	1.5-3 inches	7.7	19	10	3.2
		May 17, 1985			
10 lbs.	0-1.5 inches	5.9	123	47	3.2
sulfur/	1.5-3 inches	7.6	104	33	4.6
100 sq. ft.					

As a further example of the long-term benefits of soil applications of granular sulfur, a case history of a chlorotic pin oak of approximately 12-inch trunk diameter and 30 feet tall is also included. The tree was extremely chlorotic and was rated as a 1 on the chlorosis scale of 1 to 10. However, leaf retention was good and little twig die back had occurred. If leaf retention is poor there is little hope for recovery. A limestone driveway-walkway existed approximately 30 feet from the tree and the soil sloped so that runoff water from the driveway accumulated near the tree. On October 10, 1974 the soil was a very heavy, poorly drained clay with a pH of 7.9, 3.5 ppm available iron, 8.7 ppm manganese, and 12 ppm zinc (Table 26.2).

The tree was treated with granular sulfur on May 5, 1975 at 10 pounds per 100 square feet, well beyond the drip line. During the remaining 1975 growing season, some improvement in leaf color occurred but it was not uniform over the tree. On June 14, 1976 soil samples were again taken (2-inch diameter, 3 inches deep) and showed pH 7.7 with 21, 9.1 and 10 ppm available iron, manganese, and zinc, respectively (Table 26.2). On June 17, 1976, an additional six pounds per 100 square feet of granular sulfur was applied with some further improvement in foliage color. The treatment was repeated June 12, 1978. Beginning with the spring flush of leaves in 1979, the tree has remained green (9 to 10 on the visual rating scale). Growth was slow but this was probably due to the very poor soil conditions. Soil samples were taken on May 17, 1985 and sectioned into 0 to 1.5 and 1.5 to 3.0 inch depths (Table 26.2). The pH of the soil surface was much more acid than the sample below. The iron and manganese availability increased dramatically at both depths and probably accounts for the improved foliage color. Three applications of granular sulfur (22 pounds per 100 square feet total over a four-year period) made a sufficient adjustment in soil pH near the soil surface to increase available micronutrients to maintain good leaf color for several years. The 1985 soil test suggests that further treatments will still not be necessary for some time.

Table 26.2. Case history of a very chlorotic pin oak growing in a poorly drained heavy clay soil where part of the runoff water onto the site was from a limestone driveway.

Soil samples and treatment dates	pH	Parts/Million Available Iron	Manganese	Zinc
Very heavy clay soil Oct. 10, 1974, 0-3 inches deep	7.9	3.5	8.7	12
Treated with 96% granular sulfur May 5, 1975, 10 lbs./100 sq. ft.	--	--	--	--
Soil sampled June 14, 1976, 0-3 inches deep	7.7	21	9.1	10
Treated June 17, 1976, 6 lbs./100 sq. ft.	--	--	--	--
Treated June 12, 1978, 6 lbs./100 sq. ft.	--	--	--	--
Soil sampled June 7, 1979, 0-3 inches deep	7.5	66	16	10
Soil sampled May 17, 1985 0-1.5 inches deep	5.6	332	20	11
1.5-3 inches deep	7.2	226	58	21

A Landscape Example. Several other problem landscapes have also been studied in detail. For example, the new city hall grounds in Gainesville, Florida provided an excellent study site. One year after all construction was completed and the landscape plants were installed, chlorotic camellias and azaleas began to appear. Soil samples were taken at various locations throughout the site. A few of these are presented in Table 26.3. Fortunately, there was an area near the site where an old homestead had remained virtually undisturbed for years. No exotic plants were present and a check with the owner confirmed that no watering of any areas around the house and grounds had been done for about the past 30 years. Soil tests from this area showed a pH of 5.2 to 5.8 with iron and manganese levels of 18 and 11, respectively (Table 26.3). A planter bed of day lilies and camellias had pH from 7.2 to 7.3 and iron and manganese levels of 7 and 6 ppm, respectively. This area received little, if any, runoff from any adjacent areas, sidewalks, or other calcium sources. The primary source of calcium was the irrigation water. Adjacent to the limestone building where mortar residue could be found, the soil pH was 8.2 and only 3 ppm of both iron and manganese were present. At the base of a sloping limestone wall where azaleas had been planted, the soil pH was 8.4 with 2 ppm iron and 3 ppm manganese. In this case not only did the water supply add to the soil alkalinity, but the runoff from the sloping limestone wall plus some residue from construction combined to make an impossible growing condition for azaleas. The choices were, select more tolerant plant species or treat and/or excavate the high pH soil. Soil treatment would be slow but less expensive than soil removal and replacement.

Table 26.3. Soil pH change in the urban landscape.

Site	Gainesville, Florida City Hall		
	pH	Iron (ppm)	Manganese (ppm)
Adjacent to building	8.2	3	3
Near discharge from concrete surface	7.3	7	5
Planter bed	7.2	7	5
	7.3	6	6
Turf area	7.7	5	4
	7.2	7	5
At base of sloping stone wall	8.4	2	3
Native soil	5.2-5.8	18	11

Water Changes Soil Chemistry. Golf courses characteristically are watered frequently and heavily to maintain turf tolerant of the wear. Pines, some oaks and other species sensitive to alkalinity, frequently grow poorly on golf courses. Herbicides and high fertility levels are frequently blamed for the problem. However, the problem is generally one of decreased availability of micronutrients, especially iron and manganese and the resultant nutritional stress weakens the plants, predisposing them to various other insects and diseases.

A study of the decline and loss of many pine trees at the Mourings Golf Course in Naples, Florida revealed a distinct pattern of increased calcium in the soil and decreased levels of available iron and manganese. Soil samples taken from remote rough areas beyond the irrigation water patterns showed a soil pH range from 5.5 to 5.9 with about 500 pounds per acre calcium, 100 pounds per acre magnesium, 20 ppm iron and 18 ppm manganese (Table 26.4). Soil pH of the fairways was only 6.3, but the calcium level was over 2,200 and iron and manganese levels were 10 and 6, respectively. Irrigated rough areas had somewhat higher soil pH and calcium levels and proportionately lower levels of iron and manganese.

Native slash pines in the areas beyond the irrigation system were dark green and attractive with two seasons of needles present. All slash pine in the irrigation patterns had varying degrees of chlorosis and in general, only the current seasons needles. When leaf samples were analyzed from healthy and chlorotic trees, dramatic differences in tissue levels of copper, iron and manganese were noted. Zinc, however, was slightly higher in the trees showing chlorosis (Table 26.5).

Several key points should be noted from both this study and the Gainesville City Hall site:

a) Native levels of iron and manganese in the Florida sands were low, therefore, any appreciable increase in calcium or other bases quickly decreased their availability.

b) The 400% increase in the level of calcium in the soil at the golf course came directly from the irrigation water as did the slight increase in magnesium.

c) The soil pH gives few clues as to the change in the relationship and levels of the nutrients in the soil. A pH change from 5.5 to 5.9 up to 6.3 would generally be considered of little importance, yet note the 400% increase in calcium and 50% decrease in iron and manganese.

d) With a sandy soil (as both of these sites were) with limited buffer capacity and low levels of iron and manganese naturally, the change in available iron and manganese to the plant is quickly altered. On a heavy clay soil as in the Oklahoma studies, a much longer time and more irrigation water was required to reduce the levels of iron and manganese such that chlorosis became visible on sensitive species.

e) Note the pH of the irrigation water from the golf course was only 7.1 yet contained 69 ppm of calcium. The pH of a water supply tells nothing more than the relative proportion of acids and bases present. That water supply had enough acids present to offset the 69 ppm calcium so that the pH was only 7.1 but in addition, the acids kept the soil pH from changing appreciably even though the level of calcium had increased 400 percent. Soil pH is a much more useful indicator than water pH, but it may not reflect the critical changes that are occurring in nutrient levels and proportions in the soil.

f) On the city hall site, both the alkaline water supply plus the residues from the construction were complicating the growth of landscape plants. It is important to remember that even though the pines, azaleas and pin oaks are more sensitive indicators of nutrient availability problems, other plants are generally being affected as well. They simply are less prone to showing visual symptoms. It is unfortunate that most landscape managers react only to visual problems instead of striving to prevent problems from occurring and emphasizing true plant health, not just passive green color.

Table 26.4. Characteristics of soil and water samples from the Mourings Golf Course, Naples, Florida.

	ppm of elements in soil samples						
	pH	Ca	Mg	P	K	Fe	Mn
Native area	5.9	562	113	12	17	20	18
(undisturbed)	5.5	473	113	2	11	22	18
Irrigation water	7.1	69	0.8	.1	2.9	1.2	0.8
Fairway	6.3	2364	158	38	78	10	6
	6.3	2252	141	62	54	11	6
Rough	6.9	3248	158	94	60	7	5
	7.0	2424	128	70	36	9	7

Table 26.5. Mineral level of slash pine leaves from the Mourings Golf Course, Naples, Florida.

	Cu	Fe	Mn	Zn
Trees with no chlorosis	6.25	875	65	40.5 ppm
Trees showing chlorosis and decline	2.50	350	20	46.5 ppm

Summary. The following conclusions regarding elemental sulfur for soil acidification should be considered before plants are treated with trunk injections or other short-term treatments:

a) Granular elemental sulfur (96%) is an effective treatment for chlorosis of most landscape plants.

b) Foliage color response may not be seen for several months or until the next flush of leaves.

c) The total amount of granular sulfur needed depends on alkalinity of the soil, the element(s) involved in raising the soil pH, soil texture, chemical composition of the irrigation water, runoff water onto or away from the site in question and probably other factors.

d) The soil pH change will occur near the soil surface, therefore, soil sampling and testing procedures may reflect an increase in micronutrient availability with little or no pH change.

e) The effects of granular sulfur applied to the soil are long-term and address the cause of the chlorosis problem, not just the symptom.

f) Treat a large soil area, far beyond the outer most branches of the tree(s). In most cases, the entire soil surface on the site should be treated since tree roots extend much further than generally considered. The greater proportion of the plant root zone treated, the more rapid and long lasting the benefits.

g) Application is simple and easy with modern dust-free sulfur granules. In areas of established turf, the sequence of soil aerification, sulfur application, followed by irrigation works well. In garden areas or landscaped areas treated before planting, tilling the sulfur into the soil will speed up the soil adjustment process and to a greater depth.

h) If concern exists regarding turf or groundcover injury, a quarter- or half-rate may be made, then another application two to four months later.

A Technique for Solving Chlorosis Problems. In early 1986 this author began making lists of problems/challenges for future research. The list was then reviewed piece by piece and thoughts, ideas, possible solutions were noted again and again. One of those challenges was a practical solution to the iron chlorosis problem with trees and other landscape plants. The calcium or other bases that raise the soil pH and reduce the availability of micronutrients may be inherent in the soil or the result of residues from construction or the slow accumulation of minerals in the irrigation water or a combination of factors. The end result is poor plant growth.

The following background references were considered (3-16). Years of work in Florida where micronutrient deficiencies are rampant lead to the development of Micromax micronutrient fertilizer. The product approximates the proportions or balance of the six micronutrient elements needed for plant growth. It has been very effective in eliminating micronutrient deficiencies in the production of plants in containers. However, it's use on field soils has generally been less effective. The product is a unique combination of the correct sulfate forms of iron, manganese, copper and zinc plus sodium borate and sodium molybdate. When the product is applied directly to most soils by broadcast or general soil incorporation the micronutrients are quickly tied up by the high levels of calcium, sodium or bicarbonates. Only in high organic plant beds and the very sandy soils of central and north Florida have surface application been effective.

Several studies were done where Micromax was placed in holes in the soil around chlorotic trees in an attempt to reduce the soil tie up problem. The treatment was not effective and excavation later revealed a very hard mass of insoluble micronutrients.

In following years the focus shifted to sulfur treatments of the soil surface. An assortment of experiments in Oklahoma showed that if enough sulfur is applied, the surface of the soil can be affected, thus lowering the pH and increasing micronutrient availability. The quantity of sulfur required varies with the soil type and level of calcium and other bases in the soil. In some cases several applications may be necessary over a period of two years or more in order to make a change in soil pH without damaging or killing the grass or ground cover growing on the soil surface (12, 16). This treatment has proven very successful on landscape sites in Texas, Oklahoma, Kansas, and Florida.

Interestingly, a report from Nebraska said, "It doesn't work for us" (6).

The desirable thing about the sulfur treatment is the general increase in availability of all the micronutrients and not just iron plus the long lasting effects that address the cause of the chlorosis, not just the symptom.

The research that led to Micromax micronutrient fertilizer showed that the balance or proportion among the six micronutrient elements is very specific. If one element is out of balance with the others, chlorosis occurs even though all others may be near the correct level. Numerous experiences with what appeared to be iron chorosis were not "cured" by applying iron. In fact, on some occasions the "chlorosis" became more severe after applying iron because it was really manganese deficiency. The additional iron made the ratio of iron to manganese wider and in effect increased the severity of the manganese deficiency (16). Work in Michigan has shown that at least some of the chlorosis of trees there is manganese deficiency (8, 14). In areas of the southwest, zinc deficiency may cause chlorosis.

In spring of 1986 another review of the many factors involved in the chlorosis problem and possible solutions was made. Adding all of the micronutrients in the correct proportions to the soil seemed the "best" answer, but how? There had to be a practical way to overcome the problems noted previously. A combination of the sulfur effects and Micromax micronutrients might be the answer. On May 4, 1986, eight chlorotic pin oaks were located. They ranged from mild chlorosis to severe chlorosis with some twig death. The trees ranged in size from 5 to 8 inches DBH.

The technique chosen was to auger holes two inches in diameter and 10 inches deep in the soil, with eight holes per tree. The first four holes were drilled about three feet out from the stem at the four points of the compass. The other four holes were drilled about five feet out from the stem and centered between the first holes.

Two-inch diameter perforated plastic drain line was used as a liner to maintain the opening in the soil. In the bottom of the hole was place 1/2 lb. of Micromax micronutrients, then 1/2 lb. of granular elemental sulfur (92%) then the hole was filled with Osmocote 24-4-10 (called High-N) approximately one pound (Figure 26.5).

When the holes were drilled around the most chlorotic tree, a layer of limerock, sand and mortar remnants was encountered about five to six inches below the surface. This debris had been covered with a sandy loam topsoil. Beneath the debris was a heavy clay. The other seven trees were all growing in heavy clay soils with pH ranging from 7.2 to 7.8.

A check of the trees on May 25, 1986 showed an improvement in foliage color. Leaf color continued to improve during the growing season. The spring flush of growth in 1987 was a dark green for all trees except the specimen with the most severe chlorosis and growing conditions. A check of the trees in Sept. 1987 revealed all to have a good green color and a strong bud set for the following spring.

The year 1988 was extremely busy and the trees were forgotten. Ditto 1989. June of 1990 found me advising on a number of trees damaged by a tornado and the trees were remembered.

All of the trees were dark green and attractive, even the one on the terrible site. A check with the homeowners confirmed that only broadcast N, P, K fertilizer had been applied to the turf. Further investigation was done with the tree on the most severe site. Soil samples from just outside the piece of perforated drain contained many fine roots. Analysis of this soil showed a pH of 5.1 and 88 ppm iron and 120 ppm manganese whereas originally the pH was 7.8 and iron and manganese availability were 4.0 and 8.1, respectively.

The technique provides a long term slow release system of micronutrients and sulfur in a zone in and around each hole. The sequence of events is probably as follows:

1) the holes are drilled and the micronutrients, sulfur, and fertilizer are placed around the tree.

2) With the first wetting, the Micromax micronutrients form a hard mass and small amounts of sulfur and N,P,K are released into the soil immediately surrounding the hole.

3) With each successive rain or watering, a small amount of N, P, K and sulfur is released. The sulfur dissolved by the water forms sulfuric acid. The sulfuric acid dissolves a small portion of the micronutrients. The sulfur and the micronutrients slowly lower the pH of the soil surrounding each hole.

4) New root growth in and around each hole aids in the absorptive capacity of the tree. This is encouraged by the N, P, K as well as the sulfur and micronutrients and the improved aeration.

5) Over a period of time, a zone of soil around each hole is modified to be lower in pH and rich in micronutrients in approximately the correct proportions (Figure 26.5).

490

A plant does not require all roots to be in soil with optimum nutrient conditions for good growth. An array of studies have been done where one or more roots of a plant are in a soil or medium with favorable rates, levels or proportions of nutrients whereas the rest of the roots remain in unfavorable conditions. As long as a few of the roots are in favorable conditions of nutrient availability, plant growth is enhanced and the problem of the deficient nutrient is reduced or eliminated. In *Methods of Studying Root Systems*, W. Bohm lists an array of techniques and over 1000 references on the subject (2).

The number of holes per tree, the longevity of such treatments and other questions remain to be answered. At this early stage it appears to be an effective treatment for chlorotic trees on alkaline soils with no risk to the health of the tree and is relatively easy to install.

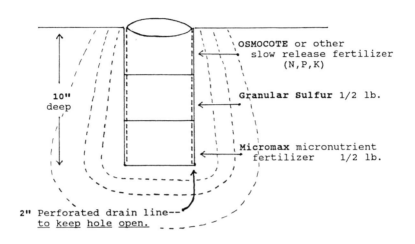

OSMOCOTE or other
slow release fertilizer
(N,P,K)

Granular Sulfur 1/2 lb.

10"
deep

Micromax micronutrient
fertilizer   1/2 lb.

2" Perforated drain line--
to keep hole open.

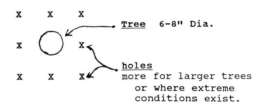

X   X   X

Tree   6-8" Dia.

X   X

holes
more for larger trees
or where extreme
conditions exist.

X   X   X

*Figure 26.5.   Diagram of the holes installed and filled with
micronutrients, sulfur, and a slow-release fertilizer (above).
The arrangement of the holes relative to the position of the trees
(below).*

Literature Cited

1. Bohm, W. 1979, *Methods of Studying Root Systems.* Springer-Verlag, New York, N.Y.

2. Clark, R.D. 1982. Iron deficiency in plants grown in the Great Plains of the U.S. Jour. Plant Nutrition 5:251-268.

3. Fischbach, J.E. and B. Webster. 1982. New method of injecting iron into pin oaks. Jour. of Arboriculture 8:240.

4. Halverson, H.G., D.R. DeWalle, W.E. Sharpe and D.G. Wirries. 1982. Runoff contaminants from natural and man-made surfaces in a non-industrial urban area. Proc. 1982 International Symp. on Urban Hydrology, Hydraulics and Sediment Control. U. of Kentucky, Lexington, Ky. p. 233-238.

5. Harrell, Mark O., Philip A. Pierce, David P. Moster and Bruce G. Webster. 1984. A comparison of treatments for chlorosis of pin oak and silver maple. Jour. of Arboriculture 10:246-249.

6. Himelick, E.B. and K.J. Himelick. 1980. Systematic treatment for chlorotic trees. Jour. of Arboriculture 6:192-196.

7. Kielbaso, J.J. and K. Ottman. 1976. Manganese deficiency--contributory to maple decline? Jour. of Arboriculture 2:27-32.

8. Messenger, Steve. 1984. Treatment of chlorotic oaks and red maples by soil acidification. Jour. of Arboriculture 10:122-128.

9. Neely, D. 1973. Pin oak chlorosis: trunk implantations correct iron deficiency. Jour. Forestry 71:340-342.

10. Neely, D. 1976. Iron deficiency chlorosis of shade trees. Jour. of Arboriculture 2:128-130.

11. Remon, James, Toby Goodale, Jim Ward, and Carl E. Whitcomb. 1977. Effects of sulfur on reducing pH of an alkaline soil. Okla. Agri. Exp. Sta. Nurs. Res. Rept. p-760:18-20.

12. Shigo, Alex L. 1983. Targets for proper tree care. Jour. of Arboriculture 9:285-294.

13. Smith, E.M. and C.D. Mitchell. 1977. Manganese deficiency of red maple. Jour. of Arboriculture 3:87-88.

14. Smith, E.M. and C.D. Mitchell. 1977. Eastern white pine iron deficiency. Jour. of Arboriculture 3:129-130.

15. Ware, G.H. 1984. Coping with clay: trees to suit sites, sites to suit trees. Jour. of Arboriculture 10:108-112.

16. Whitcomb, Carl E. 1985. *Know It & Grow It II: A Guide to the Identification and Use of Landscape Plants.* Lacebark Publications, Stillwater, OK. 720 pages.

17. Whitcomb, Carl E. 1986. Solving the iron chlorosis problem: a practical approach. Jour. of Arboriculture 12:44-48.

CHAPTER 27

PROTECTING EXISTING TREES

Protect It or Remove It - - - - - - - - 496

The Adjustment Factor - - - - - - - - - 497

Misconceptions - - - - - - - - - - - - - 498

Helpful Practices - - - - - - - - - - - 506

Root Flairs Are Clues - - - - - - - - 510

Manipulating Tree Roots - - - - - - - 512

Root Barriers - - - - - - - - - - - - 513

Shifting Support Roots - - - - - - - - 515

Protecting Existing Trees

Protect It or Remove It.   Trees existing on a site are often mutilated during construction (Figure 27.1).   Many times the efforts to "save" trees provide little or no benefit and the trees are doomed.   **Unless effective protective measures are taken, it is best to remove the trees to simplify construction, then replant.**   Half-hearted efforts to save existing trees are worse than no effort at all.   Why?   Because construction is more expensive due to the restriction of men and machines working around the trees and after they die, removal is often times very awkward and expensive when structures are nearby.   On numerous occasions this author has advised either "spend enough effort to assure that most of the trees will survive or enjoy the firewood and replant."

Figure 27.1.   These trees were marked to be "saved", yet because of the damage to the trunk, soil against the trunk, soil compaction, direct root damage and abrupt change in the root environment, their chances of survival are slim.   Trees have substantial landscape value, but only if they are treated with respect.

To tree lovers this sounds like a very cold and cruel approach. However, being a realist, unless the tree has better than a 40% chance of survival, it is better to have it removed than to die a slow lingering death. The realist view is also that if a tree takes five years to die, a tree of reasonable size planted following construction will have five years of growth on the site and will be making a significant contribution to the landscape when the dead tree is being removed.

The Adjustment Factor. Another aspect of tree growth is the adjustment factor. That is, if the tree is on the site first and environmental changes due to construction are imposed, the tree must attempt to adjust quickly which it cannot do and consequently often dies (Figure 27.2). On the other hand, if construction in completed and **then** the tree is planted into the site, it grows and adjusts to the environmental and limitation factors of the site. Trees can adjust to many environmental conditions if the adjustment occurs gradually as the tree **increases** in size. The growth rate and ultimate size the tree planted following construction attains, will generally be less than the same species on the same site without the construction limitations. However, this slower growth and size reduction is appropriate and simply reflects less favorable growing conditions. The size the top attains reflects the amount of root system support. For a tree to grow a large top with a very limited root system would amount to suicide.

Figure 27.2. Occasionally a tree survives construction and even considerable disruption of the root environment. In this case, the tree was left to grow in a very unusual situation. However, the conditions that exist on this site are unique. The soil along this part of the South Carolina coast is sandy and deep, plus a live oak is among the most tolerant species of urban conditions. For this one survivor, if this was done on 100 different sites, the mortality would probably be 99.

Misconceptions. Several misconceptions are wide-spread regarding attempts to save native trees on a site:

a. "It's a large tree so it will tolerate a lot of abuse." **False!** The larger the tree, the more delicate the balance between top and roots. In some cases, only a very minor shift in growing conditions can cause decline and ultimately, death (Figure 27.3).

b. "Trees have deep roots and taking off a few inches of surface soil will not hurt." **False!** The majority of tree roots are very shallow. Most of the effective root system of a tree is in the upper 8 to 12 inches of soil. Many trees do have a **few** roots that extend to considerable depths in the soil. However, these roots play a role only during dry periods when the penetration of oxygen into the soil is deeper, allowing them to function (Figure 27.4).

c.   "Adding a few inches of soil around the trees will be OK." **False!** **Any** change of grade around existing trees represents a **radical** change in the root environment and may make the difference between life and death. Soil aeration is a key factor influencing root function and plant health (Figure 27.5).

d.   "We'll cut back the top of the tree to adjust for the few roots lost." **False!** About 60% of the living cells in a tree are in the main stem and large branches and roots. In order to appreciably reduce the energy demand of the top, severe pruning must be done, so much so that the appearance and functional value of the tree is lost. A key point to remember if that, yes, roots may have been lost, but new roots cannot be produced without energy and growth regulators which can only come from the leaves so any reduction in leaves also reduces the rate of root recovery. It is better to spend more time and money on post-construction care than to cut back the top (Figure 27.6).

Figure 27.3. These trees were "saved" during the construction process. Now they are dying or dead and will be expensive to remove. Only the small tree to the right, which was planted following construction, is growing. Removal of the dead trees on this site will be difficult since access for equipment is limited. On the other hand, because of the liability/hazard condition of the dead and dying trees, they should be removed as soon as possible.

Figure 27.4. The artist's conception of where tree roots are located (above) is very different from their actual location (below). In the case of the bottom photo, a well-intending homeowner had plowed his yard in order to grow a good lawn. He did not expect to find tree roots just under the soil surface.

Figure 27.5. About one foot of soil was placed over the root system of this tree. Now, three years later, only a dying snag remains.

Figure 27.6. These trees were "saved" during construction. The tops were severely cut back but the trees died. The pine lived only about six months while the oak survived nearly three years. The end result was a peculiar, poorly functional parking area.

When a plant experiences stress, for any reason, the root system suffers first and most severely. This is true whether the plant is a very small seedling or an extremely large tree. Development causes various environmental changes that increase the stress level on trees even if the root system is not disturbed. Reflected light and heat, changes in the water table and surface drainage patterns are the most obvious changes in environmental conditions during construction. Add to these changes, soil compaction (Figures 27.7 and 27.8), partial loss of the root system and other damage during development and it is amazing that any trees survive the ordeal. It is unfortunate that so many sites are developed because of the existing trees, yet a few years after construction is complete, most of the trees are dead or in various stages of decline. And, once the tree begins to decline, rarely can anything be done to resurrect the specimen.

A tree dies because it starves to death. Abrupt changes in environmental conditions mean reduced energy production by the leaves. Large trees may have substantial stored reserves of starches, but as these are used and not replaced, eventually the tree dies. Death comes quickly to pines and tulip trees whereas an oak may struggle for years.

*Figure 27.7. This southern magnolia (**Magnolia grandiflora**) was growing on the site before development. Notice the sparse foliage and dead branches on the left side. Now look at Figure 27.8 for the rest of the story.*

Figure 27.8. The tree had many roots in the soil area that became a road. As the soil became more compacted and root functions declined, that side of the tree declined.

Helpful Practices. What can be done? The following steps or precautions will greatly reduce the likelihood of tree damage and decline:

a. Before development, evaluate the site to assess soil, drainage and other conditions. Trees on a deep sandy soil are somewhat more tolerant than trees on a shallow clay soil. Silt soils tend to compact as much as clays and both are more easily compacted than sand, but soils of virtually pure sand can be compacted in many instances. If the water table is likely to be affected, likelihood of tree loss is greatly increased.

b. Take a soil test and fertilize trees accordingly **before** development begins. A few dollars spent on fertilizer broadcast over the root zone areas to be left undisturbed can increase the trees' tolerance level to stress. The earlier this occurs before construction, the better. See Chapter 22 and 24 for details.

c. Allow no parking, movement or storage of any vehicle or equipment near the trees to be retained (Figure 27.9). Soil compaction is the number one killer of trees and can be caused by both machines and man. Foot traffic compacts soil more than some machines.

d. Fence or rope off the root zones of trees to be retained (Figure 27.9). Remember that the roots of most trees extend several times the distance from the trunk to the outermost branches (Figure 27.10). The more the root zone of the tree is disturbed, the more likely the tree will die.

e. Advise all construction personnel that no dumping of oil, antifreeze or other chemicals is allowed on the site. On a construction site there seems to be a tremendous temptation to dump materials among plants because "it won't hurt anything." A few meetings with construction personnel to increase their awareness of the value of trees, how long it takes to grow a tree, how vulnerable they are and how toxic materials like petroleum products and antifreeze are to trees, will greatly decrease the chance of problems.

Figure 27.9. *Where better to place one's tools than in the shade (above). This tree, that provided a respite for workmen on the site will leave a few years later. Do not allow any disturbance of, or storage of materials on the root zone of the tree if it is to be saved. The fence (below) is not sufficiently large to provide any appreciable protection for this young tree that has roots well beyond the established boundary.*

507

Figure 27.10. Roots of large trees often extend far beyond the drip line (outermost branches). Note the shade pattern of the tree from the afternoon sun and realize that many roots extend many feet beyond. Any disturbance of the root system of a tree will increase the stress level. There is no way to determine if a tree will survive the stress so, "If you value the tree, keep the disturbance to a minimum!".

f.   In some cases the foundation can be dug with a fire hose or similar hydraulic apparatus, thereby, leaving the majority of the root system undisturbed. For example, on one occasion the author was contacted regarding ways to save a group of live oaks during construction of a single family residence on a small lot in Florida. After inspecting the site, it was recommended that the contractor dig the footings and foundation with a fire hose. The foundation for the house was staked out and washing began. Whenever roots were observed, a large section was left (Figure 27.11). The washing did not injure the roots and the soil was back-filled over the roots as soon as the forms were set for the concrete footings. The house was constructed on a series of piers located wherever roots were absent. In this case a sprinkler system was also installed **under** the house. The trees are alive and well many years later.

g.   In some cases, water or other service lines must be installed adjacent to existing trees. Rather than trench and cut many roots, it is far more advisable and only slightly more expensive to tunnel **under** the tree. Trench from both directions until tree roots are observed. Then use a tunnel machine to connect the two trenches. This technique is very simple and has been used successfully many times. The machinery is commonly used for tunneling under streets and highways. A tunnel three feet or more below a large tree has no effect on its future growth or health.

Figure 27.11. Roots exposed by washing. Since tree roots are very shallow, it is very easy to wash the soil away exposing the major roots. Where roots are absent, footings can be dug either with water or by conventional means.

There is no guarantee that even with the actions listed above that a tree will survive development. Experience suggests that **the less the disturbance, the greater the likelihood of survival.** Only the amateur makes rigid predictions about tree performance following development, regardless of the precautions taken. This author has seen trees that experienced little disturbance die following development and in contrast, trees survive that were all but uprooted. These are clearly extremes, but averages are made up of extremes. In some cases the life or death of a tree can be traced back to one or two major support root systems. If the tree is disturbed on the side away from the major support roots, likelihood of survival may be 80%. But, if the tree is disturbed on the other side, the likelihood of survival may be only 20%.

Root Flairs Are Clues. With many trees, the major support root systems can be determined by examining the root flairs at the base of the trunk (Figure 27.12). Root flairs develop because the trunk expands in response to the downward flow of energy from the leaves in conjunction with the major roots. These visual responses to the distribution of the tree's root system are valuable clues to ways to reduce tree root injury during development.

Because root flairs are the major pathways from roots to leaves and vice versa, they are very sensitive. A good analogy would be a crimp in a waterhose. However, because the bulk of the translocation of water, nutrients and energy is in the outer sheath of the stem, root flair, and roots, even slight damage causes a major disruption (Figure 27.13). The downward flow of energy from the leaves is in the phloem just inside the bark. The same is true for root flairs, thus the high sensitivity to damage. There is also the factor of stem vs. root tissues. Stem tissues are adapted to tolerate low moisture contact and drying; root tissues are adapted to tolerate considerable moisture contact and, in general, can not tolerate drying. Root flairs develop in response to good root/top interaction over a period of years and generally develop bark or barklike characteristics. At this transition point between stem and root, any change in environment can cause a major disruption in the supply of water and nutrients as well as energy flow from the leaves. This is why grade changes almost always mean disaster.

Figure 27.12. Tree trunks expand more in conjunction with the major support root systems. In general, the greater the root flair, the greater contribution of that support root system to the overall growth and health of the tree. The tree above has one major root to the right, whereas, the tree below has several major root support systems. Where no root flairs are visible, be suspicious that fill soil has been added.

Figure 27.13. This tree has one very strong root flair and five minor ones (two not visible). If the major root flair is damaged, 30% to 60% of the water and nutrient support for the tree could be lost. Rarely could any tree, regardless of site and species, survive such a loss.

Manipulating Tree Roots. Roots of established trees are crucial to health and survival and should not be disturbed. However, there are situations where roots of existing trees must be cut, removed or in some way restricted. The following situations and actions are presented as suggestions **if** root manipulation must occur. It must be re-emphasized that any action that reduces, damages or restricts the activity of the established root system of a tree will place the tree in some degree of risk. If a tree is in excellent condition it will **tolerate** more stress from disturbance than if it is in marginal health. Unfortunately, there is no practical way to tell the relative level of health of a tree above some minimum. In all cases, the landscape client should be advised of the risk involved before action is taken.

Tree roots have no sense of direction or the capacity to seek out favorable growing conditions. However, when tree roots reach

512

an area favorable for root growth, they proliferate quickly. Areas where tree roots proliferate are golf course putting greens or tees. A dense mat of tree roots in such an area can greatly restrict the growth of grass roots and make grass management difficult. A similar situation can occur in flower and shrub beds, vegetable gardens and any other landscape situation where water, fertilizer, soils and aeration conditions are favorable for root growth.

Root Barriers. The practical solution may be to install a root barrier. With modern trenchers, a narrow trench three to four inches wide and 30 to 36 inches deep can be made at limited expense. The trench only needs to be wide enough to insert the barrier material. The depth of the trench is very important and must be deep enough to prevent root growth under the barrier. In areas of heavy clay soils, the barrier may only need to be 24 to 28 inches deep, whereas in most soils the barrier must be 30 to 36 inches deep.

Tree roots in a soil zone 24 to 36 inches below the surface are most active when the surface soil is dry and thus oxygen levels increase in the soil at greater depths. If a root grows under a barrier (or is present beneath a barrier because it was installed too shallow) it will grow into the high management area above and proliferate quickly. Under these conditions, the portion of the root below the barrier (and in the poorly aerated zone of soil) will function under all soil moisture conditions since it acts as a conduit from absorptive fine roots to the tree.

This same principal/process occurs with the so called "deep root" barriers being promoted to encourage tree root development at greater depths. These divices provide only a temporary delay in the development of tree roots near the soil surface.

Root barriers do restrict tree growth since a portion of the absorptive root surface area is removed during installation and the volume of soil available for root growth in the future is reduced. After installing root barriers, tree care and maintenance should be increased in order to aid in the adjustment. See the section below on shifting support roots.

Root barriers can be constructed of heavy polyethylene sheeting (eight mil or more) or six mil poly in conjunction with 40-pound roofing felt. When eight mil or heavier poly is used, it works best if it is 12 inches or more wide than the trench is deep. The poly is draped against one side of the trench and carefully backfilled. Be careful that the soil entering the trench does not draw the poly below the soil surface. A very effective technique is to use a trencher that leaves most of the soil on one side of the trench. Position the poly against the opposite side of the trench, then while standing on the top edge of the poly, draw the soil into the trench using a rake or similar device until the trench is filled. Leave the 12 inches of poly extending out of the trench until the backfill has been thoroughly watered or several rains have occurred to settle the backfill, then cut it flush with the surface. Many root barriers have been carefully installed only to have settling pull the top edge below the soil surface only to allow tree roots to grow across above the poly.

Thinner poly, four or six mil, is also an effective root barrier, but tears or punctures easily. If lightweight poly is used, use 40-pound roofing paper in conjunction to prevent punctures by the ends of the roots cut by the trencher or stones. In this case, place the roofing paper against the side of the trench, then drape with poly and fill against the poly, thus pressing the roofing paper against the sharp, cut ends of roots. Roofing paper alone makes an effective root barrier but only lasts three or four years, whereas the poly will last indefinitely.

Long rolls of poly should be used to avoid overlaps. If overlaps between rolls must occur, 8 to 10 feet should be used to reduce the likelihood of tree roots growing between the two sheets of poly and into the area to be protected. Likewise, be careful to avoid any tears or punctures of the poly that would allow roots the opportunity to "escape". When tree roots encounter a barrier of this type, the normal reaction is to grow parallel along the face of the barrier. When tree roots are cut, the adventitious roots form just behind the cut surface, thus the likelihood of a root finding an opening is fairly high (Figure 15.6).

Landscape contractors sometimes place poly beneath beds of azaleas or other difficult-to-manage shrubs, in an attempt to prevent tree root growth into the area. This is generally futile, since tree roots will generally find an opportunity along the edge of the bed, and the poly changes the water relationship and drainage of the soil or soil mix in the bed creating further complications. It is better to install a permanent tree root barrier vertically in the soil.

A word of caution: **Do Not** cut support roots of a tree such that the tree could fall in the opposite direction. In some cases trenches are made near trees and root barriers installed. This is WRONG. It is only a matter of time before a strong wind in the proper direction topples the tree due to lack of anchorage on the one side. Remember the taller the tree the greater the wind load or leverage during a storm.

Shifting Support Roots. When construction is to be done among established trees, the question often occurs regarding any action that can be done to minimize the damage to the trees. The actions mentioned earlier should be heeded carefully. In addition, the support roots (support in terms of nutrient and water absorption, not physical support) of an existing tree can be shifted. For example, when the author constructed a home and workshop among existing oak and hackberry trees, the first action taken, six months before construction began, was to heavily fertilize all of the trees to be saved on the **opposite** side from the disturbance. In this case, the native soil fertility was very low but the soil was a well aerated sandy loam, thus root development in the heavily fertilized area was rapid. As a result, all of the 32 trees disturbed are alive and well 15 years later. Remember that fertilizer should be applied only after a soil test to determine what is needed. Adding more potassium or phosphorus in the fertilizer when it is not needed can be counter-productive.

It is best if fertilizer and perhaps supplemental water can be applied to the root zone away from the disturbance a year or more in advance of construction, but even if little advanced warning exists, it is still a beneficial practice. Remember that more root growth occurs in the fall than in the spring, but some benefits will occur under most situations, any time of year. **Do not** disturb the soil surface or attempt to rototil or disc in phosphorus or other fertilizers. Remember that tree roots in an existing wooded area are very shallow and any unnecessary disturbance means additional root damage.

In situations where root barriers are installed on one side of a tree, it is a very beneficial practice to fertilize and under some circumstances water on the opposite side of the tree. This not only aids the tree in the adjustment to the barrier installation and root loss, but also reduces the rate at which roots will develop along the barrier and the likelihood of rapid root development into the protected area if a tear or puncture did occur during installation.

A quick tour of any urban area will reveal trees with little or no roots remaining on one side, but moderate growth in the entire crown. This occurs because of internal distribution of nutrients and water throughout the crown even though absorption occurs by roots in conjunction with only a portion of the normal root zone. Oaks appear to have poor internal distribution relative to other species (see Figure 28.9 in the following chapter, for example).

In summary, save as many roots as possible, while aiding root development and function in the remaining areas.

CHAPTER 28

CUT, FILL AND OTHER GRADE CHANGES

Cuts - - - - - - - - - - - - - - - - - - 518

Fills - - - - - - - - - - - - - - - - 522

Tree Wells - - - - - - - - - - - - - - 524

Retaining Walls - - - - - - - - - - - 529

Shifting the Root System - - - - - - 533

Cut, Fill and Other Grade Changes

If trees on a site to be developed are valued highly, no cut, fill or other grade changes will be allowed. There are times when this cannot be done, but it is important to emphasize to all parties concerned that the greater the disturbance, the greater the risk to the tree(s).

Cuts. Cuts or removal of soil around existing trees is nearly always devastating (Figure 28.1) . Tree roots are very shallow. A quick look below the litter on the soil surface with a shovel will reveal many small roots. The many small roots near the soil surface are the major absorbers of nutrients for plant growth and health (Figure 28.2). Between the loss of these roots and a major change in the environment that prevents the growth of replacements, there is little hope for survival.

The very small, fine roots are very sensitive to changes in environmental conditions. These fine roots are constantly dying and being replaced by new ones as the plant continually explores the soil for nutrients and water. If these fine roots are destroyed more rapidly than they are replenished, water and nutrient support for the leaves will rapidly decrease. In many cases involving construction and changes in the soil environment, most of the fine roots are lost (Figure 28.3). Survival of the tree is dependent on the development of new fine roots from the larger woody roots during or soon after the construction is completed. This procedure probably occurs on most, if not all, trees transplanted B & B or with tree spades. Thus the key to survival is the rapid development of new fine roots from the larger woody roots (Figure 28.4).

In many cases, the installation of retaining walls so that a substantial portion of the tree's root system remains undisturbed is a good choice. Retaining walls are expensive to construct and maintain but the loss of a sizable tree is also expensive. If a retaining wall is used, be sure to allow enough room for anchor roots on all sides of the tree to prevent wind throw.

Figure 28.1. Tree roots can be found in the leaf litter virtually at the soil surface (above). The roots of this live oak were exposed using a fire hose to remove about one inch of the soil (below). Note the complex mass of roots. For every root you see there were many smaller roots that were washed away.

*Figure 28.2.   Roots of a southern magnolia (**Magnolia grandiflora**) exposed by trenching.   Even though the soil is very sandy, there were few roots below a depth of about 18 inches and most were near the soil surface (the original soil surface is noted by the dotted line).   Any removal of soil from the surface will mean a devastating loss of tree roots.*

Figure 28.3.   This tree was between two major buildings on a university campus.   There was a small rise in the natural soil grade around the tree and extending into the foreground.   In order to place the sidewalk in a straight line and to have a level surface, the grade around the tree was lowered up to 10 inches. In addition, when the heavy sidewalk (for some maintenance vehicles as well as pedestrians) was installed, a further excavation of about six inches occurred.   What was an attractive and healthy water oak, first lost some of its top branches, then a few more, then the entire top, leaving only an ugly reminder of how "minor" changes can have a major impact on existing trees.

Fills. Fill placed over existing roots may or may not be devastating, depending on the nature of the fill soil used, depth applied, weather conditions, time of year, species involved, machinery used and probably other factors. However, if the trees are highly valued, **no** fill should be allowed.

A few inches of fill of a sandy soil over a sandy or clay soil may be tolerated by some species (Figure 28.4). This is the most favorable fill situation in most cases. Since water readily moves from a coarse-textured soil (the sand) to a fine-textured soil (the clay), placing a sandy soil over a clay soil allows for favorable water movement and soil aeration and unless the depth of the new soil is excessive and/or is compacted by the equipment used in spreading, root growth limitations are slight. There are exceptions even to this situation. For example, if a tree is growing on a poorly drained clay soil with good surface drainage, adding a sandy fill soil would likely spell disaster since rainfall would percolate into the sandy soil and be held on the clay soil surface. Water does move laterally in soils, however, the rate of lateral movement would probably be too slow to prevent root suffocation.

Placing a fine-textured fill soil (the clay) over a coarse-textured soil (sand or sandy loam) is nearly always fatal to existing trees. This is the reverse of the situation above. Water **will not** move from a fine-textured soil to a coarse-textured soil until the fine-textured soil becomes saturated. If surface drainage can occur, the fine-textured soil may never become saturated to a depth to force water to enter the more coarse-textured soil below. The coarse-textured soil below may be very dry while the surface fine fill soil is very wet. This condition deprives the tree of both oxygen and water since the wet fine soil may be nearly impenetrable to gases. Fine-textured soils are much more easily compacted by equipment used to spread the fill, especially if it is moist (Figure 28.5).

Never add more than two to three inches of fill soil at a time, even under the most favorable conditions. If more fill is required, do it over a year or more or remove the tree.

Figure 28.4. In this case, about four inches of fill sand was placed over the tree roots to provide a bed for the brick-on-sand sidewalk. Following completion of the walk, additional sandy soil fill was added to make a gradual slope from the surface of the walk out to the existing soil. The slope is so gradual that it is hardly noticed. The tree remains healthy and has produced new fine roots up into the fill soil. Contrast this technique with Figure 28.3 where an excavation was made for a concrete sidewalk and the tree was lost.

Never add fill soil when the existing soil or the fill soil is wet. Wet soils compact more than dry soils.

Use the lightest equipment possible and with the greatest flotation. A front loader with balloon turf tires on front and rear will compact soil less than one with narrow ag tires in front and cleated tires in rear.

Add fill soil in the fall whenever possible. Roots are most active in the fall, yet the demand for water by the leaves is low. In addition, the freezing and thawing of the soil during the winter will help loosen any compaction. By the time new leaves emerge in the spring with their higher water demand, the roots will have grown up into the shallow layer of fill soil.

Figure 28.5. This tree fell prey to cut and fill and compaction problems. The street to the left was widened, cutting back a portion of the roots. A driveway was added in the foreground that acted as a fill and quickly became compacted onto the heavy clay soil. The sidewalk was added on about four inches of fill soil. As a result of the disruption of the roots, the trees anchorage was reduced. This was an old neighborhood that was being revamped. A beautiful tree was lost because of a lack of concern for its root system.

Species native to stream banks such as willows, maples poplars, elms and other species with rapidly growing fibrous root systems are more tolerant to shallow fills than upland species such as oaks, tulip trees, pines and other conifers.

Tree Wells. Many books and other publications show elaborate systems of tree wells and other techniques that will "save" trees in areas where fills are to be made (Figure 28.6 and 28.7). **This is fiction!** Many tree wells have been installed by individuals with good intentions but almost always the tree dies. Many of these tree wells do make nice fish ponds or wishing wells after the stumps are removed, but are rarely located in the right spot in the landscape. Before allowing anyone to build a tree well, ask to see five tree wells where the trees are still alive five years after installation (Figure 28.8).

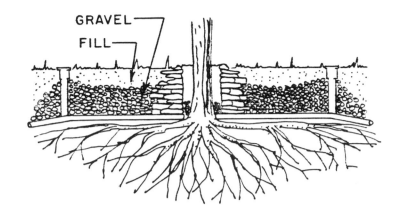

Figure 28.6. Many elaborate systems have been promoted for saving trees around which fill soil is to be placed. In this case it cannot eventually be used to make a lily pond because of the drain tile system, so it becomes a choice between fill it in or make it into a rock garden.

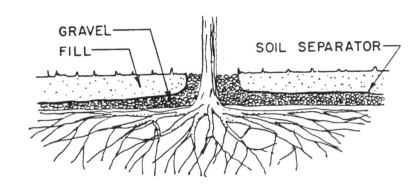

Figure 28.7. In this case, the layer of gravel over the soil surface provides an abrupt textural barrier, thus creating a perched water table in the soil above the gravel. The soil above the gravel may be very wet while the soil below may be quite dry. Only a very small fraction of the oxygen required by the root system can diffuse through the gravel. Rarely does this system work.

Those who sell these deceptive services and other misinformed people, often point to the fact that the tree lived over a year following installation so it must have died from some other cause. Not So! A large tree may take several years to die. A live oak may require five to six years or more before death, but the **cause** is the root injury due to root damage and suffocation.

Never allow fill soil, even a few inches deep, to be placed against the above-ground bark at the base of a tree. The bark has evolved to protect the above-ground trunk from dehydration and continuously moist conditions often mean stem damage and decay, or in extreme cases, girdling of the trunk (Figure 28.9). Trees are huge organisms incapable of moving or making any appreciable adjustment to their environment. A tree dies because the root system starves to death. When a tree (or any plant) becomes stressed the root system always suffers first and most. As the root system declines, water and nutrient levels supplied to the top decrease and the decline begins. The larger the tree the more rapid the decline although visual symptoms may be few at first, then develop rather abruptly. Once decline reaches a certain point recovery is very unlikely regardless of treatment(s).

*Figure 28.8.   This northern red oak (**Quercus rubra**) has survived the tree well for nearly six years, however, the sparse crown is a sure sign of decline.   The tree may "live" for another year or two, but will die a premature death compared to its lifespan without the fill soil.   This treatment does not save trees, but allows them to die a more drawn out agonizing death..*

Figure 28.9. The grade on this site was raised about one foot with a sandy loam fill soil around several large trees (above). Three years later only one tree remains but with about 50% crown dieback. The base of the tree shows the girdling effect the fill had on the bark at the trunk (below). Anytime root flairs are not visible on moderate-sized trees, some filling has probably occurred.

Retaining Walls. Where soil must be removed from one side of an existing tree and a retaining wall installed, it is better to cut the roots back two to three feet further and install good soil of moderate fertility in the gap between the old grade and the face of the retaining wall. Treating the ends of cut roots with 2000 parts per million of IBA (as discussed in the chapter on transplanting trees) may help stimulate roots into the well-aerated soil quickly enough to increase the chances of survival. On the other hand, if the cut root ends are only a few inches inside the retaining wall, there is little opportunity for the new roots to contribute, even if they form (28.10).

Figure 28.10. In this case the trench was dug and forms were installed for the retaining wall before the rest of the soil was removed. The tree may have had a greater chance of survival if the retaining wall had been moved out three feet and good fill soil placed between the back of the retaining wall and the cut root ends especially in areas where the native soil is poor.

The formation of new roots from the cut ends here is different than with transplanted trees. In most cases, since a portion of the roots have not been disturbed, and the tree top is still active, growth regulating chemicals will cause new roots to form at the cut ends of roots fairly quickly, depending on the species. This is in contrast to many transplanted trees where no new roots form at the cut ends until bud break in the spring, regardless of when the tree is transplanted.

Trees frequently do not grow, or grow less, on the side where the roots were removed or restricted, as opposed to the other side where the roots are not restricted. With an existing tree this will generally mean a decline in the branches on the affected side (see the previous chapter, for example). With a young tree it may lead to a deformed crown (Figure 28.11).

In most cases it is, in the long run, better to remove trees that cannot be allowed sufficient room to ensure a reasonable chance of survival and re-plant following construction. Trees introduced to the site following construction will grow proportionately to the new conditions of the site. They will generally not grow as large as would have occurred prior to development, but they will function for a longer time and will pose fewer safety hazards (Figure 28.12).

*Figure 28.11. This English oak, (**Quercus robur**) cannot develop roots to the right because of a deep and long-existent steam tunnel under the sidewalk. As a result, the right side of the tree has over the years, been greatly restricted compared to the left side where no root restriction exists.*

Figure 28.12. The trees on this site were introduced after construction was complete. They will adapt to the conditions of the site and grow at a proportionate rate. This is, in many cases, more cost effective than trying to save old trees with limited vigor, then eventually replacing them. Nursery-grown trees with superior root systems will establish more quickly and grow faster than trees collected from the wild. As nursery management and root modification practices improve in the future, the advantage of nursery-grown trees will become even more dramatic. A healthy, low stress tree has few problems, whereas, a stressed tree has many problems.

Shifting the Root System. When time allows, the root system of established trees can be shifted. this can be done most effectively on native sites where fertility is low. By fertilizing trees in the areas that will **NOT** be disturbed a rapid proliferation of roots occurs, thus minimizing the adverse effects of roots lost in other areas.

The greatest problem in using this technique is the lead time required. Any lead time can provide some assistance, but to be most effective at least a year is required and more would be desirable. The author has had the opportunity to use this on several occasions effectively. In areas of native woods a soil test should be done and any deficient elements should be applied to the soil surface. **Do Not** till or otherwise disturb the roots.

The least effective situations are those where the trees are already restricted or stressed by development such that any loss of roots could be devastating and there is little or no opportunity to expand root functions. On the other hand, even in developed areas, if a soil test shows any nutrients deficient, then addition of the needed element(s) to the areas **not** disturbed will be helpful.

The degree of assistance to the tree is difficult to judge in the short term, however, the cost of a soil test and fertilizer is very modest relative to the loss of a sizable tree.

CHAPTER 29

LIGHT, SHADE AND ROOT GROWTH

Light Duration - - - - - - - - - - - - 535

Light Intensity - - - - - - - - - - - 539

Shade Effects Plant Growth - - - - - - 540

Literature Cited - - - - - - - - - - - 550

Light, Shade and Root Growth

Growth of a plant, any plant, is energy-dependent. Water and all 12 fertilizer elements plus carbon dioxide from the air are the basic ingredients. Through the unique process of photosynthesis, leaves of plants capture the energy of the sun and convert it into soluble carbohydrates. The soluble carbohydrates or energy provide for all the plants respiration and growth. Any improvement in the supply or balance of the basic components (water, nitrogen, iron, etc.) will improve the total energy production of the plant **provided** the light level is correct. When energy levels decrease from insufficient light, root growth suffers most which in turn is reflected as less drought-tolerant and plant performance is poor. Three aspects of light are most important to plant growth:
1. Duration: the length of the photoperiod
2. Quality: measured in wavelengths
3. Intensity: measured in foot-candles or lux

Light Duration. Duration of light or length of photoperiod is not normally considered or modified during the production of nursery stock or maintenance of landscape plants. There are some notable exceptions: chrysanthemums, poinsettias and zygocactus (Christmas cactus). These plants require an increasing length of the dark period (a shortening of the photoperiod or duration of light) in order to flower. This occurs naturally during the autumn and crops such as poinsettias flower naturally at or near the Christmas season in the northern hemisphere. On the other hand, these crops require artificial lengthening of the dark period at other times of the year in order to be induced to flower. This mechanism is used regularly in the flowering of chrysanthemums as pot plants and cut flowers for use the year around.

Many of the coniferous trees native to northern latitudes are also sensitive to the photoperiod. The effects of photoperiod on the growth of several northern conifers were studied in Gainesville, Florida (20). Mugo pine (*Pinus mugo* 'Mughus'), white pine (*Pinus strobus*), white spruce (*Picea abies*), and Canadian hemlock (*Tsuga canadensis*) all grew better with long days as compared to the normal photoperiod of northern Florida (Figure 29.1). The fact that the plants grew similarly whether the photoperiod was lengthened or the night period interrupted, confirms that the response was due to the photoperiod and not just to a longer growing period.

Figure 29.1.   Response of white pine to photoperiod.   The longer days (LD) or interrupted (Int) both allowed the trees to grow faster than the natural Florida day length (Fla).   As the top grows larger, so does the root system.   Plants grown under the natural Florida daylength had fewer roots and as a result were more susceptible to drought stress.

A study confirmed that photoperiod is a factor affecting the growth of several species even though the 16-hour days during early summer would, at first, seem satisfactory in Stillwater, Oklahoma (19).   Austrian pine (*Pinus nigra*) and Black Hills spruce (*Picea glauca* 'Densata') both grow larger with 20-hour days as opposed to the standard 16-hour   days in north central Oklahoma (Figure 29.2).

Light intensity can be quite low and still influence photoperiod (duration).   Some conifers and many deciduous tree species are photoperiod-sensitive and respond to security lights in parking lots and other areas.   Cathey and Campbell (4) give an excellent discussion of this topic on the effects of security lighting in the October 1975 Journal of Arboriculture.   The topic is complex and can be confusing as it is mostly the red and blue colors in the light that influence plants.   For example, mercury

536

vapor lamps are low in red light, so have little effect, whereas, the newer high-pressure sodium lamps have mostly red and yellow and may influence plants. Light intensity, duration and quality (proportion of the color spectrum) all play a role in plant growth. Because of the complex interaction of these factors, each landscape site must be considered separately.

*Figure 29.2.   Arrangement of lights and plants for studying the effects of photoperiod on plant growth (above).   Austrian pine (**Pinus nigra**) and Black Hills spruce (**Picea glauca** 'Densata') (below) grew better with long days (20 hours, right) as opposed to the standard photoperiod in Stillwater, Oklahoma (16 hours, left).*

Light Intensity. The ideal light intensity for greatest photosynthesis in a leaf is much lower than the intensity of full sunlight. However, only the outer leaves of a plant canopy receive full sunlight, and the remainder receive somewhat less. The canopy of leaves of a tree or shrub contain some leaves receiving full sun, some that do not receive full sun but enough for maximum food production in the leaves, and so on to the innermost leaves that are near the compensation point. The compensation point is that light intensity where the energy produced by the leaf is equal to the energy used in respiration. When a leaf is at or slightly above the compensation point, the plant generally develops an abscission (separation) layer between the base of the leaf and the stem and the leaf drops (15).

Light intensity is rarely constant but varies with movement of the leaves as well as changes in the angle of the sun, cloud cover and other factors. Leaves that develop in high light intensity are smaller and thicker and have more but smaller chloroplasts which are generally oriented parallel to the light source (1, 3). This is a light-avoidance mechanism which allows plants to tolerate very high light levels without the chloroplasts being destroyed by the tremendous light energy. On the other hand, leaves that develop in the shade are larger and thinner and have larger chloroplasts that are generally oriented at right angles to the light source such that a high proportion of the incoming light can be captured and used in the process of photosynthesis (3, 15). Plants that are grown under shade then abruptly transferred to full sun often "sunburn". This is due to the rapid destruction of the horizontal chloroplasts by the abrupt increase in light energy received at the leaf surface. By contrast, if a shade-grown plant is moved out-of-doors on an overcast day or moved to progressively less shade gradually, little or no "sunburn" results. In this transition period, the chloroplasts reorient themselves from horizontal to vertical, in order to avoid the excess light encountered in full sun in most areas of the world (2). This "hardening off" process is of major importance on some species and of minor consequence on others.

Plants grown in full sun are generally more compact with shorter internodes and more leaves than plants grown in shade. *Ficus elastica* 'Decora' had fewer branches when grown under low light intensity as opposed to full sun (6). Sheppard and Pellet (17) grew *Cornus sericea* in full sun and under shade. They found that the shrubs grown in full sun were compact with many lateral branches but less leaf area, whereas, plants grown under 70% shade were open and had few branches but a greater leaf area.

Most woody plants are more compact and of higher visual quality with more stored energy in the stems and roots when grown in full sun or the highest light intensity practical for the species. Some work has been reported which suggests various amounts of shading for nursery stock. McGuire (16) stated that 20 percent shade could benefit broadleaf evergreens in Rhode Island but offered no data. Dewerth and Odom (7) mention that nursery stock produced under lath shade was "better and larger" than that grown in full sun. Kelly (12) reported that growth of pyracantha and holly increased slightly when grown in one-third shade and that wintergreen barberry (*Berberis julianae*) grew 80 percent more in shade than in full sun. He also reported that the fertility program had little or no effect on plants under varying shade levels. Furuta (8) reported that several cultivars of azalea set buds and flowered better when grown under 22 to 46 percent shade in southeastern U.S. None of the literature mentions root growth or possible effects of shading on development of root systems. Principles of basic physiology suggest that once light intensity is reduced below the point of light saturation for even a portion of the leaves, the root system is likely to be reduced in size. More importantly, the rate at which roots grow out into the surrounding soil following transplanting will be restricted by excess shading.

Shade Effects Plant Growth. In order to study the effects of shade and nutrition on plant growth, the following study was conducted (20):

Twenty 3.6 m. x 2.4 m. x 1.2 m. (12 ft. x 8 ft. x 4 ft.) wooden structures were built and covered with 25, 30, 47, 63 and 73 percent shade fabric (Figure 29.3). A full-sun treatment was also included. Oklahoma has light intensities in excess of 107,604 lux (10,000 foot-candles) during the summer months.

Liners (young plants) were potted into one-gallon black polyethylene containers and arranged under the shade structures. Growth medium was a 1-1-1 ratio of peat, pine bark and sand with the necessary nutrient amendments. Irrigation was provided as needed from overhead sprinklers. The study was terminated at the end of one growing season. The test plants were hetzi juniper (*Juniperus chinensis* 'Hetzi'), wateri pyracantha (*Pyracantha coccinea* 'Wateri'), evergreen euonymus (*Euonymus japonica*), silverberry elaeagnus (*Elaeagnus macrophylla*), Japanese aucuba

(*Aucuba japonica*), azalea (*Rhododendron* spp. 'Glacier' and 'Fashion'), wintergreen barberry (*Berberis julianae*), common boxwood (*Buxus sempervirens*), glossy abelia (*Abelia grandiflora*), and dwarf burford holly (*Ilex cornuta* 'Burfordi Nana').

The species fell into three groups based on the data obtained: 1) sun required, 2) shade required and 3) shade preferred. Plants requiring sun for best growth were juniper, pyracantha, elaeagnus and euonymus. As shading increased, top and root weight of juniper and pyracantha were much reduced (because of similarity only juniper data are shown) (Figure 29.4). All aspects of growth measured increased with increasing fertility level. Elaeagnus, by contrast, produced similar top weight at all but the heaviest shade level but root growth was greatest in full sun and declined with more shade (Figure 29.5). Elaeagnus shrubs in full sun were slightly shorter, more compact and had more branches than plants in 30% or more shade. The limited root system caused by the shade would probably go unnoticed in the nursery and perhaps in the garden center. However, once installed in the landscape, plants with such a limited root system would require more care and attention in order to survive.

Figure 29.3. Design and arrangement of shade structures.

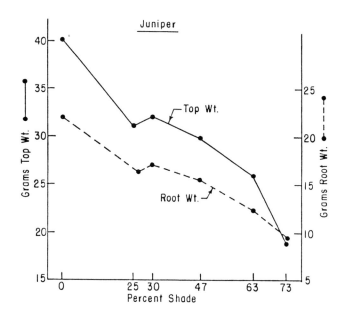

Figure 29.4. Effects of shade on top and root weight of juniper. Any shade restricted both top and root growth of juniper and pyracantha. Values are the averages of the three fertility levels used. With these two species tops and roots were restricted similarly, where with some species, the roots were affected before the top. Note the effect of shade on elaeagnus in the next figure, for example.

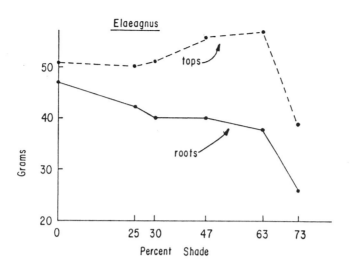

Figure 29.5. Response of elaeagnus to increased shade levels. Top growth remained about the same with increasing shade up to 63 percent. However, root production was restricted as shade levels increased leaving a top with less support and nutrient absorbing capacity.

All species tested were of higher visual quality in full sun or low shade levels when fertility level was high as opposed to when fertility was low. For example, at low fertility levels, top weights of euonymus were greatest at 25, 30, 47, and 63 percent shade, however, at the high fertility level, top weight was greatest in full sun or 25 or 30 percent shade as compared to 47 percent or more shade (Figure 29.6). Root weights of euonymus showed a similar pattern but were less with any shade when plants were grown at the high fertility level (Figure 29.7). Euonymus quality was best in full sun with only a slight decrease at the 25 and 30 percent shade levels as long as fertility level was high.

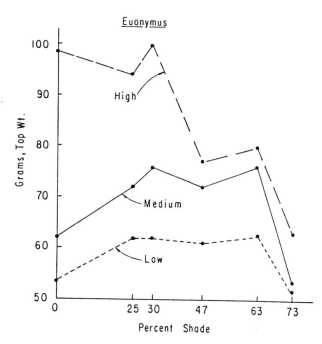

Figure 29.6. Top weight response of euonymus to shade and fertility. Note that the plants grown with low fertility (the bottom broken line) were larger under 25 to 63% shade, though plants grown with high fertility were largest in full sun to 30% shade with a steep reduction at 47% or more shade.

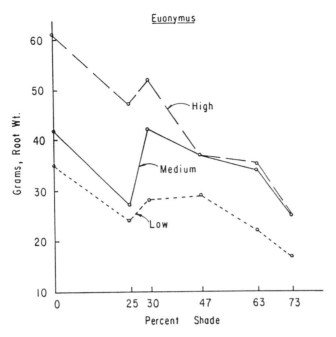

Figure 29.7. Root weight response of euonymus to shade and fertility. Root weights were much more sensitive to shading than were top weights.

Aucuba was the only shade-requiring plant in the study. As shade increased, top and root weight increased (Figure 29.8). Leaf area and visual plant quality responded similarly. Plants grew very poorly in full sun, but at 25 and 30 percent shade, aucuba was more tolerant of high light intensity when fertilizer was at the high rate as compared to the low rate.

545

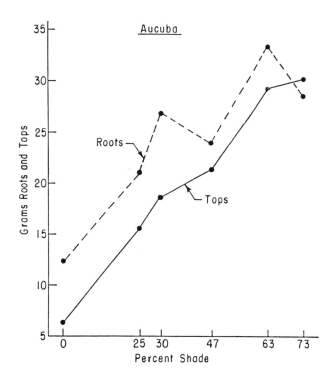

Figure 29.8. Top and root weight response of aucuba to increased shade levels. Aucuba was the only species to benefit from the 63% shade. Note that the root weight was restricted at the 73% shade level, whereas, top weight was not affected.

The shade-preferring plants were azalea, barberry, boxwood, abelia and holly. Some differences in plant response were noted, but in general they all followed the pattern of azalea as presented in Figure 29.9. As shade increased from full sun to 30 percent, weight of roots and tops increased but decreased at 63 and 73 percent shade (Figure 29.9). Notice that the greatest top weight of the plants was under 47% shade while the greatest root weight was under 30% shade. Overall visual plant quality was best under 30 percent shade.

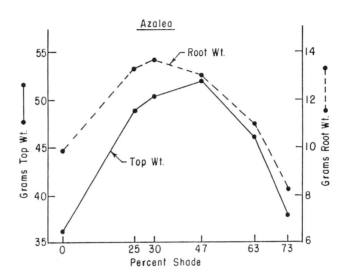

Figure 29.9. Top and root weight response of azalea to increased shade levels. Note the peak of root growth at 30% shade, whereas, top weight was similar at 30% and 47% shade.

With the exception of aucuba, there was no benefit from shade levels above 30 percent with the shade-preferring species (azalea, abelia, barberry and boxwood). Growth and quality of all species requiring full sun (juniper, pyracantha, elaeagnus and euonymus) were decidedly restricted by any shade at low fertility levels except euonymus. Shading reduced the root system before size or quality of the top growth was visually affected.

It should be emphasized that growing plants under a higher level of shade with low fertility may produce a visually acceptable top, however, the root system will be limited and stored energy reserves will be inadequate to support any stress

547

encountered, whether environmental, diseases or pests. Retail nurserymen and others have observed that when they place nursery stock under shade, it remains a good green color longer. This is "false prosperity", since the plant may look good but is actually becoming weaker and weaker internally, plus the likelihood of "sunburn" of the leaves when planted outside increases, with each day under excessive shade.

The "improved green color" is due to the more or less horizontal orientation of the green chloroplasts in the shade thus they become more visible. In contrast, outer leaves of plants in full sun have chloroplasts oriented to avoid any excess light and therefore may, at times, appear less green.

Since shade structures are expensive to construct and maintain and because root growth suffers most from excessive shading, woody nursery plants should be grown or held under the highest light intensity possible. This provides the most roots to aid establishment in the landscape while reducing the potential for sunburn usually encountered when plants are moved to full sun from moderate to heavy shade. Saran or woven shade is not as desirable from the standpoint of transferring of plants from shade to full sun ("sunburn") since the entire shade area is reduced in intensity. By contrast, lath shade oriented north-south, provides alternating strips of full sun and shade. The extent of the shade is determined by the width of the shade strips vs. the open areas.

Even though the study reported here was conducted with containers, similar plant responses will occur in the landscape as a result of variations in light intensities. The practical point is that if species such as junipers, pyracantha and elaeagnus are placed in shady locations, the rate and extent of root growth will be restricted. As a result, they will be more susceptible to drought and nutritional problems, especially in a stressful site that may also have poor soils, poor drainage or other factors that restrict plant health.

The response of the euonymus emphasizes the importance of proper nutrition in aiding plant **tolerance** to stressful sites. Euonymus on a site with low fertility will be much less drought-tolerant than if the fertility was higher. Aucuba showed a similar root growth benefit from increased fertility which also increased its tolerance for high light intensity.

Most trees require full sun for good growth and health. However, there are exceptions such as dogwood (*Cornus florida*), redbud (*Cercis canadensis*) and fringetree, (*Chionanthus virginiana*). Shrubs, on the other hand, present an array of tolerances/requirements for different light intensities. It would be very useful to the landscape architect, designer or nurseryman if the optimum light intensities and tolerance levels of all species of trees and shrubs were known. **The important premise remains that the more active the top of the plant in manufacturing energy (carbohydrates) the more extensive the root growth and the greater drought- and stress-tolerant the plant.**

There have been reports that cuttings from plants grown in high light intensities do not root as well as cuttings grown under lower light intensities (9, 10, 11, 13, 14). This is probably due to the fact that reduced light intensity is often used in conjunction with intermittent misting during propagation to reduce moisture stress of the cuttings. By contrast, when cuttings are taken from plants grown in high light intensities and placed in a propagation greenhouse with high light intensity, rooting is excellent and strong, well-branched plants are the result under a carefully designed and controlled misting system that prevents moisture stress or dehydration of the leaves. Leaves adapted to high light function poorly when abruptly placed under low light, and the leaves on a cutting are extremely important not only to rooting but to vegetative bud development and branching soon after rooting and transplanting.

As indicated earlier, shade structures are expensive to construct and maintain and because root growth suffers most from excessive shading, woody plants destined for outdoor planting should be grown and held under the highest light intensity practical. On the other hand, nursery plants destined for indoor uses should be either grown under light conditions similar to the indoor conditions, or grown under higher light intensities for rapid growth and good root development, then acclimatized, or allowed to go through a light adjustment period, prior to use in indoor conditions. Since the latter is the more economical, studies have been conducted to better understand the process of acclimatization (4, 5).

Literature Cited

1. Anderson J.M., D.S. Goodchild and N.K. Boardman. 1973. Composition of the photosystems and chloroplast structure in extreme shade plants. Biochimica et Biophysica Acta. 325:573-585.

2. Bjorkman, O. and P. Holmgren. 1963. Adaptability of the photosynthetic apparatus to light intensity in ecotypes from exposed and shaded habitats. Physiol. Plant 16:889-914.

3. Boardman, N.K. 1977. Comparative photosynthesis of sun and shade plants. Ann. Rev. Plant Physiol. 28:355-390.

4. Cathey, H.M. and L.E. Campbell. 1975. Security lighting and its impact on the landscape. Jour. of Arboriculture 1:181-187.

5. Conover, C.A. 1976. Light and fertility recommendations on production of foliage stock plants and acclimatized potted plants. U. of Fla. Agri. Res. Center. Res. Rept. RH 76-6.

6. Conover, C.A. and R.T. Poole. 1977. Effects of cultural practices on acclimatization of *Ficus benjamina.* Jour. Amer. Soc. Hort. Sci. 102(5):529-531.

7. Conover, C.A. and R.T. Poole. 1978. Production of *Ficus elastica* 'Decora' standards. HortSci. 13(6)707-708.

8. Dewerth, A.F. and R.E. Odom. 1960. A standard light-weight growing medium for horticultural specialty crops. Texas Agri. Exp. Sta. Misc. Pub. 420.

9. Hansen, J., L. Stromquist and A. Ericson. 1978. Influence of the irradiance on carbohydrate content and rooting of cuttings of pine seedlings (*Pinus sylvestris*). Plant Physiol. 61:975-979.

10. Johnson, C.R. and D.F. Hamilton. 1977. Rooting of *Hibiscus rosas-sinensis* cuttings as influenced by light intensity and ethephon. HortSci. 12(1):39-40.

11. Kawase, M. 1965. Etiolation and rooting in cuttings. Physiol. Plant. 18:1066-1076.

12. Kelly, J.D. 1959. Fertilization studies with container-grown nursery stock. Amer. Nurseryman 109(10):12-13, 79.

13. Knox, G.W. and D.F. Hamilton. 1982. Rooting of *Berberis* and *Ligustrum* cuttings from stock plants grown at selected light intensities. Scientia Hort. 16:85-90.

14. Knox, G.W. and D.F. Hamilton. 1983. A summary of research findings on the effects of light on plants. Amer. Nurseryman 158:83-91.

15. Logan, K.T. and G. Krotkov. 1969. Adaptations of the photosynthetic mechanism of sugar maple (*Acer saccharum*) seedlings grown in various light intensities. Physiol. Plant. 22:104-116.

16. McGuire, John J. 1972. Growing Ornamental Plants in Containers: A Handbook for Nurserymen. Rhode Island Agri. Exp. Sta. Bulletin 197.

17. Sheppard, R. III, and H. Pellett. 1976. Light intensity effects on red-osier dogwood. HortSci. 11(3):200-202.

18. Whitcomb, Carl E. and Lisa K. Euchner. 1979. Effects of shade levels on growth of container nursery stock. Nursery Res. Jour. 6:1-11.

19. Whitcomb, Carl E. 1984. Effects of photoperiod on growth of northern conifers. Okla. Agri. Exp. Sta. Res. Rept. P-855.

20. Whitcomb, Carl E. 1988. *Plant Production in Containers*, Lacebark Publ., Stillwater, Ok.

CHAPTER 30

THE EFFECTS OF DROUGHT STRESS

Drought Is Not Always Bad - - - - - - 553

Watering During Drought - - - - - - - 555

Summary - - - - - - - - - - - - - - 557

Literature Cited - - - - - - - - - - 558

The Effects of Drought Stress

Drought Is Not Always Bad. Drought stress generally is the result of limited moisture in the soil but may occur under a variety of other circumstances, such as:
   a) when soils are very wet and the air is hot and dry,
   b) when soils are compacted and aeration of the root zone is poor,
   c) when the root system is poor due to disease or chemical injury,
   d) when roots are not yet well developed as on recently transplanted or disturbed plants; or
   e) when the level of salts in the soil is high, thus the salts compete for the available moisture.

Most drought conditions occur in summer in conjunction with high temperature. In a situation where drought is underway or forecast the **primary objective is to keep the leaves on the plants**. Without the leaves, the chances of survival are slim. Stress from leaves damaged or lost decreases energy for developing buds for next season, stem caliper, root growth and winter stress. In addition, total reserves in the plant are quickly depleted, since all living cells in the plant continue to require energy for respiration even when the leaves are lost. Anytime a plant is stressed, the root system suffers first and longest. On the other hand, if root growth continues, additional soil is contacted as a potential source of water. As soils become dryer, aeration of the soils at greater depths also improves. Under drought conditions roots probably function at much greater depths, thereby providing critically needed moisture, but only if sufficient energy is available for root growth. **The few deep roots on most woody plants probably function only during times of drought when oxygen (aeration) penetrates far below the depth during the rest of the growing season**.

Fall fertilization of woody plants, which have held their leaves throughout summer drought stress, is very beneficial. When four temperate zone species were fertilized with various spring or fall fertilizer combinations, plant growth was greatest when a portion of the fertilizer was applied in the fall (2). When leaves are present in the fall, the active roots quickly absorb nutrients and translocate them to the leaves, where in turn, soluble carbohydrates are manufactured and returned down through the system. This increases stem caliper growth, builds energy reserves in the plant and stimulates further root growth.

Continuing nutrient absorption allows additional energy manufacturing during the fall and storage for early spring growth when soils are cold and root activity and nutrient absorption is minimal. However, if the leaves have been lost or severely damaged during drought stress, fall fertilization benefits are minimal. **Roots grow as the result of energy from the leaves (soluble carbohydrates) not from fertilizer, although the fertilizer elements are essential to the leaves.**

With many species, a major reaction to drought stress is dropping of the older leaves. Research by Gordon and Larson (1) suggests that the older leaves are the greatest contributors of energy (soluble carbohydrates) to the roots, whereas, the new leaves primarily support current shoot growth, bud development and storage in the terminals for the next flush of growth. If the older leaves are lost early for any reason (disease, insects, nutrient deficiency, herbicide injury or drought, Figure 30.1) the root system is dramatically restricted. The functional capacity of the old leaves is less than young leaves, therefore, old leaves reach the compensation point and are dropped by the plant before young leaves are affected.

Moderate moisture stress may be beneficial. When moisture is readily available and nutrition, temperature, and in some cases, photoperiod, are also favorable, new growth continues on many species of trees and shrubs. As long as new growth occurs, there is limited energy supplied to the root system to support further root development. On the other hand, as moisture stress begins, top growth is restricted. The level of energy in the plant begins to build and root growth increases (assuming there are no other limiting factors). Rapid growth of tops of plants in a landscape setting is not required like it is in a production nursery. For greatest energy levels in the plant and thereby, perhaps, greatest stress tolerance, very rapid growth is **not** desired. A good example is the high incidence of borer injury to ash (*Fraxinus* species) that are grown very rapidly in a nursery, then transplanted into a stress landscape situation without opportunity to build energy reserves. On the other hand, trees of similar size, growing more slowly suffer less internal stress when transplanted and have fewer problems with borers. Perhaps the greatest factor contributing to low energy levels in nursery stock and landscape plants is **excessive** levels of nitrogen fertilizer relative to the levels of other nutrient elements. This can cause considerable new growth, yet the leaves can only manufacture a limited amount of energy since the other nutrient elements are deficient.

*Figure 30.1. Leaf scorch drought injury to wax leaf ligustrum (**Ligustrum japonicum**). In this case the plants were placed into the landscape from three-gallon containers in early summer. No supplemental watering was provided beyond planting. Container-grown nursery stock planted in late spring through late summer is very susceptible to drought injury.*

Watering During Droughts. The universal recommendation for watering landscape plants is, "Water deep and less often" and "avoid light shallow watering". The argument against light shallow watering is that a very shallow root system will result. This **does not** occur as the root system is very shallow anyway (see Figures 26.1 and 26.2 in chapter 26, as well as Figure 27.1 in chapter 27). Watering during a dry period, even if it extends for two or three months, **will not** alter the normal root growth for the species during the remaining nine or ten months! On the other hand, consider the following situation: normal spring growth occurs, soil moisture slowly decreases and energy in the plant increases as the drought becomes more severe. The soil becomes quite dry and the plant is showing signs of drought stress (wilting, dropping of lower leaves or marginal scorch of leaves). If you water, should you water light and frequently or deep and

555

infrequently? If watering is deep, the sudden availability of water throughout the root zone may increase activity inside the plant and stimulate a flush of growth. If this occurs, new leaves that lose moisture much more quickly will **increase** the total water need of the plant over the previous level. Since droughts generally occur during periods of high temperature, the problem is compounded. This greater water requirement will continue until new root growth has occurred to increase water absorptive capacity relative to the requirement of the top. This is often when considerable crown dieback occurs while the base of the plant survives (Figure 30.2).

On the other hand, if the plant is watered lightly and frequently and no new top growth occurs, the plant is provided assistance until additional rains occur, but **without increasing** the overall water requirement of the plant. If the plant is watered lightly and frequently, then the homeowner leaves on vacation, certainly the plant will suffer. However, the stress will be somewhat less than if the plant was never provided supplemental moisture and much less than if the plant is watered deep and a soft new flush of growth occurs (Figure 30.2).

The best hedge against drought injury is a well-adapted species in the proper light intensity with a well-established root system, moderate growth rates prior to the dry period to allow good energy support for the root system, and mulching if practical. In most cases, the extent of new root growth due to relatively modest changes in the nutritional program can make dramatic differences in drought tolerance.

Leaves are cooled by the transpiration of moisture from the leaves. In short, leaves sweat or perspire. When the leaves can no longer sweat, due to lack of available moisture, the stomates close and temperature in the leaf rises quickly to the critical limit. This is similar to what happens to a person who ceases to sweat on a hot day.

The most effective time to water is after a rain, even if the rain is minimal. This is due to the higher humidity and generally lower temperatures, which reduce the loss of water to evaporation and complement the water from the rain. However, the caution concerning over-watering and stimulating new growth remains, unless the end of the normal drought period for the specific geographic area is near. These comments are based on research and experience east of the Rocky Mountains and apply throughout the eastern U.S. In the true desert areas, the most practical water management procedure may be somewhat different.

*Figure 30.2. This southern magnolia (**Magnolia grandiflora**) was watered and fertilized sufficiently during mid summer to force a new flush of growth. The homeowner then went away and on return, found the top had died. The following spring a strong new shoot emerged from near the base which suggests that the root system was only slightly injured, but the top had died from dehydration, at least partially due to the late flush of new growth.*

In summary:
a. Keep the leaves on the plant.
b. Do water, but water shallowly and frequently.
c. Do not water enough to stimulate new growth during summer's heat.
d. Keep enough water available to keep the leaves sweating and cool.
e. Fertilize in the fall, just before or after a rain, even if the leaves are lost or damaged, since some absorption will occur.
f. Moderate moisture stress and no new growth of the top means rapid building of energy reserves.

g. It is the energy (carbohydrates) from the leaves that makes the roots grow. Energy levels are highest, (thus most root growth occurs) in the fall which better supports the spring flush of growth and better provides for the plant during the next drought.

Literature Cited

1. Gordon, John C. and P.R. Larson. 1970. Re-distribution of C-labeled reserve food in young red pines during shoot elongation. Forest Sci. 16:14-20.

2. Whitcomb, Carl E. 1978. Effects of spring vs fall fertilization on the growth and cold tolerance of woody plants in the landscape. Okla. Agri. Exp. Sta. Res. Rept. P-777: 11-12.

CHAPTER 31

PRUNING

Tough Choices - - - - - - - - - - - - - 560

What to Do - - - - - - - - - - - - - - - 565

What Not to Do - - - - - - - - - - - - - 570

Wound Dressings - - - - - - - - - - - - 576

Bracing and Cabling - - - - - - - - - 578

Literature Cited - - - - - - - - - - - 584

Pruning

Tough Choices! Pruning to improve structural strength, safety, access and appearance of trees has been practiced for centuries. Pruning to improve the structural strength of a tree generally involves judgment calls on the part of the pruner (Figure 31.1). A knowledge of the species involved is also important. For example, in Figure 31.2, the narrow V fork appears questionable. Some would remove one of the limbs while others would not. If the tree were a maple, one of the limbs should probably be removed or braced. However, it is a Chinese pistache (*Pistacia chinensis*) which has very tough, durable wood and a high resistance to splitting, even in narrow V forks. Thus a knowledge of the species is very important in making decisions relative to pruning.

Since where to prune and how much are judgment calls based on the knowledge of the arborist and the intended or current use of the site, there is minimal controversy. However, there are greater differences of opinion on how and where to proceed with the actual pruning process and the treatment of the resulting wound. Dr. Alex Shigo pioneered the study of pruning, treatment of pruning wounds and the study of how trees react to pruning and the invasion of disease and/or decay organisms. The works in this area of Shigo and others have been widely publicized, thus only a practical summary is presented.

Figure 31.1. These two live oaks represent two distinct choices relative to pruning. The tree above was allowed to retain the lower limbs which "sweep" the surface of the lawn. On the other hand, the tree below has 15 or more feet of clearance under most of the canopy.

561

*Figure 31.1. (continued)   Regardless of the use of the space
beneath the tree, good branch position vertically on the main stem
as well as around the stem, are important to tree health and
structural durability.*

Figure 31.1. (continued)   If a young tree has poor branch locations on the main stem, problems loom in its future.   This young tree is attractive from a distance (above), but a close inspection of the branch structure shows many problems. Unfortunately, at this point, there is no way to correct the problems without destroying the overall appearance of the tree for several years, yet it must be done.

563

*Figure 31.2. The narrow V-fork of this Chinese pistache provides
no safety hazard because of the strength of the wood. However, if
the tree were a maple, the narrow V-fork should be removed or
braced. Note the early signs of bark entrapment between the two
limbs as each increases in diameter. It is the bark entrapment
that prevents the normal wood formation and interlocking system of
the branch with the main trunk. The limb in this photo should
have been removed when the tree was young in anticipation of this
problem in the future. At this point in time, the two limbs are
nearly the same size and to remove either one would destroy the
appearance of the crown. A cable could be installed as shown in
Figure 31.16.*

What To Do. Once it is determined that a limb is to be removed from a tree, the key point then becomes where to make the cut. In Figure 31.2, the branch angle is excellent, but the limb is too low to the ground for current use of the site and must be removed. Note the branch collar. This is not always easy to determine at first and has been marked on the photo. This is the point of distinction between trunk and limb. First cut upward from below outside the branch collar about one-third of the stem diameter (Figure 31.3). Then proceed to cut downward at the face of the branch collar until the limb drops (Figure 31.3). Once the limb drops, finish the cut ending up at the bottom of the branch collar (Figure 31.4). At first, this looks like a stub has been left (Figure 31.4), however, this is the point of distinction between trunk and limb and will provide the smallest wound with the greatest capacity to callus over in the shortest period of time.

*Figure 31.3. The limb is to be removed from the tree trunk. Note the swelling that indicates the branch collar as noted by the arrows (above photo). To remove the limb, first cut from below **outside** of the branch collar (lower photo), then cut from above at the face of the branch collar until the limb falls.*

566

Figure 31.4. After the downward cut has progressed to the point where the limb drops, the cut should be continued until it intersects with the bottom of the branch collar (see arrow in photo above). The completed proper cut leaves the smallest wound with the greatest capacity to callus over in the shortest period of time (below).

567

If the branch collar has been properly identified and the cut made correctly, the callus growth will develop from all sides (Figure 31.5). Eventually the callus growth will cover the entire wound (Figure 31.5). With time, callus growth progresses to the point where the wounds go almost undetected (Figure 31.6). By watching where the callus growth occurs first and most, relative to the surface area of the wound, one can quickly learn the optimum pruning cut location for the species.

Figure 31.5. When a pruning cut is made properly with respect to the branch collar, callus formation proceeds from all sides (above) and eventually covers the entire wound (below).

*Figure 31.6.   Callus growth over pruning wounds slowly takes on the original bark character and is   unnoticed by all but the expert.   Above, a completely covered pruning wound of a sycamore (**Platanus occidentalis**).   The large limb was removed to allow for new uses of the space beneath the tree.   About seven years were required for completion of the callus.   Below, a small limb was removed from a bur oak (**Quercus macrocarpa**), five years earlier. The casual observer would no longer notice where the limb had been removed.*

What Not To Do. On the other hand, if the pruning cut is made without the aid of a beginning cut from below, the weight of the limb will tear the branch collar at the base, exposing a much larger wound (Figure 31.7). Another common error is to "cut-flush". When a flush cut is made, the branch collar is removed and trunk tissue is damaged (Figure 31.7), resulting in a larger wound that will callus over slowly from the sides, exposing wood to organisms for a much longer time. If the pruning cut is made beyond the branch collar, the resulting stub will also pose problems. The stub will either eventually decay and fall or will finally callus over (Figure 31.8). The greater the exposure of the wood before callus is complete, the more likely the entrance of decay organisms. A stub of dead tissue is an ideal opportunity for decay organisms. Never leave a stub and never de-horn or top trees. The arbitrary topping of trees should never be tolerated. Species such as crapemyrtle (*Lagerstroemia indica*) are sometimes topped under the incorrect information that more blooms will result (Figure 31.9). This does not occur, as the plant is weakened as a result of pruning and fewer flowers are actually produced. In addition, the gnarled growth that results from repeated pruning is unattractive (Figure 31.9).

The pruning of shrubs is much more species/use specific. However, keep in mind the structure of the plant and its tolerance for shade in order to be most effective. In general, the shade tolerance of a shrub can be quickly determined by looking at the depth of the layers of leaves below the outer canopy (Figure 31.10). Prune hedges so that all of the outer surface gets some direct light unless it is a very shade-tolerant species.

Figure 31.7. When a cut is made from above only, the weight of the limb will damage the branch collar before the cut is complete and may result in stripping away the bark for several feet down the trunk (above). When a flush cut is made (below), the branch collar is removed and the resulting larger wound will require more time to callus over. When a cut is made behind the branch collar, callus formation will proceed only from the sides, whereas, if the cut is made properly at the branch collar, callus will develop from around the entire wound.

571

Figure 31.8.   A stub left beyond the branch collar provides an
excellent opportunity for decay organisms (above).   Callus growth
proceeded more rapidly on the left side of the wound since the cut
was nearer the branch collar.   Eventually this stub will callus
over, but not before decay organisms penetrate into the main stem
of the tree.   By contrast, with a proper cut (below), no stub
remains and callus formation proceeds from all sides of the wound
with a minimum of exposure.

Figure 31.9.   Top pruning, even of small trees like crapemyrtle, destroys the natural form and appearance of the tree plus reduces its structural strength and stability.

573

Figure 31.10. This viburnum hedge is well shaped plus it is a shade-tolerant species and one tolerant of pruning. As a result, this dense attractive hedge functions well as a visual screen for a work area on the other side.

Junipers are probably more abused during pruning than any other species. Spreading-type junipers are planted for their feathery, almost fernlike growth habit. yet the most common pruning technique is to shear spreading junipers into various shapes with a smooth surface. By selective removal of branches, spreading junipers can be reduced in size and spread while retaining their natural form (Figure 31.11).

Figure 31.11. The large pfitzer juniper (above) extends beyond the desired limits to the left. Note the white markers and arrows on the shrub where branches are to be removed. After removal of the branches (below), the shrubs horizontal spread has been reduced nearly three feet, yet the landscape is practically unaltered. Selective removal of branches once each year also requires much less labor than the repeated shearing so often practiced.

575

Wound Dressings. Research by Shigo and others (1-28) has shown that wound dressings are of no benefit to the formation of callus and in some cases, may be harmful. If decay organisms do enter pruning wounds, trees have the capacity to compartmentalize or wall-off the invading organisms from the remaining healthy wood (Figure 31.12). In Figure 31.12 an old pruning wound has been callused over and is hardly detectable in the bark pattern on the trunk. The tree set boundaries that prevented the invading organism from spreading throughout the trunk even though the wood at the face of the original cut decayed. The boundaries have persisted many years after the original wound (Figure 31.12).

Injuries to tree trunks **should not** be cleaned out and painted as has so long been practiced. Leaving the wound alone is probably the best practice. Callus will begin to form wherever the cambium is not damaged and will slowly cover the wound (Figure 31.13). Injuries may be from mechanical devices, cold injury or other factors. The base of the sawtooth oak (*Quercus acutissima*), in Figure 31.13 was damaged during a severe freeze very early in the fall when the hardening process was not complete. There was no initial exposed wound as the bark persisted for about one and one-half years before falling away. In this case, the callus formed at the perimeter of the damaged area and began to cover the exposed heartwood.

Figure 31.12. The callus formation on this pecan (**Carya illinoensis**) has long since covered the original wound. The callus formed over the wound has resumed growth typical of the main tree stem as though the wound had never occurred (above). A closer look at the callus formation (below) shows how the callus grew over the wound and formed in what became a cavity sometime after the limb was removed. The compartmentalization boundaries can be clearly seen including the face of the original cut and the inner penetration limits of the decay into the main stem.

577

Figure 31.13.   The trunk of this sawtooth oak was damaged by severe and early cold temperatures.   There was no indication injury had occurred for about one and one-half years as the bark remained in position.   Callus began to form at the perimeter of the injured area, eventually causing the non-functional bark to slough away.   In this case, callus is forming across the exposed heartwood from all sides.   It would be a mistake to cut away the remaining bark and damage the callus or paint the exposed heartwood.

Bracing and Cabling. Large limbs with poor branch angles or other weaknesses show that the tree did not receive proper attention in the past. Proper branch placement and development on the main trunk should have been considered while the tree was in the nursery when hand pruners could have corrected the problem. As trees grow larger, the periodic inspection for weak branches and other problems should be part of an on-going tree maintenance program. However, there are times when a limb has attained considerable size yet is weak structurally and subject to wind or ice damage. One example is given to illustrate the problem and actions that can prevent or certainly reduce the likelihood of the limb being lost at some point of stress.

The specimen in this case is a loblolly pine (*Pinus taeda*) approximately 30 feet tall with a stem caliper of about 14 inches (Figure 31.14). About 10 feet up on the main trunk is a major side branch with a poor branch angle (Figure 31.14). As the limb increases in diameter, bark will continue to be trapped between the limb and the main trunk, thus preventing the normal interlocking arrangement of the wood from the limb with the main trunk. To remove the large limb would greatly reduce the overall appearance of the tree. The action taken, in this case, was to install a tree rod of appropriate size (5/8-inch) through the base of the limb and the main trunk to prevent movement at this point (Figure 31.15). In addition, at a point approximately 2/3 of the distance from the base of the weak branch and its outer most point, a cable of appropriate size (1/2-inch) was installed to further reduce stress on the weak branch-trunk intersection (Figure 31.16). By using left and right hand thread lag screws and thimbles the cable transferred a substantial portion of the load of the limb to the main trunk. No wound dressing was used and within a few years, the tree rod nuts will be covered by callus as will part of the ends of the lag screws (Figure 31.17).

Figure 31.14. This loblolly pine has a weak major limb. If the limb were removed the appearance of the tree would be substantially changed (see arrow).

Figure 31.15. A tree rod was installed through the base of the limb and main trunk at a selected point.

This is but one example of cabling and bracing a tree. There have been many articles published on this topic if further information is needed. In this case, it was felt that the softwood of the pine, in conjunction with the weak branch-trunk intersection and the overall appearance of the tree, justified damage to the wood and the expense of installation. These are judgment calls that can only be made on a specific site with consideration for the use and safety of the site and the wishes of the owner.

Figure 31.16.   A point was selected about 2/3 the distance from the base of the weak branch and its outermost point for installation of a cable (see arrows, above).   The cable was positioned to transfer a substantial load of the limb to the main trunk, thereby reducing the load on the limb-trunk intersection (below).

Figure 31.17. The lag screws were installed so the cable could not unhook under severe conditions (above). In addition, sufficient load was transferred to the main stem to insure that the cable would not become slack for even a moment under severe winds. The head of the tree rod was not painted (below). However, the diamond washer was fitted snugly into an opening in the bark so that it pressed against heartwood. Within a few years callus will completely cover the washer and nut.

Literature Cited

1. Collins, J.F. 1924. Treatment and care of tree wounds. U.S. Dept. Agric. Farmer's Bulletin #1726. 38 pages.

2. Dooley, H.L. 1980. Methods for evaluating fungal inhibition and barrier action of tree wound paints. Plant Diseases. 64:465-467.

3. Garrett, P.W., W.K. Randall, A.L. Shigo and W.C. Shortle. 1979. Inheritance of compartmentalization of wounds in sweetgum (*Liquidambar styraciflua* L.) and eastern cottonwood (*Populus deltoides* Bartr.) USDA Forest Serv. Res. Paper NE-443. 4 pages.

4. Green, D.J., W.C. Shortle and A.L. Shigo. 1981. Compartmentalization of discolored and decayed wood in red maple branch stubs. Forest Sci. 27:519-522.

5. Houston, D.R. 1971. Discoloration and decay in red maple and yellow birch: reduction through wound treatment. Forest Sci. 17:402-406.

6. Hudler, G.W. 1984. Wound healing in bark of woody plants. Jour. of Arboriculture 10:241-245.

7. Lowerts, G.A. and R.C. Kellison. 1981. Genetically controlled resistance to discoloration and decay in wounded trees of yellow poplar. Silvae Genetica 30:98-101.

8. Marshall, R.P. 1950. Care of damaged shade trees. U.S. Dept. Agri. Farmer's Bulletin #1896. 34 pages.

9. McQuilkin, W.E. 1950. Effects of some growth regulators and dressings on the healing of tree wounds. Jour. Forestry 48:423-428.

10. Mercer, P.C. 1979. Attitudes toward pruning wounds. Arboriculture Jour. 3:457-465.

11. Mercer, P.C. 1982. Tree wounds and their treatment. Arboriculture Jour. 6:131-137.

12.   Neely, D. 1970. Healing of wounds on trees. Jour. Amer. Soc. Hort. Sci. 95:536-540.

13.   Ossenbruggen, Sharon, 1985. A properly placed cut is crucial to healthy pruning. Amer. Nurseryman, March 15, 1985.

14.   Santamour, F.S. Jr.   1984.   Early selection for wound compartmentalization potential in woody plants.   Jour. Environmental Hort. 2:126-128.

15.   Santamour, F.S. Jr. 1985. Trunk wood discoloration and decay following root wounding. Jour. Arboriculture 11:257-262.

16.   Shigo, A.L. 1982a. A pictorial primer for proper pruning. Forest Notes, Spring Issue.

17.   Shigo, A.L. 1982b. Tree health. Jour. Arboriculture 8:311-316.

18.   Shigo, A.L. 1984. Compartmentalization: a conceptual framework for understanding how trees grow and defend themselves. Amer. Review Phytopathology 22:189-214.

19.   Shigo, A.L. 1984. Tree decay and pruning. Arboriculture Jour. 8:1-12.

20.   Shigo, A.L. 1977. Compartmentalization of decay in trees. USDA Forest Ser. Bulletin #405. 73 pages.

21.   Shigo, A.L. and C.L. Wilson. 1977. Wound dressings on red maple and American elm: effectiveness after five years.   Jour. Arboriculture 3:81-87.

22. Shigo, A.L., W.C. Shortle and P.W. Garrett. 1977. Genetic control suggested in compartmentalization of discolored wood associated with tree wounds. Forest Sci. 23:179-182.

23.   Shigo, A.L. and W.C. Shortle. 1983. Wound dressings: results of studies over 13 years. Jour. of Arboriculture 9:317-329.

24.   Shigo, A.L. 1985. How tree branches are attached to trunks. Canadian Jour. Botany 63:1391-1401.

25. Shigo, A.L. and W.C. Shortle. 1977. New Ideas in tree care. Jour. of Arboriculture 3:1-5

26. Shortle, W.C. 1979. Mechanisms of compartmentalization of decay in living trees. Phytopathology 69:1147-1151.

27. Von Mayer-Wegelin, H. 1936. The history of pruning. Publ. by M. & H. Schaper, Hannover, Pa. pp. 1-61, 96-106, 166-178. Forest Serv. Translation.

28. Young, H.C. and P.E. Tilford. 1937. Tree wound dressings. Ohio Agric. Exp. Sta. Bulletin. 22:83-87.

CHAPTER 32

WHEN TREES COMPETE WITH TURFGRASS

Tree Competition with Grass - - - - - - 588

Effects on Bluegrass Growth - - - - - - 590

Effects on Seed Germination - - - - - - 598

Literature Cited - - - - - - - - - - - 601

When Trees Compete with Turfgrass

Faced with the task of establishing, maintaining, or rejuvenating turf, the landscape manager is frequently confronted by trees that are well established and of considerable size. The problem of poor turf performance beneath or adjacent to trees is often attributed to lack of light. Light does play a role but when light was removed as a factor, the competing effect of tree roots could be measured. The effects were dramatic and emphasize how great the influence of established trees can be on turf (3, 5).

Tree Competition with Grass. The studies were conducted with a series of containers with honeylocust (*Gleditsia triacanthos*) and silver maple (*Acer saccharinum*) trees (Figure 32.1 and 32.2). A minimum of 2000 foot candles at the grass surface on a sunny day (equivalent to bright shade) was maintained while having desired levels of competition. By using this procedure, light intensity was eliminated as a factor in the results (7).

Tree roots were allowed to develop free of grass competition for 4 1/2 months. Nitrogen fertilizer was added three times at the rate of three pounds per 1000 square feet from March 5 to August 19 using Nitroform (ureaformaldehyde).

On September 23, Nitroform was applied to small pots at the rate of one pound nitrogen per 1000 square feet. This provided a total of about 10 pounds nitrogen per 1000 square feet over a nine-month period. On July 18, common Kentucky bluegrass was seeded to the soil surface of selected pots at the rate of one pound per 1000 square feet and covered lightly with soil.

Grass seed germination was complete in about 30 days. Counts of established plants per pot were taken 34 days after seeding and again when the experiment was ended. Grass was clipped every week for 10 weeks at a 1 1/2-inch height beginning August 26.

When the experiment was ended, tree roots were cut where they entered the small pots. The depth of grass roots in containers was determined after the soil mass was carefully washed away. Weights of grass sod and roots and tree roots were taken as a measure of response to competition.

Figure 32.1.   Experimental set up used to study tree-grass root competition with uniform shade.   Note: Tree roots were established in both large and small containers before the grass was planted.

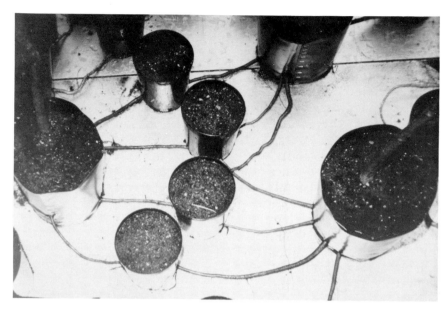

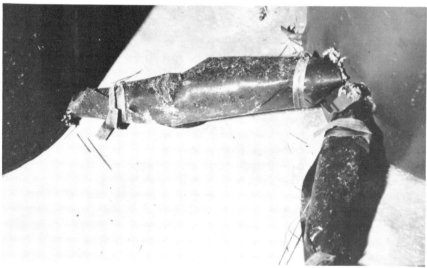

Figure 32.2. Trees were planted in large containers with selected roots extending out of the large containers and into smaller ones (above). By wrapping these roots in moist sphagnum moss and black plastic (below), the roots functioned normally, yet a specific tree root mass could be related to the performance of the grass.

Effects on Bluegrass Growth. Bluegrass foliage yields were only slightly lower where tree roots were present as compared to where tree roots were absent. Following application of nitrogen fertilizer one week prior to the first clipping date, the foliage yields of treatments containing no tree roots paralleled other yields for the first two weeks, then the clipping yields of the grass competing with the tree roots declined rapidly. A similar response was noted following the second fertilizer application.

When bluegrass sod, roots and root/sod ratios were compared at the end of the study, it could be easily seen why turf competing with tree roots is difficult to maintain. By converting the effects of tree roots on bluegrass to percentages of yields with no tree roots present, a striking contrast results (3, 4, 6).

Tree roots reduced bluegrass sod weights only 8 to 15 percent (Figure 33.3) while bluegrass root weights were reduced 63 to 80 percent (Figure 32.4). Root/sod ratios were reduced 58 to 76 percent (Figure 32.5). This shows that through some competitive factor, bluegrass is forced to maintain only a slightly reduced sod on a highly restricted root system. Such conditions place a greater demand for water and nutrients on the remaining root system and greatly increase drought sensitivity. In general, silver maple roots had a greater effect on bluegrass foliage, sod and root yields and root/sod ratios than honeylocust.

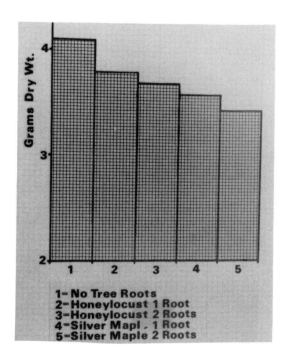

Figure 32.3. Average dry weight sod yields of Kentucky bluegrass competing with one or two established trees roots of silver maple or honeylocust.

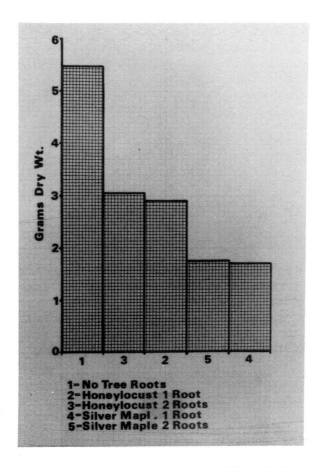

Figure 32.4. *Average dry weight root yields of Kentucky bluegrass competing with established tree roots.*

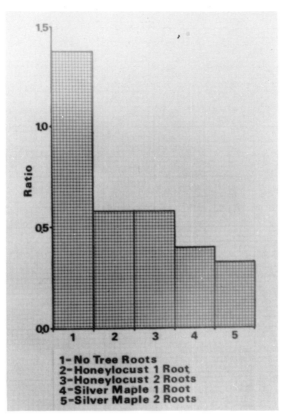

Figure 32.5. Average root/sod ratios of Kentucky bluegrass competing with established tree roots.

At the time the experiment was ended, it was observed that a mat of grass roots about 3/8-inch thick could easily be lifted from the main volume of soil where silver maple roots were present (Figure 32.6). Since silver maple roots were red and Kentucky bluegrass roots white, it was easy to detect that silver maple roots were not present in this mat at this time. This layer of bluegrass roots is of particular interest, since silver maple roots were frequently observed in this surface zone prior to bluegrass seeding (Figure 32.7).

594

Figure 32.6. Grass root layer lifted from the surface of soil containing silver maple roots that were established at the time the grass seed was planted.

Figure 32.7. Prior to planting the bluegrass seed, roots of silver maple could be easily observed near the surface of the soil mix by simply moving a thin layer (above). Likewise, when the study was ended, a dense mat of silver maple roots were present at the soil mix surface where no bluegrass had been planted (below).

That silver maple roots grew in this extreme surface soil layer became further apparent when silver maple roots in pots without bluegrass were observed (Figure 32.7). The fate of silver maple roots in this zone following planting of Kentucky bluegrass is unknown. However, it should be noted that the soil surface was not disturbed at the time the bluegrass was seeded.

During the washing operation to separate roots from the soil mix, the distance from the surface of the container to the deepest bluegrass root tip was recorded for all treatments. Bluegrass roots were found at the base of the containers and distributed throughout where tree roots were not present. Likewise, some bluegrass roots were found at the base of the containers where honeylocust roots were present and much intermingling of roots was noted with only a slight massing of bluegrass roots near the soil surface (Figure 32.8). On the other hand, where silver maple roots were present, the average distance to the deepest bluegrass root was 3.8 inches in the six-inch container. Bluegrass roots were found only next to the container wall.

This reduction in depth of penetration of bluegrass roots coupled with the drastic reduction in total weight of bluegrass roots is further evidence of the problem of establishing and maintaining good turf where tree roots are well established.

Figure 32.8. The honeylocust and bluegrass roots intermingled throughout the soil mix with no distinct zone of restriction as had occurred with the silver maple. The fine roots are bluegrass while the more coarse roots (see arrows) are honeylocust.

Effects on Seed Germination. Another aspect of bluegrass response to tree roots was found when numbers of established bluegrass plants and numbers of tillers produced per container were determined after one month and 3 1/2 months. A striking difference in number of plants was found between no tree roots and all tree root treatments for both dates (Figure 32.9). After first bluegrass counts were taken and differences noted, the question arose as to the effect on bluegrass tiller production.

The increase in the number of plants for the 11-week period was obtained by subtracting the number of established plants on the first date from the number at the final date; the difference was attributed to production of tillers. Without the competitive tree root effects, more bluegrass plants established and grew more vigorously. It was expected that these plants would also produce more tillers in a given period of time. Whatever mechanism was responsible for reducing bluegrass germination, there was little or no effect on tiller production.

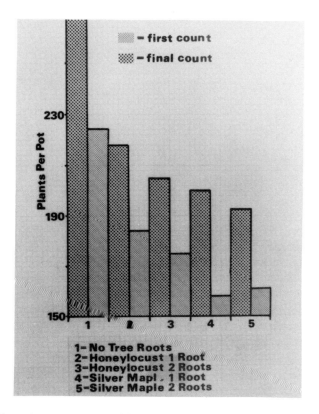

Figure 32.9. Average established Kentucky bluegrass plants per pot on two dates. Differences are attributed to tiller production.

No attempt was made to isolate or determine the mechanism by which tree roots reduced various aspects of bluegrass establishment and growth. Until further investigations are conducted, one can only speculate as to what the mechanism may be. The fact that bluegrass root weights were reduced far more than sod weights, suggests a factor present in the soil and not absorbed and translocated within the grass plant. Also, the effect on bluegrass germination suggests a volatile material or perhaps a separate mechanism from that affecting roots.

Some oxygen competition could have occurred between the well-established tree roots and the new bluegrass roots. It seems possible that established tree roots could place such a demand on soil oxygen so as to limit grass root growth. Oxygen was probably less a factor affecting bluegrass seed germination on the soil surface unless it in some way affected seedling survival rather than germination.

The possibility exists that some growth inhibitor, volatile or non-volatile, is being produced by tree roots and released into the soil mass to influence seed germination, grass root and sod development, or both. The existence of such chemicals has been recognized and studied only since the late 1940s (1, 2). Some researchers feel that plant growth inhibitors may be far more widespread and important than was first suspected. One of the most striking characteristics of some of these inhibitors is the wide gap between concentrations that inhibit growth of sensitive plants to some degree and concentrations that actually kill those plants.

Studies of this type give little indication of the nature of the factors responsible for the striking effects of tree roots on establishment and growth of turf. However, it does not support earlier theories that the primary reason for poor turf beneath trees is directly due to shade and the reduced photosynthesis or is indirectly caused by increasing disease susceptibility, although under natural conditions, these factors are probably involved.

These studies and observations suggest that once a tree becomes established, its effect on turf is dramatic. On the other hand, the effect of established turf on the root development and growth of newly planted trees and shrubs is equally dramatic. In part, it seems to be who gets there first. If the grass is present, the woody plant is restricted. However, if the woody plant survives the initial confrontation, which may last for several months to many years, depending on the site and species involved, the woody plant eventually wins and begins to restrict the turf.

Since mowing height has such a striking effect on root growth of turf, perhaps mowing the grass higher beneath or adjacent to trees will aid its tolerance level. There are differences among turf species in tolerance or ability to compete with trees. In the Deep South, St. Augustine grass is more tolerant than bermudagrass or bahia grass. In the North, tall fescue, red fescue and *Poa trivialis* are more tolerant of tree root competition than Kentucky bluegrass or ryegrass.

This is an area where much additional research is needed. Unfortunately, research that requires complex studies over many years is not viewed favorably by funding agencies, and university researchers cannot survive in the system conducting experiments that may take four or five years to provide enough information for publication. Since trees are slow to grow and such key landscape elements, their requirements should take precedence over turf which is much more easily established. Ecology of the urban landscape is poorly understood. Landscape managers should be aware of these tree-turf interactions and realize that turf beneath or adjacent to trees will require additional attention compared to turf in full sun. An alternative in some areas would be to switch to a tree-compatible ground cover.

Literature Cited

1. Bonner, J. 1950. The role of toxic substances in the interaction of higher plants. Bot. Review 16:51-65.

2. Garb. Solomon. 1961. Differential growth inhibitors produced by plants. Bot. Review 27:422-443.

3. Whitcomb, Carl E. 1969. Ph.D. Dissertation, Iowa State University, Ames, Iowa.

4. Whitcomb, Carl E. 1972. Influence of tree root competition on growth response of four cool season turfgrasses. Agron. Jour. 64:355-359.

5. Whitcomb, Carl E. 1972. When trees compete with turfgrass. The Golf Supt. 16:30-33.

6. Whitcomb, Carl E. and E.C. Roberts. 1973. Competition between established tree roots and newly seeded Kentucky bluegrass. Agron. Jour. 65:126-129.

7. Whitcomb, Carl E., E.C. Roberts and Roger Q. Landers. 1969. A connecting pot technique for root competition investigations between woody plants or between woody and herbaceous plants. Ecology 50:326-329.

Conversion Factors for the Nurseryman: English and Metric

To convert lbs./acre to kg/hectare, multiply lbs./acre by 1.121.

lbs./acre	kg/hectare	lbs./acre	kg/hectare
1/2	0.560	4	4.484
3/4	0.840	5	5.605,
1	1.121	6	6.726
1.5	1.680	8	8.968
2	2.242	10	11.210
2.5	2.803	12	13.452
3	3.363		

To convert lbs./cu.yd. to kg/cu.m, multiply lbs./cu.yd. by 0.595.

lbs./cu.yd.	kg/cu.m	lbs./cu.yd.	kg/cu.m
1/2	0.2975	5	2.974
3/4	0.445	6	3.570
1	0.595	7	4.165
1.5	0.892	8	4.760
2	1.189	10	5.948
2.5	1.487	12	7.140
3	1.784	14	8.328
4	2.380	16	9.520

To convert gallons to liters, multiply gallons by 3.785

1 gal. = 3.785 l or 231 cu.in.
2 gal. = 7.6 l
3 gal. = 11.4 l
5 gal. = 18.9 l
7.5 gal. = 28.4 l
10 gal. = 37.9 l
15 gal. = 56.8 l
20 gal. = 75.7 l
1 inch = 2.54 centimeters
1 foot = 3.048 decimeter or 30.48 centimeters

1 lb. = 454 grams
1 kilogram = 1,000 grams
or 2.2046 pounds
1 cu. yd. = 0.765 cu.m
1 meter = 39.37 inches
1 decimeter = 3.939 in.
or 0.328 ft.
1 centimeter = 0.3937 in.
1 yard = 0.9144 meter

Approximate metric equivalents:
  1 hectare = about 2 1/2 acres (2.47 acres)
  1 kilogram = 2 1/5 pounds (2.2046 pounds)
  1 meter = 1.1 yards or 3.3 feet.
  1 liter = 1.06 quarts, 61 cubic inches
  1 cubic meter = 61,026 cubic inches or 1.31 times greater than
      a cubic yard, 264 gallons.
  1 cubic foot = 7.48 gallons or 28.316 liters.
  1 gallon water = 8.326 pounds.
  1 cubic foot water = 62.43 pounds.
  1 cubic yard = 46,656 cubic inches

TO CHANGE:	TO:	MULTIPLY BY:
inches	centimeters	2.54
feet	meters	.305
miles	kilometer	1.609
meters	inches	39.37
kilometers	miles	.621
square inches	square centimeters	6.452
square yards	square meters	.836
cubic yards	cubic meters	.765
cubic meters	cubic yards	1.308
quarts	liters	.946
liters	quarts	1.057
ounces	grams	28.35
pounds	kilograms	.454
kilograms	pounds	2.205

Calculating Solutions PPM

Percent	Dilution	PPM	Grams/liter	Oz./gal.
1.0	1:100	10,000	10.0	0.35
0.1	1:1000	1,000	1.0	0.03
0.01	1:10,000	100	0.1	0.003
0.001	1:100,000	10	0.01	
0.0001	1:1,000,000	1	0.001	

One part per million (ppm):
   by weight = 1 milligram (mg) per kilogram (kg)
   by volume = 1 microliter (ul) per liter (l)

Example: You desire an 800 ppm solution **or** 800 ul per 1000 ml (one liter). The stock solution is 4.5% or 45,000 ppm.

Equation: $C_1V_1 = C_2V_2$

In this case: C_1 = 45,000 ppm (the stock solution)
   V_1 = volume of C_1
   C_2 = 800 ppm (final concentration desired)
   V_2 = 1000 ml or 1 liter

45,000 ppm (C_1) X ___?___ (V_1) = 800 ppm (C_2) X 1000 ml (V_2)

800 X 1000 = 800,000   and   45,000/800,000 = 17.87 ml

Thus, 17.78 ml in 1000 ml (1 liter) = 800 ppm

MEASURES AND EQUIVALENTS

1 inch is 2.54 centimeters. 1 centimeter is 0.394 inch

1 yard is 0.914 meter.   1 meter is 1.09 yards

1 kilogram (kg) is 1000 grams or 2.2 pounds.

1 gram (g) is 1000 milligrams or 0.035 ounce (U.S).

1 milligram (mg) is 1000 micrograms.

1 mg/liter is 1 part per million (ppm).

1 ppm is 1 mg/liter, 1 mg/kilogram, 0.0001%, 0.013 ounces by weight in 100 gallons (water).

1 liter (l) is 1000 milliliters (ml) or cubic centimeters (cc), 1.058 fluid quarts, and weighs 1 kilogram (water).

1 milliliter or cubic centimeter of water is 0.035 fluid ounces and weighs 1 gram.

1 pound is 16 oz., 453.6 grams, 0.12 gallons (water), 0.0155 cu.ft. (water), 2 1/4 cups of sugar, 4 1/2 cups of flour.

1 ounce is 28.35 grams.

1 gallon is 3.785 liters, 8.34 pounds (water), or 0.133 cubic feet.

1 cubic foot is 7.5 gallons, 62.4 pounds of water, 0.80357 bushels (U.S.)

1 gallon is 4 quarts, 8 pints, 16 cups or 128 fluid ounces.

1 quart is 2 pints, 4 cups, 32 fluid ounces, 64 tablespoons, or 0.946 liters.

1 pint is 2 cups, 16 fluid ounces, 32 tablespoons, 454 grams, 0.473 liters, or 1 pound (water).

1 ounce per 1 gallon is 7490 ppm.

Useful measurements (continued)

1 cup is 8 fluid ounces, 227 grams, 1/2 pint, 16 tablespoons, 48 teaspoons.

1 fluid ounce is 2 tablespoons, 6 teaspoons, 29.6 milliliter or cubic centimeter or 28.4 grams.

1 tablespoon (U.S.) is 3 teaspoons, 1/2 fluid ounce, 1/16 cup or approximately 16 grams.

1 percent is 10,000 ppm, 10 g/liter, 10 g/kilogram, 1.33 ounces by weight per gallon (water), 38 grams per gallon (water), 8.34 pounds per 100 gallons (water).

To convert Fahrenheit (F) into Centigrade (C), subtract 32 and multiply by 5/9; thus 68 degrees F equals 20 degrees C.

To convert Centigrade to Fahrenheit, multiply by 9/5 and add 32; thus 55 degrees C equals 131 degrees F.

Toxicities of Various Chemicals Used in Nurseries*

Toxicity Rating	Class	LD 50 (mg/kg)	Probable lethal dose for 150 lb. man
1	extremely toxic	less than 5	less than 7 drops
2	very toxic	5-49	7 drops to 1 teaspoon
3	moderately toxic	50-499	1 teaspoon to 1 ounce
4	slightly toxic	500-4999	1 ounce to 1 pint
5	almost non-toxic	5000-14,999	1 pint to 1 quart
6	non-toxic	15,000 and above	more than 1 quart

Common Name	Trade Name	LD 50 (mg/kg)
Herbicides:		
1. sodium arsenite	Atlas A, Triox	10
2. Paraquat	Paraquat	150
3. 2,4,5-T	various brands	300
4. copper sulfate	various brands	300
5. 2,4-D, 2,4-DB	various brands	600
6. cacodylic acid	Phytar 560	830
7. monosodium methylarsenate	MSMA	700
8. dicamba	Banvel D	1,040
9. vernolate, EPTC	Vernam, Eptam	1,800
10. DSMA	Ansar, Sodar	1,800
11. DCPA	Dacthal	3,000
12. dichlobenil	Casoron	3,160
13. atrazine	Atrazine	3,180
14. diuron	Karmex	3,400
15. trifluralin	Treflan	3,700
16. glyphosate	Roundup	4,900
17. simazine	Princep	5,000
18. ansulam	Ansulox 4.0	8,000
19. dalapon	Dowpon	9,300
20. alachlor	Lasso	9,300
21. benefin	Balan	10,000
Fungicides:		
1. Benlate	Benlate	9,590
2. Captan	Captan	10,000

Toxicities of Various Chemicals (continued)

Insecticides:
1. Temik	Temik	1
2. Parathion	Parathion	8
3. Toxaphene	Toxaphene	69
4. lead arsenate	(0.1 gram lethal to man)	100
5. Diazinon	Diazinon	175
6. pyrethrin	various aerosols	200
7. Chlorodane	Chlorodane	475-500
8. carbaryl	Sevin (dermal)	450
9. Malathion	Malathion	1,500
10. Methoxychlor	Methoxychlor	5,000

Fumigants:
1. B-9	2,000 ppm gas may be fatal to man)	1 mg/l

Growth Retardants:
1. B-9	Alar	8.4 gm/kg
2. Cycocel	Cycocel	670 mg/kg

Other Common Items: (for comparison)
1. gasoline		150
2. caffein	coffee	200
3. aspirin		750
4. sodium chloride	table salt	3,320

- -

*based on white rates, materials given orally

Toxicity Rating	Class	LD 50 (mg/kg)	Probable lethal dose for 150 lbs. man
1	extremely toxic	less than 5	less than 7 drops
2	very toxic	5-49	7 drops to 1 teaspoon
3	moderately toxic	50-499	1 teaspoon to 1 ounce
4	slightly toxic	500-4999	1 ounce to 1 pint
5	almost non-toxic	5000-14,999	1 pint to 1 quart
6	non-toxic	15,000 and above	more than 1 quart

GLOSSARY

Abscission layer. The partial or complete deterioration of a tissue at the base of the leaf that causes the leaf to drop.

Annual. A plant which lives for only one growing season, completing its life cycle from seed to seed.

Apical. The point or tip as of a stem or root.

Apical dominance. The suppression of side-shoot development by the terminal bud (shoot tip).

Artificial mix. Soilless mix.

Asexual propagation. Production of new plants from shoot, stem, leaf, or root pieces (by cuttings, division, layering).

Auxins. A group of hormones (plant growth regulators) that induce growth through cell elongation.

Axillary. In the angle formed by a leaf and stem.

B & B. Balled and Burlapped.

Bacterium (plural: bacteria). A one-celled microscopic plant that lacks chlorophyll and multiplies by fission. A few cause diseases but most are helpful.

Balled and Burlapped. Plants dug with roots inside soil roughly in the shape of a ball. This root-ball is then tightly wrapped in burlap to keep it from breaking apart when handled.

Bare-root stock. Nursery stock with little or no soil on the roots.

Bed. An area for growing plants, either outdoors or in greenhouses, or an area of level ground area (bed) in a greenhouse for propagation and/or growth of plants.

Bedding plants. A wide range of plants that are propagated and cultured through the initial stages of growth by commercial growers and are then sold for use in outdoor flower and vegetable gardens.

Blindness. The condition when a plant bud stops developing. It is a frequent problem of roses, during low light periods, and of the terminal buds of some tree species following transplanting.

Broad-leaved evergreens. Broad-leaved plants which retain green leaves year round.

Bud break. When resting buds resume growth.

Budding. Joining a small piece of bark (and sometimes wood) having a single bud onto the trunk, branch, or twig of a rooted plant so the single bud grows a new preferred plant.

Calcined clay. Montmorillonite clay, baked at a high temperature, which makes it rigid (it no longer shrinks or swells when wetted or dried). This material can be added to a growth medium to improve the air/water relationship.

Caliper. Diameter of plant's main stem (trunk) measured six inches above ground where the trunk is four inches or less in diameter and 12 inches above ground for larger sizes; the determining measurement in nursery stock grading, usually applied to trees and commonly expressed in inches.

Callus. Mass of cells that develops from and around wounded plant tissues, such as the base of cuttings and at the junction of a graft union.

Cambium or more correctly, cambial zone. The cylindrical zone of meristematic tissue between the heartwood and the bark of a dicot tree or shrub.

Capillarity. The movement of water through a porous material caused by the attraction of water for the particle surfaces; the smaller the particles, the stronger the attraction.

Carbohydrates. The basic food substances manufactured by the leaves generally referred to as "energy" by the author.

Chloroplast. The structure in the cells of the leaves where the chlorophyll is located. The site where carbohydrates and starches are manufactured.

Chlorosis. Leaves become yellow from the loss of chlorophyll. Can be due to nutrient disorder, virus, chemical spray injury, excessive light intensity or disease.

Compensation point. That light level where the amount of food (carbohydrates) manufactured by the leaves just equals the amount of food used by the cells of the leaf in respiration.

Conifers. Needle-leaved plants that produce seeds in cones; most conifers are evergreens; includes pine, spruce, fir, cedar, cypress, false cypress, yew, hemlock, redwood, and ginkgo.

Constant fertilization. Application of dilute fertilizer at each watering.

Container capacity. That level of moisture in a container with a specific growth medium where no further water will drain out because of the perched water table in the bottom of the container and adhesive and cohesive forces.

Culls. Undesirable or inferior plants; a relative term with many interpretations.

Cultivar. A cultivated variety; originating and persisting under cultivation; plants that are true to type from vegetative propagation; synonymous with variety.

Cutting. A portion of a stem, leaf, or root placed in a medium to grow roots and thus into a new individual plant.

Damping-off. A disease caused by a number of fungi, mainly *Pythium, Rhizoctonia*, and *Phytophthora*. The symptoms include decay of seeds prior to germination, rot of seedlings before emergence from the root medium, and development of stem rot at the soil line after emergence, causing seedlings to collapse.

Deciduous. Refers to perennial plants which lose leaves in fall or whose tops die down over winter.

Defoliation. Dropping or shedding of leaves of plants.

Desiccation. The process of drying. Desiccation of plants results from a lack of water or excessive salts.

Dibble hole. A cavity formed in a container growth medium by an object, generally the size and shape of the liner pot or tube.

Disease. A plant is said to be diseased when it develops a different appearance or when it changes physiologically from the normally accepted state. These differences are called symptoms. Disease can be caused by such unfavorable environmental conditions as temperature extremes, insects, or pathogenic organisms such as nematodes, fungi, bacteria, or viruses.

Division. Process of cutting a clump type of plant into sections.

Dolomite or dolomitic limestone. Material applied to a growth medium to supply both calcium and magnesium carbonates. It also raises the pH of the medium.

Dormant. A term applied to plants or seed which are in a state of dormancy; plants that are alive but not growing.

Emulsifiable concentrate. Formulation of pesticide or herbicide in which the pesticide or herbicide is dissolved in a petroleum solvent and emulsifier mixture, which holds the pesticide in suspension when agitated with water.

Energy. The carbohydrates and starches manufactured in the leaves of green plants.

Fertilizer injector. A machine that accurately combines a certain amount of concentrated soluble fertilizer with a known volume of water in a water line. The injector can be powered electrically or from water pressure.

Field-growing. Method of growing nursery stock directly in soil in the field as opposed to growing in containers.

Foot-candle (fc). A unit of light intensity equal to the direct illumination on a surface everywhere one foot from a uniform point source of one international candle. It is equivalent to 10.76 lux. Light intensity may vary from a maximum in summer from 10,000 fc or more to 2,000 or less in winter.

Fritted trace elements. Micronutrient elements infused in soft glass that slowly dissolve when added to a growth medium.

Fumigants. Chemicals used to fumigate soils, media, or plants; fumigants come in a liquefied or solid form, becoming a gas, vapor, or smoke when released or ignited.

Fumigation. Killing of insects, diseases, weeds, nematodes, or other organisms with a gas, smoke, or vapor.

Fungicide. Chemical that kills or suppresses fungus.

Fungus. An undifferentiated plant lacking chlorophyll and conductive tissues.

Fungus gnats. Small flies in the family *Sciaridae*; maggots feed on fungi and decaying organic matter and on plant roots and stems.

Gallon can. A metal or plastic container of 1/2- to one-gallon capacity. A very loose term referring to container volume.

Grading. Classifying plants according to quality or size.

Grafting. A method of propagation where a stem portion, with two or more buds, of one plant is joined with another plant, having roots, to form one new plant; joining a scion with the trunk, branch, or twig of a rooted plant.

Granular. Formulation in which the herbicide is mixed with a coarsely ground carrier such as coal, corn cobs, or calcined clay, to be applied dry to the soil surface and incorporated or watered-in.

Growth medium. A soilless, artificial mix or a pure material (such as peat moss or pine bark) used for growing plants; media is the plural of medium and refers to more than one growth medium.

Growing on. Plants which are to be grown further in the nursery to a larger size or desired shape before selling.

Growing season. From spring into fall as commonly used.

Harden off. Exposing plants gradually to low or varying temperatures, less humid or drier conditions, or higher light or other unaccustomed growing conditions to acclimate them to more difficult growing conditions, such as outdoors, or to being away from mist; to toughen plants to withstand handling and/or less desirable conditions.

Hardy plants. A relative term to describe plants which can withstand the cold and other weather conditions in the area where they are to be grown.

Herbicide. A chemical to control weeds.

Hormone. An organic substance produced in one part of the plant and translocated to another part where, in small concentrations, it regulates growth and development.

Host plant. A plant that is invaded by a pest or disease organism.

Humus. The relatively stable fraction of the soil organic matter remaining after the major portion of added plant and animal residues has decomposed.

Hydroponics. A system of growing plants in which water constitutes the growth medium.

IAA (indole-3-acetic acid). A naturally occurring auxin produced in apical meristems of both roots and shoots.

IBA (indole-3-butyric acid). A synthetically produced auxin.

Inoculum. The pathogen or its parts that can cause disease; that portion of individual pathogens which is brought into contact with the host.

Internode. The portion of a plant stem between two nodes. The node is the portion of the stem where one or more leaves are attached.

Interveinal. Pertaining to the space among the vascular tissues (veins) on a leaf.

Larva. The immature, wingless, and often wormlike form in which some insects hatch from the egg, and in which they remain through an increase in size and other minor changes until they assume the pupa stage.

Leaching. The most effective method of reducing high levels of soluble salts. Water the growth medium: the first application dissolves the salts, and the second watering flushes excess salts from the soil.

Leader. The dominant, central branch of a tree or shrub.

Leggy. Refers to a plant which is unattractive because it has not leafed out at the base, leaving bare and exposed trunks or branches.

Light saturation. The maximum amount of light energy that a leaf or other tissue can utilize under a given set of conditions.

Liner. A young plant of suitable size for planting in rows (lines) in the field or in containers for growing on into larger plants.

Lining out stock. Plants large enough to be planted or lined-out in a row; a nursery term.

Liquid feed. Applications of dilute fertilizer through the irrigation system.

Media. Growth media, the mix, or substrates in which plants are grown. Sand, peat moss, pine bark, and vermiculite are examples of ingredients in container growth media.

Meristem. A tissue composed of embryonic, unspecialized cells actively or potentially involved in cell division. An apical meristem is a meristem located at the tip of a shoot or root.

Methyl bromide. Chemical soil sterilant, usually sold in cans as a liquid under pressure. A dangerous gas that must be handled with care.

MHOS. Unit used to denote amount of soluble salts in a soil, determined by a Solu-bridge instrument.

Micronutrients. The trace elements required in small quantities for plant growth; specifically, iron, manganese, zinc, copper, boron, and molybdenum.

Microorganism (microbe). A small living organism that requires the aid of a microscope to be seen.

Mist propagation. System used to supply intermittent mist water sprays over the cuttings. Electrical control devices are used to turn the mist on and off.

Mycelium. The hypha or hyphae that make up the body of a fungus. Mycelium are the microscopic threadlike strands that make up the body of a fungus.

NAA (naphthalene acetic acid). A synthetically produced auxin.

Necrosis. The state of being dead and discolored.

Node. The position on a stem where leaves and buds are located.

Osmocote. A resin-coated slow-release fertilizer that can be added to a potting medium prior to planting or as a top-dressing after planting. It can be used to provide nutrition throughout the duration of a crop, or it can be used at rates that will require supplemental liquid fertilization.

Parts per million (ppm). Measurement used to denote concentration of growth regulators, fertilizer solutions, and gases. A ratio of materials; one gallon in one million gallons equals one ppm.

Pasteurization. Process whereby harmful organisms are killed; differs from sterilization, which eliminates all organisms.

Pathogen. Infectious agent that causes plant disease.

Peat moss. Partially decayed plant material, often used as an ingredient in a growth medium. Generally very acidic.

Perched water table. See page

Perlite. Volcanic rock heated to about 98' C (1,800' F), causing it to expand and become porous. The horticultural grade is a coarse aggregate and is best suited for mixing with other components for making very light-weight mixes for growing plants.

pH. A measure of the degree of acidity or alkalinity. The values range from 0, which is the most acid, to 14, which is the most alkaline, with 7 being neutral.

Phloem. A tissue in plants that transports energy downward from leaves to other plant parts, including stems and roots; the tissues outside of the cambial zone.

Phytophthora. Latin name for a genus of fungus that causes plant disease, generally a root- and crown-rot pathogen.

Photosynthesis. The manufacture of carbohydrates from carbon dioxide and water in the presence of chlorophyll, using light energy and releasing oxygen.

Phytotoxicity. Injury to a plant or plant part, caused by a chemical or environmental condition.

Post-emergent. An herbicide to kill existing weeds.

Pot-bound. Condition when the roots of a plant begin to wrap around or entwine the root ball inside of a container.

Pre-emergent. An herbicide that must be applied before the weed seed germinates

Propagation. Producing new plants from parts (cuttings, layers, division, grafts, buds, tissue, bulbs, tubers, rhizomes, corms) of whole plants, or from seeds.

Pruning. Removal of plant parts to improve the health, size, or shape of a plant.

Pythium. A fungal pathogen, water mold, soil inhabitant, and common cause of root rot and damping off of seedlings.

Respiration. Those biochemical processes which result in the consumption of oxygen and carbohydrates, the evolution of carbon dioxide, and the release of energy. Respiration has the reverse effect of photosynthesis.

Rhizome. A horizontal underground stem which forms both roots and shoots at its nodes.

Root ball. With container plants, the root system plus growth medium in which roots are growing.

Root pruning. Cutting of roots of plants to induce a more compact root system.

Rooted cutting. A cutting which has grown new roots.

Rooting compound. A chemical which promotes or hastens the rooting of cuttings.

Rooting hormone. Same as a rooting compound.

Sand. A mineral particle measuring 0.05 to 2.0 millimeters in diameter.

Scarification. A mechanical or acid treatment applied to certain seed to reduce the hard, impervious seed coat and to permit seed germination.

Seedling. A small plant grown from seed.

Semi-hardwood cuttings. Stem cuttings taken from the partially matured wood of new shoots.

Senescence. The process of growing old; aging.

Shifting. Usually means "shifting up": shifting from a smaller container to a larger one, such as from a one-gallon one to a three-gallon one.

Softwood cuttings. Stem cuttings from the soft, succulent, new spring growth.

Soil. The upper, heavily weathered layer of the earth's crust which supports plant life. It is a mixture of mineral and organic materials.

Soil mix. A mixture of bark, sand, peat, or other inorganic and/or organic materials used for growing plants. Generally no field soil is used.

Soil sterilization. Applying a chemical (soil sterilant) to a soil to prevent plant growth (especially of weeds) for one or more years.

Solenoid valve. An electrically activated valve which controls the flow of gases or liquids. Such valves can be activated by a time clock to control the rate of flow.

Solu-bridge. Apparatus that measures the electrical conductivity of a soil solution and is used to determine the soluble salt concentration.

Spider mites. Various species of mites in the family Tetranychidae that are plant parasites.

Spores. The reproductive unit of fungi; analogous to seeds of higher plants.

Steam pasteurization. A heat treatment, usually with 160 degrees F (56 C) aerated steam, for selective control of insects, diseases, nematodes, and most weeds.

Steam sterilization. A heat treatment using 212 degrees F (100 C) steam on the growth medium before planting to kill all weed seeds, insects, diseases, nematodes, and other organisms.

Sticking. Placing of cuttings into the propagation medium; "stuck" cuttings are those which have been placed into propagation medium.

Stock. Nursery plants for sale.

Stock plant. A plant from which cuttings may be taken.

Stomates. Pores or openings, generally on the underneath side of a leaf where carbon dioxide enters and water vapor is lost to cool the leaf tissues.

Strap-leaves. Leaves whose margins are partially or completely missing so that the leaf is narrower than normal, often resembling a strap.

Stratification. A seed treatment of low temperatures that is often needed to break dormancy and stimulate seed germination.

Superphosphate. (0-20-0), a granular material that can be added to a soil mixture to supply phosphorus. Contains about 9% actual phosphorus.

Surfactant or wetting agent. A chemical used to alter the surface properties of liquids. Surfactants are added to pesticide sprays to reduce the surface tension of the spray liquid, thereby enabling it to spread out more readily over the plant leaf surface. Surfactants are also used to improve the initial wetting of growth media.

Systemic. Spreading internally throughout the plant. Some pesticides are systemic, as are some pathogens.

Texture. The relative proportion of various sizes of mineral particles in a given soil or growth medium.

Tiller. Twigs or shoots that arise from the base of a plant.

Transpiration. The loss of water from the leaves of plants.

Tropism. A growth response or bending toward or away from a stimulus. Geotropism is in response to gravity: roots grow toward, and shoots away from, the center of earth's gravity. Phototropism is in response to light: shoots tend to grow toward light.

Vascular tissue. Tissue in the root, stem, leaf, or flower stem, including phloem for conducting organic substances throughout the plant, xylem for conducting water and nutrients primarily from the roots to the shoot, and supporting fiber cells. Vascular tissue in leaves is often called veins.

Vermiculite. Mica compound heated to about 738' C (1,400' F). It has a plate-like structure that enables it to retain both water and fertilizer. It is best suited for mixing with other materials for growing plants.

Verticillium. Name of a genus of fungus that causes plant disease; a root and vascular pathogen.

Wettable powder. Formulation of pesticide in which the pesticide is mixed with a finely ground clay, which holds the pesticide in suspension when agitated with water.

Wetting agent. See surfactant.

Wholesaler. One who sells to retailers; one who does not sell directly to consumers.

Xylem. A tissue in the plant that transports water and nutrients upward from the roots to the foliage. Cells connected end-to-end form xylem tubes. Vessels are the predominant xylem cells in flowering plants and have open ends. Tracheids predominate in the conifer (pines, etc.) xylem; rather than having open ends, they have pits along their sides connecting to adjacent tracheid cells. Vessel and tracheid cells are non-living at the time they carry out the function of water and nutrient transport.

INDEX

A

Abelia, 541, 546-547

Abscission, 539

Absorption, 15, 40, 48, 63, 65, 88-89, 94-95, 110, 185

Accelerated, 55, 89

Accumulation, 50

Acid, 183, 188, 218, 223, 225

Acid-forming, 136, 138

Acid-loving, 225

Acidification, 125, 218, 222, 228

Aeration, 3, 27, 39, 41, 69-70, 99, 101-102, 120, 123, 125, 127, 168, 172-174, 181, 201, 206, 209, 214-215, 218, 234, 243-244, 267, 350, 355, 357-362, 370, 373-374, 396, 454, 463, 470-471, 475, 490, 499, 513, 553

Alkalin(e)ity, 106, 218, 223, 225-226, 387, 465, 475, 480, 486, 491, 493

Allelopathy, 286, 293

Aluminum, 78, 301, 327, 387, 466

Amendments, 2-3, 6, 59, 99, 112-115, 117-119, 121, 123-125, 127, 131, 133-134, 138, 142, 146-147, 162, 168, 170, 196, 218, 232, 351, 360, 363, 372, 552, 540

Ammonia, 112, 136

Ammonium, 387, 390, 400-402, 406, 420, 423-424, 427-428, 440

Antifreeze, 506

Antitranspirants, 132, 197

Apple, 286, 296

Ash, 49, 62, 190-191, 194, 236-238, 288, 431, 554

Aucuba, 540-541, 545-548

Auger, 108

Auxin, 183, 185, 188, 283

Azaleas, 119, 121, 125, 133, 213, 218-220, 222, 223-225, 227-231, 398, 413, 415, 418, 443, 462-463, 483-484, 486, 514, 540-41, 546-547

B

Backfill, 3, 59, 112, 114-115, 119, 122, 127, 121-132, 153, 168, 175, 232, 238, 240-241, 244, 514

Backhoe, 38, 163, 235-237, 239, 241, 243, 245, 263-264

Backhoe-dug, 242-243

Bag, 37, 155

Bahia, 289

Ball, 150, 153, 155, 235, 238, 241, 243, 247

Ballast, 27

Balled-in-burlap, 3-4, 9, 13, 17-18, 21, 48-49, 71-72, 183, 187, 190, 192, 234-235, 239

Bamboo, 298-301, 307-308

Banvel, 174, 334

Barberry, 81

Bareroot, 69-70

Bark, 16, 21, 56, 66, 112-113, 117-120, 125, 127, 129, 132-133, 150, 153, 218, 223

Bark-amended, 113, 119

Base(s), 13, 29, 32, 40, 42, 52, 226

Bed-grown, 40

Berms, 373

Bermudagrass 7, 213, 289-291, 293, 296, 301, 304, 306-308, 327, 329, 332-333, 346, 476, 479, 600

Bicarbonates, 202, 218, 225, 267, 387, 441, 465-467, 488

Birch, 51, 54, 62, 64, 166-167, 584

Blackgum, 15

Blow-over, 34, 43, 45

Bluegrass, 286, 288, 295-296, 479, 588, 591-594, 596-601

Boron, 267, 385, 389, 392, 394, 403, 415, 417

Bottomless, 41, 64, 66

Boxwood, 447

Bracing, 197, 564, 579, 582, 583

Branching, 4, 6, 15, 37, 40-42, 44-45, 60, 69, 93, 163, 166, 193, 194, 197, 198, 244, 252, 256, 261, 263

Broadleaf, 13

Buds, 16, 50-54, 84, 192-193, 195-196

Buffer, 45, 48, 72

Buildup 73, 83

Burlap, 13-14, 18-19, 22-23, 70

Burn, 463

C

Cabling, 197, 564, 579, 582-583

Cacodylic, 326

Calcium, 3, 136-138, 187, 202, 218-219, 224-227, 385, 387-389, 392, 395, 400-402, 406-408, 410-412, 417, 421-424, 427, 430, 438, 440-443, 450, 465-468, 471-472, 475-476, 479, 481, 485-490, 493-494

Calibration, 319

Caliper, 24, 53-54, 60-62, 95, 118, 130, 163-166, 183, 185, 188, 207,553

Callus, 89, 565, 567-572, 576-580
Cambial, 22, 96, 252, 576
Camellia, 199
Capillarity, 55, 102, 121, 141, 146, 357, 371, 454
Carbohydrate(s), 17, 66, 88, 195, 199, 225, 252, 255, 396-397, 405-406, 416, 428, 437, 467, 470, 535, 549, 553-554, 558
Casoron, 315
Charcoal, 340-347
Chemical(s), 16, 52, 183-185
Chelate, 403
Chloride, 109, 267, 390, 401, 404, 409, 420, 423-424
Chlorophyll, 433, 442-443
Chloroplasts, 396, 539, 548
Chlorosis, 128-129, 219, 221, 226, 229, 231, 414, 431, 433-434, 437, 440, 443-445, 448, 454, 466, 473
Chrysanthemum, 406, 430, 449-450, 535
Clay, 101-102, 105, 108, 117-119, 130, 136-138, 142-143, 172, 187, 196, 218-219, 222, 225-226, 229, 236, 242, 258
Climate, 26
Clinolite, 360
Cohesive, 141-142
Cold-tolerant, 74, 79
Compacted, 101-102, 202, 214-215, 466-469, 471
Compartmentalization, 4, 6, 279, 577, 584-586
Competition, 7, 88, 212, 285-286, 289-291, 293-296, 298-300, 302, 304, 306, 309, 588-601
Compost, 29, 125,
Container(s), 9, 15, 17, 19-21, 26-31, 36-37, 39, 41-49, 51-52, 54, 56-62, 64-66, 69-74, 78-79, 81, 83, 85, 98, 116, 122, 124-125, 127-129, 132-134, 141-151, 153, 155, 157-159, 162, 166-167, 170, 172, 184, 188, 196, 225, 227, 229, 236, 244, 298-301, 305-306, 311, 317-318, 321, 332, 335, 338-339, 342, 347-348, 350-351, 353-355, 357-360, 364-366, 369, 371, 374-376, 378, 380-381, 408-410, 412, 413, 425, 463-464, 471-472, 488, 540, 548, 551, 588-590, 597
Container-grown, 3-5, 13, 26-28, 30, 36, 39, 55, 66, 69, 74, 80, 83, 85-86, 93, 119, 122, 124, 131-134, 161-162, 167-169, 232, 272, 273
Contaminants, 212
Controlled-release, 109
Copolymers, 127
Copper, 138, 385, 389, 394, 403, 425-427, 438, 445-448, 463, 466,

485, 488
Cornus, 76-77, 433, 473
Cotoneaster, 76-77
Cottonwood, 298-308, 584
Crabapple, 191-192, 196
Crabgrass, 211-212, 334, 342
Crapemyrtle, 324, 330, 455, 457, 462, 570, 573
Cut, 518, 524, 529-530, 565-568, 570-572, 576-578, 585

D
Decay, 43
Decomposition, 27, 125, 127, 129
Deficiency, 88, 113, 117, 136, 170, 209, 253, 392, 395, 398-399, 403, 309-411, 413, 417-418, 427, 430-451, 470- 472, 489, 493-494, 554
Dehydration, 10, 50, 69, 168, 196, 206, 526, 549, 557
Design, 36-37, 44-45, 47
Dessication, 52, 72-73, 83, 237
Deterioriation, 69
Detoxification, 346
Development, 191-192, 194-198
Devrinol, 315
Diagnosis, 437
Dicamba, 174, 315
Dichlobenil, 315, 346
Dicots, 96, 252
Dieback, 52
Digging, 2, 9-11, 13-16, 21-22, 51-52, 63, 92-93, 95, 99, 101, 112, 114, 234-235, 239, 249
Dilic, 326
Diphenimid, 346
Disease, 69, 88, 99, 123, 127, 465, 600
Dogwoods, 16, 20, 101, 119, 433, 548, 551
Dolomite, 137, 153, 388, 402, 409-412, 421-423, 440-441, 450, 466,
Dormant, 13, 15, 26, 28, 50-51, 70, 84, 95, 188, 190-191, 196, 198, 283
Dracenas, 437
Drainage, 2-3, 5, 19, 26, 45, 70, 102-106, 108, 123, 125, 138-139, 142, 148, 172,-174, 178, 180, 222, 279, 335, 350-360, 362, 364-366, 369, 371, 373, 375-377, 387, 428-429, 463, 503, 506, 514, 522, 548
Drains, 355, 357-358, 365-366

Drip-irrigated, 332
Drought, 92-93, 102, 109, 141, 149, 169, 191, 196, 228, 242, 253, 287-288, 327, 355, 399, 466, 536, 548-549, 553-556, 558, 591
Drought-resistant, 208
Drought-sensitive, 209
Drought-tolerant, 203, 205, 208, 535, 548

E
Ecology, 98, 601
Ecotypes, 550
Elm, 34, 38-40, 181, 197, 211, 236-239, 263, 294, 301-302, 304-308, 457-460, 585
Emitters, 219, 258
Energy, 10, 16-17, 48-51, 60, 62, 69, 88-95, 110, 161, 168, 195, 252-256, 258, 429-430, 437, 465-467, 470-471, 499, 503, 510, 535, 539-540, 547, 549, 553-558
Energy-dependent, 535
Environment(al), 56, 66, 80, 89, 94, 99, 131-133, 178-179, 188, 232, 251, 283
Erosion, 126, 214, 215, 345
Eucalyptus, 15, 155, 159
Euonymus, 76-77, 184-185, 188, 301, 307-308, 342, 344, 540-545, 547-548, 550
Evaporation, 18, 54, 556
Excavation, 175, 184
Exposure, 16, 83
Eyescrews, 279-282

F
Fabric, 5, 15, 44-45, 48-53, 55-56, 58-65, 69-70, 78, 83, 106, 108, 211-214, 216, 244
Fall-planted, 162-167, 169
Fertility, 365, 540-545, 547-548, 550
Fertilizer, 2-4, 6-7, 27, 29, 82, 93-94, 109-110, 112-113, 118-120, 129, 133, 136, 150-152, 168, 170, 175, 185-188, 190-192, 203-209, 222, 228-231, 270, 290-293, 331, 389, 391-392, 396, 399-401, 403-405, 409, 412-413, 416-417, 419-423, 425, 428-429, 431, 440, 448, 453-463, 468, 476, 488-490, 492, 506, 513, 515, 533, 535, 545, 553-554, 588, 591
Fertilization, 279
Fescue, 287-288, 291, 301, 305, 307-308, 600-601
Field, 69-72, 74,

Field-grown, 9, 13, 23, 28, 55, 62
Fill 251, 258
Flairs, 510-511, 528
Forsythia, 324, 327, 342-343, 473
Fringetree, 548
Fungicide, 187
Fusilade, 334
Fusarium, 210

G
Gardenias, 411
Geotextiles, 216
Germination, 154
Geraniums, 128-129, 410-411, 439, 441
Girdling, 56, 65, 282, 526, 528
Glyphosate, 326-327
Goal, 311, 315, 321, 324, 338
Goosegrass, 313
Granular, 219, 226, 229
Granules, 316-321
Graslan, 334
Grass(es), 5, 285-290, 295, 332, 334
Gravel, 6, 105-108, 138
Gravity, 105
Grazon, 334
Gro-bags, 53
Grosafe, 341
Gymnocladus, 15
Gypsum, 136-138, 401, 407, 409, 421, 423-424

H
Hackberry, 515
Hardiness, 74, 86, 161, 168, 199
Harvest, 22, 25, 49, 51-52, 54-55, 62, 69-70, 235
Health, 465-471, 473
Heartwood, 576, 578, 583
Heat-tolerant, 166
Heeled-in, 16
Herbicide, 79, 81, 173-174, 177-178, 187, 212-214, 311, 315-328, 334-335, 338-340, 343, 466, 485, 554
Hibiscus, 324, 336, 442, 449, 550
Holding, 69-71, 74, 80, 114, 130

Holly, 72, 97, 129, 152-153, 161-162, 164, 290, 292-293, 311, 346, 407, 434, 446, 471-472, 540-541, 546
Honeylocust, 195, 263, 286, 288, 588, 591-592, 597-598
Honeysuckle, 151
Hormone, 95, 188
Hydrogels, 127, 129, 134,
Hydroponics, 409
Hyvar, 173, 177, 335, 339-345

I
IBA, 183-188
IBDU, 109, 400, 420, 428
Ilex, 72, 76-77, 152, 159, 161. 472
Incorporation, 112, 127, 219, 222, 325, 341-345
Indolebutyric, 183, 188
Inhibitors, 212
Injury, 92-93, 110
Injury, 72-74, 78, 82-83, 85-86, 277-279, 465-466
Insect, 69, 88, 125, 253, 393, 398-399, 465-466, 471, 473
Insecticide, 187
Insulating, 47, 49, 72, 74, 79, 82-83, 173, 176, 178, 378-380
Interface, 37, 38, 39, 40
Iron, 138, 224, 226, 385, 389, 394, 403, 415-417, 427, 430, 433, 437-438, 441-444, 448, 454-455, 463, 466, 468, 473, 475-476, 478, 480-486, 488-490, 493-494, 535
Irrigation, 3, 26, 30, 102-103, 113, 115, 121, 130-133, 144, 148, 150, 164, 166-167, 178, 184, 191, 201-202, 208-209, 212-213, 218-219, 223-225, 229, 258, 289, 311, 316, 319-320, 331-332, 335, 338, 341-342, 345, 368, 391, 401-402, 409, 412, 420-422, 428-429, 431, 440, 448, 453, 465-466, 470-471, 475, 484-488, 540
Isobutylidene, 420
Ixora, 456

J
Johnsongrass, 327
Juniper, 32, 76-77, 150, 152, 161-162, 164, 166, 203, 208, 289-292, 311, 321, 329, 361, 378, 408, 540-542, 547, 574

K
K-mag, 401-402
Kalmia, 76
Karmex, 334, 336, 345
Koelreuteria, 76-77

L

Lasso, 347-348
Leached, 319, 339, 428-429
Lethal, 54, 72, 78-80, 83,
Leucothoe, 76-77
Light, 470, 473
Ligustrum, 33, 129, 132-133, 216, 290, 321, 414, 551, 555
Lilies, 484
Lime, 137, 387-388, 401, 402, 424
Limestone, 6, 481, 483-484
Liners, 187
Liquadambar, 283
Liriodendron, 283
Liriope, 298-301, 305, 307-308, 319
Loblolly, 57, 62, 64
Locust, 66
Lonicera, 151

M

Magamp, 401
Magnesium, 3, 137-138, 202, 224, 227, 253, 385, 387-389, 392, 394-395, 399, 401-403, 409-412, 417, 421-424, 427, 433-438, 440, 450, 454, 465-466, 471-472, 485
Magnesium-deficient, 435, 437
Magnolia, 76-77, 95, 97, 277, 288, 291, 432, 435, 504, 520, 557
Mahonia 76-77
Malus, 473
Manganese, 138, 224, 385, 387, 389, 393-394, 403, 415-417, 427, 433, 437-438, 442-445, 448, 454, 463, 475-476, 479-486, 488-490, 493-494
Manufacture, 88-89, 91
Maple, 6, 40, 67, 168, 170, 195, 213-214, 286, 288, 298-302, 304, 307-308, 456, 458, 493-494, 524, 551, 560, 564, 584-585, 588, 591-592, 594-598
Maturity, 74
Media, 74, 76-77, 112, 127, 132-134, 322, 346-348
Medium, 125, 127-129, 132-133, 141-148, 150, 153, 155, 162, 168, 350, 354, 357, 359, 360, 363, 379, 386, 413, 415-416, 437, 439, 441, 448, 540, 550
Microbial, 347
Microfoam, 75, 78-79, 82-83, 86
Micromax, 128, 153, 219-220, 222, 224, 403, 416, 437, 440, 488-490

Micronutrients, 125, 137-138, 218-226, 230, 389, 392, 403, 406, 410, 412-414, 416-417, 422, 427, 430, 437, 440, 447-448, 453-454, 465, 468, 475, 480, 482, 485, 488-490, 492
Micro-environment, 405
Microorganisms, 126-127, 138, 202, 340, 343
Mites, 338, 445, 447
Mix, 13, 20-21, 27, 29, 44-45, 56, 58, 70, 101, 141-145, 150, 153, 350, 352-354, 358-361, 363-366, 368-369, 371-372, 374-375, 377
Mixes, 112-113, 129-130, 162
Mockorange, 113, 342
Moisture, 113-114, 121-123, 129, 133, 142, 145-146, 148, 150, 159, 161, 164, 166, 169, 201-203, 208-210, 213, 215-216, 222-223, 228-229, 235-236, 238, 258, 267, 285, 293, 355, 358, 365, 368, 470
Molybdenum, 385, 394-395, 403, 417, 427, 438, 449-450
Mondograss, 301, 308
Monocots, 96, 300
Mulch(es), 3, 5-7, 69, 126-127, 162, 169, 178-179, 201-208, 210-216, 219, 223, 311, 324-325, 367, 463, 556

N
NAA, 183
Naphthalene, 183
Napropamide, 315
Nematodes, 210
Nitralin, 348
Nitrate, 390, 400-402, 404, 406, 420, 421, 423-424
Nitroform, 400, 588
Nitrogen, 5, 93, 109-110, 112-113, 119, 136, 150, 163, 170, 184, 190, 203, 215-216, 228-230, 253, 272, 288, 290-291, 295-296, 306, 357, 385-386, 389-392, 395, 399-400, 403-404, 406, 408, 412-413, 417-421, 423-424, 427-431, 433, 438-440, 449, 453-460, 462-463, 480, 535, 554, 588, 591
Nitrogen-deficient, 429
Nutgrass, 331
Nutrient(s), 70, 82, 88-89, 94-95, 110, 118, 125, 144-145, 150, 225, 228, 253, 255, 285-286, 302, 311, 313, 357, 360-362, 385, 392-393, 395-396, 398-400, 402, 405-406, 413, 416-420, 424, 485, 491, 510, 515, 518, 533, 553, 591
Nutrition, 4, 20, 26, 39, 66, 125, 150, 195, 459, 465, 468, 473, 540, 548
Nutsedge, 212, 327, 331-333
Nyssa, 15

O

Oak, 34, 36, 53, 66, 94, 130, 132, 161-166, 181, 183-185, 188, 190, 195, 197, 203, 208-209, 226, 283, 288, 331-333, 373, 457, 475, 480-481, 483, 493, 498, 402-503, 515, 519, 521, 526-527, 531, 569, 576, 578

Ornamentals, 73, 86,

Oryzalin, 212, 315

Osmocote, 109, 128, 150, 153, 219, 228-231, 390-401, 407-409, 418-420, 425, 428, 489

Overwintering, 47, 71, 74-75, 83

Oxadiazon, 311, 315, 348

Oxyfluorfen, 311, 315

Oxygen, 6, 101, 126, 161, 201, 214, 240, 246, 313, 340, 343, 390, 427, 499, 513, 522, 525, 553, 600

P

Pachysandra, 301-302, 306, 308

Palm, 96, 252, 437

Paraquat, 326-327

Parkinsonia, 67

Pathogen, 234, 370

Peach, 191, 193, 195, 199, 327

Pear, 188, 190-191, 193, 197-198, 327

Peat, 112-114, 116-119, 121, 125, 127, 129-130, 132-133, 138, 150, 153, 162, 196, 218-225, 229, 322, 359, 412, 431, 441, 447, 540

Peat-amended, 113-114

Pecan, 188, 191, 218, 228, 443-444, 454, 577

Perched, 19, 105, 125, 141-142, 525

Percolation, 2, 102-103, 117, 124, 126, 141, 144-145, 355, 369, 428, 475

Periwinkle, 301

Perk, 440

Perlite, 360-361, 363, 441

Permeable, 358

Pests, 375

Petunias

pH, 6, 118, 125, 137-138, 216, 218, 222, 225-226, 230, 385, 387-389, 395, 403, 440, 442, 448, 453-455, 465-466, 475-490, 493

Phloem, 48, 252, 255

Phosphate, 113, 400-401, 423, 427-429, 439

Phosphorus, 3, 5, 93, 109-110, 228, 230, 253, 385, 389-390, 392, 399-401, 406-409, 413, 417, 420, 422-424, 427, 429-431, 433, 438, 441-443, 450, 453-454, 468, 515

631

Photinia, 84,
Photoperiod, 554
Photoperiod-sensitive, 536
Photosynthesis, 199, 425, 535, 539, 550, 600
Physiology, 97, 216, 270
Phytophthora, 26
Phytotoxicity, 128-129, 315, 347
Picloram, 334
Pieris, 76-77
Pigweed, 311, 323, 342
Pilea, 78
Pine, 6, 94, 98, 113, 117-120, 127, 129, 133, 161-162, 164-166,
    207, 214, 218, 223, 236-238, 240, 242-243, 252, 290, 292-293,
    301-305, 307-308, 322, 324, 339, 359, 378, 381
Pistacia, 52, 117, 161-162, 164, 166, 560, 564
Pittosporum, 113-114, 116, 131, 289, 321, 433, 436
Planetree, 40, 258, 263
Planta-Gel, 127, 129
Planted, 298, 300-301, 589-590, 595-596, 600
Planters, 362
Planting, 2-7, 9-10, 13-17, 30, 38, 44, 51, 53, 55-56, 59-60, 63,
    65, 112-121, 124, 120-134, 142, 147, 150-152, 154- 156, 159,
    161-170, 172-174, 178-181, 183-185, 190-192, 194, 196-198, 210,
    215-216, 218-219, 222, 224, 229, 231-232, 234-235, 238, 240,
    243, 245, 247, 249, 251, 256, 258, 260-262, 266-267, 270, 272,
    274, 276, 279, 290-291, 315, 319, 342, 344, 370, 376, 391, 417,
    555
Plastic, 37, 44
Platanus, 40, 94
Plum, 196, 199
Podocarpus, 433, 436
Poinsettias, 128-129, 433, 535
Polyacrylamide, 133
Polymer, 129, 132-134
Pomifera, 40
Ponderosa, 473
Poplars, 524, 584
Populus, 89
Porosity, 121, 126, 138, 350, 354, 360, 362, 377
Porous, 5-6, 70, 101-103, 105, 126, 215-216
Post-emergent, 311-312, 316, 326, 331, 334
Potash, 385, 401-402, 423-424

Potassium, 93, 109, 150, 228, 230, 253, 385, 389-390, 392, 399-402, 409, 412-413, 417, 419-421, 423-424, 427, 431-433, 438, 440, 453-454, 456, 515
Pramitol, 173, 335, 340, 345
Pre-emergent, 174, 311-312, 315-316, 321-328, 331, 335
Princep, 315, 324
Prometon, 340
Propagation, 66, 154, 170, 184-185
Protection, 73, 75, 78-81, 83, 85-86, 276
Pruning, 4, 7, 88-95, 97-98, 159, 190-194, 196-199, 256, 258-260, 262, 267, 270, 283, 285, 287, 438, 499, 560-561, 568-570, 573-574, 576, 584-586
Prunus, 190-191, 196, 198, 473
Pyracantha, 32-33, 76-77, 150, 152-153, 166, 169, 184-186, 289, 311, 327, 378, 434, 473, 540-542, 547-548
Pyrus, 190-191
Pythium, 26, 210

Q
Quercus, 94, 161, 165-166, 184

R
Rainfall, 3-5, 99, 113, 115, 121, 126, 130,
Redbuds, 16, 20, 101, 190, 306, 548
Redwood, 223
-Regeneration, 67, 94, 97, *188, 283
Respiration, 254, 535, 539, 553
Restricted, 22, 24, 29, 48, 51, 65, 71, 95, 172-174, 178-181
Restrictions, 141, 155
Rhododendron, 76-77, 131, 134, 218, 225, 228, 232, 418, 443, 462-463, 541
Rhizomes, 299, 326, 333
Rodents, 79
Ronstar, 311, 314-316, 321-322, 324, 347-348
RootBuilder, 44-45, 47, 70
RootMaker, 41, 42
Root(s), 3-6, 9-17, 19, 21-22, 24, 26-27, 29, 32-45, 48-51, 54-60, 62-65, 67, 69, 70, 72-74, 76-79, 82-83, 85-86, 88-98, 99, 101-104, 108, 110, 112-116, 119, 121-124, 126-127, 129, 136, 141-150, 152-158, 161-165, 167-169, 173, 175, 177-178, 181, 183-188, 190-192, 195-199, 202, 206-207, 209-211, 214-216, 225, 228, 234-235, 237-241, 243-244, 246-247, 251-256, 262-267, 270, 272-273, 276, 279-280, 283, 285-286, 288-289, 293, 295-296,

298-301, 304, 306, 309, 311, 313, 321-322, 324-326, 333, 338,
350, 352, 355, 360, 367, 370-371, 375-381, 387, 389-390, 393,
396-399, 404-405, 410, 413, 415-417, 421-422, 429, 437-438,
442, 454-456, 458-460, 463, 466-468, 470-471, 475, 487, 490-
491, 493, 496-499, 502-503, 505-508, 510-516, 518-520, 522-524,
529-531, 533, 536, 540, 542, 546, 548, 553-558, 588-601
Root-absorbed, 331
Root-bound, 5, 28-30, 32-37, 51, 152-155, 169
Root-branching, 44
Root-modifying, 41
Root-pruning, 44, 70, 89, 91-97, 300
Root-trapping, 44, 46, 70
Rootstocks, 191
Rose, 252, 270, 447
Rose-of-sharon, 336
Rosetting, 445
Roundup, 174, 187, 213, 289, 312, 326-334, 346
Rout, 321
Run-off, 126
Ryegrass, 601

S
Salix, 89
Salts, 109-110, 129, 133, 137-138, 174, 202, 228-230, 404,
409, 416, 420, 424, 429, 457, 462, 476-477, 480, 553
Salt-sensitive, 110, 228
Sand, 113, 117, 119, 129-130, 162, 174-175, 179, 196, 360-362,
364, 429, 447, 540
Sandy, 137, 191, 215, 218-219, 222, 229, 388, 391, 394, 405, 409,
412, 418, 459, 462, 485, 488, 490, 498, 506, 515, 520-523, 528
Sassafras, 15
Saturated, 352, 354, 357-358, 367-371, 377, 522
Sawdust, 112-113, 359
Scale, 231, 260, 475, 481-482
Schefflera, 438
Scorching, 73, 555
Seedling(s), 29, 40-41, 64, 66-67, 94, 97-98, 128, 130, 184, 187-
188, 191, 197-198, 236, 238, 258, 380
Shade, 6, 21
Sidewall, 41, 44, 46, 59, 72
Simazine, 334, 336, 338, 345-346
Slow-release, 5, 93-94, 109-110, 113, 150, 168, 175, 228-231,
390-391, 400-401, 406, 409, 416, 418-420, 428

Sodium, 109, 136-138, 187, 202, 218-219, 222-230, 232, 267, 385, 387, 400, 403, 404, 417, 420, 423, 453-456, 458-459, 462-463, 465-466, 488, 537

Soil(s), 2-6, 9-14, 16, 19-22, 24, 27, 29, 30, 33, 38, 40, 43, 45, 48-49, 51, 54-56, 58-63, 65, 69-72, 74, 79, 86, 99-110, 113-114, 117-119, 121-123, 125-126, 130, 136-139, 141-148, 150, 152-155, 158, 161-164, 167-170, 172-178, 180, 184-185, 187, 190-191, 196, 201-203, 206-207, 209-210, 213-216, 234-239, 242-244, 246, 248-249, 251, 253, 256, 258, 263-265, 267, 269, 272-273, 275-276, 279-280, 285, 288-289, 311, 315-316, 319, 321-322, 324-328, 331, 333-335, 338-345, 347, 350-351, 353, 355-369, 371-378, 380-381, 385, 387-392, 394, 404-405, 408-409, 411-413, 421, 438-429, 431, 440-441, 444-445, 448-449, 465-471, 473, 475-493, 506, 513, 548, 588, 594-600

Soilless, 13, 19-20, 70, 162

Space, 4, 25, 28-29, 45, 56, 58, 70, 75, 81, 272

Spade, 234-239, 242-244, 245, 248-249

Spade-dug, 3, 6, 55, 187, 251, 258, 261-262, 267, 279

Spray(s), 47, 183, 187-188, 325, 331, 403, 437, 442

Spreader, 316-318, 342, 388

Sprinklers, 164, 204, 267, 269, 476, 508, 540

Spruce, 13, 94, 535-536, 538

Stak(es)ing, 4, 47, 59, 272-276, 279-280, 283

Starch(es), 50, 67, 127-128, 393, 396, 465, 503

Starch-polyacrylonitrile, 127

Starch-sucrose, 199

Stem, 4-6, 37-42, 48, 51, 55-56, 62-63, 70-71, 74, 163-166, 206-207, 215, 251-253, 255-256, 258-259, 263-266,

Sterilant, 173-174, 335, 338-340, 345

Stimulators, 183-184, 187-188

Stress, 2, 4, 13, 16-17, 19-20, 29, 33, 42, 45, 52, 69-71, 78-80, 82-83, 99, 109-110, 117, 121, 128, 141, 148-150, 152-153, 272, 275, 283, 360, 371, 374, 376, 465, 466-468, 480-471, 473

Structures, 75, 78, 82-84

Stunting, 430, 438, 445

Styrofoam, 176

Subsoil, 101, 117-119,

Suckers, 191-194, 258-260, 267

Sudan, 125

Sudex, 125

Suffocation, 4-5, 19-20, 56, 69, 124, 142-144, 174, 377, 522, 526

Sugars, 48

Sulfate, 136-138, 427, 431, 437, 439-440
Sulfur, 3, 136-137, 218-230, 385, 387-389, 392, 400-403, 406, 409, 422, 454, 476-483, 487-493,
Sulfur-coated, 109, 136, 228-231, 390, 400, 420, 428
Superabsorbent, 119, 127, 129-130
Superphosphate, 109, 429, 439, 450
Surfactant, 327, 332
Surflan, 212-213, 315
Sweetgum, 196, 199, 406, 584
Sycamore, 24, 54, 63, 91, 288, 569

T
Taper, 43, 44, 45, 46
Taxus, 20, 74, 76-77, 86, 473
Temperatures, 26, 52, 55, 70-74, 76-78, 82, 84-86, 89, 93-94, 121, 129, 173, 178, 355, 378, 380-381, 470
Terra-Sorb, 127-130
Textiles, 216
Texture, 141-144, 352-353, 357-372, 377
Tile, 104-106, 525
Tilth, 136-138
Tolerance, 6, 71-72, 74
Top-pruning, 195-197, 356, 258, 262-263, 267
Toxic(ity), 54, 119, 225, 326, 392, 413, 418, 427, 438, 440, 445, 448-451, 466, 601
Traffic, 467, 469
Translocation, 48, 95, 225, 326-327
Transpiration, 54, 381, 556
Transplant, 2, 7, 10, 29, 33, 51, 62, 65-66, 69, 88, 90, 95, 132, 188, 232, 258, 270
Transplanting, 2, 6, 9-10, 13, 17, 20, 22, 29-31, 34, 39-40, 50-52, 55-56, 59-60, 62, 65-67, 101-102, 110, 130, 132-134, 141, 147-150, 152-155, 183, 191-192, 194-199, 234-240, 242-244, 246, 249, 251-252, 255-256, 258-259, 261-262, 269-270, 272, 283, 285, 300, 540, 549
Treflan, 79, 81, 219, 312, 315, 321, 324-325, 328, 331, 347-348
Trench, 508-509, 513-514, 520, 529
Triazine, 343
Trimec, 174, 334
Trunk, 5-6, 95,
Tunnel, 531
Turf, 386, 425, 456, 479, 484, 487, 490, 523, 588, 591, 597, 600-601

Turface, 360
Turfgrasses, 289, 294-296
Typar, 212-214

U
Ulmus, 38-39, 66, 94, 236
Uracil, 346
Urban, 375, 465-467, 473, 475, 484, 490, 498, 515
Urea, 109-110, 136, 228-229, 231, 390-391, 400, 402, 420-421, 423, 428, 459, 480
Ureaformaldehyde, 109, 390, 400, 428, 588

V
Vermeer, 60-61, 236, 242, 258
Vermiculite, 113, 117, 316, 360, 363
Vertical, 4, 59, 105,
Viburnum, 76-77, 473
Vinca, 301, 303, 307-308
Volatilization, 325

W
Wall, 72-73, 83
Water, 2-5, 13, 15-17, 19-20, 27, 29, 31, 39, 40-41, 45, 48, 53-55, 63, 65, 89, 93-95, 113-114, 117, 121-125, 127-131, 133-134, 141-144, 161-162, 164, 172-174, 178, 183, 184, 187, 190, 193, 199, 201-202, 209, 212-214, 216, 218-219, 223-225, 227-228, 236, 242, 253, 255, 258, 265, 267, 269, 286, 302, 311, 313, 320, 322, 324-327, 330-332, 334-335, 341, 345, 350-355, 357-358, 360-363, 365-366, 368-371, 376-377, 380, 393, 396-405, 409-412, 416, 419-420, 422, 424, 440, 448, 462-463, 465-467, 470-473, 475, 481, 483-488, 490, 503, 506, 508-510, 512-515
Water-absorbing, 129, 132
Water-conserving, 54
Water-holding, 127-128, 130, 132
Water-loving, 127
Water-soluble, 400, 420
Weather, 90, 93
Weed(s), 4-6, 88, 202, 208, 210-214, 216, 469
Well, 88, 93-94, 96
Well-aerated, 3, 126
Well-drained, 102, 108, 119
Willow, 524
Wilting, 128-129, 131, 420

Wintercreeper, 342
Wire, 22-24, 66, 279-280, 282
Wounds, 4, 89, 560, 565, 567-572, 576-577, 579, 584-586

XYZ
Xylem, 48, 252, 255, 406, 424
Yucca, 319, 321, 328
Zeolite, 360
Zinc, 385, 389, 394, 403, 417, 427, 438, 448, 454, 480-481, 484, 485, 488, 489